WOMEN AND SOCIAL ACTION IN VICTORIAN AND EDWARDIAN ENGLAND

Women and Social Action in Victorian and Edwardian England

Jane Lewis

Stanford University Press
Stanford, California
1991

Stanford University Press
Stanford, California
© Jane Lewis 1991
Originating publisher: Edward Elgar Publishing Ltd., Aldershot, England
First published in the USA by Stanford University Press
Printed in Great Britain
ISBN 0-8047-1905-5
LC 90-71680
This book printed on acid-free paper

Contents

Acknowledgements

I would like to thank the Nuffield Foundation for enabling me to take a term's leave at a crucial time in the research for this book. The manuscript was finished in Stockholm, where, as the visiting Kerstin Hesselgren Professor with the Swedish Council for Research in the Humanities and Social Sciences (*Humanistisk-Samhällsvetenskaplega Forskingsrådet*) I was able to enjoy somewhat more time for writing than is habitually the case at the LSE. I am also indebted to many librarians and archivists, particularly to Dr Angela Raspin, of the British Library for Political and Economic Sciences.

Versions of many of the chapters in this book have been presented at various seminars: the Women's History Seminar and the Victorian and Edwardian Seminar at the Institute for Historical Research, the University of London; at an international conference sponsored by the Nuffield Foundation on the Social Survey in Historical Perspective (1989); at the Booth Centenary Conference organized by the Open University (1989); and at the Social History Society's Annual Conference (1990). I am grateful to the participants for their comments. The ideas exchanged in an informal reading group originally called together by Catherine Hall and myself to discuss new developments in historical writing have proved invaluable.

Perhaps my greatest debt is to the many friends and colleagues who have shared ideas with me and provided so much support during the writing of this book. I would especially like to thank: Sue Bruley, Clare Collins, Carol Dyhouse, Catherine Hall, Yvonne Hirdman, Angela John, Elizabeth Lebas, Barbara Meredith, David Piachaud, Brenda Pratt, Susan Richter, Ruth Roach-Pierson, Lyndal Roper, Sally Sainsbury, Lloyd Trott, Jeffrey Weeks and Meta Zimmeck. I am extremely grateful to those who undertook to read all or part of the manuscript: Anne Bindslev, Catherine Sandbach-Dahlström, Leonore Davidoff, Denise Riley, Michael Rose, Mark Shrimpton and Ulla Wikander. Edward Elgar continues to be a sympathetic and interested editor.

Introduction

Patterns of achievement

The five women who are the subjects of this book were all notable public figures. When I first started the research more than five years ago, I began work on Helen Bosanquet (née Dendy) and Beatrice Webb (née Potter), because their lives seemed to touch and diverge in a manner that promised to open up issues regarding approaches to social questions in late Victorian and Edwardian England; the part played by the female social activist, as social worker, social investigator and social reformer; and the way in which feminism, or perhaps more accurately consciousness of 'the Woman Question', touched their lives in their public and private aspects.

The decline of the linear 'origins of the welfare state' interpretation of late nineteenth- and early twentieth-century measures to tackle poverty, unemployment and sickness has reopened many issues of historical importance. For the most part, nineteenth-century women social activists have been portrayed as *grandes dames* with firm ideas as to individual morality and self-help, Beatrice Webb's increasing sense of a 'class consciousness of sin' and conversion to Fabian Socialism excepted. In fact, four of the five women treated in this book – Octavia Hill, Helen Bosanquet, Mary Ward and Violet Markham – were strategically located within what was arguably the mainstream of social theory and social action. This linked the solution of social problems firmly to the family and to social work performed voluntarily by middle-class women who thereby fulfilled their citizenship obligations. Individualism was by no means a simple creed feeding a belief in self-interest and self-help. Indeed, by the early twentieth century, individualism in the sense of holistic social work with the individual in his or her family context, undertaken with the aim of producing a fully participative citizen, could even coexist with a measure of state collectivism.

An analysis of the 'lived lives' of these women shows how their ideas about the proper relationships between individual, family and the state were forged in relation both to their gendered (and often contested) concepts of duty and citizenship, and to their shared conviction that on the commitment to social action depended social progress. Just as it has become impossible to talk about a single late nineteenth- and early twentieth-century feminism, so it is misleading to refer to a movement from a simple individualism to collectivism. There were many

1

individualisms as the subjects of this book demonstrate. The only major unifying force was the powerful commitment to social action, which each woman had to reconcile with an equally strong commitment to domestic duties and to late Victorian ideas about female propriety.

Both Helen Dendy and Beatrice Potter began work outside the home under the auspices of late nineteenth-century philanthropy, to which Helen remained faithful, becoming an authoritative voice within the most influential charitable organization of the day, the Charity Organisation Society (COS). Beatrice soon became disillusioned with the philanthropic world and turned into one of the most powerful critics of both its philosophy and methods, favouring instead the development of administrative machinery and expertise by the state as a means to solving the problem of poverty. In the 1880s and 1890s, this meant going against the grain in two important respects, first in questioning the dominant role of charity in the relief of the poor, and second, in abandoning philanthropic endeavour, which was considered virtually the only appropriate work for middle-class women beyond the home, in favour of the more masculine pursuit of 'a science of society'. Yet Beatrice took up an anti-suffrage position during the 1880s, not lending her support to the cause until 1906. Helen Bosanquet publicly endorsed the suffrage, opting also to support the radical claim of votes for working women rather than merely for women with property (that is, on the same terms as men). Both married rather later than was usual (in their mid-thirties) and remained childless. Marriage brought the peace of mind that accompanied the knowledge that spinsterhood would not be their fate, yet despite the careful negotiation of the marital bargain, which is minutely documented for Beatrice, marriage also brought the threat of submersion of a public persona constructed against the odds.

Octavia Hill was of an earlier generation, born some twenty years before these two, but an understanding of the context of her work in housing management, begun in the mid-1860s, and as a founder member of the COS (in 1869) became important for appreciating the nature and magnitude of the continuities and changes in the thinking and practice of those women activists who did not become prominent until the 1890s and 1900s. Beatrice Potter began work outside the home as a rent collector trained in the Octavia Hill system, although not working directly for her. Octavia's strongly held principles regarding the middle-class duty to serve – men through policymaking at the local and national levels and women through individual social work with the poor – lived on in modified form in later generations of women, even in those who, like Beatrice, rejected her idea that individual social work undertaken voluntarily as a matter of conscience was the only valid way of achieving social change. Alone of the five women, Octavia never married, but she believed that the family should be the main focus of middle-class women's lives and that their primary obligation should be the welfare of their own families. After that, in the case of middle-class women, the needs of the poor, considered within their family context, demanded their attention.

Mary Ward, slightly closer in age to Helen Bosanquet and Beatrice Webb than to Octavia Hill, provided (as did Helen) a powerful strand of continuity in terms of the importance she attached to the family as both agent and object of social reform. As the best-selling novelist, Mrs Humphry Ward, she portrayed a world in which family responsibilities took priority for both men and women and in which strict codes of moral behaviour were delineated for both sexes in order to sustain the social discipline that she believed found expression in the bourgeois family form. Mary Ward also followed Octavia firmly in her stand against women's suffrage, grounding her ideas about women's rights and obligations as citizens in participation in local affairs, which were, she argued, of direct relevance to family life in a way that national and imperial matters were not. In this she differed from Helen Bosanquet, who showed the other face of female philanthropy by supporting votes for women. But in her thinking about the mechanisms for fulfilling women's wider – 'social maternalist' – obligations to the community beyond their immediate families, Mary Ward proved a more transitional figure. Unlike the other four women, she did not engage in individual social work, nor was she ever a member of the COS. Instead her social activism went into the founding of a Bloomsbury settlement house, which in the tradition of the late nineteenth-century British and American settlements was designed to provide a base from which the middle class might seek direct contact with the poor via the organization of clubs and lecture programmes, and, in the case of Mary Ward's settlement, work with neighbourhood children. She proved willing to treat the needs of poor children regardless of the rights and wrongs of their parents and if necessary to invoke the aid of the state.

Born in 1872, some fourteen years after Beatrice Potter, Violet Markham represents a third generation of social activism. She remained committed to the idea of personal social work, but from 1911 publicly dissociated herself from the COS, to which both Octavia and Helen remained loyal, advocating instead an active partnership between the voluntary sector and the state. She also provided, with Mary Ward, the main female leadership for the organized anti-suffrage movement. Unlike Mary Ward, she abandoned the 'Antis' in the middle of World

War I, but without changing her views about the proper social roles of men and women. Violet Markham left the slightest inheritance in terms of an original corpus of ideas and practices, and yet she achieved the most in terms of public appointments, serving on numerous war-time committees and most importantly, during the 1930s, becoming the only woman member on the Unemployment Assistance Board. In some measure, this was a function of the passing of time. For all that Octavia Hill was invited, in 1887, to celebrate Queen Victoria's Golden Jubilee in Westminster Abbey, as one of three women who had most influenced the course of Victorian Britain (the other two were Josephine Butler and Florence Nightingale), she was passed over for membership of the Royal Commission on Housing in the mid-1880s. Only once did she serve on a public body, just before her death (and together with Helen Bosanquet and Beatrice Webb), on the Royal Commission on the Poor Laws between 1905 and 1909.

But there are larger issues surrounding the assessments made of the contribution of these women by contemporaries and by historians. Three, Octavia, Beatrice and Mary, became household names. Leslie Stephen's second wife, Julia Duckworth, apparently set her children three role models: Octavia Hill, Mary Ward and Florence Nightingale.[1] By the 1920s, many considered Beatrice Webb to be the best-known woman in England. But as Deborah Epstein Nord remarked in her book on Beatrice: 'prominent women in particular seem to have suffered from the disturbing powers of time, memory and popular prejudice'.[2] As early as 1924, Elizabeth Robins, actress and writer, was complaining about the 'bald inadequacy' of the accounts of Mary Ward's work printed after her death, which Robins linked to the 'animus shown by men of letters in private' towards her work during her lifetime.[3] Historians have tended to label anyone as determinedly loyal to the COS as Octavia and Helen as rank individualists, who ignored the structural causes of poverty in their conviction that personal social work under the auspices of the voluntary sector rather than the state would provide the means of training or disciplining the poor into an independent and self-maintaining existence.[4] Nor as Epstein Nord's words indicate, has Beatrice Webb, who took a very different view, escaped opprobrium. Both contemporaries (H. G. Wells being perhaps the most famous) and later commentators tended to portray her as something of a female Gradgrind, always emphasizing the rational and scientific, in short as rather masculine.

My picture of these women is more nuanced. Only Octavia Hill was certain as to the manner in which to combine public work with family responsibilities; the others tended to reflect consciously both on women's conflicting obligations towards, and indeed the attractions of, a public life as against the home. The image of the upright Victorian figure, confidently directing the business of her own home and extending her rule to the homes of the poor, whether through the pursuit of scientific charity or a science of society, dissolves into a more complicated series of problems and contradictions. Not all were sure of how to negotiate the boundary between public and private in their own lives (Beatrice Webb was a conspicuous example) and most were conscious of the kind of moral dilemmas and conflicting choices between family and career that were posed sharply in Mary Ward's novels. The vote represented the most conspicuous boundary issue of the period, forcing all five women to express a view sometimes reluctantly, sometimes willingly, as to the extent of women's sphere. All were more keen to stress women's obligations than their rights. That was part of the language of duty to which all subscribed and which underpinned the injunction to serve.

The impetus to social action which all shared did not only consist of the pursuit of a more scientific treatment of poverty and the poor. The spiritual element in their visions of how to achieve a better society never disappeared. Nor was the focus of attention simply the role of the state as against that of charity in addressing social problems. They were equally preoccupied by the importance of the relationships between the individual, the family and the state. Indeed, in their dealings with the poor, as in so much else, the nature of their work defies simple classification. They aimed to change behaviour, inevitably in accordance with middle-class norms and values. Yet in the case of Octavia Hill and Helen Bosanquet in particular, their sympathy with the conditions of the poor, especially of poor women, and their respect for the autonomy of the working-class family was real enough.

Rather than attempting an assessment of their lives and work chiefly on the basis of what we know of outcomes, whether expressed through the confident air of the officially commissioned portrait, or through the undoubted harshness of much of the work of women social workers in practice, my aim has been to express the contradictions that existed both between motives and outcomes in their approaches to social problems, and between public and private worlds in their own lives and in their prescriptions for other women. I have also tried to make clear their own priorities, concepts and frameworks of analysis, which have tended to be obscured by those historians whose main concern has been to locate their work in relation to a much larger canvas, most typically the shift from individualism to collectivism and the growth of the welfare state.

Women's rights and obligations

All the subjects of this book wanted to lead 'useful' lives. Thus even Octavia Hill, who quite accepted her friend and mentor John Ruskin's conviction as to the importance of home and family for women, rejected the idea that women should confine themselves to reigning as 'Queens' over their own hearths.[5] She believed, in accordance with religious traditions set much earlier in the nineteenth century, in the national importance of women's role as moral guardians and educators within the home, and she built on existing ideas that the moral influence of women should be exercised through the medium of philanthropic visiting beyond their own families.[6] Indeed in the case of both Octavia Hill and Helen Bosanquet, the business failures of their fathers forced them to engage in paid work, something that women's obligations to their families dictated that they should do in the event of necessity, but which firm notions of middle-class propriety decreed to be otherwise undesirable. Middle-class women in possession of a male relative able to support them very rarely worked for pay.[7]

Given her firm convictions as to women's duty to serve, Octavia Hill strongly supported women's improved access to education. This position was common to all five women. Beatrice Potter's early diary was dominated by the quest for self-education and, almost a generation later, Violet Markham remained profoundly dissatisfied with her skimpy formal education. Helen Bosanquet was the only one of the five to take a degree and, like Octavia Hill, became involved in the effort to give women social workers a more rigorous training. Mary Ward took part in the struggle to open Oxford University to women. The feminist issue causing division between them was the suffrage, although even here friendship networks were, with some difficulty, preserved; for example between Mary Ward, Violet Markham and many of their suffragist friends. In addition, suffragists and anti-suffragists continued to work together on other social issues. Thus Helen Bosanquet, Beatrice Webb and Mary Ward, who were also divided in terms of their party politics (Helen was a Liberal, Beatrice a Fabian Socialist and Mary as a Liberal Unionist supported the Conservatives), worked together to extend protective legislation in the form of the Factory Acts to a greater number of women workers.[8]

In large measure, continued friendship and cooperation was possible because of certain shared assumptions regarding the position of women, irrespective of divisions over the vote. As Sandra Holton has noted, a broad spectrum of women accepted the tenets of Victorian (male) social and medical scientists on sexual difference, which held that women's capacities were biologically determined and therefore different from those of men.[9] Sexual difference, unlike class difference, was deemed to be a 'natural' phenomenon and women's lives were therefore inevitably going to be dictated by their capacity to bear children. Hence it was argued that women's chief occupation would be that of wife and mother.[10] There is evidence that three of the subjects of this book actively feared spinsterhood as potentially unsexing. It was some recompense for the unmarried woman if she believed that she could lead a useful life within the community and retain an element of 'womanly feeling' by engaging in work with the families of poor women. But both true womanhood and happiness were believed to depend on the achievement of marriage and preferably also motherhood.

Belief in natural sexual difference also determined the idea of women's citizenship, which was additionally fractured by social class. Whereas (middle-class) men's world comprised both public and private spheres and their obligations involved the responsibility to protect both, middle-class women's obligations were to their own families and, it was argued by philanthropists, to those of the less fortunate. This gendered concept of citizenship obligations did not necessarily entail acceptance of separate spheres for men and women in the sense that social theorists such as Herbert Spencer (Beatrice Potter's mentor) and Frederic Harrison (known personally to Beatrice and to Mary Ward) conceived of them, with the domestic world firmly isolated from the public and subordinated to it.[11] Mary Ward, who accepted the idea that women's primary obligations should be to home and family, also represented women's work as being of fundamental importance to state and nation. Both Helen Bosanquet and her academic philosopher husband Bernard argued that the family mediated between the individual and the state. It was not therefore perceived as a private and separate sphere, but rather as the fundamental unit of the polis and as such the agent of social progress as well as the object of social reform.

The campaign for the vote has usually been depicted as a claim made on the basis of a desire for equality with men, but the vast majority of both supporters and opponents of the suffrage began from a position of 'difference'. The arguments of suffragists often included a tactical appeal to sexual difference as well as to women's equal capacity to exercise the franchise,[12] for example, many argued for the 'balancing' powers of the woman's vote in the national equilibrium. Given the importance attached to women's role in the family by the majority of late nineteenth-century philanthropists, attitudes towards votes for women within this community were going to be determined primarily by whether it was considered that the suffrage would threaten to undermine women's domestic responsibilities. In fact, the suffrage campaign split the world of philanthropy.[13] Women like Helen Bosanquet believed in women's need to pursue fulfilment in any area they chose, including the political, if they were to be good wives and mothers. However, women like Mary Ward viewed what she perceived as the rapidly changing position of women, especially in terms of their greater mobility outside the home, as a threat to their traditional responsibilities. She saw the vote as one more claim that was likely to distract women from their locally based responsibilities to the family, and which would in addition involve women acting alongside men, something that she firmly believed to be impossible because sexual attraction would inevitably imperil working relationships. But those women opposing the vote did not necessarily believe that women should be confined to their own homes. Both Mary Ward and Violet Markham argued strongly for women's domestic talents to be put to use in local government and in local institutions – in workhouses, hospitals and schools – as well as in the homes of the poor within the local community. In this formulation, the demand was for a place for women within social administration which would allow them to exercise their familial influence more broadly, rather than for legislative power. When Beatrice Webb and Violet Markham changed their minds about opposing votes for women, both cited as a reason their perception that matters of social administration were becoming national rather than local concerns as social policies became matters of high politics.[14] Thus women's proper concern with 'domestic politics' required the exercise of the franchise. Violet Markham made it quite clear that her convictions as to the existence of fundamental sexual difference had not changed at all.

The problem was that in claiming the territory of the social beyond their own homes, middle-class female social workers and social investigators confronted the vigorous ideology of separate spheres.[15] Herbert Spencer, for example, believed that society was evolving towards the point when all women would be able to stay at home and the separation of spheres would be complete, while Frederic Harrison's vision also confined women to the family and pictured men alone mediating between the family and the larger world. Despite being attracted to this emphasis on the importance of evolutionary progress and familial order, no woman social activist, whether pro- or anti-suffrage, was able to accept such views because they meant that female citizenship would vest only in motherhood. Women actively involved in addressing social questions claimed that their obligations as citizens involved service, not only to their families but to others within the local community.

But women social activists remained extremely sensitive as to where the boundary should be drawn in respect of their activities. Octavia Hill insisted that while women had a duty to serve the families of the poor, any work they did had to be not only domestic in nature, but 'quiet' and 'out-of-sight'. Not only the content of the work, but the manner of doing it had to fall within the bounds of propriety.[16] All five women deplored female assertiveness. Beatrice Webb, for example, had great difficulty overcoming her antipathy to the idea of women speaking in public. All were appalled by the activities of the militant suffragettes. Octavia Hill had difficulty bringing herself to write a letter to a newspaper editor expressing her opposition to votes for women, but ironically Violet Markham enjoyed perhaps the most highly developed career as a public speaker, largely as a consequence of her prominence in the anti-suffrage campaign. For Violet Markham and Mary Ward, if not for Octavia Hill, it was a case of temporarily stepping beyond the bounds of propriety in order the better to safeguard those bounds in the long term.

The fear that all five women shared of violating norms of womanly behaviour arose from the understanding that if they were perceived to be overtly intent on crossing the boundary between men's and women's worlds, then they risked the withdrawal of male protection.[17] When Beatrice Webb told Frederic Harrison that she regretted signing the 1889 petition against women's suffrage, he apparently spoke of the 'future massacre' of women that would come when men were driven beyond male patience.[18] Having accepted that women were first and foremost wives and mothers and that their primary obligation was to home and family, it followed that they were dependent on men as husbands and legislators for protection. Women like Mary Ward and Violet Markham believed additionally that the chivalrous niceties of middle-class male behaviour rested on women being seen to abide by the canons of propriety that served to police the boundary of woman's sphere. They were convinced as to the fragility of the carefully con-structed middle-class social order and feared that women's claims to greater autonomy, whether to easier divorce or to the vote, would result in men abandoning civilized behaviour towards women in the manner predicted by Harrison and shown by the police towards suffragette demonstrators.[19] All five women were agreed that the boundary between male and female spheres had to be respected, but they were not agreed on exactly where it lay or, in particular, on the degree to which the suffrage threatened to erode it.

The nature of social action
The commitment to social action shared by all five women transcended their political differences in terms of both feminism and party politics.

None adopted a *laissez-faire* approach, believing rather that the problem of poverty in the towns required the active consideration of all better-off citizens. Four of the five women began by 'visiting' the poor, either under the auspices of the COS, or as rent collector/social workers, under the Octavia Hill system of housing management. Vast numbers of Victorian middle-class women undertook such work.[20] Many visited the poor at the behest of the local parish church and continued to distribute coal and food tickets as well as spiritual advice, much to the disgust of the COS, which insisted that to give material relief without proper investigation of the applicant's circumstances could only result in further demoralization. But 'taking a district' or visiting the inmates of the local workhouse was something that large numbers of young middle-class women felt obliged to do before marriage, and many carried on the work throughout their adult lives. Middle-class men were also expected to serve at the local as well as the national level, albeit more in a decisionmaking role. In terms of philanthropy, they tended to give more generously of their money than of their time. The active work of philanthropy was gendered; men served mainly on the committees of charitable organizations but did not visit the poor, and in the male settlement houses they were more inclined to give lectures and form clubs than to venture out into the community to undertake work of personal service.[21]

The motives for middle-class women's extensive involvement in a variety of charitable endeavours, of which visiting the poor was only the most common, were complicated. Some historians have emphasized a variety of self-interested reasons for taking up the work. Feminists have stressed the way in which philanthropic work represented one of the few acceptable bridges to the world beyond the home.[22] Martha Vicinus has described the spirit of adventure in which many women embarked on work in the settlement houses.[23] Certainly the simple desire to do something interesting and challenging should not be underestimated. Philanthropic work also offered a sense of community to unmarried women, whether through the settlements, as part of Octavia Hill's band of 'fellow workers', or through membership of an organization like the COS. Beatrice Webb sensed this when she very briefly celebrated the dignity of 'glorified spinsterhood'. The small number of late nineteenth-century female university graduates commonly ended up, like Helen Bosanquet, as residents of settlements, often working under the auspices of the COS. Increasing numbers of women expanded their activities into the work of local government, but it was not easy to go far beyond this. Only a few women, Beatrice was one, were able to use philanthropy as a stepping stone to other work in the public sphere.

Philanthropic work remained within the bounds of propriety and middle-class women's sphere, whereas most other public activities involved crossing the boundary into unwomanly behaviour.

Work among the poor, especially that of house-to-house visiting, was often far from pleasant. Many must have shared Beatrice Webb's revulsion from the smells, dirt and brutality. And yet small armies of women continued to do it. It may have been that middle-class women were as eager to save their own souls by ministering to the poor as to provide spiritual comfort, or, among the more secular, to hold at bay what Beatrice Webb referred to as the growing 'class consciousness of sin'.[24] In this interpretation, direct involvement with the poor helped assuage middle-class guilt.

But perhaps most significantly, women's call to serve others was inspired by their perception of 'duty' and was perceived to constitute their main obligation as citizens. The language of 'duty' together with that of 'feeling' and of 'character' was central to the social vocabulary of the late nineteenth century.[25] Woman's duty to love and serve was, as Lynda Nead has pointed out, conflated with her nature.[26] Ideas about sexual difference made absence of feeling for others abnormal in women. Furthermore, the injunction to serve was substantially re-inforced by ideas of Christian obligation. Octavia Hill in particular was affected by the huge moral seriousness that F. D. Maurice, a Christian Socialist, attached to human relationships and she insisted that all Christians were obliged to search their consciences in respect of their contact with others, especially the less fortunate. Three of the five women had close contact with Unitarianism, which shared with Utilitarianism a belief in the perfectibility of man and society. It inspired a strong commitment on the part of men and women to social action, which they were expected to fulfil in appropriately gendered ways. The strength of the religious impulse to serve was probably strongest for Octavia Hill's generation. Both Mary Ward and Beatrice Webb struggled explicitly to reconcile religion and the doubt inspired by science, which resulted not so much from Darwinism as from, in the case of Mary Ward, the new German historical criticism applied to miracle, and in the case of Beatrice, from the difficulty in retaining a vision of society derived from moral and spiritual concerns alongside a preoccupation with the best mechanical, administrative means of achieving it. Moral and spiritual concerns remained long after organized religion relaxed its grip. Indeed the importance attached to the family, guarded and nurtured by women, may be understood in terms of the way in which the home itself became sacred, the chief prop of a moral order no longer so firmly buttressed by belief.[27] As Leonore Davidoff

has shown, upper middle-class women felt that their domestic routines
– running a home and controlling servants, together with the rituals of
card leaving and visiting – were duties performed in the interests of the
wider society. The claims of the social order linked such duties to God
and made them very hard to resist.[28] A more generalized duty to society
could be extended to concern about – including a desire to regulate –
the families of the poor, or, as Martha Vicinus has shown, it could
sometimes be transmuted to a community of women.[29]

The duty to serve the poor was also genuinely felt and continued to
occupy a central place in the ideas of those to whom the language of
political obligation spoke as loudly as that of Christianity. Both Helen
Bosanquet and Mary Ward were concerned that individuals should
develop their 'best selves' and that social bonds between rich and poor
in the community should be strengthened. Both were substantially
influenced by British Idealism, Mary Ward by T. H. Green, its leading
exponent, and Helen Bosanquet by the work of her husband. Green
stressed above all the importance of individual self-development and
the building of character, but his inheritance was mixed in terms of the
means considered necessary to achieve this.[30] Bernard Bosanquet and
C. S. Loch, the General Secretary of the COS, who had been a pupil
of Green, insisted that it was a matter of individuals working to improve
the characters and to change the behaviour of their less fortunate
fellows. This put a high premium on the individual social work that was
performed by women and tied its practice firmly to social theory.
However, an opposing view, which gathered substantial numbers of
adherents after the social disturbances of the mid-1880s, advocated a
more substantial role for state collectivism in creating an environment
in which every individual might develop to his fullest potential.[31]
Beatrice Webb went furthest along this road, fighting not only for
collectivist means, but an objective that centred on a vision of a socialist
society rather than on reformed and empowered individuals. Mary
Ward and Violet Markham adhered firmly to personal social service as
the means of achieving social change, but were increasingly prepared
to accept help from the state in carrying it out, as the early twentieth-
century language of 'national efficiency' created awareness across the
political spectrum of the burden that high levels of poverty and physical
unfitness created for the body politic.[32] However, to Octavia Hill and
Helen Bosanquet, state intervention threatened to erode the very sense
of personal responsibility that individual social work was designed to
foster. Thus to all except Beatrice Webb, social work remained the main
vehicle for achieving both social reform – by changing the mind-set and
behaviour of the poor – and social progress. The duty to serve others

was therefore conceptualized as an obligation of citizenship and achieved a position of considerable importance within the social theory of the late nineteenth and early twentieth centuries.

Social action in the form of social work was inspired by more than self-interest, but there remains the issue as to whether its practitioners were effectively little more than the handmaidens of classical political economy, undertaking to discipline the poor. Women's social work focused on the family in the belief that social problems were susceptible to solution by the proper exercise of family responsibilities: of husbands to provide; of wives to manage; and of both parents to play their part both in socializing children into habits of industry and thrift, and in imbuing them in their turn with a sense of responsibility towards the needs of not only the children they would have but also their elderly parents. Specialist visitors focused on particular areas of behaviour, for example the lady health missioners (later 'health visitors') concerned themselves with infant welfare and hygiene.[33] The emphasis that proponents of social work placed on the development of character, on personal responsibility and on the family as the chief provider of welfare fitted easily into well-established Victorian beliefs regarding the causes of poverty and its solution.[34] The 1834 Poor Law worked on the premise that individual moral failure was the root of destitution and that the provision of relief outside the workhouse could only serve further to demoralize the recipient and sap his incentive to provide for himself.[35] This diagnosis was broadly accepted by the COS, which sought both to work in cooperation with the poor law authorities and to build a philosophy of personal social work designed to restore the character of the individual.[36] Settlement workers were concerned primarily with educational work rather than with the problems associated with the relief of the destitute, but their desire to spread the benefits of what was a middle-class culture among the poor paralleled the middle-class norms and values employed by visitors of the poor when assessing applications for relief and seeking to achieve changes in behaviour.[37]

Women social workers have been adjudged unrelenting individualists who sought to impose on the poor the gendered obligations associated with the bourgeois family form. Workers such as Octavia Hill and Helen Bosanquet were certainly individualists in the sense that they believed the fulfilment of personal responsibilities within the family, which were conceptualized differently for men and for women, to be both the only proper object of social intervention and the only means of achieving further social progress. But they were not opposed to any and all state intervention. Octavia Hill, for example, was not opposed to either public health legislation or building codes, but she attacked any legislation that threatened to subvert the responsibility of family members each for the other's welfare (such as proposals for old age pensions or the provision of meals for schoolchildren). Lasting social reform, it was believed, could only come by reforming people. Armies of social workers were therefore essential and the willingness of the middle class to undertake such work also became a crucial test of their citizenship obligations to their fellows. Thus Octavia Hill and Helen Bosanquet insisted that social work be voluntary and resisted the idea of a major role for the state as an employer in this regard.

Nevertheless, Bernard Bosanquet was inclined to see individualism and collectivism as positions on a spectrum rather than as dichotomous. This would appear to be a more accurate description of the turn of the century debate than the depiction of a battle between 'friends' and 'enemies' of the state to be found in many accounts of the period.[38] As Stefan Collini has observed, there existed a hegemonic set of assumptions regarding 'the ideal of service, the duty to contribute to the common good, the need to make the best of oneself, the duty of self-development and so on'.[39] Such assumptions often resulted in common approaches to the problem of poverty. For example Beatrice Webb continued to share the high regard of the woman social worker for the respectable poor, and probably showed as much or more enthusiasm for disciplining the intractable poor – 'the residuum' – than did Octavia Hill or Helen Bosanquet.

In fact, individualism signified more than anti-statism. In terms of the practice of voluntary social work, it encompassed a method as well as a vehicle for treating the poor. When Mary Ward invoked the financial aid of the state for her work with children, and when Violet Markham went on to advocate a new 'partnership' between the state and the voluntary sector, they both retained their faith in social work with individuals as the solution to social problems. Individualism referred to the preference on the part of philanthropists for tackling social problems by treating the needs of individuals in a holistic fashion within the context of the family, as well as for keeping state intervention to a minimum. Accounts of the 'origins' of the welfare state have tended to subsume the first of these under the second, but positions on the individualism/collectivism spectrum become more complicated when the two meanings of individualism are separated. For example, female social investigators within the Fabian Women's Group shared common ground with Helen Bosanquet in terms of their qualitative analysis of the fabric of working-class women's lives, even though they differed radically in their advocacy of state intervention.[40] Beatrice Webb, on the other hand, found herself in fierce conflict with Helen Bosanquet on all fronts. First, she became a believer in the study of aggregates rather than of individuals. Second, she favoured treating social problems by diagnosing their cause and then allocating the individual to a particular authority, rather than using a social worker to investigate the position of the family as a whole. Thus if the cause was deemed to be unemployment, the individual would be sent to an official at a Ministry of Labour; and in her scheme for reforming the treatment of those seeking poor relief, different family members would find themselves being treated by different authorities. Third, she believed that state bureaucracy should fully supersede voluntary effort.

The aim of social workers working within the ambit of the COS was to secure the self-maintenance of the individual applying for assistance, which involved exercising particular pressure on men to provide, although it was also strongly believed that wives could do much to ameliorate the situation of their families by careful housewifery. But in terms of ideals, social workers cared for more than the relatively narrow ambition of making sure that applicants for relief achieved material independence of both charity and the state. People like Helen Bosanquet put a much higher premium on the achievement of participation as full citizens than on material well-being *per se*. In the case of working-class women she extended this concern to advocating the granting of the vote. Helen attached considerable importance to the idea of enabling the individual to take control of his or her life, a concept not dissimilar from the modern social work idea of empowerment. The values of political economy were substantially modified for Octavia Hill by Christian obligation and for Helen Bosanquet by the tenets of Idealist philosophy, which stressed the importance of ethical individualism. This required the fulfilment of obligations to fellow citizens, rather than the atomic individualism characterized by the injunction to self-help.[41] Above all, the problem of poverty was conceptualized as a moral rather than as an economic issue.[42] The *idea* of social work was therefore informed by much more than simple classical political economy.

However, it is more difficult to assess the outcome of the *practice* of the social work that was dominated by women and which often involved interaction between the middle-class visitor and the working-class wife. Pat Hollis has concluded that the work of women who visited workhouses significantly improved the lot of the inmates.[43] But the ordinary, usually ill-trained house-to-house visitor may have understood little of the higher motives of those providing the rationale for social work. It is therefore likely that the attempts of a COS visitor to determine whether an applicant for relief was 'deserving' or 'undeserving' and whether, regardless of moral fault, he or she possessed the moral qualities that would enable the social worker to give effective help was likely to prove both intrusive and stigmatizing.[44] Even the texts produced by the leaders in the field were themselves replete with contradictions when it came to dealing with clients. Helen Bosanquet could show great empathy with the position of working-class women, and yet be extraordinarily condescending. Middle-class women may well have acted as the advocates of working-class wives and mothers,[45] but nevertheless have ended by treating them more as victims than anything else. Eleanor Rathbone confessed to a friend that her work for the COS in Liverpool continued to appeal to her despite its growing unpopularity (in Edwardian Britain) because of its small-scale nature and the fact that it was possible to 'save' a family from the workhouse by dint of personal effort.[46] The main source of authority used by the middle-class woman visitor in her work was after all that derived from her social class position.

The vast majority of women's social activism was contained within the voluntary sector, Beatrice Webb's commitment to social investigation and to propaganda on behalf of state collectivism was exceptional. In the histories of social policies which have tended to focus on the growth of the state, women's contribution has therefore been over-looked.[47] More seriously still, their ideas were also lost within the growing bureaucracy of the welfare state, for while they came to occupy paid positions in social work, policy was made by a civil service that was almost entirely male in its upper echelons.[48] In the scramble to wash the charity and hence, it was believed, the stigma out of welfare provision, social work was separated from social theory and ideas as to the importance of social participation were divorced from the provision of an adequate standard of material well-being, which became the sole goal of the welfare state. But this was a long process. More immediate was the effect of World War I in signalling the end of hopes of social progress to the women social workers who sought to promote moral regeneration and reform as well as economic self-maintenance. Beatrice Webb also suffered a severe bout of pessimism and depression during the war, a reminder that she shared first, the commitment to social action that was the outstanding characteristic of all five women, albeit that her diagnosis of and solution to the problem of poverty became very different; second, their faith in social progress; and third, a vision that was as much moral and spiritual as material.

Public and private lives
When they addressed questions of women's rights and obligations these

five women did not conceive of the family as 'sealed off' from the public sphere. Yet they also understood that there was a dividing line between male and female spheres in the middle class; what constituted its transgression was a matter of debate. Hence in their own lives these women faced difficult decisions about whether and how to establish a public identity, where to delineate its boundary, and how to integrate it with the family life that all agreed should take priority for women. Sometimes dilemmas inherent in women's position were posed publicly and explicitly, as, for example, by Mary Ward in her novels, and sometimes they were articulated in private without any evidence that they were being connected to the more general position of women in society, as in Beatrice Webb's discussions of her situation in her diary.

All five women valued education highly, but there is evidence that some feared its effect on womanly qualities. It is striking that while Mary Ward fought to open Oxford to women, neither of her daughters attended university. Beatrice Webb constantly feared that her pursuit of knowledge was unnatural and indeed beyond the capacity of a woman. Thus even in regard to the one feminist claim they all supported, their personal feelings were equivocal. At some hard-to-define point the pursuit of knowledge might become unwomanly. Clara Collet, a contemporary of Beatrice Webb and Helen Bosanquet, who joined Beatrice in her work of social investigation and who went on, much more unusually, to become a civil servant at the Board of Trade, summed up these feelings in a short story she wrote. One woman, aged about thirty, remarks to her friend (a settlement worker) of a third woman who has chosen an academic job: 'What good does she do to anybody with her middle English? Marion, why did we never learn at Newnham that we should be women some day, not merely sponges to absorb knowledge and give it out again?'[49]

Ostensibly all five women practised what they preached and put family obligations first. Octavia Hill embraced her duty to care for her sick sister with enthusiasm; Beatrice Potter did not question her obligation to care for her father, but did not enjoy it; while Violet Markham admitted that she had needed to be prompted to do similarly for her mother, but was afterwards relieved to have done her duty. Family support was also very important to all five women. Octavia Hill relied enormously on her mother and sisters and Mary Ward on first her niece and then her elder daughter. Violet Markham came rather to enjoy her status as family matriarch and Beatrice Webb also enjoyed keeping in touch with the doings of her large number of nephews and nieces, although her relationship with her sisters was more problematic.[50] For four of the women, their husbands provided substantial support as well as ensuring 'womanly fulfilment'. But marriage also posed the problem of how to achieve a proper balance between the private identity of wife, and in the case of Mary Ward, mother, and an often painfully created public persona.

Three of the four married women remained childless. Mary Ward was very unusual in getting married extremely young, at twenty-one (to an Oxford academic who became a journalist on *The Times*) having three children, and still managing to create a public identity. In two cases, those of Beatrice Potter and Violet Markham, marriage is known to have been a matter of conscious calculation, something Pat Jalland also observed in her study of some fifty late Victorian and Edwardian political families.[51] All four marriages appear to have worked, possibly because in all cases the women were able to redress the power imbalance which is arguably part and parcel of the marriage contract and the marital relationship.[52] Beatrice, Helen and Violet all married late, after their commitment to a public life was clearly established. Beatrice married a man who was both unprepossessing in appearance and of a lower social class, and both she and Violet had not inconsiderable private incomes of their own. Mary Ward also gained satisfaction and autonomy from earning a large amount of money from her novels. Beatrice and Helen chose men who shared their intellectual interests and whom they might reasonably have expected to become partners; Violet married a man from an entirely different world, whom she considered ideal because he raised no objection to their continuing to live quite separate public lives. Violet seems to have also been able to keep up her considerable friendship network after marriage. However, many of Beatrice's friends recoiled from her decision to marry a social inferior and a socialist. While Beatrice would have had difficulty managing the predominantly male world of first the social survey and then the study of institutions without Sidney's support, marriage also involved her in some compromise as far as the use of her own methods of social investigation were concerned. The women who stuck to the more female dominated world of philanthropy and social work had an easier time in this respect.

It is not easy fully to reconstruct these women's expectations of marriage. In her work on the worlds of Edwardian working-class women, Ellen Ross has concluded that the marital relationship did not enjoin romantic love or verbal and sexual intimacy, but rather required financial obligations, services and activities that were gender specific.[53] Romantic love does not seem to have bulked large in what personal correspondence remains for the five women considered in this book either, which is not to say that it did not exist. But the ideal in marriages as much as in public life, was articulated not in terms of personal desire, which could only be selfish, but rather in the language of service. Marriage was a matter of social discipline involving mutual respect and loyalty. The partners' proper aim was to serve each other and thereby enrich the wider community. The family was after all conceived of as the fundamental unit of society and marriage was its underpinning, which meant that it was to be taken extremely seriously. None of the five favoured relaxing the divorce laws.

All five women achieved a public voice, although in the case of Beatrice Webb, it was more often than not joined to that of her husband. But they differed widely in the extent to which they were seen to occupy public spaces. Octavia Hill deliberately sought to avoid them and all except Violet Markham experienced considerable anxiety and ambivalence as to the propriety of taking the public platform. Violet was also alone in eventually taking up a genuinely public career as the token woman appointee on government committees. Probably she was temperamentally better suited to this work than someone like Beatrice, for example, whose first such experience – as a member of the Royal Commission on the Poor Laws – was distinguished by her difficulty in finding a way of operating in a male dominated forum. Those who remained associated with the more acceptable work of philanthropy and those who, like Violet Markham, were content to confine their public interests to matters defined as 'women's issues' found it easier to move about in the public world.

The amount that it is possible to know about these five women's struggle for identity and for integration of their public and private lives varies. The papers and writings of the five women permit very different levels of contact to the reader; something that finds expression in my (inconsistent) decision as to how to name them in the text. There are virtually no personal papers in the form of letters and diaries for Helen Bosanquet, and what remain for Octavia Hill were carefully vetted by her relatives. The other three left large quantities of correspondence; Violet Markham, a short-lived diary; and Beatrice Webb an enormous and famous diary that she kept faithfully from adolescence to her death. The difficulties of using such source materials are well known. In particular, the point at which outpouring overtakes consciousness of self is often hard to establish.[54] Clara Collet was well aware of this when she wrote in her diary: 'The most difficult thing in a diary is to write totally for yourself; try as hard as one will there is always the *arrière-pensée* about what people would think of as they read it'.[55] Concern as to propriety may well have pervaded private documents as well as dictating public utterances and behaviour. For example, Octavia Hill was, like the American settlement house worker, Jane Addams, always careful to insist that she had been 'called' to her work rather than risk asserting her own agency.[56]

Examining both public and personal records, I have focused on two main themes: the issues regarding women's rights and obligations at the personal and prescriptive levels, and the meaning of social action. The main aim has been to examine the nature of the connections the five women made and to explore the often contradictory messages they offered.

Notes

(All places of publication London unless otherwise stated.)
1. Noel Annan, *Leslie Stephen* (Weidenfeld & Nicolson, 1984), p. 120.
2. Deborah Epstein Nord, *The Apprenticeship of Beatrice Webb* (Macmillan, 1985), p. 1.
3. Anon. (Elizabeth Robins), *Ancilla's Share* (Hutchinson, 1924), p. 89. I am grateful to Angela V. John for this reference. Of course women too were antagonistic towards Mary Ward. Rebecca West was perhaps her most constant and harshest critic, albeit in public rather than in private.
4. Perhaps the most influential has been Gareth Stedman Jones, *Outcast London* (Harmondsworth: Penguin, 1976).
5. John Ruskin, 'Of Queens' Gardens', in *Sesame and Lilies* (Smith Elder, 1865).
6. For the earlier tradition see: Leonore Davidoff and Catherine Hall, *Family Fortunes. Men and Women of the English Middle Class, 1780–1850* (Hutchinson, 1987).
7. While M. Jeanne Peterson's *Family, Love and Work in the Lives of Victorian Gentlewomen* (Bloomington: Indiana University Press, 1989) has shown that in the Paget family paid employment was certainly not unknown, there is as yet no evidence to suggest that this was more generally true of Victorian middle-class women.
8. This provides additional support for P. F. Clarke's argument regarding the existence of a 'progressive movement' in England. See his 'The Progressive Movement in England', *Transactions of the Royal Historical Society* 24 (1974).
9. Sandra Stanley Holton, *Feminism and Democracy. Women's Suffrage and Reform Politics in Britain, 1900–1918* (Cambridge: Cambridge University Press, 1986), pp. 9–28.
10. For the most recent comprehensive discussion see Cynthia Eagle Russet, *Sexual Science. The Victorian Construction of Womanhood* (Cambridge, Mass.: Harvard University Press, 1989).
11. On Herbert Spencer see Carol Dyhouse, 'Social Darwinistic Ideas and the Development of Women's Education in England, 1880–1920', *History of Education* 5 (Feb. 1976); and Jill Conway, 'Stereotypes of Femininity in a Theory of Sexual Evolution', in Martha Vicinus (ed.), *Suffer and be Still* (Bloomington: Indiana University Press, 1973). On Frederic Harrison, see Martha S. Vogeler, *Frederic Harrison, The Vocations of a Positivist* (Oxford: Clarendon, 1984); and Christopher Kent, *Brains and Numbers. Elitism, Comtism and Democracy in Mid-Victorian England* (Toronto: University of Toronto Press, 1978), pp. 58–77.
12. I am not altogether convinced by work that shows feminists in the past to have been wholly inspired by ideas of either equality or difference, for example Joan Scott, *Gender and the Politics of History* (New York: Columbia University Press, 1988), especially chapter 9; and Karen Offen, 'Defining Feminism: A Comparative Historical Approach', *Signs* 14 (Autumn 1988).

13. See Brian Harrison, *Separate Spheres. The Opposition to Women's Suffrage in Britain* (Croom Helm, 1978), p. 84.
14. José Harris, 'The Transition to High Politics in English Social Policy, 1880–1914', in Michael Bentley and John Stevenson, *High and Low Politics in Modern Britain* (Oxford: Clarendon, 1983).
15. Mary Poovey, *The Proper Lady and the Woman Writer* (Chicago: University of Chicago Press, 1984), p. 242 has discussed the paradoxical commands of propriety in relation to sexual behaviour.
16. I am indebted to Denise Riley's discussion of late nineteenth-century women and the social in *Am I That Name?* (Macmillan, 1988).
17. Mary Poovey, *Uneven Developments. The Ideological Work of Gender in Mid-Victorian England* (Virago, 1989), 1st edn 1988, p. 11, identifies the nature and function of protection.
18. Vogeler, *Harrison*, p. 217.
19. For a perceptive account of the violence associated with suffragette demonstrations, see Martha Vicinus, *Independent Women. Work and Community for Single Women, 1850–1920* (Virago, 1985), chapter 7.
20. On women and philanthropy see especially Frank Prochaska, *Women and Philanthropy in Nineteenth Century England* (Oxford: Clarendon, 1980). On the extension of this work to local government see Pat Hollis, *Ladies Elect. Women in England Local Government, 1865–1914* (Oxford: Clarendon, 1987).
21. Prochaska, *Women and Philanthropy*; and Seth Koven, 'Culture and Poverty: The London Settlement House Movement, 1870–1914', unpublished PhD thesis, University of Harvard, 1987.
22. Anne Summers, 'A Home from Home: Women's Philanthropic Work in the Nineteenth Century', in Sandra Burman (ed.), *Fit Work for Women* (Croom Helm, 1979).
23. See Vicinus, *Independent Women*, chap. 6.
24. Brian Harrison, 'Philanthropy and the Victorians', *Victorian Studies* 9 (1966), provides an excellent discussion of the concept of and motives for philanthropy.
25. Stefan Collini has already shown the importance of the idea of character to Victorian political thought, 'The Idea of "Character" in Victorian Political Thought', *Transactions of the Royal Historical Society* 35 (1985).
26. Lynda Nead, *Myths of Sexuality. Representations of Women in Victorian Britain* (Oxford: Blackwell, 1988), p. 28.
27. See Davidoff and Hall, *Family Fortunes*, especially Pts One and Three.
28. Leonore Davidoff, *The Best Circles* (Croom Helm, 1975).
29. Vicinus, *Independent Women*.
30. On T. H. Green see Melvin Richter, *The Politics of Conscience: T. H. Green and his Age* (Weidenfeld & Nicolson, 1964); Andrew Vincent (ed.), *The Philosophy of T. H. Green* (Gower, 1986); and W. H. Greenleaf, *The British Political Tradition*, Vol. 2 (Methuen, 1983).
31. On individualism and collectivism, see especially Stefan Collini, *Liberalism and Sociology. L. T. Hobhouse and Political Argument in England, 1880–1914* Cambridge: Cambridge University Press, 1979), chap. 1.
32. On national efficiency, see G. R. Searle, *The Quest for National Efficiency* (Oxford: Blackwell, 1971).
33. On health visiting and its origins, see Celia Davies, 'The Health Visitor as Mother's Friend: A Woman's Place in Public Health, 1900–1914', *Social History of Medicine* 1 (April 1988); and J. Lewis, *The Politics of Motherhood: Maternal and Child Welfare in England, 1900–1939* (Croom Helm, 1980).
34. Stefan Collini has made a similar point regarding the thought of Bernard Bosanquet in 'Hobhouse, Bosanquet and the State: Philosophical Idealism and Political Argument in England, 1880–1918', *Past and Present* 72 (Aug. 1976).
35. On the nineteenth-century poor law, see Derek Fraser, *The Evolution of the Welfare State* (Macmillan, 1973).

36. On the Charity Organisation Society, see Charles Loch Mowat, *The Charity Organisation Society, 1869–1913* (Methuen, 1961).
37. Koven, 'Culture and Poverty'. See also Standish Meacham, *Toynbee Hall and Social Reform, 1880–1914* (New Haven: Yale University Press, 1988).
38. For example, Rodney Barker, *Political Ideas in Modern Britain* (Methuen, 1978).
39. Collini, *Liberalism and Sociology*, p. 49.
40. See Magdalen Stuart Pember Reeves, *Round about a Pound a Week* (G. Bell, 1915).
41. In this I am inclined to follow the work of A. W. Vincent, 'The Poor Law Reports of 1909 and the Social Theory of the Charity Organisation Society', *Victorian Studies* 27 (1984) and Andrew Vincent and Raymond Plant, *Philosophy, Politics and Citizenship* (Oxford: Blackwell, 1984), rather than either A. M. McBriar, *An Edwardian Mixed Doubles: The Bosanquets versus the Webbs. A Study in British Social Policy, 1890–1929* (Oxford: Clarendon, 1987), who writes of the influence of economic ideas on Helen Bosanquet, or Judith Fido, 'The Charity Organisation Society and Social Casework in London, 1869–1900', in A. P. Donajgrodski (ed.), *Social Control in Nineteenth Century Britain* (Croom Helm, 1977), who depicts the social theory of the Bosanquets as a rather crude exercise in social control.
42. The importance of moral as opposed to social or economic debate in Victorian Britain has been stressed by Stefan Collini, 'Political Theory and the "Science of Society" in Victorian Britain', *Historical Journal* 23 (1980); and Peter Clarke, *Liberals and Social Democrats* (Cambridge: Cambridge University Press, 1978). See also the related argument of P. Nicholson, 'A Moral View of Politics: T. H. Green and the British Idealists', *Political Studies* 35 (March 1987).
43. Hollis, *Ladies Elect*, pp. 284–5. The American literature also stresses the worthy aspects of the 'domestication of politics': Paula Baker, 'The Domestication of Politics: Women in American Political Society, 1780–1920', *American Historical Review* 89 (June 1984); and Ann Firor Scott, 'On Seeing and Not Seeing: A Case of Historical Invisibility', *Journal of American History* 71 (June 1984).
44. Certainly this is the conclusion of Ellen Ross from her study of working-class wives, ' "Feeding the Children": Housewives and London Charity, 1870–1918', unpub. paper presented to the Davis Center Seminar, 2/5/86.
45. Cf. the findings of Linda Gordon, *Heroes of their own Lives. The Politics and History of Family Violence in Boston, 1880–1960* (New York: Viking, 1988).
46. Cited by Ronald G. Walton, *Women in Social Work* (Routledge & Kegan Paul, 1975), p. 74.
47. Frank Prochaska makes this point in his *The Voluntary Impulse. Philanthropy in Modern Britain* (Faber & Faber, 1988), p. xiv.
48. On women's position in the civil service, see Meta Zimmeck, 'Strategies and Stratagems for the Employment of Women in the Civil Service, 1919–1939', *Historical Journal* 27 (1984) and 'Jobs for the Girls: The Expansion of Clerical Work for Women, 1850–1914', in Angela V. John (ed.), *Unequal Opportunities. Women's Employment in England, 1800–1918* (Oxford: Blackwell, 1986).
49. Collet Papers, Warwick University Modern Archive, MSS 29/3/13/4/6.
50. Barbara Caine, *Destined to be Wives. The Sisters of Beatrice Webb* (Oxford: Clarendon, 1986).
51. Pat Jalland, *Women, Marriage and Politics, 1860–1914* (Oxford: Clarendon, 1986), p. 46.
52. Phyllis Rose, *Parallel Lives. Five Victorian Marriages* (New York: Knopf, 1984), pp. 266–7 suggests that women must transgress some barrier, for example that of class or age, in order to redress their power disadvantage in marriage. There is surprisingly little by way of sociological studies of power in marriage. The main work remains that of R. O. Blood and D. M. Wolfe, *Husbands and Wives: The Dynamics of Married Living* (Collier–Macmillan, 1960).
53. Ellen Ross, ' "Fierce Questions and Taunts": Married Life in Working Class London, 1870–1914', *Feminist Studies* 8 (1982).

54. See Revel Guest and Angela V. John, *Lady Charlotte. A Biography of the Nineteenth Century* (Weidenfeld & Nicolson, 1989), p. xix.
55. Clara Collet's Diary, 27/2/78, Collet Papers, MSS 29/8/1/14. Carolyn Steedman, *Childhood, Culture and Class in Britain; Margaret McMillan, 1860–1931* (Virago, 1990) has drawn attention to the idea of 'fictions of the self' that may be a part of autobiography.
56. Bella Brodzski and Celeste Schenck (eds), *Life/Lives. Theorizing Women's Autobiography* (Ithaca: Cornell University Press, 1988), p. 69.

1 Octavia Hill, 1838–1912

Sidney Cockerell, a businessman and close friend and adviser of Octavia
Hill, described her to his sister in 1871 as 'an unobtrusive and plainly
dressed little lady, everlastingly knitting an extraordinarily fine piece of
work'. He went on to comment on her 'power of mind and sweetness
of character . . . a lady of great force and energy, with wide open and
well-stored brain, but without as gentle and womanly as a woman can
be, and possessed of a wonderful tact . . .'[1] Octavia Hill would have
been pleased with the description. She liked to think of her work as
homely and womanly and eschewed any explicit pursuit of a public
persona. However, her fellow workers, as she called them, were more
likely to write of her toughness. Margaret Wynne Nevinson, who was
sent by Samuel Barnett of Toynbee Hall Settlement to talk to Octavia
about rent collecting, found her to be 'a fierce, militant, little body'.[2]

The cumulative effect of Octavia Hill's letters, published by her sister
and brother-in-law after her death, is to emphasize what Sidney
Cockerell would probably have described as her womanly qualities. As
she is shown forcefully directing the increasing numbers of rent
collector/social workers and acquiring the some 1500 properties she
controlled by her death in 1912, she talks about her activities in terms
of 'quiet, detailed work', for which 'feelings and sympathy' are the most
important qualifications. Her language of moral earnestness and
Victorian spirituality suffocates the modern reader. Yet her letters to
the Sidney Cockerells, both father and son, reveal a quite different
aspect of her thought and personality. The sharp enquiries about
accounts, personal investments and the running of particular aspects of
her work betoken a liking, as well as an aptitude for, and toughness
about, matters of business. This must have been the side of her
character she often showed to fellow workers such as Margaret Nevinson, or indeed to tenants. It is the main strength of Gillian Darley's new
biography that she manages to get behind the Octavia Hill carefully
constructed by her relatives for public consumption.[3]

A recent assessment of Octavia Hill has sought to reconcile her
apparent inconsistencies by reference to her theology.[4] While it is an
advance on the popular representation of Octavia Hill to recognize that
she was not just a simple, hard-nosed adherent of the tenets of classical
nineteenth-century liberalism and political economy, condemning
handouts to paupers and pitilessly squeezing rent out of poor tenants,

it is not especially helpful to represent the contrasting elements in her character and behaviour as inconsistencies. Octavia Hill certainly saw no inconsistency, and it is possible to reconstruct her thinking to show how the parts fitted together. Her Christian principles, derived in large part from F. D. Maurice, a Christian Socialist, were certainly crucial both as the root of her commitment to social action and as the source of her extraordinary confidence; Octavia was something of a conviction politician who yet openly scorned party politics and the public sphere. As crucial were her beliefs about the nature of women's contribution to the welfare of the wider community and her need to reconcile the primacy she accorded family duties with her social work.

In many ways her own background was extremely unconventional. After her father's bankruptcy in 1840, she, her sisters and her mother earned their living first by managing a toy workshop for the Christian Socialists and later by running one of the home-from-home girls' schools that were becoming increasingly common in the third quarter of the nineteenth century.[5] When she was twenty-one, she rose at 5 a.m. to do some needlework before a day that included teaching, copying work for John Ruskin and running the toymaker's workshop. Two evenings a week she taught drawing and did her accounts and mending on Saturdays. At this point she was also trying 'to go a little more into society' because it rested her mother. Octavia Hill was, however, contemptuous of both society and ladies. Paradoxically, given Ruskin's influence over her, her notion of the womanly woman in no way corresponded with his particular idea of women as 'angels in the house'. While she did not consciously formulate her desire to serve others as a species of social maternalism in the manner of Anna Jameson at the end of the 1850s,[6] the way in which she talked about her work reflected her strong desire to keep it familial and domestic (and thereby on a scale that she was comfortable with), as well as to strive above all to improve the welfare of poor families.

Work was compulsive for Octavia. From an early age she drove herself to the point of breakdown. Nor did she ever question the fundamentals of the course she pursued. The core of her activity was social work with individuals (chiefly women) and families. Convinced of its rightness, the important thing seemed to be to get on and do it. More than once, including in a conversation with Beatrice Webb,[7] she poured scorn on talkers and theorizers. Social action was to be realized through social work. There was therefore a rigidity in her approach that became more problematic in view of the enormous influence she achieved. She called women into the field of social work and indeed contributed to their training and sense of corporate if not professional identity (she remained committed to the idea that the majority of women workers would be volunteers). But she also set firm limits on the nature of their work and of their participation in the public sphere that were to prove difficult to break. So many women started their working lives outside the home (paid or unpaid) in one of the three areas of social work that Octavia Hill was involved in: Charity Organisation Society (COS) work, housing management and settlement work. Octavia's ideas as to the limits of the possible by no means constrained all of them. For example, while Nevinson found it very difficult to master the art of keeping rent books and accounts, these skills came in handy when she joined the suffragettes. Octavia would have been appalled. It was possibly more difficult still to break out of the narrowly conceived social work of Octavia Hill into social investigation than to be swept into the suffrage movement. Certainly Beatrice Webb found it so, and experienced many more tensions and anxieties than did Helen Bosanquet who stayed within the mould established by Octavia Hill, albeit moving towards theory and away from practice.

The commitment to social action

Octavia Hill's first love was art rather than social work. In 1856, she wrote to Ruskin about her passionate commitment to art, which she nonetheless feared to be fundamentally flawed because it was inherently selfish: 'I care immensely, almost exclusively, for decorative art . . . I have puzzled people because I have set myself resolutely to become a painter, and yet have cared for people; so very much. If I did NOT care for them, would not all that is not selfish in my artistic plans be lost?'[8] Two years later, she reiterated that without caring for people even her 'cherished dream of the attic I mean to possess, if ever I have time and money to procure a little spot to be alone in, would lose its principle charm'.[9] Such dreams caused Octavia Hill considerable distress. At about the same time she also told Ruskin that it was impossible for human beings to be happy if they began by thinking about their own feelings. Yet 'forgetfulness of self' was the most difficult thing to attain. Ruskin's declaration that he had been thinking of nothing but himself did not moderate Octavia's sense of the importance of duty to others. Years later she revealed some of the feelings that must have influenced her move towards social work when she tried to advise Sidney Cockerell junior on his choice of career. He was feeling miserable at the thought of pursuing a career in the family firm of coal merchants (something he did for seven years before going on to do more congenial work cataloguing books and manuscripts for William Morris, which led to a distinguished career in the world of books and museums).

Octavia counselled in favour of business over art in the belief that it would 'give continuity and reality' to his life which might otherwise go the way of 'so many artists' ' lives into 'freaks and fancies instead of into practical serviceable work, glorified by imaginative thought, high ideals and artistic joy'.[10] But when Sidney Cockerell finally decided to leave the firm, she wished him well, commenting only that she was unable quite to understand it, believing as she did in 'the wholesomeness of a steady foundation of business'.[11] Thus in her rejection of work as an artist, she was probably influenced by both the importance of duty to others and a sense that social action in the form of housing management (which she developed first) was based more firmly in the 'real world'. Nevertheless, Octavia Hill's love of colour and space never left her and she applied it in her housing work: in the Kyrle Society, which she founded with her sister Miranda to bring beauty into the lives of the poor (the Society was strongly supported by William Morris); and in her campaigns to save open spaces (which will not receive detailed consideration here). The image of a woman concerned only with the virtues of utilitarian apartments and bare whitewashed walls, perpetuated in no small measure by Beatrice Webb, will not do.

The mainspring to social action that Octavia Hill most freely acknowledged was that of duty. Her business acumen was never trumpeted, for although in her later writings she acknowledged and even stressed its importance for women intending to be housing managers, she felt obliged to consider the criticism that it might make women 'hard' and unwomanly.[12]

Ruskin declared roundly that he hated 'duty and all belonging to it in this curiously cramped and false shape it has got into in this age'.[13] Later, in 1877, Octavia Hill and Ruskin were to quarrel irrevocably when, after a long series of letters, Octavia was provoked into writing that she thought him incapable of managing practical work. Ruskin was angered as much by the apparent lapse in the loyalty of a pupil as by the accusation, but they never spoke again.[14] By the early 1870s, social work had become central in Octavia's life, and in moving so strongly towards it she owed much more to the other major influence on her thinking, the ideas of F. D. Maurice, a broad churchman and Christian Socialist, than she did to Ruskin. Her concept of duty to serve others was derived from Christian principles and only very rarely did she appeal to others to offer themselves for service on the basis of self-interest rather than obligation.[15]

In an 1891 lecture on the 'Reformation of Society', Maurice drew attention to the danger that material progress would increase selfishness, which was, he felt, profoundly anti-social. Wherever the 'highest and noblest human will and reason' has prevailed, the 'selfish principle' had been combated by the promotion of cooperation as an antithesis to competition.[16] Were the selfish principle to hold sway, the logical end would be the disappearance of all care and support in society including 'family feeling'. In his lectures to the members of the Working Men's College he had founded and in his writings on social morality, Maurice continued to stress self-sacrifice as the cardinal principle of human morality. Only when people sought the interests of the whole society and extended family feeling to the broader community were they truly human.[17] This idea as to the importance of self-giving as a manifestation of Christian obligation was central to Octavia Hill's thinking and indeed to many Victorian female social reformers (Mary Ward is a further example). It underpinned the work of the Winkworth sisters (also followers of Maurice) in the 1860s and 70s, whose letters about social work emphasized that self-denial was not enough; only through giving to others would joy and happiness be achieved.[18] And at the end of the century it remained the organizing principle behind the idea of women's mission to women, whether to poor mothers or to prostitutes.[19]

From time to time Octavia Hill taxed herself with the thought that she might be behaving selfishly.[20] Her letters that have been preserved exhibit an almost superhuman moral earnestness. The single reference to a summer filled with melons and theatre visits (albeit juxtaposed with reference to the importance of forgetfulness of self) is striking because it is virtually the only one of its kind, yet as Darley has shown, she did possess a 'streak of gaiety'.[21] As early as 1856, when she was 18, Octavia wrote in reply to a query from a stranger about Christian Socialism that the core beliefs were that 'fellow work' was stronger than isolation, union than division, and generosity than selfishness. This at least is what she took from Christian Socialism. Octavia believed strongly that God was with those who gave themselves: 'I think our Father especially speaks to those whom he honours by asking them to make sacrifices. I at least have learnt to thank Him so very much for having called me to this humble out-of-sight work . . .'[22] Thus while Octavia and other Victorian social reformers were to all intents and purposes firm believers in classical political economy, they did not adopt as their guiding principles the tenets of Utilitarianism and in particular the pursuit of self-interest. Indeed, Octavia commented of John Stuart Mill that he 'would never win my heart, he is decidedly an able man, and I liked watching him [in the House of Commons], as one would a finely contrived machine'.[23] She was unable to accept that the basis of a society should rest solely on the private accumulation of wealth and a *laissez-faire* ethic.

Octavia Hill's idea of duty was based on the promotion of family ties and corporate feeling as the measure of good citizenship, but its Christian root meant that she, like Maurice, relied on the impetus for service and social reform coming from within each individual. While she stressed the obligation to aid others, respect for personal autonomy made it impossible either to impose that obligation on someone else or indeed to act to effect fundamental change in social relations. To this extent she may be seen to straddle the great modern divide between those who would argue for positive welfare rights based on an obligation to aid others (to be fulfilled via social institutions, especially the state) and those who argue for negative rights and eschew any such obligation to aid others for fear of interfering with the autonomy of persons.[24] Octavia Hill believed that all Christians were obliged to try to do the right thing. She wrote to Henrietta Barnett in 1873: 'I fight so desperately to be right, to see right, to do right'.[25] Above all she believed that if everyone sincerely pursued 'right action' good would prevail. Pondering Sidney Cockerell's desire to leave the family firm she wrote: 'Certainly you did not choose from any temptation leading you, it seemed to you right and you chose it at some sacrifice. It seemed to you, I must say it seemed to me . . . the path of duty'. Despite a business career having seemed to have represented right action, she was prepared to countenance the idea that God was calling him in another direction and she encouraged him to 'feel his way' forward according to the best dictates of his conscience.[26] One of her pupils recalled much later being taught that she should do a thing because it was right without question as to personal desire.[27] Octavia's emphasis on motivation and means rather than ends, and on self-giving and duty rather than self-interest distance her (and other Victorian social reformers) from nineteenth-century *laissez-faire* and from the enterprise culture of the late twentieth century in almost equal measure.

To those of her followers who worried as to whether they had interpreted God's will correctly and were indeed doing right, she offered some comfort: 'the burden of absolutely right action . . . is not with you, only the duty of trying to see and do right. If you keep this steadily before you, your Father will be continually bringing out of all your feeble efforts and clumsy mistakes all manner of great joy, and help, and wonderful results you never thought of'.[28] God cared, she believed, more for what people were than for what they achieved. Octavia Hill's unswerving belief in a divinely revealed right action proved another issue separating her from Ruskin, who felt that as soon as someone did things to please God all 'natural' sense of right disappeared. Such a division between Christian belief and moral sense was impossible to Octavia. In his turn Ruskin expressed impatience with both Octavia's optimistic faith that God would not allow right action to fail and her lack of attention to fundamental social relations. Writing in 1871, some six years before their rift, he praised her efforts in housing management but commented that 'the best that can be done in this way will be useless ultimately, unless the deep source of misery be cut off'.[29] While Octavia was successfully 'moralizing' a couple of acres, many more were being demoralized by uncaring and/or grasping landlords.

But Octavia saw no possibility of changing systems or the behaviour of masses of people. Change could only be achieved by slow, patient work, by setting an example that others would also come to feel was right; 'giving nobly' was the key to making 'the things of this world fair and orderly'.[30] Furthermore, she had no patience with those who tried to force their ideas on others. She pointed out that Ruskin, who gave her her first houses to manage, had never signed anything to prevent him taking back control of them and nor should he, because 'he is bound, as all men are, to do what seems to him right'.[31] Similarly, when she tried to preserve the Quaker burial grounds as open space for the people, she 'owned to an amazed sorrow' that the property should be sold, but she refused to go and address the Quaker meeting to put her case: 'I think I must really leave it in their own hands. The responsibility is wholly theirs'.[32] The belief that everyone had a right to do as they wished as long as they thought sincerely about it and searched their consciences, and yet the equally strong belief that her own position represented right action, resulted in a language of heavy moral suasion that is particularly characteristic of Octavia Hill. However, implicit warnings as to divine displeasure were often insufficient in face of market forces.

In respect of those requiring help, by implication the poor and downtrodden, Christian-inspired duty dictated an effort to know them and above all to extend sympathy and to feel with them. By entering into their suffering the social workers would be able to achieve a sense of communion with the poor: 'it is suffering that endears all to us, and binds us into one, for it calls out faith, it calls for sacrifice, for patience, and as all strong feeling felt by two people draws them together and makes them understand one another, so I bless all sorrow in my deepest heart, only asking that it may do its appointed work of uniting not separating'.[33]

This was written when Octavia was young, but her later writing showed little departure from these sentiments. In some situations this approach was both humane and in its way radical. For example, she wrote movingly of visiting a poor woman whose baby had died and of the importance of understanding what it meant to experience such pain. But in the case of a family servant who returned from a visit home hungry and with the news that her infant sister had died, Octavia's pleasure at the girl's sad fatalism before the will of God is hard to stomach and makes Ruskin's impatience easier to comprehend. Even though Octavia's faith stressed self-giving rather than, like evangelicals, pain and renunciation, she consistently spoke of finding unity and corporate strength through suffering rather than through shared happiness. The sorrow of a mother faced with the loss of a child, or the struggles of an old bedridden woman represented lives to be reverenced and admired. However, beyond showing a respect for the lives of the poor that was novel, she gave little indication as to how matters were to improve. Octavia fell back on her twin convictions that the awareness of the rich as to their obligations to the poor would gradually awaken, and that the character of the poor would improve by virtue of their increased contact with their social betters: 'infinitesimally small actions' by individuals would eventually produce social change.[34]

Duty is gendered

While it was the duty of the rich, male and female, to give of themselves (which meant giving time as much as money), the tasks of men and women were clearly differentiated. Frank Prochaska has observed the way in which men controlled finances and committees in the world of nineteenth-century charity, while women raised funds through bazaars and balls and visited the poor.[35] Similarly, Seth Koven has described how in the work of the settlements women tended to undertake personal visiting, become school-board managers and run schemes such as the Children's Country Holidays Fund, moving eventually into professional social work, while men concentrated more on lecturing, social investigation and local politics, often moving into positions of power and influence as civil servants and politicians.[36] Octavia Hill subscribed to this broad gender division of labour and called for middle-class men to give their time as poor law guardians, vestrymen and COS committee men, but she did her best to persuade them, her half-brother Arthur included, of the moral worth of such lowly work of public service and of the need for able men to stay in it. If a man tried for Parliament and failed, 'no one misses you very much. But if, instead of trying to get high up, you were to try to get down low, what a position of usefulness you would have!'[37] Women were asked to go lower still and get to know the poor on an individual basis. Octavia's emphasis on the different but complementary work of men and women followed the lead of Maurice, who insisted that their roles in wider society should reflect the proper relation between husbands and wives. Women's part was to cultivate 'the feelings which embrace and comprehend truth', while men cultivated 'the understandings which were destined to supply us with the outward and visible expression of it'.[38] Maurice's explanation of such differences (in the pre-Darwinian period) appealed to their God-given nature rather than to biology. Octavia Hill often referred to the importance of feeling in her work, by which she meant more than mere sentiment. Right action depended on depth of feeling. Nor were feelings wholly intuitive, they had to be nurtured and developed. Mary Ward was to develop this use of the term 'feeling'. Like Anna Jameson who preceded her in appealing for the extension of woman's role as sister, mother, nurse and helper beyond the family, and like countless women, feminist and non-feminist, who followed her, Octavia Hill accepted and built on contemporary ideas as to gender divisions.

Women's special province was considered to be that of patient, personal service, something Mary Talbot, warden of the St Margaret's House women's settlement (a female branch of the Oxford Settlement) described as a 'practical witness' to the Christianity which bade women to care.[39] Octavia Hill was attracted by the work of the Oxford Settlement rather than by that of Toynbee Hall (despite her close connection with its founder, Samuel Barnett, who served as curate to the Marylebone parish in which she worked and who married one of her best rent collectors), because of its greater emphasis on spirituality. Maurice encouraged women to begin their mission to other women with their own servants: 'if you shrink from a hearty patriarchal sympathy with your own servants, because it would require too much personal human intercourse with them, you are like a man who, finding that he had not powder enough to fire off a pocket-pistol, should try to better matters by using the same quantity of ammunition in an 84lb gun'. He invited middle-class women to consider how they might go to 'poor creatures as woman to woman', in order to minister to their 'diseased and anxious minds' and to extend sympathy to calm their perturbed spirits.[40] He was impressed by the example set by both Mrs Jameson and, later, Josephine Butler in her work to defend prostitutes against the Contagious Diseases Acts. During the 1850s and early 1860s, Octavia Hill sought to train her school pupils to be 'sweetly serviceable', while voicing her own admiration for the kind of heroic service performed by Florence Nightingale, notwithstanding the disapproval expressed by a friend's parents of the latter's work. Some sixteen years later, Nightingale returned the compliment, praising Octavia's work in a review of George Eliot's *Middlemarch*, in which she condemned the range of choices (two inappropriate husbands) that Eliot had offered her heroine, Dorothea.[41]

In Octavia's view, women's duty was to do useful work, but she gave priority to detailed, patient, gentle work in the homes of the poor, which had the benefit of coming closest to women's family duties in both its nature and scale.[42] In addition, while Octavia acknowledged the idea of women's mission to women, justifying home visiting more on the grounds that it was a natural extension of women's sphere and in terms of what it might do for domestic morality generally, the particular form of personal social work that she developed around the task of rent collection meant that the collectors came into contact most frequently with poor wives and mothers. Despite Octavia Hill's desire, in the classic manner of late nineteenth-century scientific charity, to make contact with and enforce a sense of responsibility in the male bread-winner, it was working-class women who dealt with visitors of all kinds: inspectors from the National Society for the Prevention of Cruelty to Children, school-board attendance officers, district visitors and COS workers.[43] C. P. B. Bosanquet (a founder of the COS and Helen Bosanquet's brother-in-law) remarked in the handbook he wrote for visitors of the poor in London: 'The London poor are accustomed to the notion of being visited and are more inclined to complain of being neglected than to look on a visitor as an intruder'.[44] And, by the last quarter of the nineteenth century, the large numbers of unpaid visitors were middle-class women, bent on leaving their homes in order to instruct working-class women how to manage theirs.[45]

Individual work
The individual work of personal service was crucial to Octavia Hill's realization of her duty to help others. In her housing and COS work and in her association with the Women's University Settlement, per-sonal visiting comprised the core activity. This is not to deny the shrewdness with which Octavia pursued her business dealings, especi-ally in respect of acquiring buildings and courts to manage, or her knowledge of the wider issues to do with housing which she displayed before the government inquiry of 1882 or the Royal Commission on Housing of 1885. But her letters and published writings showed her determination to put the work with individuals first: 'Oh it is easy to work early and late, to keep accounts, and manage housekeeping etc., but the gentle voice, the loving word, the ministry, the true tender spirit, these are great gifts, and will endure when the others have perished'.[46] Octavia made a deliberate decision not to broaden her activities in housing to encompass building projects of her own, her

interests being strictly confined to 'managing the lowest' class of tenant.[47]

She regarded individual work as the only lasting way of effecting social change. The human intensity of the work mattered to her because of the possibilities it opened up to increase direct communication between rich and poor and because personal contact represented a line of action grounded solidly in Christian morality. In 1889, she reminded her fellow workers that irrespective of what action was taken in the future on issues such as the provision of school meals by the state, 'for you and me there remain much the same eternal duties, love, thought, justice, liberality, simplicity, hope, understanding, for ever, still human heart depends on human heart for sympathy, and still the old duties of neighbourliness continue'.[48] Were her fellow workers to be attracted by the idea of free meals, free primary school education and subsidized housing, she bade them first to remember that someone had to pay the bill, and second to make sure that the advocates of such policies were not motivated either by cowardice or ambition; Octavia found it difficult to believe that people holding such views had sincerely searched their consciences to determine what actions were right.

Octavia Hill profoundly distrusted systems and machinery and feared that working on a larger scale would mean working for a system: 'I would rather work in the unsought-after, out-of-sight places, side by side with my fellow workers, face to face with tenants than in the conspicuous forefront of any great movement'.[49] Settlements also began with a distrust of machinery, according to Samuel Barnett, although E. J. Urwick, the subwarden of Toynbee Hall in the early 1900s and later the Director of the COS's School of Sociology and then the London School of Economics' (LSE) Department of Social Administration, felt that this distrust rapidly faded and that the work of settlements became routinized.[50] Octavia Hill, however, never wavered in this regard. For example, while she supported the main objects of the 1875 Artisans Dwellings Act, she was nevertheless pleased that when Kay Shuttleworth referred to her work in his House of Commons speech, he cited not dry facts and figures but rather the human aspects of her face-to-face work with the poor.[51] Similarly, as a member of the Royal Commission on the Poor Law between 1905 and 1909, she continued to maintain that the solution to the problem of poverty depended 'not on machinery which commissions may recommend . . . but on the number of faithful men and women whom England can secure and inspire as faithful servants'.[52] Unlike the male settlement workers, Octavia Hill was singularly unconcerned with power outside her small sphere of operations.

As early as 1855, Maurice had stated his opinion that if ladies would visit the poor their mere presence in the neighbourhood would help to secure (moral) improvement.[53] Similarly in her evidence to the 1882 Select Committee on Artisans' and Labourers' Dwellings, Octavia expressed her opinion that a great deal of the degradation of the poor stemmed from the absence of a middle-class presence and middle-class opinion in poor areas.[54] Such a view was commonplace in the 1880s.[55] In the words of the Manchester Ladies Health Society, which started its sanitary education work early in the 1860s, no one was more fitted to break the ground between social classes than ladies: 'comparatively unfettered by the vexed relations between labour and capital, with their more ready sympathy and common interests with all other women, they would begin hopefully where men would have little chance'.[56] Later, women social investigators, such as Lady Bell, who conducted a door-to-door investigation of Middlesbrough, continued to feel fewer inhibitions (as well as more interest) in observing family relationships and interactions than their male counterparts. Octavia Hill shared this optimism as to the possibilities for class contact, although she stressed that men as well as women had to come forward for service, albeit in different ways. And as long as all tried sincerely to do the right thing, she held that they would prosper in their endeavours. She believed firmly that only individual work 'lightened by love and softening the pain by near sympathy' could bring those who had fallen by the wayside back into society and only by personal contact was it possible for the giver to see the effect of the gift, whether of time or money. Individual work would serve to re-establish 'natural human intercourse' between rich and poor, but would also serve to reveal the facts of life among the poor to what Octavia feared was a largely sentimental public.[57]

The idea of individual work 'down among the poor' was not new. Maurice had advocated a form of contact that emphasized education rather than the stereotypical lady bountiful approach, and during the 1860s considerable effort was made to extend visiting networks. Missions employed working-class women to distribute Bibles and middle-class women distributed tracts as well as health advice on behalf of their sanitary associations, approaching the poor in a spirit of 'friendly inspection'. Parish visiting by middle-class women remained bound up with the distribution of coal and food tickets as well as tracts. While it seems that she may have been inspired particularly by the example of the Bible women visitors,[58] none of these models suited Octavia Hill's concept of personal work with the poor. The motivating force behind her work was her strong sense of Christian obligation rather than a more traditional and often condescending paternalism.[59]

Indeed, she felt that she was espousing a radically different approach and attitude towards the poor although in *practice* there were significant continuities between the well-off-lady-doing-good and Octavia Hill's visitors. While historical assessments of her work in housing and for the COS, with which she was closely involved from the first, have stressed her apparent disregard of the structural causes of poverty, Octavia herself emphasized the importance of thoroughly knowing the personal characters and circumstances of the poor, and then of loving and befriending them. In 1873 her sister Miranda wrote approvingly of Samuel Barnett who had just married Octavia's best rent collector, Henrietta Rowland, as a man who had intimate knowledge of the poor, strong personal sympathies and who was a strong Radical 'with a horror of class distinctions, and practical disregard for them, which you don't find in all Radicals'.[60] The comment was a shrewd one and could also have been applied to Octavia Hill. This is not to say that she was in shape or form a natural egalitarian in her efforts to communicate with the poor; but she insisted on the importance of treating the poor as people rather than as a separate species labelled pauper. Early on, when she was a teenager and helping to run the toymakers workshop, she wrote fiercely to Miranda about the Ragged School meeting she had attended: 'Oh, to hear how people talk of others, and think they are treating them as Christians; I'd rather be a table than a Ragged School child'.[61] At the most basic level, knowing, loving and befriending the poor did translate into an insistence on the observation of common courtesies in dealings with poor women, but beyond this it is not clear that Octavia reached any profound understanding or appreciation of working-class life and culture such as was achieved later by some of the early twentieth-century women social investigators like Lady Bell, Margery Loane or, in a rather different context, Beatrice Webb.

Octavia's aim in undertaking personal social work among the poor was after all to change their behaviour: 'my only notion of reform is that of living side by side with people, till all that one believes becomes clear to them'.[62] Octavia's unshakeable belief in her obligation to pursue what her Christian conscience decreed to be right action inevitably produced imbalances in her relations with the poor. Knowing, loving and befriending easily became at best teaching and leading, and at worst controlling: 'I would not set my conviction, however strong it might be, against your judgement or right, but when you are doing what I know your own conscience condemns I, now that I have the power (as housing manager) will enforce right'.[63] Thus despite her insistence that all people, rich and poor, must reach their own decision as to what they chose to do, Octavia found it easy to justify the rightness of her ideas as opposed to those of the poor by resort to a line of argument that had much in common with the Marxian concept of false consciousness. In her evidence to the Royal Commission on Housing in 1885, she referred to her tenants' need for 'paternal supervision'.[64] It was rare that she used language of this kind to describe her social work. But the work did involve supervision and control, as well as a genuine effort to work side by side with the tenants. And above all there was paternalism in the relationship. In the end all the cards lay with Octavia.

However, her paternalism was not that of the old lady bountiful kind. Here again, Octavia could lay claim, perhaps better claim, to a new and radical approach. In her evidence to the 1885 Royal Commission, she referred to the need for a mix of business and philanthropic instincts.[65] Her philanthropy was geared to achieving a fulfilment of obligations on the part of rich and poor in crowded, urban slums. The vehicle for the expression of these obligations was the right use of money. In her major work of housing management, the lady managers (on behalf of the landlord) kept accurate rent books and accounts, carried out repairs and still made sure that the property paid its way, while tenants were obliged first and foremost to pay their rent. Individual work with the poor took place on the occasion of rent collection. Ellen Chase, an American who worked with Octavia for many years in Deptford, the area in which Octavia experienced the most difficulty, wrote simply and without further reflection or comment, of friendship growing out of the business relationship. This was Octavia's own way of reconciling the apparently irreconcilable: business and paternalism. In some respects, her approach mirrored that of many nineteenth-century industrialists. Judy Lown has described the way in which Courtaulds, for example, used 'new paternalism' to promote a harmony of interests between employers and employed within the context of the teachings of political economy, which insisted that relations between master and servant were governed by immutable laws. Samuel Courtauld believed that it was his duty to assist working-class self-help by establishing institutions to encourage self-improvement through habits of thrift, sobriety and, in regard to his largely young female workforce, a proper sense of domestic virtues.[66]

Octavia believed that the key to changing the behaviour of the poor lay in strengthening character. As Stefan Collini has pointed out, the idea of character depended on a prior notion of duty and invocations of character 'in fact presupposed an agreed moral code'.[67] Unlike Helen Bosanquet, Octavia Hill did not spend time elaborating this idea or explaining the importance of character as a cause of poverty. She simply assumed, in common with the vast majority of legislators and policy-makers of the nineteenth and early twentieth centuries, that 'habits' were a crucial determinant of social status. However, one of her early biographers was incorrect in stating categorically that she believed that bad habits alone created bad conditions.[68] The commissioners of 1885 were careful to press all their witnesses for their views on this absorbing question of nature versus nurture. Octavia stated clearly that she felt 'the improvements of people and dwellings must go hand in hand'.[69] Her views in this respect were virtually identical to those of other witnesses, for example of G. R. Sims, whose journalism on the condition of the poor in the East End had fuelled the debates on the housing crisis during the 1880s. He replied to the commissioners that 'it is the men and the circumstances together; you cannot say which it is'.[70] In her housing work Octavia sought to ensure a basic standard of amenity in the properties she controlled, but after that her main interest lay in individual work with the poor, which was directed towards changing habits and building character. She felt that the constant need to judge character was both the most crucial and the most difficult part of her work in housing:

> The management depends very much on judgement of character. You must notice when the man is doing any better, and when he is not. You cannot bring that up before a committee and prove it. You must say to this man, 'Go', and you must say to that one, 'stay', and you must devise a plan which shall make that man gradually feel the benefit of his own care.[71]

She recognized that 'earnest workers' found all this difficult to reconcile with the Biblical injunction to 'Judge not', but she believed that disaster would follow if character were ignored in charitable work. Approaching the poor in the spirit of knowing, loving and befriending them was a way of making the business of character assessment and modification possible and palatable.

A large part of knowing the poor meant knowing their characters, but 'by knowledge of character more is meant than whether a man is a drunkard or a woman is dishonest, it means knowledge of the passions, hopes and history of people; where the temptation will touch them, what is the little scheme they have made of their lives, or would make, if they had encouragement, what training long-past phases of their lives may have afforded; how to move, touch, teach them'.[72] She insisted on the importance of knowing the whole person in a manner not dissimilar from Ruskin, claiming proudly and in terms that ran counter to the growing statistical movement, that 'my people are numbered; not merely counted, but known, man, woman and child'.[73] The numbers she could thoroughly know were inevitably small, but thorough work with small numbers of people was, she believed, the only way to effect permanent change in people's behaviour. Anticipating criticism of the scale of her work, she demanded only whether the mass of people were not 'made up of many small knots'. All that was needed were armies of workers prepared to approach the poor in a new way.

Octavia Hill was extremely critical of older patterns of district visiting, whereby ladies began their work with the intention of helping the poor rather than of knowing them, the problem being that they were then more likely to think of the poor not primarily as *people*, but as *poor* people'.[74] In this Octavia endeavoured to have her cake and eat it, for while she genuinely insisted on the common humanity of rich and poor, she nevertheless believed in the superiority of middle-class culture. Yet in the context of contemporary attitudes towards the poor, and in particular in relation to the fears surrounding the urban crisis of the 1880s, Octavia's willingness to work alongside the poor was commendable. In a sharp riposte to the members of the 1882 Select Committee, she insisted that while it was possible to 'hunt' the poor, they could never be reached without an effort to get to know them.[75] In a paper published more than a decade earlier, she had stressed what it meant to the poor that somebody took the trouble to get to know them properly.[76] An effort to know and then to love would eventually evoke a 'satisfactory' response on the part of the poor.

Loving the poor was something many middle-class workers must have found difficult. Beatrice Webb was probably not untypical in experiencing a sense of revulsion from the noise, smells and brutality of life in the courts.[77] But Octavia insisted that 'you cannot learn how to help a man, nor even get him to tell you what ails him till you care for him'.[78] She urged all visitors to think of the poor as their husbands, sons and daughters, and to deal with them accordingly. By making the effort to sympathize and to feel with them, by entering thoroughly into their lives, the visitor would be able to befriend the visited, a necessary preliminary to effective individual work. With friendship came trust, the 'most beautiful trait' in the character of the poor, and then the visitor could be sure that the people were ready to listen. 'Unpalatable truths' could only be conveyed as from one friend to another: '[The rich are] thoroughly cowardly about telling them [the poor] any truth that is unpalatable, and know too little of them to meet them really as friends, and learn to be natural and brave with them'.[79] Mrs Henrietta Barnett, trained by Octavia, referred to friendship as 'our weapon'.[80] As Anthony Wohl has observed, it was perhaps easier to gain entry to a working-class home as a friendly visitor than as a paid official. Certainly the women's sanitary associations thought so and eagerly promoted the woman visitor as the 'mother's friend'.[81] However, Octavia Hill deplored their idea of 'friendly inspection' as something bound to subvert natural friendship and trust. In her evidence to the 1885 Royal Commission, she rejected the idea of inspection, strongly favoured by other witnesses, because in her experience the poor dreaded it.[82] In large measure her views in this regard were sound. Popular dislike of the 'kid-catcher' (school attendance officer) and the 'cruelty man' (National Society for the Prevention of Cruelty to Children inspector) was strong and there is clear evidence of a more general working-class dislike of inquisitorial and stigmatizing welfare in the late nineteenth and early twentieth centuries.[83] This is not to say, as some recent accounts would have it, that the poor resented all forms of welfare provision.[84] For example, attendance records and autobiographical accounts suggest that early twentieth-century infant welfare clinics were popular with working-class mothers while health visitors were less so.

The position regarding Octavia Hill's own individual work with the poor, which relied on home visiting, is less clear. It is easy to criticize her notion of building friendship and trust as naïve, but we are too far from perfecting social work relationships in the late twentieth century to sweep aside her practices in a cavalier fashion. She would have insisted that her particular mix of business philanthropy protected her rent collectors from just this sort of criticism. They visited for a purpose and trust grew not just out of friendship but out of the fulfilment of the mutual obligations of landlord and tenant, that is out of the business relationship.

Octavia Hill believed in principle that the poor as much as the rich had to arrive at a sense of right action that could only come from within. She hoped to lead them to such an understanding, in other words, to an appreciation of her own sense of what was right. Maurice recognized that every social class had its own standard, its own notion of right and wrong, justice and injustice and Octavia herself reminded her readers that the poor shared as much in the 'two primary blessings' of divine love and family love as the rich.[85] However for her, as much as for those active in the settlement movement, the goal was to impart middle-class values and culture, whether through friendship, teaching or frank 'training', and thereby to change habits. She was nevertheless anxious to avoid directly imposing her will. The path of true liberalism, after all, lay in having the patience to wait until by dint of careful teaching the people chose the right way. Octavia envisaged something, at least, of a two-way process whereby those working with the poor endeavoured to further their best hopes while also trying to persuade them of the beneficence of middle-class values: 'I further believed that any lady who would help them to obtain things, the need of which they felt themselves, and would sympathize with them in their desire for such, would soon find them eager to learn her view of what was best for them, that whether this was so or not, her duty was to keep alive their own best hopes and intentions, which came at rare intervals, but fade too often for want of encouragement'.[86] Standards could only be raised gradually. Octavia cited the example of her effort to get a woman who dreaded exposing her 'bits of things' to public view to rent an extra room on a higher floor.[87] However, in the end leading tended to take second place to teaching, training and controlling. Octavia herself admitted that she had 'a tremendous despotism' justified only by her desire to exercise it 'with a view of bringing out the powers of the people, and training them as responsible for themselves within certain limits'.[88]

Like other women social reformers, her extraordinary authority over the poor derived in large measure from her social class.[89] In a piece published in 1871, she told the story of a woman tenant who locked her door and shouted loudly that she would not pay rent until something was done about her rooms. Octavia reported that only 'perfect silence would make her voice drop lower'.[90] In their dealings with the poor, middle-class women counted in large part on a measure of deferential behaviour towards well-spoken ladies. But in many cases, Octavia's included, authority gained an additional edge because of the belief that it was literally God-given. In 1869, Octavia described the 'awed sense of joy' she felt in taking over her first court and having 'the moral power to say, by deeds that speak louder than words, "where God gives me authority, this, which you in your own hearts know to be wrong shall not go on . . ." '[91] Geoffrey Best's judgement reached some twenty-five years ago seems most accurate in terms of its assessment of the outcome, if not the intention, of all this: the poor would be helped if they would submit.[92]

Maurice had stressed the importance of teaching the poor. For example, a lady visitor could teach poor women to 'feel' the sacredness of home life by extending middle-class courtesies to them and by communicating to them her reluctance to intrude upon them. But teaching was bound to shade into more didactic forms, given Octavia Hill's sense of rightness and her consciousness of her power and authority; she urged her fellow workers to act as '*Queens*, as well as *friends*' in their particular domains.[93] She told the Select Committee of 1882 that she believed the poor to be 'improvable', but the class she managed was destructive and required training.[94] Constant supervision by rent collectors and playground supervisors created a 'wonderful hold' over the people and made it easier to help them.

Even when placing the emphasis on controlling rather than on knowing, loving and befriending the poor, Octavia Hill was anxious to stress the importance of courtesy and respect in the dealings between her fellow workers and poor women. Maurice gave considerable attention to the issue of communication between rich and poor, urging visitors to do as they would be done by and not to reprove or find fault, as well as being aware that the barriers to social intercourse might be different among working people.[95] He warned that paupers had for 'so long been used as anvils for other people to hammer out their own goodness on'[96] that it would take time to put relations with the poor on a normal footing. Octavia Hill explained to her cousin and friend Mary Harris that she deplored the way haggard, careworn women tenants came 'cringing down' to her. She felt that she wanted to say: 'don't treat me with such respect. In spirit I bow down to you, feeling that you deserve reverence, in that you have preserved any atom of God's image in you, degraded and battered as you are by the world's pressure'.[97] She told her fellow workers that they must 'show the same respect for the privacy and independence and should treat them with the same courtesy that I should show towards other personal friends'.[98] How far this was followed, even to the extent of knocking on a door before entering is not clear, for the advice was repeated at frequent intervals by women social workers throughout the late nineteenth and early twentieth centuries, and still found a place in Emelia Kanthack's advice to health visitors, published in 1907.[99]

Octavia Hill usually inspired awe and respect from both fellow workers and the poor. Henrietta Barnett admired her enormously but criticized what she perceived as a cordiality towards the poor born of *noblesse oblige*.[100] There was certainly paternalism, but it was of a new style. There was no quick sally into a quarter to distribute gifts and a little advice followed by a quick retreat. On the contrary, Octavia deplored the giving of money. Her fellow workers were invited to give of their time and their superior wisdom. Beatrice Webb as well as Ruskin felt exasperated at Octavia's overwhelming conviction that she was right, her belief that such small-scale activity was the only way of effecting lasting change and her willingness and indeed her delight in immersing herself in minutiae. But as far as Octavia was concerned, the root of the social problem could only be the individual and she set out to moralize social relations in industrial urban society by seeking to persuade the rich of their Christian obligation to aid those less well-off and by improving the character of the poor. There were profound tensions between business and philanthropy in her practice of individual social work but her approach was important above all for the way in which it completely rejected the creed of self-interest preached by utilitarians and classical economists. Accepting the rules of the market and the social structure as she found them, Octavia Hill nonetheless preached selflessness rather than greed, and a caring capitalism.

Charity organization and the relief of poverty

Octavia Hill was a founding member of the COS and the only female member of its council. Her work for, and writing about, issues concerning the society further illuminate her attitudes towards poverty. She has been portrayed as something of a hard-line COSer. Certainly she refused to countenance 'doles' for the able-bodied poor and was a firm believer in a large role for voluntary charitable endeavour through a society like the COS. But in the society's harshest period (its first decade, 1869–79), she was often critical of it and the source of her differences was the priority she accorded to thorough individual work with the poor. Yet during the last quarter of the nineteenth century and until she died in 1912, Octavia remained a staunch member of the COS when others, such as Samuel Barnett, were leaving it and when organizations such as the Guilds of Help and the Personal Service Association were being set up as a result of dissatisfaction with the COS, albeit with aims that still had much in common with Octavia's in terms of their commitment to individual social work.

When she was eighteen, Octavia relayed a story to Mary Harris about a man watching a blind owl being fed by a raven. The man decided, on the strength of this, that he would be taken care of if he stopped working. Someone else asked why he had not identified with the raven. The moral, Octavia decided, was that 'one should remember that one is a raven or an owl *alternately*, as it seems best to God'.[101] The notion that there was a divine plan meant that little could be done about the external factors involved in causing poverty, rather the individual should prepare to face periods of misfortune. Octavia vehemently opposed relief to the able-bodied, whether via the poor law or voluntary funds such as the Lord Mayor of London's Mansion House Fund, which was activated during the periods of acute distress during the late nineteenth century. Such money could effect no long-term improvement in the condition of the poor and only thwarted any effort to persuade the poor to prepare for periods of distress by living prudently and practising thrift in good times. She believed too that the irregular alms distributed by district visitors and other philanthropically inclined persons only succeeded in keeping 'a whole class on the very brink of pauperism who might be taught self-control and foresight if we would let them learn it'.[102] Indeed, such relief had been nothing short of cruel in its kindness and was serving merely to undermine the self-respect of the poor:

> I am quite awed when I think what our impatient charity is doing to the poor of London: men, who should hold up their heads as self-respecting fathers of families, learning to sing like beggars in the streets – all because we give pennies; those who might have a little fund in the savings bank discouraged because the spendthrift is at least as abundantly helped when time of need comes . . . Is family life forgotten that we seem determined to set up all manner of great institutions with charitable subscriptions, instead of encouraging each member of the family to do his or her work?[103]

In fact, as Booth and Rowntree's social investigations of London and York were to show, as many as one third of the population had no means of saving in the way Octavia Hill and the COS suggested. More recent research has also pointed out how middle-class effort to persuade working people to use savings banks was based on a fundamental lack of appreciation of the precarious nature of the working-class family economy and the importance of the place of credit as well as saving within it.[104] Working-class family budgets painstakingly collected by Edwardian female social investigators showed that saving was more likely in respect of funerals than old age.

Regarding relief to the able-bodied, the evidence suggests that Octavia Hill was among the sternest of COS members. In 1875, a case was submitted to the COS Council by the St George's District Committee concerning a deserted wife who was unable to earn enough to clothe and feed herself and her children. The St George's Committee admitted that whatever relief it could give was unlikely to effect permanent improvement, one of the cardinal considerations of COS relief practice, but on the other hand the woman was deserving and her need was great. Octavia opposed relief but was in this instance outvoted on the ground that the COS should give to all cases considered suitable for charitable assistance who were not going to be helped by any other society.[105] Octavia's attitude towards the non-able-bodied, particularly the elderly, was quite different. She consistently sought donors for the provision of adequate pensions for deserving chronic cases and became increasingly angry at the difficulty COS committees and pensions societies experienced in raising subscriptions for the provision of pensions while 'money for free meals for hundreds who should support themselves flows in freely'.[106]

Octavia Hill refused to accept that the duty of the rich towards the poor could be commuted into cash. The old charity of the lady bountiful was selfish and self-indulgent in that people gave in order to be able to put the problem of the poor out of their minds. This was to over-simplify the complicated motives behind the gift,[107] but the COS used the double accusation of guilt – in terms of the demoralization of the receivers and the selfishness of the givers – to great effect.

Octavia Hill insisted that 'doles darkened friendship'[108] and that what was really needed was people prepared to spend time with the poor, getting to know their real needs and how best they might be helped. She bade potential COS workers to 'decide for yourselves quietly what amount of time you are justified in devoting to such work'.[109] Charity was a duty and all duties had to be done thoroughly, but of course the first call on women's time had to be their own families, hence the importance of thinking through their commitment. It was incumbent on the giver to make sure the gift was beneficent. It would only be so if it came 'as a witness of real love'.[110] Wise charity (Octavia did not use the word scientific as many members of the COS did, preferring to allude to the Christian derivation of her beliefs and practices) was fully of the heart as well as of the head and lost 'nothing of its lovingness'.[111] However, her injunction not to give cash to the able-bodied poor was susceptible to extremely narrow interpretation. Octavia recognized this when she warned that the philosophy of the new charity did not mean that the rich could cultivate their own elegant tastes 'in happy satisfaction that the poor cannot be bettered by our gifts (and) in fact must learn self-help'.[112] But as early as 1869, Ruskin criticized the way she presented her views, saying that she laid too much emphasis on the evil of almsgiving and not enough on the importance of the gift of time and personal sympathy. He felt that had she put the latter point more strongly to her audience, comprised in 1869 of the Association for the Promotion of Social Science, she would not have found them so sympathetic.[113]

Ruskin may well have been right. Certainly Octavia herself spent much time in the 1870s warning that the COS committees were neglecting individual work among the poor and concentrating too much on the prevention of mendicity. There was, she felt, a danger that the COS committees 'with their systems of rules' would crush out 'the personal element'.[114] Without face-to-face visiting the work of the COS became hard, dry, abstract and systematized. Visitors were the 'living links' in the system. Furthermore, without workers 'in the field', the COS ran the risk of not 'knowing' the poor.[115] In 1877 she wrote: 'The COS is suffering grievously at its centre; the tone gets harder, the alienation deeper. They ought to be brought into close contact with the workers among the poor'.[116] Only the visitor could report fully on the character of applicants for relief, thus enabling committee members to reach wise decisions. Visitors were also crucial in explaining the 'wise decision' to the disappointed applicant. In 1874 she wrote passionately to the vicar of St Mary's in Marylebone, Mr Fremantle, about the shortcomings of the organization of relief in the parish:

> A man comes up, the committee decides to do nothing, he ought to save, an elder lad ought to go to work, he ought to send some child to a hospital. Nothing to be done! No nothing by the Committee perhaps, nothing definite at a given time by the visitor, but the refusal can hardly be a help to the man unless it is again and again gently explained, unless advice is given, information procured . . . the more they resolve to pursue a system of relief which is in the end a blessing to the poor, but which for the moment appears less merciful, the more tenderly gentle, the more patiently watchful, should be the messengers and interpretors of those decisions.[117]

The poor had to be educated in the ways of the new charity, just as Harriet Martineau endeavoured to teach them the logic of political economy.[118] Margaret Sewell, the head worker of the Women's University Settlement, who worked closely with Octavia Hill in the 1890s, added her voice to Octavia's, arguing that the follow-up of 'unassisted cases' by visitors was crucial to the success of charity organization.[119]

In many respects, the struggle between the 'hard and drys' and the 'wets' (albeit in terms of the work of personal visiting rather than advocacy of any relaxation in relief practices) was also a gendered division between the committee men and the women visitors, although Octavia Hill never presented it as such. Nor is it clear that her faith in the powers of lady visitors to explain matters to the poor was justified. A. L. Hodson, who worked in the Women's University Settlement, apparently experienced considerable difficulty in applying COS principles to the cases she visited. She agreed that most applicants had some failings of character and should not be given relief, but after that she felt that her way was unclear. She found COS ideas 'interesting, generally convincing, but a little paralysing'.[120] Obviously this worker felt that patient and gentle explanation of the committee's decision was not enough.

The primary aim of the COS at its inception in 1869 was to organize charity. In fact, during the 1870s, it seemed more keen to promote its second objective, the repression of mendicity, and from the beginning of the 1880s, it became increasingly involved in a kind of individual casework by committee, whereby the investigation by the visitor as to the character of the applicant was the crucial determinant of whether relief was granted. It was in fact Octavia Hill who set up the only really successful experiment in the organization of charity in Marylebone during the 1870s. There, she took up the job of secretary to the parish visitors, attending meetings of the COS committee and the parish relief committee. All applicants for poor law relief were first passed to the COS committee for investigation and the weeding-out of those not 'deserving' of help. Visitors supplied information on which the decision was based (relayed through Octavia as secretary) and visited those referred back to the poor law in order to explain matters to them.[121] Only in Marylebone did the COS achieve its ideal of fully-fledged cooperation with both the clergy and the poor law authorities. In their *Economics of Industry* (1879), Alfred and Mary Marshall cited her work in support of their arguments regarding state and voluntary aid in poor relief.[122] Elsewhere both the church and the poor law tended to remain aloof. Octavia was frequently scathing in her denunciation of the attitudes of the clergy and their district visitors in particular. In 1876, she pleaded with them for 'God's sake' to cooperate in stemming the flood of ruinous doles. Otherwise the COS would fail or, more likely, because the COS workers were full of 'earnest young blood' and were finding 'humanity in science', the COS system would supersede that of parish visiting. 'Why risk warfare when there could be peace?' she asked.[123] However, appeals for the clergy to work with the COS continued in vain throughout the 1870s and early 1880s, until the Society became well and truly focused on the task of investigating cases applying for relief.[124]

Octavia compared the Marylebone system to the Elberfield scheme in Germany, a much-vaunted model for British administration of relief in the late nineteenth century.[125] The appeal of Elberfield for Octavia and many others lay in the close personal supervision of each applicant for relief by an unpaid worker who was in fact obliged by law to offer his or her services, a degree of compulsion that did not fit Octavia's philosophy and which she conveniently overlooked when citing merits of the scheme. The Elberfield workers also had the power to decide the rate of relief to be given, something Octavia realized would be impossible until British voluntary workers were better trained, and which would in any case have been virtually impossible to achieve given the well-developed nature of British local administration compared to the German. Octavia admitted that in print the scheme looked 'dry and formal' but she insisted that 'anyone who reflects will see how the most intimate, loving, friendly way of reaching the poor through the efforts of kind visitors (each of whom visits chiefly amongst those she knows best) has been secured'.[126] She urged a similar system with firm control from the centre in the form of a paid or unpaid secretary on her close friend, Mrs Jane Senior, who was considering promoting a system of visiting for poor law cases (women visitors had already gained access to the workhouse).[127]

However, the popular verdict remained that the COS was hard and dry. Hodson referred to applicants to the COS district committee as leaving hope outside the door.[128] By the late 1880s, the COS itself was prepared to admit that its image left much to be desired. An article in the *Charity Organisation Reporter* for 1882 described applicants coming either before a paid agent, who might be untowardly brusque, or before a huge committee, which proved extremely daunting for the applicant. 'Is it altogether wonderful that some people do not like us?' the author asked.[129] In its annual report for 1887 the Society acknowledged that it was often accused of being an instrument of political economy, administering relief on 'mechanical and material principles'. Adding that this was not true, the Report nonetheless admitted that the criticism touched points of weakness.[130] The story of the COS showed how easy it was for the caring element to disappear from work embodying so many of Octavia Hill's ideas.

Yet Octavia remained loyal to the COS. Indeed, she seemed to delight in taking a share in its unpopularity. She freely confessed that her own efforts in Marylebone resulted in considerable resentment, believing that this was inevitable until the poor understood the new ways.[131] At the 1891 annual general meeting of the society, while disclaiming any power of public speaking, she expressed her 'profoundest desire to identify myself, so far as possible with its [the COS's] work – so to identify myself that I may be included, if I may be so honoured, in any unpopularity or censure that may be heaped on it'.[132] In the same year she wrote to Sidney Cockerell about the help the COS had given with the organization of a cadet corps in her Southwark buildings and remarked that there was a tendency to accept the help of the COS and then to avoid any identification with it.[133]

Octavia's attachment to the Society was based on more than loyalty. In her view, notwithstanding its tendency to dryness, the COS promised more than any other organization involved in the question of poverty to uphold certain principles she believed to be crucial to successful work among the poor. These were: the voluntarist principle, because Octavia believed that each person had to come to his or her own conclusion as to what constituted right action, which made any state intervention that might erode personal responsibility anathema; and the defence of family responsibility, which she believed to be the source of all fellow-feeling in the community, again against incursions by the state.

Samuel Barnett, who unlike Ruskin, stated his firm approval of Octavia's 1869 speech to the National Association for the Promotion of

Social Science and who was instrumental in stopping all outdoor relief to the able-bodied in Whitechapel, nevertheless began to show signs of moving away from some COS principles in the mid-1880s. In 1884, Henrietta Barnett accused the COS of lacking heart in its dealings with dock labourers seeking relief and in an 1886 article, Samuel Barnett advocated the organization of unskilled labour, albeit at the same time reiterating his old position on outdoor relief.[134] By 1895 he was prepared to launch a full-scale attack on the COS, accusing it of dogmatism and of turning saving and opposition to state intervention into idols.[135] Octavia, who was already suspicious of his churchmanship, and who had chosen to throw her weight behind the Oxford House and Women's University Settlements in preference to Toynbee Hall, rallied to the COS. Her early work in Marylebone had in fact included a scheme to provide those in need with work rather than relief. Similarly in her housing work she was prepared to employ young women and elderly men in painting and cleaning work in the buildings. But while she felt that the charitable provision of work was safer than the giving of doles, she was concerned about its distorting effects on the labour market and on wages. She could not, like Ruskin, rejoice in any proposal to reform the labour market such that competition was reduced. To the end, the idea of public works provided by the state remained anathema. She was alone on the Royal Commission on the Poor Laws in objecting to proposals for public works, arguing that 'the work should be recognised as relief or training, wherever it was not needed and carried on in the real market of the open world'.[136]

It was this same sticking-point that probably accounted for the fact that she did not participate in the new twentieth-century initiatives in the form of the Guilds of Help and the Personal Service Association. The Guilds of Help also claimed to be an adaptation of the Elberfield system and emphasized 'moral and friendly influence and support' using voluntary helpers.[137] However, they did not want to judge character and separate the deserving from the undeserving or, as the COS had tried to do from the later 1880s, the helpable from the unhelpable. In addition, the Guilds were very much a response to the unemployment crisis of 1904–5 and one of their chief aims was to work with local authorities and indeed to further the state provision of employment.[138] Violet Markham, who was involved in both the Guild of Help movement and (as a founder) the Personal Service Association, wrote a letter to the *Spectator* criticizing the COS's attitude towards the state, which she explained more fully in correspondence with the Society itself in 1912. She eschewed both the view that poverty was solely the fault of the individual (which she saw as the COS position) and that it was purely a creation of social circumstances. While she supported the COS principles of relief in terms of the emphasis they placed on investigation, casework and regard for the self-respect of the individual, she felt that relief was not the only issue. She argued, for example, that the state could no longer afford to tolerate the waste of human capital represented by the hungry child. For charitable organizations to hold aloof from the state merely meant that local and central government were to be deprived of crucial help and guidance.[139]

While Markham may have been right in labelling the COS in general as a rankly individualistic organization, Octavia Hill was not disposed completely to ignore social circumstances in cases of poverty, although she did not make these the main focus of her work. But then nor did the Guilds of Help. However, although Octavia was prepared to use volunteer visitors as a caring leaven to the social costs resulting from the operation of market forces, she could not follow New Liberals, like Markham, and see state action on behalf of those in need (whether through the medium of school meals, old age pensions or national insurance) as a positive, creative and enabling, rather than demoralizing force. Most of the proponents of the Guilds of Help were New Liberals, whose efforts would result by the 1920s in what Elizabeth MacAdam was to call the 'new philanthropy'.[140] This consisted of a mixture of state and voluntary services, which if not exactly practising close liaison, did not indulge in open hostility. But Octavia Hill remained a nineteenth-century liberal in her view that any financial aid to the poor from the state was but another form of dole. Pensions given to an elderly person by a charitable society after careful individual work by a visitor who assessed the old person's family circumstances and character were fine, but state pensions given to all over 70 years of age (from 1908) with minimal checks as to character (even these were abandoned as unworkable in 1919) and set at a rate that was by no means high enough to ensure adequate relief in all cases were not.

Similarly, both the COS and Octavia Hill whipped themselves into a frenzy of concern over the issue of providing school meals for children. In Octavia's words: 'women were standing gossiping or quarrelling, dirty and draggled, about on doorsteps, while we are cooking at school for their children the dinner they should be preparing in the tidy house'.[141] The whole point of personal work with the poor was to teach them ways of becoming self-supporting, to strengthen individual character and thereby family ties and responsibility so that children looked after their elderly parents and parents their young children. To Octavia's mind, people like Samuel Barnett greatly underestimated the family as the essential source of joy and support in people's lives; as Darley has suggested, her idealization of family life may well have stemmed from the early disruption of her own.[142] She was prepared to countenance state intervention in but two areas, that of setting building regulations and in the preservation of open spaces (culminating in her work to establish the National Trust) but neither of these directly touched the crucial matter of personal responsibility.

Housing management

Followers of Octavia Hill often spoke of being trained in the Octavia Hill system of housing management, and certainly their practices were sufficiently distinctive to warrant the label. However, Octavia herself always denied that she worked according to a set of rules or that she had evolved a system. She deplored systems and liked to stress the way in which her work consisted of an individual response to each and every tenant. She worked with what she described to the Royal Commission on Housing in 1885 as the class of tenant below that housed by the model dwellings companies, who tended to be destructive and who required careful training and supervision.[143]

She insisted that her principles were worked out rather than thought out and that they were infinitely flexible. She believed that she had come 'to much better results from doing things simply because they came in her path, than I have ever done when I have made plans of what I would like to do'.[144] It was really theory that Octavia deplored more than system, method or principle. She put a premium on experience; principles could be learned quickly but experience could not be acquired overnight:

> There is indeed some technical knowledge essential – more, perhaps, than people realise who seem to think they can manage houses without training. But success in this depends no more on any plan than does that of a young lady who begins housekeeping. Certain things she should indeed know, but whether she manages well will depend mainly on what she is.[145]

In other words, it would depend on her capacity to work individually with the poor. In words strongly reminiscent of Mrs Thatcher's analogy between her prime ministerial duties and domestic housekeeping, Octavia Hill thus sought to demystify and play up the commonsense element in her work, thereby also making the point that it was suitable work for women to do.

As with her COS work, she was anxious to encourage personal contact with the poor and was contemptuous of those who lacked knowledge of their day-to-day lives. Only theoreticians, she felt, could believe that the provision of new blocks of flats at cheap rents was all that was necessary to solve the problem of housing for the poor, ignoring both the destructive tendencies of the class she worked with and their need for housing near their work, which made them hold fast to their older tenement dwellings. She always favoured rehabilitating old dwellings if possible and favoured cottages over blocks of flats, in part because she felt that blocks lacked the individuality of the family home, although in her article prepared for Booth's study of London life and labour, she placed the problem of regulating large numbers of the undisciplined and untrained ahead of what she realized would be labelled a 'sentimental' concern such as this.[146] Theoreticians were also just plain dull: 'I cannot well express how sure I am of the unutterable dullness of abstract truths, however gloriously expressed'.[147] The only thinkers she had time for were Ruskin and Maurice. Abstract concepts seemed to her a poor vehicle for capturing life; as she advised a correspondent, 'if you want people to understand love you must say mother'.[148] Much to Beatrice Webb's dismay, she showed little or no interest in new ideas about the question of poverty, preferring to immerse herself in the minutiae of individual work with the poor:

> it is not often that I turn away from the very engrossing detail of work here to think much about general questions . . . It is with me here almost as with the poor themselves, a kind of fight for mere existence – references, notices, rents, repairs, the dry necessary matters of business, take up almost all time and thought.[149]

Octavia believed that such behaviour brought her into closer sympathy with the poor, but it scarcely encouraged any serious reflection on the nature of her achievement. She often expressed her concern to bring theorists and practical workers into communication but when asked to speak was apt to demur: 'But what can I say? There has been so much said. Is it not better just now silently to do?'[150] In general, she believed that only if more people would get to know the poor would the best way of helping them become evident. No theory could provide the answer. As a member of the Royal Commission on the Poor Law she felt that many of its recommendations should have been tested first by years of practical work and small-scale experiments.[151]

Octavia's strong preference for practical experience over theory and above all for personal social work with tenants was nevertheless premised on very strong ideas as to fundamental housing principles. The aim of her work was to remoralize relations between landlord and tenant, such that both fulfilled their obligations. She had no interest in getting into the business of building new dwellings, which she considered of peripheral importance in the solution of the housing problem.

Rather, she concentrated on getting landlords to provide security of tenure and to keep their property in good repair, and on getting tenants to pay their rent and treat the property with respect. It was important that each relationship be worked out individually. Her work would set an example as to what might be achieved, the hope being that more landlords would then feel their way to emulating it. Coercion was of course out of the question. Each property owner had to manage his investment according to what he felt was right. The essence of the relationship was a business one. The critical point of contact between landlord and tenant was at the point of paying rent and it was when they collected the rent that the lady visitors were able to engage in their more 'paternalistic' work of knowing, befriending, training and controlling the poor. In her 1883 letter to her fellow workers, Octavia likened the landlord/tenant relationship 'with all its mutual attachments and duties' to that which existed in many rural areas.[152] It was not often that she employed any such backward-looking analogies, but the emphasis she placed on the establishment of a landlord/tenant relationship that was paternal as well as businesslike led naturally to the invocation of a (fictional) rural and (implicitly) pre-industrial model.

But money was central and Octavia's attitudes towards money were complicated. From the days of running the toymakers' workshop, she had shown considerable shrewdness in managing it. At the age of nineteen, she successfully negotiated the sale of the toys to a wholesaler, who doubtless meant to test her business capacity by asking her if she properly understood the meaning of the discount she proposed. Octavia held her ground and rejoicing in her victory added in typical fashion: 'I felt that quiet truth had overcome noisy selfishness'.[153] Just a little later she wrote to Mary Harris: 'You hardly know how solemnly I feel about money, so that the want or possession of it are serious lessons to me . . . I feel in all that concerns money how life and hope are untouched by troubles'.[154] Early in the 1870s she felt that her own relative poverty was an asset, keeping her 'low and humble and hardy' and closer to the poor people she served, and balancing her somewhat 'intoxicating power'.[155] In 1874, her financial worries ceased when friends invested a considerable amount of money in trust for her. Later, she exhibited concern about the investments she acquired but told Sidney Cockerell, her financial adviser, that she had a 'profound contempt for inquietness about money'.[156] It would seem that part of her wanted to let sleeping dogs (in this instance her Russian bonds) lie, especially as she believed in the justice of the Russian cause; part was frustrated at not comprehending the workings of financial markets; and part was happy to accept advice from a trusted friend. It was impossible, however, for Octavia not to take an active part in her own business affairs.

Both rich and poor had a duty to manage their money 'nobly'. Those who failed to do so had, she feared, some 'rottenness at the heart'.[157] The rich were obliged to watch carefully over and safeguard their investments, as well as making sure that they knew how their charitable gifts were spent: 'if we want to ease our consciences by giving money and yet will not take trouble about it; if we want to make a great effect with little money; if we want to do what is popular; assuredly our alms will bring curses'.[158] In 1878 she advised her supporters frankly that because of her own ill-health (brought about by the quarrel with Ruskin and a broken engagement) her sister would be taking over the administration of the contributions they had made to help deserving tenants. But because her sister was inexperienced in social work, they should 'review the wisdom of sending money' to her in the coming years.[159] (The donations fell by some £75 to £375.) Yet her letters asking and thanking donors for money were often extremely sentimental and contrasted strongly with the businesslike line of her correspondence regarding the balance sheets for her properties and her own financial affairs. One commentator has suggested that letters to potential and actual donors were harder for her to write.[160] This may be so, but it is clear that she was also seeking to express the sense of fellowship and communion that she felt was being built between those who expressed their sympathy towards her work by giving.

As a housing manager, she undertook to protect the landlord's investment. From the first, Ruskin, who gave her her first houses to manage, insisted on a 'fair' rate of interest of 5 per cent, first because money should be used properly and produce some return, and second so that other landlords would be willing to follow his example.[161] Octavia always insisted that housing for the poorest could be made to pay if the accommodation was kept simple and if the management of lettings, repairs and rents was sufficiently careful, even when ground rents were relatively high.[162] She firmly opposed any state subsidy for housing in the form of municipal building. She was happy to go so far as to promote the Artisans Dwelling Act of 1875, confessing that she had realized that there were obstacles to the work in certain courts and districts which societies and individuals could not overcome.[163] For example, the Drury Lane court that she worked was surrounded by others whose owners had no interest in securing more sunlight. She argued that just as the abolition of slavery had been entirely necessary despite being costly, so the provision of thorough ventilation would inevitably be a charge on the community. But she insisted that the buildings erected according to the new building regulations should pay their own way. She contended that subsidy was wrong in principle because it was effectively another rate in aid of wages akin to poor relief. Once again she was drawing a careful line between state action that directly touched individual responsibility and that which did not. She also felt that municipal authorities could not at once represent the ratepayers and provide subsidy to the poor.[164] However, Wohl has suggested that 5 per cent was such a low rate of return that it effectively constituted a subsidy.[165] Even more pertinent was the way in which the success of Octavia's scheme rested largely on the unpaid labour of lady rent collectors. Only those who needed a salary to support themselves received one. Thus Emma Cons was paid, while the wealthy Henrietta Rowland was not.

On the tenants' side, the fundamental obligation was the payment of rent. At first some remissions were given in respect of prompt payment, but these were later abandoned because it undermined the idea that such behaviour was a duty incumbent on all. Tenants who did not pay up were evicted. The strictness with which this principle was enforced was explained in terms of first, the need to ensure a return on the property (unremunerative rents would in any case merely act as a rate in aid of wages and result in lower wages); second, as a means to keeping rents at a reasonable level (Octavia told the 1882 Select Committee that the reason why rents were so high was that so many did not pay and while this explanation was partial, she certainly tapped a source of injustice felt by the poor themselves); and third, the regular payment of rent would increase the tenant's sense of self-respect and hope of doing better.[166] During the 1890s, she developed complicated systems whereby tenants would also pay their own rates, a move that was far from popular but which she felt would ensure that tenants would see how rates were rising and would vote accordingly.[167] Octavia wrote of tenants preparing for her visits to collect the rent by cleaning their flats, and of their pleasure in such preparations and in seeing her satisfaction. The visits also served as occasions for getting to know the tenants and for offering advice. Describing her very early efforts to collect rent in dark and lawless courts among drunken tenants, Octavia recalled pondering the principles she would use in ruling her tenants. Rent collection provided the vehicle for exerting moral and financial discipline.[168]

Octavia was convinced that the regular visits of rent collectors would eventually result in better habits among tenants. Landladies, she felt, were a more influential force than teachers in the lives of the poor.[169] She encouraged her collectors to take an interest in every detail of their tenants' lives; everything was a part of life and therefore mattered and people could only be understood as wholes. Rent collection was significantly different from district visiting and, Octavia believed, more important and more demanding. It had to be carried out on an absolutely regular basis and continuously throughout the year.[170] In return, progress on the part of those visited was more marked. Octavia Hill undoubtedly sought to inculcate middle-class values, something which always makes modern hackles rise, but the major redeeming feature has to be that she did genuinely know and care for 'her' poor. Her interpretation of what was best for them may be questioned but the importance of her understanding of the need for some kind of careful management of rented homes has been rediscovered in the 1980s.[171]

The main work of the rent collector was to bring order, cleanliness and quiet out of chaos and dirt, and to raise the 'standard' of the tenants. Collecting worked on two fronts: to encourage both changes in personal habits and a corporate sense of belonging in the dwellings. Octavia Hill noted the passing of deferential relations between rich and poor in the city and condemned the way in which no sense of duty had taken its place, only talk of rights.[172] Her best reward was when her mother reported to her that a tenant was grateful that her court had become 'so quiet and respectable'.[173] Rent collectors got to know their families. They made careful investigations (not unlike the COS) of employers, kin and previous landladies before taking on a new tenant, and they attended to repairs (Octavia had to give up the management of a court where the landlord refused her control of these).[174] In 1871, she reported that she and her fellow workers were doing 'indestructable repairs on the drains first'.[175] The difficulties of financing and carrying out repairs in what were very run-down buildings were enormous, but after some initial hiccoughs, it would seem that Octavia Hill maintained a better standard of basic repairs than have many local authorities in the post-war period. Rent collectors also judiciously gave out scrubbing work in the buildings to a deserving widow or to a girl too young for domestic service; arranged a country holiday for a child; a sewing class; or a party or excursion for a group of tenants. When the most respectable member of a court died, Octavia wrote of the importance of leaving his friends to help his widow, but of then stepping in 'with strong quiet lasting aid and help to earn or something of that kind'.[176] Collectors also made sure that respectable working people did not have to suffer drunken neighbours and they endeavoured to resolve long-standing quarrels, for example between women over the use of a wash tub. Octavia was fond of describing the work as quiet, detailed and continuous: 'For the work is one of detail . . . day after day the work is one of such small things, that if one did not look beyond and through them they would be trying – locks to be mended, notices to be served, the missing shilling of the week's rent to be called for three or four times, petty quarrels to be settled, small rebukes to be spoken, the same remonstrances to be made again and again'.[177] Beatrice Webb for one found it impossible to 'look beyond' such tedious minutiae, but Octavia revelled in it and fretted when health broke down or pressure of business prevented her from getting 'down among the poor' for 'individual work'.

At an appropriate moment, the rent collector would be able to suggest to the tenant that another room be taken, thus encouraging tenants always to aspire to the 'next standard'. Because she believed that tenants would raise their standards but slowly, Octavia opposed the new model dwellings with their self-contained flats which did not afford the possibility of tenants renting another room. Similarly she believed that amenities had to be kept basic. There was no need to pipe water to each flat; as long as there was a tap on each floor it could easily be carried. This would of course also reduce the cost of the initial improvement to dwellings taken over for management, a not inconsiderable matter. Octavia felt that the people who planned artisans' dwellings always wanted to do too much at once. It was impossible to move the lowest class of tenant out of a cellar dwelling into an 'ideal home'. Appliances and facilities could only be improved gradually.[178] Tenants participated in the decision as to how any surplus from the repair funds would be spent, an important element of housing management that has frequently been overlooked.

Beatrice Webb passionately denounced Octavia Hill's ideas as to what standard of amenity was appropriate for poor tenants. On the other hand Octavia's repeated reference to her class of tenants as 'destructive' was not without foundation; vandalism was a major problem. She did not deny the importance of gradually improving amenities and was a lifelong campaigner for introducing as much natural beauty, light and air into the slums as possible. She wrote passionately about watching the air disappear from the London courts with the continual advance of speculative builders: 'This is different from reason and science: this is life, this is pain'.[179] She supported the efforts to decorate public buildings and she spent a large amount of time soliciting voluntary subscriptions to collectively purchase anything from open spaces the size of Parliament Hill Fields to brightly coloured tiles for the outside wall of one of her properties, which spelled a suitably uplifting message: 'Every house is builded by some man but he that built all things is God'.[180] She made several attempts to fence the garden of her first set of properties and then to plant it, describing her struggle in terms of a battle for order.

> You know something of how hard I worked for it [the first houses on Freshwater Place] long ago; my difficulties in building the wall, and in contending with the dirt of the people, how gradually we reduced it to comparative order, have paved it, lighted it, supplied water cisterns, raised the height of the rooms, built a staircase, balcony and additional storey, how Mr Ruskin had live trees planted for us and creepers, and by his beautiful presents of flowers, helped to teach our people to love flowers. You know or can imagine, how dear the place is to me.[181]

The imposition of order was thus not entirely a matter of disciplining tenants, Octavia Hill's own efforts were substantial.

Octavia Hill's preoccupation with natural beauty was very much in keeping with late nineteenth-century fears as to the morally degenerate quality of urban life. Certainly she was inclined to paint a romantic picture of the effect of days in the open air upon slum dwellers.[182] The Barnetts started the Children's Country Holiday Fund in order that urban children might experience morally improving rural life and, as Margaret Sewell explained, the chief criterion of selection was the degree to which the child needed 'civilizing'.[183] But Octavia Hill also sought to build a sense of corporate identity through her tenants' use of gardens and in Southwark, a community hall. She was delighted when a woman in a mending and needlework class held weekly for married women and older girls used the expression 'one of us', signalling to Octavia Hill her 'consciousness of corporate life'. Similarly she wrote to Sidney Cockerell that she was delighted by the 'beautiful corporate life' in the Women and Girls' Institute in Southwark and the 'manly' and independent relations being built in the boys club.[184] Octavia Hill was aware of the possibility of educating parents through their children long before the early twentieth-century proponents of mothercraft lessons for schoolgirls and of child welfare advocates, such as Margaret McMillan. Probably she drew, as did McMillan, on the work of Ruskin in this regard.[185] She and her fellow workers in Southwark organized a May Day festival and Octavia watched the progress of the children's play anxiously. Playgrounds were supervised and the children taught games: 'we had our playground festival yesterday, with all its wonderful memories, and the blessed sense of progress . . . And Oh, Mary! what a progress in the people . . . The cottages looked so neat and clean . . . Then how the children have improved! What a number of games they know!'[186]

The picture Octavia liked to paint was one of improving tenants and ever-widening sympathies among the rich. Many of her co-workers provided a rather more balanced view. Ella Pycroft and Ellen Chase, both rent collectors, wrote in a down-to-earth tone and were obviously as caught up in the minutiae of the work as was Octavia herself. Ellen Chase, for example, wrote to Octavia in the mid-1880s to report on the difficult work in Deptford:

> King [a tenant] had torn his garden all to pieces and broken pale of fence and windows here and there, and did not show himself at all. We were nonplussed. First I hoped to slip a notice under the door, but the weather-board was too close, that is a reason against putting it on. Then we debated how legal a service pinning to the back door would be . . . Mrs. T had the cheek to offer nothing, so I took her notice. I gave out several jobs of cleaning to even off the £7. Mrs. Sandal's cistern was leaking worst sort. Matthews and Arter both said floor too old to pay for removal. My unlets have come down 10/-.[187]

Octavia's letters to Ellen Chase after the latter's return to America were written in a similar vein, with snippets of news about the behaviour of particular tenants in the street reported much as the doings of characters in a soap opera might be discussed today. But the accounts of Chase and Pycroft stopped short of the high moral tone that Octavia usually adopted at some point. Ellen Chase confessed that she did not sleep the night before having to evict a tenant and recalled having to face a hostile crowd, with children throwing pebbles into her hat and making ribald remarks on her clothing.[188] She won herself a little leeway by laughing back at them but was thankful when she pushed through the crowd and was able to hurry off for her train home. Margaret Wynne Nevinson remembered the number of cases of wife beating and Miss Pycroft's pluck in living in the buildings for a period to try and stop it, but without success.[189] Miss Hodson, who collected rents as part of her training at the Women's University Settlement, did not venture into her district on Monday afternoons because she hated to see the fights and the drunkenness.[190] And Beatrice Webb was straightforwardly repelled by the noise and brutality and was, unlike Chase and Pycroft, depressed and bored by the work.[191] The younger Sidney Cockerell, who helped Octavia run the boys' club in Southwark, also declared himself bored with the work by the early 1890s.[192] Not all were as able as Octavia to take spiritual comfort in the thought of being called to 'quiet detailed work' and not all were as convinced of its worth.

Octavia was singularly free from doubt, although from time to time she did express a certain amount of unease as to her power of communicating with the poor. In 1875 she wrote to Sidney Cockerell expressing her admiration of the work done by two rent collectors who had achieved 'the most perfect terms of quiet, gentle power and happy intercourse with their people, noticing and managing cleansing, repairs, rents and everything. I am so thankful'.[193] She felt that she lacked the 'glad bright sympathy' showed by these workers in their relations with tenants. She was unable, for example, to make the classes for girls go well. She wrote to Mary Harris in 1875 that she was

> sensible how much I lack swiftly turning perception, and unfailing gentleness, and a certain cautious reservation of speech. My only chance among the people is trying to be all right, so that it mayn't matter their seeing right through me. I have no powers of diplomacy; these I don't regret, but the power of non-expression might be advantageous.[194]

Despite her injunctions to her fellow workers to do quiet work, Octavia apparently found difficulty in keeping her own counsel. Certainly there is some evidence that tenants found her strict and unapproachable, for all her efforts to befriend them. Her sister Miranda reported the words of one old Deptford woman who was surprised and pleased to find Octavia did have feelings after all.[195] And, writing in 1961, a former pupil in her school recollected that while she loved Miranda Hill, who was gentle and understanding, she had found Octavia stern, uncompromising and 'sometimes a bit sarcastic'.[196]

On the whole, Octavia did not allow her occasional bouts of self-questioning to perturb her unduly. Just as with her COS work, she tended to rejoice in a certain degree of unpopularity which, she felt, tested her workers and drew them together: 'In these days when benevolence is popular, I think we may be thankful to have difficulty to surmount'.[197] It was in any case important never to be downcast. She remained convinced that God would not let the good thing she worked and prayed for fail. She was but His instrument. Given the very real difficulties she faced in her work of housing management, a considerable measure of confidence was necessary. Doubtless she was right in her estimation that 'all successful management of finance depends on walking open-eyed forward, having weighed possibilities and results'.[198] But her singular conviction as to the rightness of her work did make her impatient of any attempts to measure its success. The only judge she cared about was the Almighty and she felt that what concerned Him was the spirit in which the work was carried out rather than the outcome. This attitude was of course perfectly consistent with her desire to moralize relations between rich and poor rather than to change the structural underpinnings of those relationships. But the way in which she attached as much (or more) importance to means as to ends found later echoes in socialist thought, for example in the thinking of Tawney.[199] In any case, she felt that unpopularity and even defeat was to be expected in the early stages of any great cause, hence her philosophical acceptance of opposition.[200] At the beginning of her housing work she encountered the hostility of the local Marylebone medical officer of health, who condemned several of her properties as insanitary. Octavia found the public debate difficult to handle and coped only by deliberately shutting out the controversy, comforting herself by reading Cromwell and Carlyle and relying on her friends to see her through, while worrying lest she be considered despotic and arrogant.[201]

Concrete evidence of two problematic areas in Octavia's housing work serve further to illuminate some of the tensions that existed in practice for her and her fellow workers in their work with tenants. The boys' club run by Sidney Cockerell and, until 1877, by Edward Bond, caused her considerable heartache. Interestingly Koven, in his study of London settlements, has observed that the working-class men's clubs often posed particular difficulties for settlers who were anxious to promote democracy on the one hand and good administration on the other;[202] certainly Mary Ward had her share of conflict with the leaders of the club at her University Hall settlement. In 1875, Octavia expressed her satisfaction with the 'manly independence' shown by the club members, but a few months later she was complaining that the club was behind with its rent and also said that she had no desire to attend its meetings which promised to be 'uncivil'.[203] When the club took the initiative in letting space to the School Board for an infant class in the mornings, she was furious and wrote an extremely sarcastic note to Cockerell. She wanted to retain control over the club's finances and wanted to make sure that the rent from the School Board went to defray the subsidy the club received. Nor could she allow the club to open on Sundays, although it bothered her to enforce a direct prohibition. The club members considered themselves: 'the best judges of their own affairs. This was the only consideration that made me pause. I do not like to tyrannise'.[204] However, when push came to shove, respect for what the club members believed to be right action was subordinated to her own sense of what was fit, and working with these tenants in a spirit of friendship gave way to the exercise of firm control.

Octavia experienced problems on a much larger scale in Deptford, where Ellen Chase acted as her faithful lieutenant for many years. Deptford tenants did not seem to respond to the best efforts of the rent collectors. Ellen Chase described Deptford as 'less advanced' and wrote that it had been a struggle to 'get a sense of truth into the people' and to imbue them with an idea of their obligations as tenants and citizens.[205] In her letters to her fellow workers, Octavia made many weary references throughout the 1880s to 'poor Deptford':

> sometimes I fancy it is a little better, and often I remind myself that such work as is given to it, and the presence of such workers as it has up and down among its people, must tell, but it seems really hardly to move. Still I am sure it will, and God grant me and those who are with me in spirit to hope and wait.[206]

But in 1889 she recorded that while it was possible to make good tenants comfortable, improving the bad was a lost cause; it was impossible to 'exercise any just and wise rule or to secure order'.[207] A year later, in spite of a lot of money having been spent on repairs, drainage, cleansing and redecorating, and the noting of all 'delapidations' every three weeks, the street remained 'disgraceful'.[208] The tenants were not in the least deferential and faced with their refusal to cooperate, the rent collectors could do little.

Octavia for once declared herself defeated: 'what more to do I do not know, I don't want to throw all the blame on the tenants of whom I am fond, whom we have failed to help better'.[209] She reassured her fellow workers that because the spirit of their work had been good, they would be bound to reap some rewards. She congratulated them on setting a good example to the tenants and for their 'self-forgetfulness, humility, gentleness, patience, utter indifference to what is popular, thought concentrated only on the people and what is good for them'. By 1894 she had decided to pull out of Deptford altogether. Her incapacity to reach this group of tenants was due primarily to the short leases on the properties and to the shifting nature of the population, but it may also have signalled the beginnings of other difficulties elsewhere. In 1907 she was unable to pay the owners of 'one or two small properties' any dividend at all and in the case of others it had diminished. And by 1909, her lettings were 'quite despairful'.[210] She blamed the building of municipal blocks of subsidized dwellings for distorting the rental market but it may also have been the case that given a choice, many tenants chose not to put themselves under the Octavia Hill system of management. However, rents in the municipal blocks were no lower than those charged by Octavia Hill during the 1890s, and Darley has concluded that tenancies in Octavia's blocks were sought after.[211] Certainly the relatively low turn-over of tenants she achieved contributed conspicuously to her success in managing all but Deptford.

Finally there is also evidence that by the 1890s and 1900s Octavia Hill was experiencing some difficulty in getting enough co-workers as well as tenants. She had put as much energy into building up a community of fellow workers (she hated the term rent collector) as she had into tenant and building management. The term 'fellow worker' came from Maurice, and Octavia Hill conscientiously built on Maurice's ideas as to the importance of unity among co-workers. In 1902, she wrote that just as the years had justified the use of the phrase 'one of us' in respect of tenants, so she felt that there was 'among those I am proud to call "my fellow workers" a certain real link', even though at several stages in her career she bemoaned the fact that many workers were as strangers to one another.[212] In some respects, she experienced very similar problems in her relationships with her co-workers as with her tenants. She liked to extol the relationships she built with them on simple grounds of human sympathy, just as she liked to talk about the growth of friendship and trust with tenants.[213] But the goal of a community of united and yet independent workers proved difficult to achieve. In a telling letter to Sidney Cockerell after a birthday party she said that she 'did feel as if you were all my children even those much older than I'.[214] The irresistible impulse to paternalism and even despotism proved strong indeed. She confided to Mary Harris that she was worried about the amount of power she wielded and whether she was becoming overbearing, but so few people offered her any advice as to where she might be wrong.[215]

Octavia never quite felt able genuinely to delegate portions of the work to others. In 1873, she wrote angrily of the 'little power of growth' in her work whenever she herself withdrew, even though she said that she tried to see it as an opportunity for bringing out the character and power of her co-workers. Again in 1874, she marvelled at how things 'got on' when she did them herself.[216] In theory she recognized that it was impossible to get the 'full benefit of heart, head and active will' without giving those who served responsibility, and early on she did give Emma Cons, another strong personality, control over some buildings on Drury Lane. Miss Cons employed her own rent collectors, kept her own accounts and reported to the owners direct. It is not clear how Octavia Hill viewed this. She and Emma Cons were old friends and she merely remarked that Miss Cons's ways were very different from her own; certainly Beatrice Webb noted that Emma Cons moved away from the ideas of the COS during the 1880s.[217] But such divergent practices were rare. Octavia wrote to her fellow workers in rather a patronizing fashion in 1874:

> I think few of you fully realised that this [taking responsibility for their buildings] is what I mean when I ask you if you will take charge of houses,

you think of it as collecting and then rendering an account to me here, you think the responsibility of action lies here. Will you try in future to believe that though I am quite ready to resume the charge of my district when you are unable to carry on the work there . . . all the kingdom is your own while you hold it, to make of it what good thing you can . . .[218]

When Octavia broke down in 1877, went abroad and set aside her housing work for four years, some rejigging of her work was essential. In her 1878 letter to her fellow workers (she wrote one each year) she reported that while her previous efforts to get workers to function independently had not been very successful, since she had left London they had 'consented most kindly to accept more responsibility than of old'.[219] However she was far from satisfied with much of their work. Some showed administrative power with little real sympathy for the people, others the reverse.[220] In other words, few achieved the mix of business and paternalism that Octavia considered crucial for success. In some measure Octavia's dilemma must have been real. Not only was the work tough and continuous, but few had both facility with account books and a liking for personal social work. By the 1890s, Octavia was deploring the relative abundance of financial contributions she received compared to paucity of volunteer workers and was ready to consider a more formal attempt at training new workers.

The Women's University Settlement and the training of social workers
Many rent collectors experienced considerable difficulty with the work. Octavia's deep regard for the importance of money and its wise use made her insist on neat rent books and accounts, even though the strong-minded Miss Cons apparently felt such things were a waste of time.[221] Octavia herself anxiously sought Sidney Cockerell's advice as to how to make the proper entries in her ledgers and declared herself 'DREADFULLY ashamed' when she lost track of a cheque for £5.[222] In 1876, she had to deal with a bookkeeper, Mrs Allen, whose accounts were faulty:

> She is very unwilling to send them [the books] as she hates inaccuracy – but dreads to be found out in it yet more – and she hopes things will come right if they are kept quiet. You [Sidney Cockerell] on the other hand, abhor and detest unbalanced, uncompared books, and I feel wretched till these are absolutely proved to agree with ours, or the mistakes hunted down. And I being responsible am the person to decide. . . . She has the elements of a good bookkeeper however, all except more courage to face and clear up a mistake at once . . .[223]

Margaret Nevinson certainly found rent collecting 'an expensive hobby', not least because she was soft hearted and tended to give food before collecting rent. She would then have to spend hours trying to make the totals tally. But she recorded cheerfully that the discipline she learned in this respect came in handy in the suffrage movement.[224] One volunteer writing in the *Charity Organisation Review* in 1887 recorded how humiliating it was to find that so many women's desire to take up the work died a sudden death when they found they had to keep accounts.[225] In 1892, a Miss Pawl apparently broke down when put in charge of the accounts in Deptford and left suddenly.[226] Given the poor quality of most middle-class girls' education, especially in mathematics, all this was hardly surprising. During her time as a teacher in the 1850s and 1860s, Octavia had given her full support to Emily Davies's campaign for higher education for women and for the extension of university local examinations to girls' high schools. She checked through all her workers' books with them, offering a running commentary which some, like Mary Clover, who became secretary of Girton College in 1903, found useful.[227] Others must have found it devastating.

But Octavia Hill had a contempt for the traditional amateurism of ladies. It mattered not that her workers were volunteers, they were expected to develop expertise in the law relating to housing and the complexities of the London rating system, as well as in keeping accounts. In 1879, she wrote to her fellow workers after her return from a period abroad that everyone was 'building and buying, but that she was appalled to learn how few were doing anything towards training volunteers'.[228] Octavia felt very anxious that training schemes should not favour the production of paid workers. She claimed that it was impossible for paid workers to deal with her 'destructive' class of tenants, because the paid rent collector would only collect from the honest, who then subsidized the dishonest.[229] But here she was referring primarily to her preference for middle-class female collectors over working-class paid (and usually male) officials. Middle-class women were crucial to the enterprise of social work attached to rent collection. And middle-class women were in the late nineteenth century going to be for the most part volunteers. Furthermore, a system of 'professed' [professional] workers would mean that they would 'quickly begin to hug our system and perhaps want to perpetuate it even to the extent of making work for it'.[230] Octavia's deep suspicion of systems and theories gave her considerable insight into an aspect of the process of professionalization that has become the subject of fierce debate in the late twentieth century.

The COS went through a prolonged period of discussion as to the wisdom of paying its district secretaries during the 1880s.[231] Again, one of the major issues in the debate was the problem of attracting 'superior' workers to paid posts. The Society had used paid agents to take down cases from an early stage, and these were usually ex-servicemen or policemen who, by the mid-1880s, were felt to have contributed to the 'hard' treatment of applicants.[232] But district secretaries were usually of a higher social class and, more difficult still, some of them were women. By the early 1890s some secretaries were being paid; Helen Bosanquet was one. However the COS continued to emphasize the importance of a flexible body of volunteers attached to each district office. Octavia Hill denied that her commitment to volunteers presented any difficulties, despite the continuous nature of the work. She picked her workers, knew when they would be absent and arranged things accordingly. The problem remained of 'how to unite the fresh, loving, spontaneous individual sympathy with the quiet, grave, sustained and instructed spirit of the trained worker'.[233] Octavia addressed this issue forcibly during the early 1890s and Mrs Rose Dunn Gardner produced an influential paper on the training of volunteers for the COS late in 1894.[234] Mrs Gardner emphasized the need to capture the interest of volunteers and to make them feel a sense of responsibility. This involved taking the time to introduce them to the work of each department.

The work of conceptualizing a system of training for the social work done by the COS district committees and by Octavia Hill's rent collectors was taken up by the Women's University Settlement (WUS, founded in 1887), in conjunction with the COS and with Octavia Hill. Octavia sat on the executive committee of the WUS from 1888. The stated aims of the settlement were manifestly in tune with her own. At the annual general meeting of 1888, Mrs Alfred Marshall stressed from the chair that they proposed to strengthen character rather than seeking directly to diminish suffering.[235] The first head worker, Miss Gruner, who like many settlers was recruited from Newnham College, Cambridge, insisted that 'the work should be carried on quietly, with no straining after opportunities, (and) no public appeals for assistance . . .'[236]

This was all very much to Octavia's taste, although she initially harboured great reservations about settlement work for women, believing strongly that the best workers were women who lived with their own families and who were preferably wives and mothers, not women living in the 'artificial' environment of a settlement:

> Is she not the most sympathetic, most powerful, who nursed her own mother through the long illness, and knew how to go quietly about the darkened

room, who entered so heartily into the sister's love and marriage, and obeyed so perfectly the father's command when it was hardest?[237]

Margery Loane, a district nurse who wrote at length about the poor during the 1900s, also advised girls wishing to take up district nursing to practise their skills first on their families.[238] Octavia agreed that 'home training and the high ideal of home duty' was the best preparation for work among the poor. Much earlier she had replied to some approving comments of Ruskin's on the subject of convents in a negative manner, seeing them as an escape from important duties, and it seems that her later distrust of both missions and settlements as a site for female social work arose from similar feelings.[239] When she joined the executive committee of the WUS she explained her action in the following terms:

> I have complied with the request not because I have very much confidence in the beneficial result of many settlements of workers bound together by no family ties, and with no natural connection but a district; but because the settlement is the practical outcome and centre of a very large association. (I believe some 580 of the young, highly educated and thoughtful ladies of England.) and because a small group of these, settled in the heart of the south London poor, may be of the greatest use.[240]

Women's duties were first to home and family and second to others in need beyond the family. Ideally these could be combined, but the efforts of settlement workers would bear little fruit if they were undertaken as a substitute for home and family duties. Octavia strongly disapproved of those who preferred '*chosen* duties' to 'fulfilling the duties *laid* upon them'.[241] As she wrote to Miss Schuster, who wanted to join her in social work, but who was nursing her father: 'It is for the sake of the homes that we are all working and it is in our own that what we do tells most deeply'. Miss Schuster was strongly advised to stay put.[242] Octavia was also convinced that lady workers needed the brightness and warmth of their family homes if they were to be effective workers in the slums.[243] The strain of living in the worst places would be too much for educated people. On this, she and Beatrice Webb saw eye to eye. But many of the more successful rent collectors, for example Ella Pycroft and Emma Cons, did live among the poor for long periods. Others, if the fictional account by Alice Stronach is anything to go by, transferred from one world of female comradeship (Newnham) to another (in the WUS), but eventually came to the realization that there was 'something missing' in the form of marriage and family life in a manner that would have warmed Octavia's heart.[244] However, another visitor to the settlement, also from Newnham, found the settlers rather too earnest, critical and dowdy.[245] This was more in keeping with the stereotypical picture of the woman graduate and of social workers that Beatrice Webb proved anxious to avoid.

Octavia Hill was vastly reassured as to the purpose and possibilities of the WUS when Margaret Sewell became its head worker in 1891. Sewell stressed that 'the idea, if idea it can be called, is to do consciously and with a definite purpose, where population was dense, that which is done unconsciously, and without effort, almost everywhere else'.[246] She was similar to Octavia both in terms of her ideas and, one suspects, personality. Like Octavia she emphasized the need for social workers to 'know the poor and to direct their work towards strengthening the family unit'. Female settlement workers were much more devoted to the idea of work with families than were male settlers; indeed both Octavia and E. J. Urwick were critical of Barnett and Toynbee Hall on this point.[247] The training of women at the WUS aimed to give them an intimate knowledge of the 'normal' life of the people and Margaret Sewell encouraged them to follow COS practice and get to know the circumstances of each family. They should try and work with the ideals of the people even if they were not as high as the social worker felt they should be and even though at the end of the day it was once more the social worker's own values of thrift, order and quiet that would prevail.[248]

Miss Gruner felt training to be a distraction from the main objects of the settlement and resigned in 1888.[249] A year later Sewell signalled a move towards emphasizing the training of workers as part of the settlement's agenda, and a lecture series was started in 1891 with the assistance of Bernard Bosanquet. In keeping with her suspicion of writers and theories, Octavia Hill was very anxious that workers obtain practical experience. As late as 1905 she reiterated her view (at a meeting of the COS) that the vast bulk of any training programme should be practical and that 'the most instructive thing possible was really to know a few people'.[250] Octavia persuaded the settlement to adopt her early Marylebone scheme as a model for its work and the women settlers were exposed to as wide a variety of local relief agencies and committees, voluntary and statutory, as possible. The settlement was rigorous in screening the organizations to which it was prepared to send its workers. Despite outcry from the COS, Miss Sewell vetoed any further contact with the Metropolitan Association for Befriending of Young Servants (MABYS, founded by Henrietta Barnett and strongly supported by Octavia Hill's close friend Jane Senior) because of the inefficiency of their local office.[251] Notwithstanding Octavia's doubts, the theoretical side of the training also developed and in 1896 the WUS joined forces with the COS and the National Union of Women Workers (originally a conservative philanthropic and religious organization of middle-class women, which became the National Council of Women during the World War I) to set up a course of joint lectures. This was eventually absorbed by first the COS's School of Sociology, established in 1903, and then the LSE's Department of Social Administration in 1912. By 1900, Octavia was also making a concentrated effort to train women as housing managers and in 1903 acceded to a request by the COS's School of Sociology to allow their students to work with her as rent collectors.

The number of women training at the settlement was substantially bolstered by a £2,500 bequest from Emily Pfeiffer who promoted the cause of women's education within the bounds of accepted gender divisions. Pfeiffer's attempt to counter the case of doctors and scientists against more rigorous education for adolescent girls was, not untypically, convoluted: 'The equality I would claim is not as things at present stand, not DE FACTO, but in original capacity, and even so, an equality in difference, and to some extent of compensation'.[252] Margaret Sewell and Octavia Hill's ideas of the qualities required of women social workers would have appealed to her. One of the Pfeiffer fellowships was held by Mary Sheepshanks, who went on to become the vice-principal of Morley College, of which Emma Cons was one of the founders.[253]

Despite her commitment to training, Sewell was sufficiently a follower of Octavia Hill to insist that

> important though we believe education and method to be, we do not hold them of FIRST importance. We do not suppose that by training and teaching we can dispense with, or render superfluous, that loving zeal which yearns for the souls of men, that instinct to come at all costs to the help of the helpless.[254]

The first requirement of women settlers, as with rent collectors, was that they be womanly women. They operated within a severely circumscribed sphere. Indeed, when Octavia Hill sought a new secretary for the National Trust, she was quite clear that this was a man's work and would not consider a woman for the position.[255] Furthermore, when the premises which Octavia had used to legitimize the mixing of housing management with personal social work were called into question with the rapid expansion of public housing after World War I, women lost their hold on the profession.[256] They could no longer sustain their claim in the name of 'social maternalism' when the paternalist aspect of their work stood condemned, and it was the paternalist side of it that had legitimized their involvement in what might otherwise have been considered a man's world of business.[257] While many of the men trained in the settlements went on to careers in politics and the civil service, women were confined to a relatively narrow sphere of social work and, even there, their rise was slow.

Public and private life

Unpaid work outside the home dominated Octavia Hill's life. While it was to her way of thinking clearly a Christian obligation, its meaning was nevertheless complicated in terms of its relationship to the private world of home and family and to the public sphere of paid work and political participation.

Octavia saw her work as essentially domestic in character and regretted any increase in its size and complexity that threatened to make it less so. She wrote to her fellow workers in 1877:

> you will notice, or at least I notice, very sadly, how year by year this little letter has to do with larger and more public questions . . . My work becomes less home-like, more struggling; there is in it necessarily more of opposition; it brings me into contest with people further off, whom I do not know well, nor care for at all.[258]

In her passion for detailed personal work 'down among the poor' there was the desire to isolate herself as far as possible from a world she both instinctively felt and rationally believed did not belong to her, as well as a conviction that this was the way to achieve long-term social change. She steadfastly refused all offers of more public work[259] until she became a member of the Royal Commission on the Poor Laws in 1905, seven years before she died. Similarly she made every effort to practise what she preached and made sure that she put her own family's needs before those of the strangers among whom she worked. However, she was strong-minded, strong-willed and a shrewd businesswoman and there were conflicts that she did not usually acknowledge in her determination to do the work of a womanly woman.

Octavia's feelings about the importance of family and of putting duty to family first were very similar to those of F. D. Maurice who told ladies intending to learn about visiting the poor that they were 'only studying what you may practise at infinite advantage at home, if a sick relative should confine you to it, your labours among the poor should be suspended'.[260] Octavia had every intention of obeying these strictures, just as she reiterated them to her fellow workers. In 1880, she told a friend that home claims were very strong and she had had to put her housing work in second place, but welcomed this: 'I often think that now people want more to see how noble private life should be and can be, than to take up public work – at any rate exclusively'.[261] In 1890 she stayed at home to nurse her sister and wrote to Sidney Cockerell that she would be

> deeply interested if anyone is good enough to report any facts to me, if in the intervals of nursing, I get downstairs, but I would ask friends kindly not to expect replies *on any subject* till we see whether we are through the worst or not. The nursing devolves on me, and *nothing* can divide with it my thought.[262]

The effect of these words was substantially undermined by their position in the middle of a letter full of instructions as to how she wanted the work in hand to proceed. Nor was she always as dogmatic on the issue of family duties. In the case of Olive Cockerell, sister of Sidney junior and Octavia's goddaughter, she was very upset at the way in which another Cockerell widower brother, resident in the USA, was exploiting Olive's services as a housekeeper and carer for his son. She was anxious that Olive should return to England and develop her artistic talents: 'You know how deeply I feel as to family duties, but I do myself firmly believe you ought to come [home]'.[263] She had also tried to understand Sidney Cockerell's dilemma about his career some years previously, eventually respecting his decision to leave the family firm, again, in order to pursue a more artistic and literary career.

While Octavia stressed the home-like qualities of her work, she also acknowledged her own home as a refuge in terms of its brightness and warmth compared to the squalor of the slums, and as a place distinctly separate and different from her work, no matter how many linkages she sought to make between them. In 1890, Margaret Sewell asked Octavia to serve as the warden of the WUS and to come and live in Southwark. Octavia was sufficiently attached to Miss Sewell and her work to be seriously tempted, but she decided that her home and her sisters were rooted in Marylebone, as well as believing that she might be too well-established and powerful a presence in the settlement.[264]

Octavia relied as much on the support of friends as on her family, although early on her deep attachment to Sophia Jex Blake, who made a brave attempt to become the first woman to get a medical degree in the teeth of parental and medical opposition, was broken when her mother found Sophia's presence in the household too difficult.[265] In her housing work Octavia came to depend on the support of a number of less intimate friends. In 1876 she invited only her personal friends to her annual party (excluding after some anxiety, her tenant friends), and she acknowledged her debt to those who had believed in her and who had 'kept alive in me the memory that life meant more than work, more than sacrifice, more than mere action . . .'[266] She poured out her heart, tried out her ideas (mainly on duty and God) and reported her reactions to Ruskin and Maurice and to her friend of young womanhood, Mary Harris. One of her greatest friends of the 1860s and 1870s was Jane Senior who, in 1874, was appointed the first female Poor Law Inspector and who wrote an influential and controversial report on the fate of girls educated in the workhouse. They shared ideas about poverty and the importance of visiting the poor, and offered each other comfort at times of stress related to their work. When Jane died, Octavia wrote a long and very emotional letter to Sidney Cockerell: 'she loved me as few do . . . the thought that I can never again in human word receive any message from her shakes me with passionate sobbing . . .'[267] She leaned heavily on the advice of the Sidney Cockerells, father and son, and also on that of Edward Bond who helped to run the boys' club in Southwark. In 1877 Octavia Hill became engaged to Bond and it was the breaking of the engagement together with the quarrel with Ruskin that occasioned her long breakdown, beginning in 1877. The letters explaining the circumstances of the engagement and its ending were destroyed by Octavia's relatives after her death but it is clear that her one desire afterwards was to get 'out of sight'. She retreated to the country and then abroad, and when she returned to her housing work she was never happier than when immersed in the detailed 'out-of-sight' work with tenants.

But it is much too easy to explain Octavia Hill's work as some kind of sublimation. A number of powerful forces pushed her towards 'quiet individual work' long before her broken engagement. The end of the relationship with Bond merely served to exacerbate the driven character of that work. She acknowledged the importance of rest but was never able properly to relax. From her teenage years she worked extra-ordinarily long hours, from five in the morning until late at night, six days a week. And like most other late Victorian women social reformers, she actively pondered what was useful work. All her efforts were directed towards building a web of human relationships with her fellow workers and with her poor, as she called them, and her delight in losing herself in the minutiae of the work was derived from the sense that it was serving this larger end.

Octavia felt at home with and probably also fully in control of the little world she created and worked in. She was able to justify the core of the work as detailed, patient and gentle women's work, thereby avoiding any accusation that it was not a proper part of a woman's sphere, something that would surely have caused her pain and anxiety. But the line between home-like work and more public campaigns and activities became a hard one to draw. She was full of regard for those, male and female, who eschewed high-profile work for the more out-of-sight quiet work. In 1903, she wrote to Charles Booth about her 'extreme desire for silence about all we are doing, I believe all our work goes on so much better in silence'.[268] But she was less conscious of the more subtle behavioural divides within the world in which she moved. Her sister commented, justly, that Octavia was something 'of a Cecil in her sphere'.[269] Catherine Winkworth welcomed the fragmented, detailed work of personal social work with the poor as women's Christian duty, but all the same pondered the question of when it might be appropriate to assert herself.[270] Octavia was always asserting herself, albeit that she couched her requests and directions in thanks to the Almighty for telling her what to do. She was also prepared to take up the cudgels on behalf of the poor in the Victorian periodical press, arguing not only for her scheme of housing management but also for the preservation of open space. In 1875, she explained to Sidney Cockerell that she had written a letter to the national daily press on the latter because 'I rather long to have my say for the poor publicly and that soon'.[271] Not unlike the settlers of Toynbee Hall, Octavia advocated quiet work and then trumpeted it.[272] But she found debate in public much more difficult. When faced with a public trial such as that involving the conflict with the medical officer of health in Marylebone in 1874, she retreated, finding it 'troublesome and trying', and relied on her friends to see her through.[273] Her sympathy with Jane Senior's difficulties in facing the controversy raised by her report on workhouse girls was sincere, and she assured her that while newspapers and partisans would be unpleasant, there would be 'one at least (one who is probably the sample of many)' who would 'be thinking of you with love and perfect trust'.[274] In a culture in which middle-class women could hold no public position it would have been difficult for them to have dealt with such moments of conflict, even if every attempt was made to minimize these, without the support of friends and family and without a strong belief that they had God on their side.

There are but few references to Octavia's public persona. She disliked public speaking and often prefaced the rare speeches she made to the COS with a disclaimer as to her capacity to do it.[275] When she attended a public meeting her pattern throughout her life was to sit quietly and only near the end to say 'a few words of common sense' in a 'quiet and gentle' tone.[276] Her contributions must nevertheless have often been forceful. Bishop Temple for example, admitted that she had bested the

Ecclesiastical Commissioners in getting them to revise their plan for managing their properties.[277] When she took the chair at a cadet meeting in her own realm in Southwark, one man present compared her to Queen Elizabeth I, her 'mouth closing up tight like an unyielding steel trap when she was displeased', and described her as full of 'indomitable resolution' and 'scrupulous regard for every halfpenny spent or received'.[278] In the more public fora of the Ecclesiastical Commissioners' meetings or, in her final years, those of the Poor Law Commissioners, there must have remained a considerable touch of the image first reported by Sidney Cockerell in 1871: of a womanly woman, strong and yet rather silent.

She found the *modus vivendi* she achieved for herself satisfying and had no hesitation in prescribing it for her followers. Indeed, she heartily opposed any more spirited attempt to participate in the public sphere, particularly via the women's suffrage movement. It was not that she was implacably opposed to all feminist campaigns. She had supported both the movement to improve girls' education and Barbara Bodichon's campaign for a married women's property Act. But she considered the suffrage movement to entail a horrifying amount of self-advertisement.[279] She opened her uncompromising letter to *The Times* in 1910 on the subject in typical fashion: 'I am sorry to enter into the political world even so far as to write about the question of women's suffrage'. She sadly acknowledged the difference between her and many of her 'earnest young fellow workers' on the issue; Emma Cons, for example, became the vice-president of the London Society for Women's Suffrage but significantly her friendship with Octavia survived her sympathy with the call for votes for women. Octavia reiterated her belief in the differences between male and female spheres and the duty of men and women to serve to the best of their capacity within their respective spheres, so providing mutual support for each other. For women to step into the male sphere of political power would 'militate against their usefulness in the large field of public work'. In addition, national politics were for Octavia very much the world of imperial politics and therefore by definition a male domain. Only if women sought and respected the 'out-of-sight, silent work' would they really achieve something. Like other anti-suffragist women social reformers, Octavia Hill did not want to exclude women from all work outside the home but rather to restrict such work to a narrowly domestic form, practised at the local and not the national level and ideally within the very homes of the poor. She believed firmly that God called women to care for the sick, the old and the poor; 'Let the woman seek the quiet paths of helpful real work, be set on finding where she is wanted, in her duties, not her rights', only then would she fulfil God's will.[280] But for many, personal service represented but another form of self-denial, in terms both of personal time to read and reflect and of public time to become involved in larger issues and debates.

Notes

1. S. Cockerell (Sr) to Lucinia Franks, 5/9/91, D. Misc. 84/3, Octavia Hill Papers, Marylebone Public Library. (All references to D. Misc. material are to be found in this library.)
2. M. Wynne Nevinson, *Life's Fitful Fever* (A. & C. Black, 1926).
3. Gillian Darley, *Octavia Hill. A Life* (Constable, 1990).
4. Nancy Boyd, *Josephine Butler, Octavia Hill and Florence Nightingale* (Macmillan, 1982).
5. Carol Dyhouse, *Girls Growing Up in Late Victorian and Edwardian England* (Routledge & Kegan Paul, 1981).
6. Anna Jameson, *Sisters of Charity and the Communism of Labour* (Longman, 1859).
7. Beatrice Webb, Diary TS, 12/5/86, f. 660, BLPES.
8. Emily Maurice (ed.), *Octavia Hill: Early Ideals* (Allen & Unwin, 1928), pp. 126–7.
9. Ibid., p. 142.
10. Octavia Hill (hereafter OH) to Sidney Cockerell (Jr) (hereafter SC Jr), 6/7/89, Item 92, D. Misc. 84/2.
11. OH to SC Jr, 25/7/92, D. Misc. 84/2.
12. Maurice, *Early Ideals*, p. 95 (OH to Miranda Harris, hereafter MH), 1867.
13. Ibid., p. 161, John Ruskin to OH, 1863.
14. E. T. Cook and A. Wedderburn (eds), *The Works of John Ruskin*, Vol. XXIX, Fors Clavigera Letters 1873–1896 (Allen & Unwin, 1907), Letter 86, Feb. 1878. Darley, *Octavia Hill*, pp. 192–5, has the fullest account of this quarrel.
15. Octavia Hill, *Our Common Land* (Macmillan, 1877), p. 136, when she appealed to the middle-class fear of disease emanating from the slums.
16. Rev. Prof. Maurice, 'On the Reform of Society', Lecture on the opening of the Working Tailors' Association (Southampton: Forbes & Knibb, 1851), pp. 13–22.
17. F. D. Maurice, *Social Morality* (Macmillan, 1893), p. 364.
18. Margaret J. Shaen (ed.), *Memorials of Two Sisters: Susanna and Catherine Winkworth* (Longman, 1908), p. 303.
19. Baroness Burdett Coutts, *Women's Mission to Women* (Sampson Low Marston & Co., 1893).
20. OH to Mrs Cockerell, 7/8/77, Item 47, D. Misc. 84/3.
21. Maurice, *Early Ideals*, pp. 138–9, OH to MH, 1858; Darley, p. 67.
22. OH to SC Jr, 8/10/88, Item 60, D. Misc. 84/2.
23. Maurice, *Early Ideals*, p. 100, OH to MH, 1868.
24. Raymond Plant, 'Needs, Agency and Welfare Rights', paper presented to the conference on Political Philosophy and the Welfare State, Suntory Toyota International Centre for Economics and Related Disciplines, LSE, June, 1988.
25. OH to Henrietta Barnett, 26/12/73, Coll. Misc. 512, British Library of Political and Economic Sciences.
26. OH to SC Jr, 23/3/90, Item 107, D. Misc. 84/2.
27. Maurice, *Early Ideals*, p. 73, pupil of Nottingham Place School to Mrs C. E. Maurice, 1912.
28. Octavia Hill, Letter to My Fellow Workers, 1879, p. 6, D. Misc. 84/5 (all the Letters are to be found under this classification in Marylebone Public Library).
29. Clive Wilmer (ed.), *John Ruskin: Unto This Last and Other Writings* (Penguin, 1985), p. 312.

30. Octavia Hill, 'District Visiting', reprinted from *Good Words* (Longman, 1877), p. 14, paper read to a meeting of district visitors and clergy at the Bishop of Colchester and Bristol's house.

31. Rev. W. H. Fremantle for St Mary's Bryanston Sq., *Pastoral Address and Report of the Charities for the Year 1870*, Appendix B, Miss Hill's Report of the Walmer Street District, 31/12/70, pp. 29–30.

32. Hill, *Common Land*, p. 130.

33. Maurice, *Early Ideals*, p. 52, OH to MH, 1857.

34. Octavia Hill, 'Organised Work Among the Poor; Suggestions Founded on Four Years Management of a London Court', *Macmillans* 20 (May–Oct. 1869).

35. Frank Prochaska, *Women and Philanthropy in Nineteenth-Century England* (Oxford: Clarendon, 1980).

36. Seth Koven, 'Culture and Poverty: The London Settlement House Movement, 1870–1914', unpublished PhD thesis, Harvard, 1987.

37. Hill, *Common Land*, p. 102.

38. Frank McClain, 'Maurice on Women', in Frank McClain, Richard Norris and John Orens (eds), *F. D. Maurice: A Study* (Cowley Publishers, 1982); Maurice, *Social Morality*, p. 56.

39. Mary Talbot, 'St Margaret's House (B. Gr.) Ladies Branch of Oxford House', in John M. Knapp (ed.), *The Universities and the Social Problem. An Account of University Settlements in East London* (Rivington, Percival & Co, 1895).

40. F. D. Maurice, *Lectures to Ladies on Practical Subjects* (Macmillan, 1855), pp. 55 and 89–90.

41. William Thomson Hill, *Octavia Hill: Pioneer of the National Trust and Housing Reformer* (Hutchins, 1956), p. 39.

42. Hill, Letter to My Fellow Workers, 1883, p. 7.

43. J. Lewis, 'The Working Class Wife and Mother and State Intervention', in J. Lewis (ed.), *Labour and Love: Women's Experience of Home and Family, 1850–1940* (Oxford: Blackwell, 1986).

44. Charles Bosanquet, *A Handy Book for Visitors of the Poor in London* (Longman, 1874), p. 15.

45. Anne Summers, 'A Home from Home: Women's Philanthropic Work in the Nineteenth Century', in S. Burman (ed.), *Fit Work for Women* (Croom Helm, 1979).

46. Maurice, *Early Ideals*, p. 40, OH to MH, 1857.

47. PP, 1882, 279, Select Committee on Artisans' and Labourers' Dwellings. Minutes of Evidence, Vol. VII, Q. 3359.

48. Hill, Letter to My Fellow Workers, 1889, p. 11.

49. Hill, Letter to My Fellow Workers, 1882, p. 4.

50. S. Barnett, 'University Settlements', in W. Reason (ed.), *University and Social Settlements* (Methuen, 1898), p. 11.

51. C. Edmund Maurice, *Life of Octavia Hill* (Macmillan, 1913), p. 322, OH to MH, 1875.

52. Ibid., p. 565; OH to Fellow Workers, 1907.

53. Maurice, *Lectures to Ladies*, p. 126.

54. PP, 279, Q. 3298.

55. G. Stedman-Jones, *Outcast London* (Harmondsworth: Penguin, 1976), 1st edn 1971.

56. *Ladies' Health Society of Manchester and Salford* (Manchester: Richard Gill, 1893), p. 5.

57. Hill, Letter to My Fellow Workers, 1880, pp. 3–4, and for 1891, p. 7.

58. Darley, *Octavia Hill*, p. 73.

59. On paternalism see: David Roberts, *Paternalism in Early Victorian England* (Croom Helm, 1979).

60. Maurice, *Life of Octavia Hill*, p. 281, Miranda to Mrs Durant, 1973.

61. Maurice, *Early Ideals*, p. 28, OH to MH, 1856.

62. Ibid., p. 211, snippet, nd.
63. Octavia Hill, *Homes of the London Poor* (Macmillan, 1875), p. 37.
64. PP, 1885, C. 4402-I, Report of the Royal Commission on Housing of the Working Classes, Vol. II, Minutes of Evidence, Vol. XXX, Q. 9123.
65. Ibid., Q. 8986.
66. Ellen Chase, *Tenant Friends in Old Deptford* (Williams & Norgate, 1929), p. 203; and Judy Lown, *Women and Industrialization. Gender at Work in Nineteenth-Century England* (Cambridge: Polity Press, 1939), pp. 96–7.
67. Stefan Collini, 'The Idea of "Character" in Victorian Political Thought', *Transactions of the Royal Historical Society* 35, 1985, pp. 36-7.
68. Hill, *Octavia Hill*, p. 15.
69. PP, C. 4402-I, Q. 9172.
70. Ibid., Q. 5788. See also G. R. Sims, *How the Poor Live* (Chatto & Windus, 1883).
71. PP, C. 4402-I, Q. 8865.
72. Maurice, *Life of Octavia Hill*, p. 258.
73. Hill, 'Organised Work among the Poor', p. 224.
74. Hill, *Common Land*, p. 48.
75. PP, 279, Q. 3260.
76. Hill, *Homes of the London Poor*, p. 58.
77. Beatrice Webb, Diary TS, 7/11/86, f. 745.
78. Hill, Letter to My Fellow Workers, 1875, p. 7.
79. Hill, Letter to My Fellow Workers, 1884–5, p. 4.
80. Henrietta Barnett, *The Work of Lady Visitors* (Metropolitan Association for Befriending Young Servants, 1881).
81. Anthony Wohl, 'Octavia Hill and the Homes of the London Poor', *Jr. of British Studies* 10 (May 1971); Celia Davies, 'The Health Visitor as Mother's Friend: A Woman's Place in Public Health, 1900–1914', *Social History of Medicine* I (April 1988).
82. PP, C. 4402-I, Q. 8901–5.
83. Pat Thane, 'The Working Class and State "Welfare" in Britain, 1880–1914', *Historical Journal* 27 (1984).
84. Ferdinand Mount, *The Subversive Family: An Alternative History of Love and Marriage* (Allen & Unwin, 1983), 1st edn 1982.
85. Maurice, *Social Morality*, p. 3; Octavia Hill, 'Colour, Space and Music for the People', *Nineteenth Century* (May 1884), reprinted by Kegan Paul Trench & Co., p. 1.
86. Hill, *Homes of the London Poor*, p. 14.
87. PP, 279, Q. 3412.
88. PP, C. 4402–I, Q. 8967.
89. Dorothy Thompson, 'Women, Work and Politics in Nineteenth Century England: The Problem of Authority', in Jane Rendall (ed.), *Equal or Different: Women's Politics, 1800–1914* (Oxford: Blackwell, 1987).
90. Hill, *Homes of the London Poor*, p. 82.
91. Hill, 'Organised Work among the Poor', p. 220.
92. Geoffrey Best, *Temporal Pillars* (Cambridge: Cambridge University Press, 1964), p. 480.
93. Hill, Letter to My Fellow Workers, 1874, p. 10.
94. PP, 279, Q. 3259; PP, C. 4402-I, Q. 8864.
95. Maurice, *Lectures to Ladies*, pp. 61 and 107–8.
96. Ibid., p. 279.
97. Maurice, *Early Ideals*, p. 190, OH to MH, nd.
98. Hill, *Homes of the London Poor*, p. 77.
99. Emelia Kanthack, *The Preservation of Infant Life* (H. K. Lewis, 1907), p. 2. See also M. Loane, *An Englishman's Castle* (Edward Arnold, 1909), p. 139.
100. Boyd, *Josephine Butler, Octavia Hill and Florence Nightingale*, p. 134.
101. Maurice, *Early Ideals*, p. 34, OH to MH, 1856.

102.   Hill, *Common Land*, p. 54.
103.   Octavia Hill, *The Charity Organisation Society*, Occasional Paper #15 (COS, 1896), p. 17.
104.   Paul Johnson, *Saving and Spending: The Working-Class Economy in Britain, 1870–1939* (Oxford: Clarendon, 1985).
105.   'Proceedings of Council', *Charity Organisation Reporter*, 5/5/75, p. 70.
106.   Octavia Hill, 'The Need of Thoroughness in Charitable Work', *Charity Organisation Review* (Nov. 1898), pp. 233–9; Letter to My Fellow Workers, 1891, p. 7.
107.   Brian Harrison, 'Philanthropy and the Victorians', *Victorian Studies* 9 (1966).
108.   Hill, *Common Land*, p. 60.
109.   Hill, 'The Need of Thoroughness', p. 237.
110.   Octavia Hill, 'A Word on Good Citizenship', *Fortnightly Review* XX (July–Dec. 1876), pp. 322–3; Maurice, *Life of Octavia Hill*, pp. 227–8, OH to Florence Davenport Hill (sister), 1867.
111.   Hill, *Common Land*, p. 64.
112.   Ibid., p. 90.
113.   Fremantle, Pastoral Address. Supplement to the Report. 'An Attempt to Raise a Few of the London Poor without Gifts', Letter from John Ruskin, TS, 30/8/70.
114.   Octavia Hill, 'The Work of Volunteers in the Organisation of Charity', *Macmillans* 26 (May–Oct 1872), p. 441.
115.   Hill, *Common Land*, pp. 65–6.
116.   Hill, Letter to My Fellow Workers, 1877, p. 10.
117.   OH to Rev. Fremantle, 1/11/74, Coll. Misc. 512, BLPES.
118.   Harriet Martineau, *Illustrations of Political Economy* (np, 1834).
119.   Margaret Sewell, 'Some Aspects of Charity Organisation', *Charity Organisation Review* (Jan. 1898), pp. 8–24.
120.   A. L. Hodson, *Letters from a Settlement* (Edward Arnold, 1909), pp. 22–33.
121.   Octavia Hill, 'The Elberfield System in London', *Charity Organisation Reporter*, 4/11/74, p. 317; Hill, 'District Visiting', pp. 9–10; Hill, *Homes of the London Poor*, pp. 117–57.
122.   Alfred and Mary Marshall, *The Economics of Industry* (Macmillan, 1879), pp. 34–5.
123.   Hill, Letter to My Fellow Workers, 1876, p. 12.
124.   'The Clergy and Charitable Relief', *Charity Organisation Reporter*, 26/4/77, pp. 70–1; 'Charity Organisation in its Relations to Clergy and Ministers of Religion', ibid., 26/5/81, pp. 118–24.
125.   Michael Rose, 'The Crisis of Poor Relief in England, 1860–1890', in W. J. Mommsen, *The Emergence of the Welfare State in Britain and Germany* (Croom Helm, 1981), pp. 50–70.
126.   Hill, 'Work of Volunteers', p. 444.
127.   Maurice, *Life of Octavia Hill*, p. 298, OH to Jane Senior, 1873; and Pat Hollis, *Ladies Elect: Women in English Local Government, 1865–1914* (Oxford: Oxford University Press, 1987).
128.   Hodson, *Letters from a Settlement*, p. 178.
129.   'Applicants in the Office', *Charity Organisation Reporter*, 9/3/82, p. 63; 'Charity and Humanity', ibid., 5/7/83, p. 217.
130.   Charity Organisation Society, *Eighteenth Annual Report, 1887*, p. 6, GLC Archives, A/FWA/C/B1/4.
131.   Octavia Hill, 'Further Account of the Walmer St. Industrial Experiment', 1872, D. Misc. 84/5.
132.   'The Annual Meeting', *Charity Organisation Review* (June 1891), p. 243.
133.   OH to SC Jr, 1/2/91, Item 130, D. Misc. 84/2.
134.   Mrs Barnett, 'What has the COS to do with Social Reform?', *Charity Organisation Reporter*, 19/4/84, pp. 128–9; and Samuel A. Barnett, 'Distress in East London', *Nineteenth Century* 20 (Nov. 1886), pp. 678–92.

135. Canon Barnett, 'A Friendly Criticism of the COS', *Charity Organisation Review* (Aug. 1895), pp. 338–44.
136. Hill, Letter to My Fellow Workers, 1908, pp. 13–14.
137. W. Milledge (Bradford City Guild of Help), 'Guilds of Help', *Charity Organisation Review* (July 1906), pp. 46–57.
138. N. Masterman, 'The Guild of Help Movement', *Charity Organisation Review* (Sept. 1906), pp. 139–50. See also T. Cahill, 'The New Philanthropy: The Emergence of a Bradford City Guild of Help', *Journal of Social Policy* 9 (July 1980), p. 359.
139. 'Miss Markham on the COS', *Charity Organisation Review* (March 1912), pp. 128–43.
140. Elizabeth Macadam, *The New Philanthropy: A Study of the Relations between the Statutory and the Voluntary Social Services* (Allen & Unwin, 1934).
141. Hill, 'The COS', p. 17.
142. OH to SC Jr, 31/3/92, Item 173, D. Misc. 84/2; Darley, *Octavia Hill*, p. 29.
143. PP, C. 4402-I, Q. 8864.
144. Maurice, *Early Ideals*, p. 141, OH to Ruskin, nd; Hill, *Homes of the London Poor*, p. 78.
145. Hill, 'Colour and Space', p. 12.
146. PP, 279, Q. 2980; and Octavia Hill, 'Influence on Character', in Charles Booth, *Life and Labour of the People in London*, Vol. 3 (Macmillan, 1892), pp. 29–37.
147. Maurice, *Early Ideals*, p. 233, snippet from letter, nd.
148. Ibid.
149. Maurice, *Life of Octavia Hill*, pp. 227–8, OH to Miss Florence Davenport Hill, 1867.
150. Hill, 'Colour and Space', p. 12.
151. Hill, Letter to My Fellow Workers, 1908, p. 11.
152. Hill, Letter to My Fellow Workers, 1883, p. 8.
153. Maurice, *Early Ideals*, p. 45, OH to Miranda Hill, 1857.
154. Ibid., p. 57, OH to Miranda, 1858.
155. Maurice, *Life of Octavia Hill*, p. 270, OH to Miss Mayo, 1871.
156. OH to SC Sr, 11/5/76, Item 24, D. Misc. 84/3.
157. OH to SC Jr, 20/7/89, Item 94, D. Misc. 84/2.
158. Hill, Letter to My Fellow Workers, 1890, p. 4.
159. Hill, Letter to My Fellow Workers, 1878, p. 9.
160. Lucy Jonckheere, 'Octavia Hill', *Help* 8 (Jan./Feb. 1969), pp. 17–22.
161. Maurice, *Early Ideals*, p. 170, Ruskin to OH 1867.
162. PP, 279, Q. 2980.
163. Hill, *Homes of the London Poor*, Preface, p. 3.
164. Hill, Letter to My Fellow Workers, 1906, p. 6.
165. Wohl, 'Octavia Hill'.
166. 'Report of the Special Committee on Dwellings', *Charity Organisation Reporter*, 9/4/73; PP, C. 4402-I, Q. 3399; Hill, *Homes of the London Poor*, pp. 104–5.
167. Hill, Letter to My Fellow Workers, 1895, p. 6; 1896, p. 9; 1901, p. 9. Rates were local property taxes. Government's rationale for changing the system of local taxation to a 'community charge' (effectively a poll tax) in 1990 had much in common with Octavia's desire to make sure that tenants were aware of movements in local taxation.
168. Hill, *Homes of the London Poor*, pp. 86 and 75.
169. Ibid., p. 20.
170. Hill, Letter to My Fellow Workers, 1879, p. 4; see also 'The Relations between Rich and Poor as Bearing on Pauperism', *Charity Organisation Review* (June 1901), p. 311.
171. See Anne Power, *Property before People* (Allen & Unwin, 1987).
172. Hill, Letter to My Fellow Workers, 1884–5, p. 4.
173. Maurice, *Life of Octavia Hill*, p. 387, Mrs Hill to OH, 1879.

174. Hill, Letter to My Fellow Workers, 1891, p. 4.
175. Hill, *Homes of the London Poor*, p. 84.
176. OH to SC Sr, 6/5/75, Item 18, D. Misc. 84/3.
177. Hill, *Homes of the London Poor*, p. 105.
178. PP, 279, Q. 3002; PP, C. 4402-I, Q. 8852; Hill, *Homes of the London Poor*, p. 193.
179. Octavia Hill, 'More Air for London', *Nineteenth Century* XXIII (Jan.–June 1888), p. 181.
180. List of donors and tile letters, Item 11a, D. Misc. 84/3.
181. Maurice, *Life of Octavia Hill*, p. 293, snippet, 1873.
182. Hill, *Our Common Land*, p. 3.
183. M. A. Sewell, *Children's Country Holidays*, Tract No 4 (NUWW, 1897), p. 3.
184. OH to SC Sr, 3/10/75, Item 21, D. Misc. 84/3; Hill, 'Organised Work among the Poor', p. 220.
185. OH to SC Sr, 21/12/73, Item 8, D. Misc. 84/3; Carolyn Steedman, *Childhood, Culture and Class in Britain. Margaret McMillan, 1860–1931* (Virago, 1990).
186. Maurice, *Life of Octavia Hill*, p. 276, 1872.
187. Ibid., p. 458, Ellen Chase to OH, 1884 or 1885.
188. Chase, *Tenant Friends*, pp. 132–43.
189. Nevinson, *Life's Fitful Fever*, p. 91.
190. Hodson, *Letters from a Settlement*, p. 136.
191. Beatrice Webb, Diary, 7/11/86, f. 743.
192. Wilfred Blunt, *The Life of Sydney Carlyle Cockerell* (Hamish Hamilton, 1964), p. 24.
193. OH to SC Sr, 28/4/75, Item 16, D. Misc. 84/3.
194. Maurice, *Life of Octavia Hill*, p. 320.
195. Ibid., p. 458, Miranda Hill to Edmund Maurice, 1885.
196. M. Card (née Meyrick Jones) to (?), 3/12/61, D. Misc. 84/5.
197. Maurice, *Life of Octavia Hill*, p. 459, OH to Mrs Edmund Maurice, 1885.
198. OH to SC Sr, 8/12/76, Item 14, D. Misc. 84/3.
199. Norman Dennis and A. H. Halsey, *English Ethical Socialism: Thomas More to R. H. Tawney* (Oxford: Clarendon, 1988), pp. 149–69.
200. Hill, Letter to My Fellow Workers, 1893, p. 8.
201. Maurice, *Life of Octavia Hill*, p. 313, OH to Ruskin, 1876; and OH to SC Sr, 28/4/75, Item 16, D. Misc. 84/3.
202. Koven, 'Culture and Poverty', p. 222.
203. OH to SC Sr, 3/7/76, Item 28; 5/7/76, Item 29, D. Misc. 84/3.
204. OH to SC Sr, 13/4/77, Item 43, D. Misc. 84/3.
205. Chase, *Tenant Friends*, p. 15.
206. Hill, Letter to My Fellow Workers, 1887, p. 7.
207. Hill, Letter to My Fellow Workers, 1889, p. 7.
208. Hill, Letter to My Fellow Workers, 1890, p. 7.
209. Ibid.
210. OH to Miss Schuster, 16/7/09, Item 27, D. Misc. 84/1.
211. Darley, *Octavia Hill*, p. 254.
212. Octavia Hill, Letter to My Fellow Workers, 1902, p. 11; OH to SC Sr, 28/4/75, Item 16, D. Misc. 84/3.
213. OH to SC Sr, 3/1/74, Item 10, D. Misc. 84/3.
214. OH to SC Sr, 7/12/73, Item 6, D. Misc. 84/3.
215. Maurice, *Life of Octavia Hill*, p. 310, OH to MH, 1874.
216. Ibid., p. 287, OH to MH, 1873, and p. 305, OH to MH, 1874.
217. Octavia Hill, Letter Accompanying Account of Donations for 1876, p. 5, D. Misc. 84/5; Beatrice Webb, *My Apprenticeship* (Cambridge: Cambridge University Press, 1979), 1st edn 1926, p. 266, fn. 1.
218. Hill, Letter to My Fellow Workers, 1874, p. 10.
219. Hill, Letter to My Fellow Workers, 1878, p. 3.

220. Maurice, *Life of Octavia Hill*, p. 355; and OH to SC Sr, 4/1/77, Item 38, D. Misc. 84/3.
221. OH to SC Sr, 26/10/73, Item 5, D. Misc. 84/3.
222. OH to SC Sr, 3/10/75, Item 21, D. Misc. 84/3; and OH to SC Jr, 9/6/88, Item 52, D. Misc. 84/2.
223. OH to SC Sr, 27/6/76, Item 27, D. Misc. 84/3. Mrs Allen replaced Sophia Peters, who left to marry C. S. Loch, General Secretary of the COS.
224. Nevinson, *Life's Fitful Fever*, p. 90.
225. A Volunteer, 'Women's Work in the Housing of the Poor', *Charity Organisation Review* (Oct. 1887), p. 375.
226. OH to SC Jr, 16/10/92, Item 187, D. Misc. 84/2.
227. Mary Clover (1877–1965), biographical information file, Blackfriars Settlement.
228. Hill, Letter to My Fellow Workers, 1879, p. 8.
229. PP, C. 4402-I, Q. 8869.
230. Hill, 'District Visiting', p. 7.
231. 'District Committees and Organisation', *Charity Organisation Reporter*, 10/3/81, pp. 58–9; 'District Secretaries', ibid., 1/6/82, p. 161; 'Paid and Unpaid', ibid., 4/10/83, p. 291.
232. N. Masterman, 'The COS of the Future', *Charity Organisation Review* (June 1885), p. 241.
233. Octavia Hill, 'Trained Workers for the Poor', *Nineteenth Century* XXXIII (Jan.–June 1893), p. 36.
234. Mrs Rose Dunn Gardner, 'The Training of Volunteers', *Charity Organisation Review* (Jan. 1995), pp. 2–6.
235. Minutes of the 1888 Annual General Meeting, Blackfriars Settlement Archives, C1a.
236. Minutes of the Executive Committee, Vol. I, 27/6/87, Blackfriars.
237. Hill, 'District Visiting', p. 6.
238. M. Loane, *Neighbours and Friends* (Edward Arnold, 1910), p. 121.
239. Maurice, *Early Ideals*, p. 124, OH to Ruskin, 1857.
240. Hill, Letter to My Fellow Workers, 1889, p. 10.
241. Hill, 'Trained Workers for the Poor', p. 38.
242. OH to Miss Schuster, 7/8/04, Item 4, D. Misc. 84/1.
243. Hill, *Homes of the London Poor*, p. 140; Maurice, *Life of Octavia Hill*, p. 455, OH to Mother, 1885.
244. A. Stronach, *A Newnham Friendship* (Blackie & Son, 1901).
245. Sybil Oldfield, *Spinsters of this Parish. The Life and Times of F. M. Major and Mary Sheepshanks* (Virago, 1984), pp. 52–3.
246. M. A. Sewell and E. G. Powell, 'Women's Settlements in England', in Reason, *University and Social Settlements*, p. 95.
247. OH to SC Jr, 31/3/92, Item 173, D. Misc. 84/2; and E. J. Urwick, 'The Settlement Ideal', *Charity Organisation Review* (March 1902), pp. 119–27.
248. 'Report of Sub-Cttee. on the Training of Students', 22/5/02, Blackfriars; and M. A. Sewell, *District Visiting* (SPCK, 1893).
249. Minutes of the Executive Committee, 26/11/88, Blackfriars.
250. 'The Training of Friendly Visitors', *Charity Organisation Review* (Dec. 1905), p. 310.
251. MABYS to Sewell, 2/3/05, Blackfriars, A12 and 13.
252. Emily Pfeiffer, *Women and Work* (Trubner, 1888), p. 163.
253. Oldfield, *Spinsters*, p. 67.
254. M. A. Sewell, 'Method and Education in Charitable Work', *Charity Organisation Review* (Dec. 1900), p. 379.
255. OH to SC Jr, 31/10/96, Item 209, D. Misc. 84/2.
256. *House Property and its Management. Papers on the Methods of Management introduced by Octavia Hill and adapted to Modern Conditions* (Allen & Unwin, 1921), pp. 83 and 88.

257. This point has been elaborated by Denise Riley, *Am I that Name?* (Macmillan, 1988).
258. Hill, Letter to My Fellow Workers, 1877, p. 14.
259. Hill, Letter to My Fellow Workers, 1882, p. 4.
260. Maurice, *Lectures to Ladies*, p. 18.
261. Maurice, *Life of Octavia Hill*, p. 438, OH to Mrs M. Shaen, 1880.
262. OH to SC Jr, 10/11/90, Item 125, D. Misc. 84/2.
263. OH to Olive Cockerell, 17/5/93, Item 3, D. Misc. 84/3.
264. OH to Sewell, 3/12/90, Packet, Blackfriars.
265. E. Moberley Bell, *Octavia Hill* (Constable & Co., 1942), pp. 52–9.
266. OH to Henrietta Barnett, 12/11/76, Coll. Misc. 512.
267. OH to SC Sr, 21/3/77, Item 42, D. Misc. 84/3.
268. OH to Charles Booth, 10/9/03, University of London MS 797/I/4912.
269. Maurice, *Life of Octavia Hill*, p. 306, Miranda to Edmund Maurice, 1874.
270. Shaen, *Memorials of Two Sisters*, p. 292.
271. OH to SC Sr, 16/7/75, Item 19, D. Misc. 84/3.
272. Standish Meacham, *Toynbee Hall and Social Reform, 1880–1914* (New Haven: Yale University Press, 1988).
273. OH to SC Sr, 17/11/74, Item 13, D. Misc. 84/3.
274. Maurice, *Life of Octavia Hill*, p. 307, OH to Jane Senior, 1874.
275. 'Report of Annual Meeting', *Charity Organisation Review* (June 1891), p. 243.
276. Maurice, *Life of Octavia Hill*, p. 324, Ld. Shuttleworth to Edmund Maurice, 1875.
277. Ibid., p. 486, Miranda to Ellen Chase, 24/2/89.
278. Mr Nevinson, TS, nd (circa 1890), on cadet corps meeting presided over by OH, D. Misc. 84/2.
279. Maurice, *Life of Octavia Hill*, p. 263, OH to Miss Mayo, 1868.
280. 'Women and the Suffrage', Letter from OH to *The Times*, 15/7/10, D. Misc. 84/2.

2 Beatrice Webb, 1858–1943

Unlike Octavia Hill, Beatrice Potter grew up in an extremely affluent family which provided handsomely for all ten daughters.[1] However, by the 1880s Beatrice was experiencing the classic ennui of the unmarried middle-class daughter at home, caring for her widowed father and a difficult younger sister. The early entries in her diary, which she kept faithfully from 1869 to her death in 1943, are full of the frustrations imposed by a narrowly domestic life, such as Florence Nightingale described so powerfully in 'Cassandra',[2] and of the struggle for self-education.

Philanthropic work provided the only acceptable route into the world beyond home and family and Beatrice spent from 1883 to 1885 working for the Charity Organisation Society (COS) and as a rent collector. But unlike Octavia Hill, she had little enthusiasm for the work. She found it boring but because she accepted the ideas of Victorian social and medical scientists (especially those of her mentor, Herbert Spencer) as to natural sexual difference and female inferiority, she also felt anxiety at the idea that she might be behaving in an unwomanly fashion, laying claim to work beyond her 'natural' capacity. For by 1886, Beatrice was much involved in Charles Booth's social survey of London, which provided her with work that she found considerably more congenial. But she continued to worry about leading a celibate life fearing, as did Mary Ward also, that 'dry' spinsterhood prohibited the true and full development of female personality.

By the late 1880s, Beatrice was also impatient with the results achieved by Octavia Hill's brand of personal social work. The extent of poverty uncovered by Booth appeared vast, and from her own investigation of dock labour and the sweated trades Beatrice concluded that what was needed was a large measure of social reform and administrative reorganization. She could not understand Octavia Hill's lack of interest in social investigation, which seemed to her to provide the facts from which it was possible to derive the principles of social intervention. Beatrice became as strongly committed to scientific research and to the search for efficient machinery as Octavia Hill was antipathetic.

Beatrice's marriage to Sidney in 1892 symbolized her leaving the women's world of philanthropy and her commitment both to developing scientific research methods and to campaigning for the reorganization of society in accordance with socialist principles. However, in their major studies of social institutions, trade unions, local government and the poor law, the relationship between facts and principles, and between scientific research and polemic, frequently became blurred. Beatrice was additionally perturbed that their methods did not address the crucial question of what ends they should work towards. Science could only provide the means. In an increasingly secular society, Beatrice felt more and more strongly the need for a common spiritual purpose. In this she differed greatly from Sidney (who did not feel any compulsion to consider existential questions)[3] but had much in common with other women social reformers.

Beatrice's great gain in marrying Sidney was the consolidation of her identity as a social investigator, although she also feared the submersion of that identity beneath the duties of wifehood. The work of investigation was largely the private work of library research and writing; after her marriage, Beatrice's special skills as an interviewer and observer tended to take second place to the consideration of documentary evidence, which, under Sidney's influence, she came to regard as a more rigorous form of research. Increasingly, the lives of the Webbs became more public, with the founding of the London School of Economics (LSE) and the role Sidney played on the London County Council. Beatrice, however, found it difficult to cross the boundary between the semi-private work of research into the public world of committees and public speaking, and experienced considerable confusion as to how to behave in undertaking her first major task of this kind as a member of the Royal Commission on the Poor Laws between 1905 and 1909.

In marrying Sidney, who was perceived to be very much her social inferior, Beatrice also suffered considerable isolation, both because many friends (including the Booths) boycotted the marriage and because she became part of a male-dominated world of political manipulation and empirical research. But nevertheless it proved, as both the Webbs had calculated before their marriage, that together they wielded more influence than they could have hoped to apart. Indeed, Beatrice saw her marriage as a continuation of her commitment to social service. Her picture of her marriage as a loyal and faithful working partnership was a microcosm of what she hoped for the wider society, which was why she felt such concern when increasing numbers of marriages among those in her circle either appeared to lack such qualities or broke down altogether.

However, Deborah Epstein Nord has argued strongly and convincingly that Beatrice failed to achieve either her goal of integrating love and work in her marriage or of integrating science and faith within Fabianism, and that the syntheses she sought were breaking down even at the very time she wrote optimistically about them in her auto-biography during the early 1920s.[4] Certainly tensions between Beatrice's perceptions of her wifely duty and her work, and between Sidney's larger commitment to public work and their mutual work of private research and writing, never disappeared, but the bonds of affection and mutual respect between them were crucial in supporting Beatrice in her endeavours. Of the two failures of integration perceived by Nord, it seems that the second caused Beatrice more conscious torment. By the late 1920s and 30s, she felt anxious about unemploy-ment and whether the Webbs' hopes for gradual evolution towards more rational progressive legislation would be fulfilled, and also about the apparent lack of moral purpose in social life, which she felt was symbolized in the breakdown of traditional sexual morality. In her declining years she embraced Soviet Communism because she felt it provided a solution to both these issues.

Beatrice's image among contemporaries was all too often that of a rather rigid, unimaginative, humourless, truth-seeker. The much more complicated (and human) personality revealed in her autobiography came as something of a shock to most of them. Subsequently biog-raphers have charged that Beatrice turned her back on music, drama, art and literature in deference to Sidney.[5] But the Beatrice of the 1880s had no such aspirations and while Sidney certainly constrained Beatrice's originality as a social researcher by giving priority to methods that were his province (and more usually that of men generally) rather than hers, Beatrice's own conviction as to women's limited capacities and essential inferiority relative to men would likely have proved a major barrier to substantive independent, creative achievement. While Beatrice expressed clearly the dilemmas of late nineteenth- and early twentieth-century women, she had no feminist consciousness. Indeed her abandonment of the female world of philanthropy involved adopting an anti-feminist stance in the form of opposition to votes for women. She also tended to attach much less importance to any extension of democracy than to reform of administrative machinery, which to her was the key to getting things done. In large measure the tensions and conflicts in her ideas and behaviour are complicated because she carried with her so many of her early beliefs, particularly the importance of spirituality and of moral purpose.

Social work and personal identity
In 1883 Beatrice Webb recorded in her diary her belief as to the 'goodness' of 'going amongst the poor' and the importance of selfless-ness in charitable work. However, at the same time she began to

develop doubts about the value of the work such as apparently never troubled Octavia Hill. She recorded: 'One thing is clear in my mind, it is distinctly *advantageous to us* to go amongst the poor. We can get from them the experience of life which is real and interesting'.[6] To some extent Beatrice was speaking for herself. She was quite open about her hope that COS work would 'work in well with my "human" study. One learns very little about human nature from Society'.[7] She never openly questioned the sincerity of those working for the COS or in housing management. In the chapter of her autobiography which is devoted to the COS, and written more with the benefit of hindsight and less from diary entries than any other in the book, Beatrice referred to the value of the principles on which the COS was founded: patient and persistent personal service, the acceptance of personal responsibility for the ulterior consequences of charitable assistance and the application of the scientific method to each case. But there is an edge to her choice of verb in her description of COS workers as 'yearning to serve'. At worst the result could be, she thought, 'pharasaical self-congratulation'.[8] Beatrice had already struggled with religious doctrine that seemed to her in the end to pander to the selfishness of the individual: 'the idea of working out your own salvation, of doing good . . . in order to arrive at eternal bliss . . . is . . . selfishness . . . immoral'.[9] In view of the close relationship between women's charitable endeavour and Christian obligations her feelings about philanthropy were in all likelihood tinged with the same reservations, although she was careful not to attribute directly such moral confusion to others. In fact her reasons for turning away from social work were complicated and involved a rejection at the personal level as well as profound doubts as to the value of the work itself.

Beatrice very much shared the desire of women like Octavia Hill to do useful work. However her diary for the late 1870s and 1880s is the record of almost unceasing struggle between perceived female duty to home and family and her desire for an education and employment. Unlike Octavia Hill, she was quite unable to integrate both elements in a single model of God-given duty. In 1879, on her return from a trip to Germany at the age of 22, she wrote of the strain imposed by 'the quiet and perfectly lonely life and the want of employment which makes life almost torture', and linked this explicitly with the ill-health that was a feature of her youth.[10] But Beatrice nevertheless accepted the idea that women should ideally take their place at home and perform any other useful work without show or fuss. She took over her mother's work at home on the latter's death in 1882, supervising the household and caring for her younger sister Rosie. In 1885, her father suffered a stroke which forced her to give up her philanthropic work and she became more than ever tied to the house until his death in 1891. Her sisters provided her with a four-month break each year from her nursing duties, which she used to work on Charles Booth's London Survey. She always referred to this work as a 'holiday'.[11] Duty, to Beatrice, involved her work at home and her social obligations. The three hours reading she managed to squeeze in between 5 and 8 a.m. and her desire to become an active social investigator she considered mere self-indulgence and a stimulus to unworthy ambition. She nevertheless vigorously defended this time to herself. A sister who not only interrupted her before breakfast but criticized her reading was told: 'This is *my* room and *my* time – go away'.[12] But the domestic burden was a heavy one. In January 1886, she recorded in her diary: 'the position of unmarried [sic] daughter at home is an unhappy one even for a strong woman; it is an impossible one for a weak one'.[13] Beatrice was obviously not weak but rather possessed an indomitable will.

In her diary Beatrice recorded her respect for women who stuck to their traditional sphere of home and family. In 1884, she expressed her admiration for Mary Booth's 'gentle and loving contempt for any *special* work outside the ordinary sphere of a woman's life; her high standard of excellence which should discourage any vain attempt to leave the beaten track of woman's duty'.[14] Louise Creighton, wife of Mandell Creighton (who became Bishop of London in 1897) was described in similar terms, although Louise was also admired by Beatrice as the author of several English and European history textbooks. (After Mandell Creighton's death in 1901, Louise was to become more active in the philanthropic world, playing a leading role in the affairs of the National Union of Women Workers.) Like Beatrice, Louise opposed women's suffrage in the late 1880s and had also changed her mind by the late 1900s. Her admiration for 'womanly women' did not mean that Beatrice also favoured the social round of card-leaving and -calling intermixed with those pretty accomplishments that were considered so appropriate for middle-class women. She deplored such idle behaviour as much as Octavia Hill and Florence Nightingale before her. In 1883, she wrote of a party at the Speaker's: ' "Ladies" are so expressionless. Should fancy mental superiority of men greatest in our class. How could it be otherwise with the daily life of ladies in Society . . . How can intelligent women wish to marry into the set where this is the social regime?'[15]

She agreed, however, with Octavia Hill that any useful work performed by women should also be quiet work. Writing to her father in 1885 of her sister Kate's work in rent collecting, Beatrice praised the way she kept in the background 'and refused to become an authority. Clever women who take up work so often like to be *in evidence*'.[16] This was also Octavia Hill's *bête noir*. The problem for Beatrice was that she did not want the kind of work, whether in the private or public sphere, that would keep her in the background. Whether in the form of marriage to a major political figure, such as she contemplated to Joseph Chamberlain, or publishing and speaking (although the latter caused her great difficulty initially) on the results of her social investigations, she envisaged exercising considerable social power. But until she decided at the end of 1888 once and for all to opt firmly for a life of social investigation Beatrice continued to equate the building of character with her 'real domestic duties', and to oppose it to selfish and inappropriate intellectual ambition beyond her sphere. In 1882 she 'earnestly prayed' that 'no foolish vanity' would lead her away from 'the thorough accomplishment of my real duties'.[17] Whereas Octavia Hill found joy in self-giving within her family circle, Beatrice Webb experienced anguish and frustration. But as many commentators have observed, the tendency to self-denial that resulted from the priority she accorded family duties never altogether left her. Nord has concluded that she confused morality with asceticism and that her search for a punishing morality was linked to her mistrust of her own consciousness and to her fear of vanity and egoism.[18]

Beatrice argued with herself over her duty to her family and her desire for useful work in the context of rigid late-Victorian ideas about sexual difference. She must have gained a close knowledge of contemporary opinion on the issue through her friendship with Herbert Spencer, perhaps the most influential writer on the subject on both sides of the Atlantic. Spencer maintained that sexual difference should be understood in terms of the early arrest of women's individual evolution in order to permit the conservation of their energies for reproduction. He argued that sex roles were a product of mankind's successful adaptation to social survival and that the more highly differentiated they were, the higher the social progress of society. Thus Spencer conflated sex and gender difference and neatly justified the rigid separation of spheres experienced by middle-class Victorian women, whereby they were confined to the private and the familial.[19]

Beatrice freely acknowledged male mental superiority and agreed with Spencer that women's education needed, above all, to include instruction in household duties:

> One thing seems clear to me from my own experience and from Mr Spencer's theoretical demonstration, that there is a fatal mistake being made in the

'improved education of women' in that it is a purely intellectual one, and restricted even in its intellectuality in as much as it neglects one great faculty of the intellect, observation.

(The latter Beatrice was to remedy in her own experiments in social investigation some five years later.) She went on to agree that women should learn to 'apply *Method* to the practical duties of life', especially to housework but confessed that personally she cared only for brain-work, something she feared to be an 'evil' and at a deeper level still, unnatural.[20] Because she felt that her own thirst for intellectual stimulation conflicted with her proper duties she labelled it a self-indulgence and felt additionally guilty about its pursuit.

Despite her acknowledgement of women's true vocation as wives and mothers, Beatrice found it impossible to suppress her desire for intellectual inquiry. Battling her way through the work of the neo-classical economists before breakfast in 1882, she staunchly declared her refusal to believe that mathematics could be the 'highest faculty of the brain' because she found it so difficult.[21] Yet she was also racked by self-doubt which was undoubtedly a product of both her attempt at self-education and her knowledge that established opinion decreed the existence of fundamental sexual difference and female inferiority. She wrote: 'All my duties lie in the practical direction, why should I, wretched little frog, try and puff myself into a professional'.[22] She allowed only that intellectual effort might have a part to play in influencing her moral development. But she feared too that her attempt to come to terms with social science might be thwarted by her female propensity to elevate the intuitive and the spiritual over the rational and scientific. She set up the first part of her autobiography in the manner of the late nineteenth century as a struggle between religion and science, but in the case of a female writer this was complicated by Victorian ideas of sexual difference. In keeping with these, Beatrice reiterated that it was 'impossible for women to live in agnosticism'.[23]

Throughout the 1880s she made continual reference to her limited faculties and her doubts as to her ability to undertake intellectual work, fearing that her ambitions were merely a product of vanity. Beatrice's struggle for self-education was after all carried on in relative isolation. While she corresponded with friends about her reading and confided in them her religious doubts, her sisters did not understand her efforts. Beatrice noted that they thought her 'aim absurdly out of proportion to my capacity'.[24] And yet she also recorded her underlying faith in her own capacities, which was strong enough to provide the spur to all her efforts: the 'old faith in individual work . . . the sanctity of any moral and intellectual conviction', whose welcome return was heralded in the privacy of her diary in 1887.[25] While it was natural that her sisters should have doubted her capacities, especially given her own propensity to downplay them, it was also understandable that given her strong conception of what she should be doing and her genuine doubts as to what she (or any woman) was capable of, she kept her ambitions largely to herself, which only served to increase her isolation.

In the wake of a particularly harsh bout of self-doubt and criticism in 1883, Beatrice decided to devote herself to her proper duties for five months and go into Society. She also resolved to make a sympathetic effort to get to know the people she met there, partly it would seem out of commitment to the task but partly out of the unquenchable determination to develop the art of social observation:

> I would like to go amongst men and women with a determination to know them . . . without sympathy there is an impassable barrier to real knowledge of the inner working which guide the outer actions of human beings. Sympathy, or rather *accepted* sympathy is the only instrument for the dissection of character.[26]

But here she reached another impasse, for was there not a danger that 'cold blooded inquiry' would take the place of heartfelt sympathy? And was not sympathy central, in the Octavia Hill manner, to womanly feeling? She concluded that the impetus to purely scientific inquiry must be 'shaken off sternly'. In a slightly later conversation with Spencer she expressed the fear that rationality in women was necessarily antithetical to sympathy and that 'rational woman [sic] are generally odiously dull and self-centred'.[27] On this occasion Spencer proved somewhat reassuring, citing the example of George Eliot as someone who had managed successfully to combine rational thought and sympathetic feeling.

Ideal womanhood in Beatrice's estimation was inspired first by religious feeling and sympathy, which prompted attention to family duties, and second, by selfless work for others, eschewing any form of development outside a woman's proper sphere. At the age of 23, on holiday in Italy, Beatrice recorded her impressions of a fellow female unmarried tourist in glowing terms: 'a life of continual communion with a spiritual ideal, and of continual work for others. She is one of those rare women, who seem to be perfect human beings', adding, 'a possibility denied to the masculine nature?'[28] Perfect women, ruling by definition in their own sphere, were not therefore inferior to men. Only if a woman stepped out of her sphere and competed with men did she run such a risk.

In 1883 she began working as a rent collector. Charitable work was at least practical service to others and as long as it was carried out in a self-effacing manner was socially acceptable. The problem was that Beatrice did not find charitable work congenial and in the end came to question its worth as a solution to the problems of poverty. Work for the COS or as a rent collector involved above all, as Octavia Hill put it, 'detailed work'. Beatrice Webb found the work of rent collection in particular took all her energy and dulled her mind. At the end of the day she felt too tired 'to think or feel' and 'when overtired, the tenants haunt me with their wretched, disorderly lives'. Rent collection required collectors to enter whole-heartedly into their tenants' worlds in order to know their circumstances and habits, and thereby to bring them to a more orderly management of their affairs. But Beatrice experienced revulsion at the 'bottomless pit of decaying life' she saw represented both in the conditions of the buildings themselves and their inhabitants, and found it difficult to summon up the necessary enthusiasm for the task.[29] In September 1885, she recorded that she had succeeded in getting one family to pay its rent and failed with another because of 'the difference in my manner'.[30] She found it extremely difficult to be at once firm in the exercise of rules and yet gentle, and concluded that such 'practical work' was not to her taste.

When compared with Octavia Hill there is no doubt but that Beatrice lacked the capacity for sympathetic interaction with the poor. Mulling over the work of rent collection in her diary, she once referred to the 'loveable qualities which a lady raises into activity and appreciation', and the capacity of the poor for improvement and self-control once their affection had been gained, but she was not able to love the poor as lady visitors were bidden to do. Certainly Beatrice could not contemplate living among the poor: 'the East End life, with its dirt, drunkenness and immorality, absence of combined effort or common interests saddens me, weighs down my spirit. I could not live down here; I should lose heart and become worthless as a worker'.[31] Where Octavia Hill saw affection and hope, Beatrice saw brutality and decay.

Beatrice collected rents in Katherine Buildings which were run by the East End Dwellings Company, whose directors included Edward Bond and were all close associates of Octavia Hill. The contrast between Beatrice and her fellow worker in the Buildings, Miss Ella Pycroft, was striking and serves to highlight the particular qualities needed by the successful late nineteenth-century social worker. Ella Pycroft was a Devonshire doctor's daughter who served as a rent collector until 1890 and later became the Chief Organizer of domestic economy subjects under the Technical Education Board of the London County Council. Like Beatrice she had a strong will, a desire to do useful work, and religious doubts; both found it very difficult to understand the purpose of the kind of suffering they witnessed in Katherine Buildings. But unlike Beatrice, Ella revelled in the work of sorting out tenant squabbles and prising improvements out of the reluctant directors of the buildings. She lived quite happily among the tenants with few creature comforts, although even she was put out when two eminent local philanthropists, Canon and Mrs Bradby, visited her and criticized the fact that she had more than one deal table and chair in her room. Describing the incident to Beatrice Webb, she inquired with mock humility: 'Is there anything so very 'umble in my appearance that this most economically furnished room should be considered "sumptuous" for me?'[32] Beatrice made a point of sending Ella flowers, eggs and cream during 1886, after she had left the Buildings to nurse her father.

Philanthropic work assumed that lady visitors would be able to wield a natural authority. Of course few possessed Octavia Hill's kind of personal authority. Ella Pycroft was perfectly able to handle outbursts of violence at the concerts she spent so much time organizing, disputes on hot summer nights and 'bullying' by those she had evicted for not paying their rents, but, unlike Octavia, she admitted that she was often both unsure of her course of action and frightened:

> The Fishers are gone at last and Mrs F is such a good hearted woman in spite of her rowdiness that I hated giving her notice – her husband burnt the notice before my eyes and they shouted at me 'till I was really frightened, but we parted the best of friends – poor things.[33]

Beatrice Webb commented early on in her autobiography about the way she acquired the 'marks of her caste' and how later, in 1886, the woman in charge of the sweatshop where she went (disguised) to work as a trouser hand picked her out as one able to give orders and exert power over others.[34] Beatrice was right to be uneasy about the exchange between rich and poor and about the true basis of the friendship upon which it was supposed to be built.

Ella Pycroft used the hard detailed work of rent collecting almost as a form of escape, both from her own troubles and from larger social problems. Both she and Octavia Hill sought to carve out a manageable territory of individual work, as she commented to Beatrice: 'it would not help me at all to have a spell of "passive" life, thinking of all the trouble of the world, without being able at any rate to try and help other people through theirs'.[35] Both Ella and Octavia Hill had experienced unsuccessful love affairs which Ella referred to in a letter to Beatrice:

I am sorry for you not having work enough to keep you from looking forward, I think that is the most miserable habit and it is only to be escaped by constant employment. Mercifully for me, I never look forward now – except to the chance of making the arrears less next week, and that hope generally fails me. I think it is no use blinding the facts that nothing can make up to us women for the loss of humanities – I know nothing will ever to me; one may bury one's cares for a time under a load of work, but they are always ready to come up again.[36]

This element of sublimation in charitable endeavour bothered Beatrice Webb intensely. She was convinced that women needed the comfort and connections of homelife and children, with definite family duties to fulfil and someone dependent on their love and care, if they were to achieve health and happiness. Her own longing for a child and bitterness regarding the difficulties celibacy posed for women confirmed her in her belief in the importance of traditional home duties.[37] Like many other late-Victorian women, feminist and non-feminist, Beatrice was able to acknowledge female sexuality in the context of her desire for motherhood, while otherwise abhorring the free expression of sexual feelings. Her attraction to Chamberlain in the mid-1880s was sexual. But because Chamberlain also demanded a political wife and a *'femme complaisante'*, she knew that it would be dishonest to her true self and principles, albeit that she was still far from being completely sure of these, to pretend that she would be able to accede to his every wish and argument.

Beatrice engaged most fully in the COS and rent collecting work in the aftermath of her 'affair' with Chamberlain and referred to the work as a 'narcotic'.[38] But she neither wished nor approved of women substituting service to others for service to family and commented in her diary that both Ella Pycroft and Octavia Hill would have been 'much more' if happily married. Of Ella she said: 'She is a true woman and will never be fairly happy out of marriage. For that it needs that your passion should go elsewhere into truth-seeking philanthropy, religion – it matters not into which'.[39] Ella had after all made plain to Beatrice that she felt nothing could make up to a woman for 'the loss of humanities', and despite her endeavours to bury her sense of personal isolation under work, she not infrequently succumbed to what she called in her letter 'the City of dreadful night'. Her only solace in such dark periods was religion: 'I had to take to the "Imitation of Christ" as a soothing influence. It is strange how one gathers calm from those old devotional books full of faith in which one has no share'.[40] Beatrice felt the same, and used the ritual of the Church of England (she regularly attended communion at St Paul's) to a very similar purpose, which must only have strengthened her belief as to the essential difference between men and women in regard to religion.

Beatrice's recognition that many leading women philanthropists lacked a family life of their own caused her to reflect on the position of unmarried women in late-Victorian society. After a visit to Octavia Hill's lieutenant, Miss Emma Cons, she attempted to describe her:

> Not a lady by birth? With the face and manner of a distinguished woman, a ruler of men. Absolute absorption in work – strong religious feeling – very little culture or interest in things outside the sphere of her own action . . . Did not attempt to theorize in her work . . . spoke to her people with peculiar mixture of sympathy and authority which characterizes the modern class of governing women . . .

Beatrice recognized that notwithstanding the attention to detail and the evocation of those qualities of sympathy considered supremely womanly, women such as Cons and Hill were powerful leaders. Beatrice went on to generalize about the new 'governing and guiding' women:

> Unlike the learned women – the emotional part of their nature is fully developed – their sympathy kept almost painfully active. Their eyes are clear of self-consciousness and bright with love and pity from which it springs. They have the dignity of habitual authority. Often they have the narrow-mindedness and social gaucherie of complete absorption, physical and mental, in one lot of feeling and ideas. The pure organiser belongs to a different class . . . [for example the hospital matron, and] is to a certain extent unsexed by the justice, push and severity required.

Beatrice felt that the governing and guiding woman-manager used moral suasion, but the organizing woman had to employ 'technical justice'. 'Push and severity', she continued, 'are not the prominent qualities of the governing and guiding woman. For the guidance of men by personal influence, *feeling* more than thought is required,[41] (author's itals). For the unmarried woman, therefore, charitable work represented the best option for womanly work. Both academic and paid work, even when in a caring role, lay beyond women's sphere and would inevitably erode femininity and thus threaten sexual identity.

Women involved in philanthropic work also ran some risk in this respect. In a letter to Beatrice, Ella Pycroft commented adversely on the 'prim old maid' the Barnetts had persuaded her to take on as a rent collector: 'I should say she must be the descendant of many generations of single women – or at least that's what I should say if I believed in miracles'. This woman remained a thorn in Ella's side and did nothing to improve her stock when she told Ella that the 'power' in her forehead reminded her of Miss Susan (actually Sophia) Jex Blake. This caused Ella to remark heartily: 'I am thankful my name isn't Susan or Sophia Jex Blake and that I am not a female doctor'.[42] In Ella's and Beatrice's view this woman rent collector had lost all womanly feeling. She had become the dry, spinsterish figure they feared most. It was not just a matter of regretting the failure to achieve the status of a married woman; both Ella and Beatrice were able to take some pleasure in their own company and that of other women of their own kind. Ella freely admitted that there were not too many people who could 'manage' her and was able to delight in an evening alone after a tiring day 'writing to a sympathetic soul' and smoking.[43] On the other hand, she hated the occasional outing she was expected to take with her unmarried female relations:

> There were four old maids, all peculiar (two strong minded, and two yielding and universally enthusiastic), one dull widow, and three girls who mostly giggled . . . here am I tired out with one afternoon of such society, while they stand it all their lives and yet can go on contentedly smiling.[44]

But, both Beatrice and Ella were fundamentally convinced that women needed marriage and motherhood if crucial womanly feelings were to be kept alive. It was the image of the spinster as essentially unsexed that they abhorred.

Beatrice discussed the role played by marriage in women's lives with Frederic Harrison in 1886 and recorded it in some detail in her diary. They agreed that unmarried life could not be happy for women but 'disagreed on the usefulness of it'. Harrison took the view that

> marriage was absolutely essential to the development of character, that it alone gave the restfulness necessary for true work. I maintain that if unmarried women kept their feelings alive, did not choke them with routine idleness, practical work or with intellectualism, though they must suffer pain, they were often for that very reason more sympathetic than married women.[45]

Harrison disagreed that this could possibly be so. This conversation occurred in the middle of a period when Beatrice, having given up the idea of marriage to Chamberlain, had committed herself not only to her work of rent collecting but also to the life of a 'glorified spinster'. Her diary reveals her identifying with her fellow unmarried women workers but her convictions as to the centrality of marriage and motherhood to female happiness remained undiminished and her hope that she might keep womanly feeling alive was probably barely strong enough to survive Harrison's denial. Just as she was given no encouragement by her family for her work of self-education, so she found no reassurance that unmarried women might have their compensations or even be able to live a 'normal' life. Margaret Harkness, a close friend of Beatrice during the latter's young womanhood who later became a novelist under the pseudonym of John Law, had written long letters to Beatrice on the subject of marriage versus a career during her nurse training. Her verdict, delivered in 1878, was: 'I think an unmarried woman living a true life, is far nobler than a married woman, but I doubt if she does as much good, or if she makes as many people happy as a married woman'.[46] This was very close to the view taken by Beatrice during the 1880s. Throughout 1887 and 1888, Beatrice continued to refer to the importance of showing 'charity and sympathy' towards single women of her own class and commented on the inevitable cooling of her relationship with Mary Booth and the greater ease of friendships with women in circumstances similar to her own.[47] Nevertheless when she and Ella Pycroft read a 'cleverish' article in *Macmillans* magazine on 'glorified spinsters . . . a new race of women not looking for or expecting marriage . . . self-dependent, courageous and cool headed', she remarked only that ' "glorified spinsterhood" is at present gilded by the charm of novelty and youth'.[48] She had no faith that it could last.

Beatrice's feelings about her fellow social workers were thus, to say the least, ambivalent. Practical work may have represented the only acceptable call to duty for the unmarried woman and the best hope of retaining some womanly qualities, but in the end Beatrice was not interested in the nature of the work and found most of its practitioners rather dull and narrow. When she stopped working as a rent collector in 1885 in order to nurse her father, she also began to write on social issues; her first article on unemployment was published in 1886. Beatrice relied on her female friends, particularly Bella Fisher (who had written a history text for children) for criticism and advice in her early attempts to study and write, and it was Margaret Harkness who introduced Beatrice to the idea of working in the British Library.[49] Herbert Spencer, however, began to warn Beatrice that her work was unsuitable: 'You have your duty to your relatives, and your duty to society to consider. Though you doubtless are prompted by what you think is your duty to society, yet you labour under a mistaken view of that duty'.[50]

By 1888 Beatrice was as fully involved in work on dock labour and the sweated trades for Booth's survey of London as caring for her father permitted, and increasingly certain of her role as a social investigator. At the end of 1888 she recorded in her diary that Charles Booth wanted her to go on to investigate women's employment in the East End and she noted that female labour was a subject of growing importance. But she had already set her heart on study of the cooperative movement. In March 1889 she went to the Creightons for dinner and was engaged in conversation by the economist, Alfred Marshall. The conversation began, she recalled, with 'chaffing' about the roles of men and women. Holding women to be subordinate and marriage to represent an altruistic sacrifice of male freedom, Marshall warned: 'If you compete with us we shan't marry you', while Beatrice

> maintained the opposite argument; that there was an ideal of character in which strength, courage, sympathy, self-devotion, persistent purpose were united to a clear and far-seeing intellect; that the ideal was common to the man and to the woman, that what you needed was not different qualities and different defects, but the same virtues working in different ways.

This was not exactly the opposite argument; Beatrice was in fact making a case for companionate marriage and finding sufficient courage to depart from her previous Spencerian belief in the existence of innate sexual difference. Women's duties might lie in a different direction from those of men but there was not necessarily any female inferiority of intellect and capacity. Later they discussed her projected history of cooperation. Marshall thought her course unwise and advised: 'There is one thing that you and only you can do – an inquiry into that unknown field of female labour'.[51] Again Beatrice had sufficient courage (albeit privately) to disagree, perceiving the logical inconsistency of his position. If her skills as a social investigator were good enough to look at the uncharted territory of female labour, then they were good enough to look at cooperation.

The conversation touched on subjects that Beatrice had pondered at great length and over which she felt both deeply and profoundly ambivalent. It must have been painful; certainly she recorded it at great length in her journal. And it took great determination, reflecting the strength of her underlying belief in her capacities, to pursue her isolated course, again in the face of disagreement from eminent sources. It is also significant, however, that despite the obvious impression made by the conversation and the doubts that it must have stirred anew, Beatrice recorded her enjoyment of the conversation and her liking for Marshall. She delighted in intellectual debate and was very quick on her feet, and on the whole found suitable sparring partners, not surprisingly, in the form of men rather than women. She preferred intellectual work and the company of male collaborators. Time and again she revelled in the feelings of ease and equality she experienced in the company of educated working men, whether she was smoking in the company of Kerrigan, the school board visitor, who provided her with valuable information during her work for Booth, or sitting with the cooperators of Bacup. As early as 1880 she recorded in her diary that it was so much easier to get on with men: 'They seldom criticise a girl who is willing to make herself pleasant to them – And then their wider knowledge of human nature makes them more interesting as companions, and enables one to be freer in conversation with them'.[52] Beatrice's art of conversation unquestionably relied heavily on the feminine art of making herself pleasant, even when uttering an acerbic remark, although a friend once criticized her 'unattractively combative' manner in argument. Beatrice admitted the fault, commenting wryly that it was hard to be 'womanly, adaptable and earnest' at the same time.[53]

In seeking the world of social investigation she was not only rejecting the world of 'practical women' but actively seeking the company of men and also claiming a right to investigate 'male' subjects, which would in turn mean that she would have to be reckoned with in the male world. By the time she decided to undertake her study of cooperation, Beatrice had decided that, for better or worse, she had a 'masculine intellect'.[54] Her new study of cooperation opened up copious opportunities to pursue issues of importance to women, especially women's role as consumers, but unlike many women of the period including COS women such as Helen Bosanquet and the members of the Fabian Women's Group, she chose not to do so. In her study of dock labour she had recognized the importance of the relationship between the workplace and the home, but thereafter Beatrice omitted gender from her analysis.

In Nord's view, it was Beatrice's rejection of the women's world of social work and her move towards the male world of social investigation that prompted her to sign the anti-suffrage petition organized by Mrs Humphry Ward and published in the *Nineteenth Century* in June 1889.[55] But, as Brian Harrison has pointed out, the philanthropic world was split by the suffrage struggle.[56] In fact, rejection of the female world probably played less of a part in Beatrice's decision to sign the anti-suffrage petition than did her eagerness to be accepted by the male world. She explained her action weakly, saying that she felt that she had not yet done enough to speak as a representative of the class of women Mrs Fawcett wanted to enfranchise – celibate women.[57] Certainly Beatrice would not have wished to be associated with what she perceived to be single women's cause. But in 1889, it is doubtful that she thought very much at all about the women involved, other than to wish to distance herself from an issue that was unpopular with the vast majority of men. In so far as she thought about the matter in anything but a self-serving manner, her comment in 1906, when she publicly changed her views, rings true. She contended that she had always been more concerned about obligations and duties than about rights, and that in 1889 she had not been convinced that formal politics were important.[58] Octavia Hill felt the same. Both women were adept at political intrigue, but neither believed political democracy to be a very important factor in the solution of social problems.

Beatrice must have realized that she had sealed what promised to be a lonely as well as exciting fate at the 1889 Cooperative Congress when the male cooperators accused her of taking the view she had on suffrage because she was 'rich and strong'. She escaped from this situation with an exit line that had always served her well in male company: 'I will go anywhere for a cigarette'[59] (on a previous occasion she had remarked that smoking had 'a more fatal power' than the vote for women).[60] However, she found herself more annoyed that she felt she should be in the company of men by the way in which the 'little clique of exceptional women, with their correct behaviour and political aspirations', gave her the 'cold shoulder'.[61] Beatrice Webb had decided to give up work that she found dull and increasingly of questionable merit and become one of the boys. The brief days of identity with 'glorified spinsterhood' were over, but her choice exacted a heavy price. Early in 1891, she again remarked on her relative isolation. Octavia Hill had objected to her being asked to preside at a meeting because she tried 'to float' herself and her work through her 'personal influence on men'; furthermore the 'same impression' had apparently reached Florence Nightingale, while Annie Besant, whom Beatrice much admired, had, Beatrice felt, never trusted her.[62]

The value of social work in question

With the benefit of hindsight Beatrice described the COS as

> an honest though short circuited attempt to apply the scientific method of observation and experiment, measuring and verification to the task of delivering the poor from their miseries by the personal service and pecuniary assistance tendered by their wealthy and leisured fellow-citizens.[63]

Such judgements in her autobiography are politically astute, but have benefited from mature reflection; there are relatively few passages in her diary relating to the period of her COS work. She identified the principal concern of the COS as a 'belief – it may almost be called an obsession – that the mass misery of great cities arose mainly, if not entirely, from spasmodic, indiscriminate and unconditional doles'.[64] This analysis did less than full justice to the importance COS leaders attached to developing individual social work as a means of building character and promoting both self-maintenance and a fuller citizenship, but it pinpointed the major outcome of the COS approach as far as poor-relief policy went and accurately described both Octavia Hill's and Helen Bosanquet's position on the question of outdoor relief. Furthermore, such a position was, as Beatrice shrewdly observed, politically controversial. For while almsgiving had always been considered a Christian virtue, the COS struggled to convince Victorians that it represented but a 'mean and cruel form of [middle-class] self-indulgence'.[65]

During her work as a rent collector, there is evidence that Beatrice experienced considerable difficulties in deciding how to treat the poor. So did Ella Pycroft, who had far fewer doubts about COS philosophy generally. Such confusion must have been fairly widespread (see p. 46). While Octavia Hill emphasized the importance of befriending the poor, she also insisted that the worker might have to be cruel to be kind. If the person in distress was so placed because he spent too much money on drink, then it was argued that there was little point in giving him more money to spend on it. Octavia Hill's letters to her fellow workers were full of strictures as to the importance of thinking through the effect of giving money and of taking responsibility for the additionally harmful effect that doles might be expected to have. However, this was a difficult lesson for many tender-hearted middle-class women who wanted to act correctly in helping the poor but who found almsgiving both the most satisfying way of assuaging their 'consciousness of sin' and most productive of a ready response in the recipient.

Ella Pycroft's co-worker, Maurice Paul, a medical student and son of the publisher, admired her 'hardness' in the treatment of tenants but was himself extremely soft-hearted, going so far as to break one of Octavia Hill's cardinal principles by lending money to tenants. Ella herself told Beatrice of a case where in the midst of a heavy day she had forgotten to tell the broker not to take away the bed from a couple on whom she had levied a distraint in order to effect an eviction. As a result she was 'pursued and bullied' by the couple 'till I didn't know whether I weren't the brute they seemed to think me'.[66] Many tenants took up considerable time and energy. For example, Ella spent long hours talking to a Crimean War veteran who felt a grave sense of injustice about his small war pension and the behaviour of his commanding officer on the battlefield, and who was prone to bouts of drinking. He was soothed somewhat by Ella's visits, during which she persuaded him to make a flannel shirt for hop-picking, and taught both him and his wife to herringbone.

In the case of Sherman, a tenant who was out of work due to sickness, unable to pay his rent and therefore facing eviction and the poor law, Ella struggled for correct guiding principles. She reasoned that because the man's health would take months rather than weeks to mend, he therefore could not justly be maintained in a COS convalescent home, the only obvious way of saving him from the poor law. And there remained the problem of finding him light work afterwards. In her worst moments she reflected on social Darwinistic theory:

> when one has the power of making one's life useful one has no right to be overwhelmed by one's own trouble then – but I don't see what use Sherman's life can be to anyone, unless to keep pity alive in other people's breasts – Ugh, what a vile theory that is![67]

Perhaps it was therefore better to abandon the helpless entirely. But a month later found her having appealed successfully to Beatrice for a pension to keep the man off the poor law and in his flat, and also found her speculating on the possibility of him taking tolls at the entry to an old clothes market in the neighbourhood once he had recovered.

Beatrice recorded, albeit more briefly, an instance of her own profound confusion when confronted by such problems at the individual level. Visiting an opium eater and his wife and three children in 1883 she pondered in her diary: 'One is tempted to a feeling of righteous indignation against the man, but did he make himself? And is he not on the whole more pitiable?'[68] Nevertheless it seems that in this instance she toed the COS line for in 1886, reflecting on the difficulty of applying COS principles in 'hard cases', Pycroft recalled Beatrice's story of denying the opium eater relief some years before as a model of good practice.[69]

However, the decision was not taken either as lightly or as easily as contemporary critics of 'scientific charity' and historians have often implied. Ella Pycroft sought guidance from socialist literature as well as from her Octavia Hill training. She considered Lassalle's (socialist) 'arguments about the people raising themselves from serfdom and becoming active citizens' to be of great merit. He lost her sympathy only when he suggested that 'people aren't to work for themselves in future, the state will manage it all'.[70] To Ella and other more reflective workers, their ultimate purpose was individual empowerment, which seemed incompatible with socialism as they understood it. But this did not mean that they accepted and unthinkingly practised all the principles of scientific charity.

In 1883, in the manner of a good Spencerian, Beatrice was concerned that no matter how it was practised, charitable relief must favour the weak to the detriment of the strong.

> But can these general considerations have any weight when we come face to face with individual misery, and do these economic facts bear any proportion in importance to the moral facts with which 'charity' is concerned? Does not the advisability of charity depend on the moral qualities which are developed in the relation of giver and receiver. . .?[71]

She shrewdly perceived a tension between the moral principles which motivated people such as Octavia Hill and the practical outcome of their thinking which tended to accord with the prescriptions of the classical economists. Albeit that in the case of Octavia, these were effectively reconciled by her religiously inspired belief in 'right action' as the basis for achieving social change (see pp. 29–30). In particular Beatrice became critical of the distinction the COS made between those deserving and those undeserving of charitable help. (The undeserving were those of poor character, such as the drunkard or the opium eater.) She noted that the deserving were often those whom it was impossible to help effectively within the framework of COS principles; Sherman was a case in point. She concluded that while some such principles were 'almost forced upon any systematic private philanthropists', it was difficult to see how 'they could be made consistent with the duty persistently inculcated of personal friendship with the poor'.[72] Beatrice's perception of a double tension at the level of theory and principle, and at the level of practice, was acute. Even those workers like Ella Pycroft who did not question the principles of scientific charity found conflicts in their practice.

As for rent collecting, by 1885 Beatrice Webb felt that Katherine Buildings were 'an utter failure' and were in no way an influence for good despite Ella Pycroft's best efforts. In the first place there was the condition of the buildings themselves. In her autobiography she noted Octavia Hill's complaint to the 1885 Royal Commission on the Housing of the Working Classes that reformers wanted to do too much at once, moving the poor out of damp one-roomed cellars into ideal homes. Better, Octavia argued, to rent out one or two rooms above ground and let tenants move into more spacious and better quality accommodation as their standards improved. In Beatrice's view, Katherine Buildings were the dreary, undecorated outcome of this policy. She described one of the directors of the Buildings as a 'cut and dried philanthropist, with little human nature, who was determined that the tenants *should* like nothing but what was *useful*'.[73] This director's view showed how easy it was for Octavia Hill's prescriptions to be meanly interpreted. There is no reference to Octavia's passion for flowers and lawns in the accounts of the Katherine Buildings. As Beatrice put it to her father a year later, the directors seemed not to be aware that 'the class *willing* and *fit* to live in dwellings where all the arrangements are so wanting in charm and privacy are much more limited than they suppose'.[74] Certainly Ella Pycroft provided a detailed account of the Buildings' deficiencies, from the lack of privacy in the communal latrine to blocked sinks and lack of shelving for saucepans. In her annual report for 1885, she reported that 56 tenants had left because of the poor conditions.[75] One benefactor offered to pay for more cleaning on the stairs which Pycroft accepted, knowing that it alone would not result in any great improvement. The benefactor then wrote to complain about the number of drunken tenants on Saturday night and to ask if she could not evict them. She replied that she could if they proved incorrigible but that out of 200 tenants, 20 or 30 were bound to be drunk on a Saturday night.[76] Busybody benefactors were matched by the intransigent opposition of some directors to her pleas for more caretaking staff and improvements.

In the second place there were the tenants themselves, who in Beatrice's view remained a brutalized and degenerate mass:

> The respectable tenants keep rigidly to themselves. The meeting places, there is something grotesquely coarse in this, are the water-closets. Boys and girls crowd in these landings – they are the only lighted places on [sic] the buildings – gamble and flirt. The lady collectors are an altogether superficial thing. Undoubtedly their gentleness and kindness bring light into many homes – but what are they in face of this collected brutality?[77]

Beatrice was convinced that while on balance scientific charity had not made things worse, it had not resulted in any significant improvement.

Beatrice was disgusted by the residuum, whom she encountered as a COS worker and whose members were regularly evicted from the buildings, and was impatient of their improvement, reserving her sympathies for the respectable working class. She wrote in her diary that the destitute were no more representative of the working class than the 'sporting set' were of London society. More representative, she felt, was the Lancashire village of Bacup, which she visited in disguise with Martha Jackson (a poor relation who acted as her mother's maid) and which influenced her strongly as a model working-class community. She described it as being steeped in religion and cooperation and, as a result, full of moral purpose. Making the comparison with the residuum, she commented crossly in her diary: 'mere philanthropists are apt to overlook the existence of an independent working class, and when they talk sentimentally of "the people" they mean merely the ne'er-do-wells'.[78] Beatrice used the word philanthropists loosely. Just as with hindsight she was partial, although perceptive, in her criticism of the COS, here it suited her, in the manner of the COS worker she then was, to class all philanthropists as sentimental.

In 1885, despite her acute restlessness with charitable work for both personal and philosophical reasons, Beatrice Webb showed no sign of having formulated an alternative strategy to the individual work of philanthropy. She was however convinced that the practical work of rent collection was not for her and that she was much more likely to develop her ideas by undertaking some project of social investigation. Above all she was convinced that all philanthropists, whether scientific or otherwise, were people whose love of detailed work signalled a narrowness of vision. Her autobiography contains repeatedly derogatory references to 'hard working philanthropy'.

She had been consistently shocked at leading women philanthropists' lack of interest in analysing the nature of their work. When she met Emma Cons, she noted that while she was completely absorbed in her work, 'no description of tenants [was] kept. Did not attempt to theorise about her work'. Similarly, Octavia Hill objected that there was too much 'windy talk' and too little action.[79] Beatrice herself had a clear idea of the kind of information she ideally wanted to collect about her tenants: the number of children per family, their occupations, income, race, place of birth, religion, whether of London stock or recipients of charity.[80] Indeed, it was her perception that many of the Katherine Buildings' tenants were in-migrants to the capital that supplied her with the idea (used in her first two articles) that there was a causal connection between the existence of a pool of such labour and casual work at the docks. In short, Beatrice was not content to confine her efforts to personal social work. Nor was she greatly interested in more ambitious schemes of social administration. Her failure to convince the directors of the Buildings as to the proper course of improvements led her to suggest a scheme to the Reverend Samuel Barnett of Toynbee Hall whereby all agencies for housing would be associated in one body. Barnett was very struck by the idea and wanted her to elaborate it, whereupon she got cold feet about her capacity to carry it through.[81] She was preoccupied increasingly more by intellectual work than by social-work practice and in particular by the idea of social investigation and its methods.

Becoming a social investigator

Methods
Beatrice spent considerable time thinking about how she might attempt

the work of social investigation. She recorded in her autobiography that Spencer had been the first to teach her the value of facts, even though she was later to deplore the way in which he used them.[82] Interestingly, it was the methods of Francis Galton, remembered chiefly for his dubious work in the field of eugenics, that stayed in her mind during the 1880s:

> the most relevant of Galton's many gifts was the unique contribution of three separate and distinct processes of intellect: a continuous curiosity about, and a rapid apprehension of individual facts . . . the facility for ingenious trains of reasoning; and . . . the capacity for correcting and verifying his own hypotheses.[83]

Beatrice respected the first gift because she was always deploring her own lack of capacity in this regard. For example, she felt that she had no gift for the rapid reading and judgement of original documents and that any facility she developed in this regard was painfully acquired. Her identification of Galton's second and third gifts was faulty in the extreme. Galton's 'ingenious trains of reasoning' mitigated against the verification of his hypotheses. While his methodology was more rigorous than that of Spencer, his work was open to much the same charge of a selective use of facts to bolster preconceived ideas. That Beatrice (and others) could believe that Galton had achieved value-free social scientific investigation merely demonstrated how the use of scientific forms – observation, hypothesis-forming and verification – could disguise the way in which assumptions undermined those very processes.

Beatrice was committed to seeking a solution to social problems through value-free social investigation, a commitment inspired and sustained by the secret hope that she would provide *the* solution to those problems. When Samuel Barnett stated his belief (similar to that of Helen Bosanquet) that ideas had more influence than facts because ideas influenced character and the development of character was the key to life, Beatrice noted that she believed in ideas, but in ideas following facts. She went on to plan an article on 'social diagnosis' to show how far action had been influenced by fact. She felt that the historical record could be made to show how social sentiment had been formed by descriptions of social facts, which in turn had given rise to political action, an argument which itself owed as much to conviction as to observable fact.[84]

Indeed, Beatrice's relationship to 'social facts' was an increasingly uneasy one. In the course of her investigation into cooperation in 1889, she complained about the 'treadmill of disjointed facts, in themselves utterly uninteresting and appallingly dry', but noted, 'however it is satisfactory to feel that one will never be beaten for lack of industry'.[85] She certainly did not share Florence Nightingale's reputed enthusiasm for chewing on a good fact. By the time she came to work (with Sidney) on the massive amount of material they collected for their study of trade unions, she declared herself to be sick of 'these ugly details of time work and piece work'.[86] To Beatrice, facts in and of themselves were as boring as the detailed practical work of rent collection. During her marriage to Sidney she often 'broke down' with a sick headache while note-taking, work that she could not stick at for more than a few hours a day. Her devotion to facts was a species of duty; there is in her diary-entries the feeling, worthy of Octavia Hill, that the diligent and exhaustive search for facts represented 'right action', from which good prescriptions were bound to emerge. The key she believed was to assemble the facts without prejudice.

The relationship between fact and explanation remained elusive, as the Webbs were forced to admit in their study of trade unions where, despite their best efforts, the search for a theoretical framework proceeded deductively rather than arising (inductively) out of the facts.[87] In 1894, while working on the second volume of the study, Beatrice recognized that it was 'silly . . . to suppose that *facts ever tell their own story* – it is all a matter of arranging them so that they may tell something – and the arrangement is purely a subjective process'; and a month later she admitted the divorce between thesis and description: the facts 'are not much good as the basis of our structure – they are only the ornament'.[88] The process of deriving an explanatory framework, of seeking a pattern in the data, was for Beatrice a largely intuitive one. By mid-1897, she recorded triumphantly in her diary that she and Sidney had '*found* our theory' (author's itals) and that 'every previous part of our analysis seems to fit in perfectly; and facts which before puzzled us range themselves in their places as if "by nature" '.[89] But Beatrice continued to express honest doubts as to whether this was social science or merely compiling and chronicling.[90] In the case of their massive work on local government, which followed the study of trade unions, the process of merely disentangling the facts and marshalling them one after another into a coherent narrative proved an exhausting task. Beatrice found this sort of labour profoundly enervating and much preferred the work involved in writing something like the *Constitution for the Socialist Commonwealth*, which required more creative thinking and less close attention to the use of evidence.[91]

In the midst of work on the trade union study, Beatrice acknowledged that it was difficult to act both as investigator and agitator: 'We are trying, in our humble way, to lead both lives – to keep our heads clear to see the facts – without losing that touch of the political market which leads to efficient propaganda'.[92] The struggle became harder rather than easier. Two years before the Royal Commission on the Poor Laws was appointed, Beatrice again perceived the discrepancy between the role the Webbs played as advocates in their political work and their search for 'truth' in their work of social investigation.[93] On the Royal Commission, Beatrice insisted on proper social research but produced a report that was more a propaganda document. The work Beatrice did (in close cooperation with Sidney) for her Minority Report to the Royal Commission on the Poor Laws had the old problems as to the relationship between facts and theory, but in a more exaggerated form. The Minority Report showed little commitment to the method of social science she had so painfully evolved. She wrote energetically to Sidney in May 1908:

> With seeming impartiality and moderation every word of that Report [the Minority] has to tell in the direction of Breaking-up the Poor Law, the argument has to be repeated in any conceivable form so that the reader cannot escape from it. It must be a real work of Art; we can dismiss Science. It will be High Jinks doing it and we will get to work at once. The more saturated it is with argument the less will they be able to adopt any part of it without the conclusions – but the argument must be cunningly wrought – so as to seem a mere recital of the facts. The Wood shall absorb the Trees.[94]

This revealing passage not only forecast accurately the nature of the finished report but also exposed its lack of firm foundation. Beatrice was extremely critical of the method of the Royal Commission, complaining that witnesses were questioned for too long on matters they knew little about, with the result that the method of cross-examination became more a means of political point-scoring than of fact-seeking.[95] She employed her own investigators to collect the data she required. However the relationship between the facts she had such high regard for and her final report was hazier than ever.

Knowing the solution they wished to promote, Beatrice set about 'discovering' the principles to underpin it and collecting facts to support them. The collection of data for this in mid-1906 proceeded hand in hand with the research for the Webbs' history of local government in what Beatrice admitted was a baffling mix of notetaking and drafting by Beatrice and her secretaries.[96] In a Memorandum submitted to the commission, she described the principles of the 1834 Poor Law as national uniformity, less eligibility and the workhouse system, amounting together to a policy of *laissez-faire*. She argued that these had been progressively abandoned in favour of three new principles: curative treatment (the sick, for example, had been excepted from the principle of less eligibility); universality (her examples included the provision of vaccination, sanitation and elementary education); and compulsion (lunatics and even the able-bodied could, by 1907, be compulsorily detained). All that had to be done was to develop a policy that clearly embodied these new principles to provide a national minimum standard of life for all, under the auspices of local authorities, with an element of compulsion reserved for those who might prove unwilling to live useful, cooperative lives. She felt that the new principles embodied

> the doctrine of mutual obligation between the community and the individual. The universal maintenance of a definite minimum of civilised life – seen to be in the interest of the community no less than in that of the individual – became the joint responsibility of an indissoluble partnership.[97]

Beatrice's reading of poor law history in this fashion was entirely inaccurate, as Helen Bosanquet perceived when she subjected Beatrice's so-called principles to a justifiably scathing attack.[98] Beatrice had committed one of the cardinal sins of social investigation that she herself had identified: distorting the facts to fit preconceived ideas.

Similarly, in structuring the specific recommendations of her report, Beatrice sought principles to fit her preconceptions. In the case of the medical treatment of the destitute, her ideas were stimulated by a flash of inspiration that illness should be treated as a public nuisance. Thinking this while listening to COS evidence in favour of restricting medical relief to the technically destitute, she began 'to cross-examine on this assumption bringing out the existing conflict between the poor law and health authorities, and making the unfortunate poor law witnesses say they were in favour of the public health attitude'.[99] She jumped from this to making a link with the idea of universal medical inspection and treatment, as in the case of smallpox vaccination, and to her curative principle. The argument was cogent but consisted essentially of a series of propositions. Beatrice had most trouble, as did the majority of the commissioners, with the problem of the able-bodied pauper. In April 1907, she confessed that she was 'blest if I know yet what to do with the able-bodied', and in July was still unsure as to whether there should be a national authority to deal with them.[100] At the beginning of 1908 she and Sidney were working at high pressure but still could not quite see the wood for the trees; nevertheless Beatrice declared that she had 'ample confidence in our methods'. Having 'discovered' the principles of 1907, they were busy 'manufacturing the heavy artillery of fact that is to drive both principles and scheme home'.[101] In the end, the majority decided there would have to be a central destitution authority and Beatrice decided there would not, representing her decision quite falsely as a logical outcome of principle founded on empirical investigation.

While the gap between Beatrice's theory of social investigation and her practice often resulted in work that was particularly vulnerable to methodological criticism, as in the case of the Minority Report to the Royal Commission on the Poor Laws, it was also the case that her most original contributions came from penetrating flashes of insight that had little relation to the painstaking scissor-and-pasting of each and every fact in endless permutations and combinations,' such as she described in *Methods of Social Study*.[102] In her study of cooperation, Beatrice managed to stand the stated ideals of cooperators on their head to reach the conclusion that the importance of cooperation lay in its discovery of consumers and demand rather than in its stated goal of moving towards cooperative production and profit-sharing. In her preface to *The Cooperative Movement*, Beatrice described how important it had been to watch the directors of the Cooperative Wholesale Society at work and to get a feel for what exactly they were concerned about.[103] Her ability to see right round an issue was demonstrated again in her work on the Royal Commission on the Poor Laws, when she was suddenly able to reconceptualize illness as a public nuisance to be suppressed in the interests of the community.

Such flashes of insight arose in the first instance from an effort to rethink the research questions, even though she later deplored the idea of starting an investigation with questions because these inevitably would be loaded with assumptions arising from personal prejudices or political ideas.[104] Beatrice was particularly derogatory about the way philanthropists selected facts for their most sensational impact. She remarked dryly about her paper on tailoring that it 'will be too matter-of-fact for the taste of the public – too much of a study of economic life and not sufficiently flavoured with philanthropy'.[105] Beatrice's rejection of the part played by research questions as opposed to hypotheses was bound up with her determination to reject Spencer's tendency to 'palm off illustrations as data' and to transcribe biological laws into the terms of social facts and then to reason from them as social laws.[106] Her well-founded criticism of Spencer's methods is dotted throughout her autobiography; it made her determined to develop more rigorous methodology. Unfortunately, Beatrice remained seemingly ignorant and increasingly neglectful, in the name of social science, of the main sources of her own originality.

After her marriage Beatrice was confirmed in her belief that the scientific practice of social investigation would be a step towards the development of a fully-fledged science of society. This grand aim required meticulous attention to the scientific method, described by Beatrice as the collection of all the facts, conjecture as to the cause and effect and verification by renewed observation of the material. But as many critics have noted, in the end the relationship between the Webbs' central beliefs about the ideal structure of a social democracy and their data remained unacknowledged and untested.[107] Increasingly they insisted that the solution to the problem of bias lay in the collection of *all* the facts, a herculean task. Not surprisingly, they relied extensively on research assistants, the first of whom, Frank Wallis Galton, was hired in 1892 at the salary of £100 a year, which to his disgust was not increased during his six years with them.[108] They defied any attempt to establish which facts might be relevant out of a conviction that patterns would emerge from them; that they would speak for themselves. But this in turn increasingly stifled Beatrice's capacity for lateral thought which depended not so much on the magpie approach to researching social problems as on her capacity, developed during the late 1880s, imaginatively to synthesize the crucial elements of a problem and then to turn the result through various angles for analysis.

The second source of Beatrice's originality derived from the inspiration provided by the mixture of research methods she used. During the period of her transition to the role of social investigator in the mid- and late 1880s, she showed less obsession with the neutral acquisition of facts from which 'truth' would emerge and a greater commitment to building up a picture of the social problem that incorporated the views of all the major actors. During this period Beatrice conducted a lively debate in her diary over the appropriate mix of research tools and ways of deciding the scope of a particular study. Working for Booth on dock labour, she recorded that 'the difficulty lies in keeping off by-ways, mastering the *leading facts* thoroughly and not attempting to study all the excrescences'.[109] Similarly at the beginning of her study of cooperation, she declared that she had not yet decided what sort of facts she was looking for. During this phase of her work as a social investigator, Beatrice tended to feel her way into a subject. In regard to her study of cooperation, she remarked that the facts provided her with a 'bunch of keys', in terms of important events, societies, technical terms and personalities, which she could then use to gain the confidence of interviewees and thereby move the research onto another plane.[110] Documentary facts at this point were reviewed more for their contribution to the whole. Later they came to occupy pride of place in the process of data collection.

During her work with Booth, Beatrice was especially aware of the choice to be made between the collection of statistical material, whether from census data or by interview, and the qualitative data produced by social observation. Beatrice's position, which she began to work out in her paper on social diagnosis and elaborated in an unpublished paper in 1887 on 'Personal Observation and Statistical Enquiry', held that investigators should 'know and realise distinguishing qualities and peculiar conditions' before they could enumerate the people possessing those qualities or living in those conditions.[111] Crucially, both methods were necessary for the construction of social facts. To establish a finding as a social fact, the investigator had to show those qualities to be characteristic of enough people. (Beatrice was impressed by the potential of Booth's method of 'wholesale interviews' for eliminating bias and for serving this purpose of verification.)[112]

The idea that social facts were the product of more than one research method was important. In particular, personal observation was crucial to Beatrice's success as a social investigator. As early as 1883, she recorded in her diary that 'it would be amusing to make studies of human beings with the same care I bestowed on imitating bits of rock, stick and root'.[113] Her delight in first-hand observation, particularly when it involved disguise as in her investigation of the tailoring trade, is obvious from the pages of her diary in the late 1880s. As Nord has remarked, it allowed for a dramatic and sympathetic identification with the people she observed.[114]

Interviewing provided a similar, although not quite so relished, method of obtaining information. In 1887, Beatrice provided an early demonstration of her understanding of this particular method. Accompanying Booth to interview a factory inspector, she reflected that they had gained little information because Booth had failed to show sufficient sympathy with the man's wounded vanity: 'Although I was sorry I had not been alone with him; I should have managed him better, with softer and less direct treatment', a skill, as she was later to recognize (and hence to deprecate), that was also found more often in women than in men.[115] A few years later she was to comment in a similar fashion on her skill as an interviewer when compared to Sidney's awkwardness.[116] On the Royal Commission on the Poor Laws, her interviewing skills received public recognition,[117] but by that time she was more intent on using them to political effect. She confessed that interviewing as a means to gaining information had lost all its charm.[118]

Very early on Beatrice noted that if she had followed her taste and temperament she would have become 'not a worker in the field of sociology, but a descriptive psychologist', using either the novel or scientific observation. She recognized that what roused and absorbed her curiosity were 'men and women, regarded – if I may use an old-fashioned word – as "souls" '[119] This inclination towards psychology was shared by Helen Bosanquet, who turned to the work of psychologists to provide an explanatory framework for the human perceptions that she regarded as being the key to the development of character. However, Beatrice was by no means sure that it was possible for the investigator to observe mental characteristics that he/she did not possess and she found herself turned off psychological texts by the apparently arbitrary definition of mind in the abstract. She felt that 'both observation and the power of correct reasoning from certain data, are best trained where the connection between cause and effect is more directly cognisable than where this is left to the imagination'.[120] Nevertheless, Ella Pycroft for one was astute enough to realize the crucial role played by personal observation in the development of Beatrice's ideas. In 1886, she wrote apropos of the publication of Beatrice's first article:

> you are very different [from me] and can go on very well for a time thinking out generalisations from your own, or other people's observations – only it will be well for you to make a few fresh observations now and then, or you will be taking your own theories as facts to start from again.[121]

The last part was to exaggerate the case but certainly, after her marriage, Beatrice tended to confine herself more and more to documentary research and to lose her imaginative and sympathetic grip on the whole.

Booth agreed with Beatrice that social investigation was not a matter of making a choice between qualitative and quantitative methods and suggested in a confused and long letter in 1886 that

> the statistical method was needed to give bearings to the result of personal observation or personal observation to give life to the statistics. It is to me not so much verification – the figures or the facts may be correct enough in themselves – but they mislead from want of due proportion and from lack of colour – but it is very difficult as you say to state this – to make it neat and complete enough.[122]

He nevertheless went on to state his aim to be the construction of a large statistical framework, 'built to receive accumulations of facts out of which at last is evolved the theory and law and the basis of more intelligent action'. In the end Beatrice declared his approach to produce only a static snapshot which failed to reveal causality: 'the actual processes of birth, growth, decay and death'. Nevertheless, it provided clues through the 'affiliations and concomitants [correlations]', for example, between poverty and poor sanitation or infant mortality.[123] Here, as with her study of cooperation, Beatrice seemed to show a more realistic awareness of the limitations of method than she did in the later, historically-based studies she carried out with Sidney, where it seemed that she expected cause and effect to emerge automatically.

Beatrice came to believe that it was the qualitative methods of observation and more particularly the use of documents that enabled the investigator to study process, while the statistical method served to check the observations. In fact, the Webbs came to rely almost exclusively on charting the development of institutions and despite Beatrice's criticism of Spencer's confusion of induction and deduction, and of process and ends, her understanding of process was derived almost entirely from Spencerian evolutionary ideas and therefore involved implicit notions of progress.[124] On Spencer's death, Beatrice acknowledged the influence he had had on her thinking and methods:

> He taught me to look on all social institutions exactly as if they were plants or animals – things that would be observed, classified and explained and the action of which could to some extent be foretold if one knew enough about them . . . The importance of functional adaptation was at the basis of a good deal of faith in collective regulation [I] afterwards developed.[125]

For Beatrice, the terms historical, evolutionary, kinetic, and comparative methods were interchangeable. However, in comparison with her audience of sociologists in 1906 which, like Spencer, saw no problem in ascertaining 'laws of development' which would enable them 'to see in a general way the future course of history',[126] Beatrice's understanding was advanced and her claims modest. But in concentrating after the 1880s on the study of the life history of institutions, she became not only more limited in her choice of research methods and more rigid in her conception of methodology, particularly in terms of the importance she attached to the accumulation and shuffling of facts, but also more narrow in her approach. In 1887 she advocated the study of social institutions in order to arrive at a more accurate understanding of social processes, citing her investigations of dock and sweated labour. But the evolutionary approach to the Webbs' study of trade unions in the 1890s, for example, was more narrowly administrative and tended, as Marshall has observed, to be divorced from consideration of the wider social, economic and political fabric.[127] When Beatrice ceased to observe, she also seemed to lose sight of the actors and to become absorbed only in the workings of machinery.

There is no doubt but that Beatrice followed Sidney's lead in giving priority to the written record, in large measure because she had so little faith in women's capacities. She repeatedly acknowledged Sidney's superior ability to deal with written documents. She claimed the 'craft' of observation and interviewing as her own but immediately proceeded to devalue her expertise. In the Preface to *Industrial Democracy*, the Webbs (most probably Beatrice) reviewed their methods, reiterating the importance of documentary evidence and suggesting that women were particularly good at 'passive observation'.[128] Beatrice continued to believe that woman's spirituality left 'her consciousness more the prey of irresponsible undirected ideas'.[129] Observation and the interview were in her view 'womanish' because they were more open to subjective interpretation and therefore inferior. In a talk she gave for the BBC in 1929 on methods, she said: 'I have been wondering whether any historian has listened to my talks on observation and explanation, and on the interview. "Just like a woman" I can hear him explain to his wife, "just like a woman to think that running about, looking at things, and gossiping about them with other people is *research* or anything approaching *research*" '. She went on to say that while her imaginary historian was wrong to deny any place to observation and interview, he was right to stress the overwhelming importance of documentary evidence.[130] This conclusion had as much to do with the sexual division of the work as with her view about the importance of objectivity.

Analysis
Beatrice was even less clear about what principles to appeal to in the early steps towards a more analytical approach to social problems than she was about methods. Puzzling over the problem of drunkenness in Katherine Buildings in 1885, she was tempted to think state prohibition the only solution. But thinking about state education the same year, she condemned legislation for asserting 'that the poor owing to a lack of right instinct and right judgement are incapable of being dutiful, only capable of obedience to the sense of duty of a superior class'.[131] Such a defence of working-class independence of character could have been penned by Helen Bosanquet, but was usually reserved by Beatrice during this period for the respectable poor, such as the cooperators of Bacup. In her first article, 'A Lady's View of the Unemployed', which was published in 1886, she described her point of view as one of a rent collector in a block of flats close to the docks, having 'the lowest class of working poor' (a description which was reported by Ella Pycroft to have outraged many of the tenants when she brought the article to their attention).[132] In her analysis of the causes of increased unemployment, Beatrice noted the movement of the docks downriver and the changing structure of occupations in the capital, but gave priority to the drift of unskilled labour into the city, attracted by the low amusements of city life. She followed this with a warning against the provision of public

works which would only encourage more in-migration.[133] When Chamberlain wrote asking her further to explain her opposition to public works, she added that her objections were based solely on the conviction that the conditions to which the state labourer would be subjected would prove hopelessly demoralizing.[134] Such a view was very similar to the one taken by the COS more generally. Ella Pycroft reported that the 'better class' of men in Katherine Buildings agreed that if they accepted unskilled labouring work under the auspices of a public-works programme they would sink permanently into the ranks of the unskilled.[135]

In 1886 Beatrice had apparently not reached the point where social observation led her to conclusions that differed significantly from those of scientific charity. Indeed her instincts were probably similar to those of Ella Pycroft who, for all her tender-hearted devotion to her tenants, wrote some six months later:

> I am coming to see more and more that it is useless to try and help the helpless, that the truly kind thing is to let the weak go to the wall and get out of the strong people's way as fast as possible. And yet in individual cases it is so hard to act up to one's knowledge . . . I wonder if in the next generation people will be strong enough to crush their compassionate feelings and act wisely.[136]

Early social workers could not avoid the way in which the ideas of scientific charity as to the proper treatment of their clients impinged on their relationship with them. It was, as both Ella Pycroft and Beatrice Webb had already observed, very difficult to be cruel to someone in order to be kind, and all in the spirit of friendship.

Beatrice was not alone in endeavouring to address such problems at a more abstract level. By 1886 Samuel Barnett also came to condemn COS practice as 'not always inquiring into the causes of a family's poverty in Christ's spirit of tenderness'.[137] He wrote to Beatrice after the publication of 'A Lady's View of the Unemployed', stating his commitment to the COS view about the pauperizing dangers of doles. But he also had more radical ideas than Beatrice on the causes of distress, which he believed to be primarily ill-health and inequality. By 1888 Barnett wanted the 'best things', libraries, parks and baths, made free, for the poor could 'not pay for the pleasure which satisfies and without which the people perish'.[138] In her later comments on Barnett's break away from strict COS philosophy, Beatrice noted that he was no reasoner or scientific observer, and that he was still working on the Octavia Hill basis of what constituted right action.[139] She was probably correct. Barnett never developed a coherent theoretical position in respect to the issue of poverty and well into the 1890s his thought contained contradictory elements. Nevertheless, by the late 1880s the incompatibility at the one-to-one level of a loving charity with the denial of material assistance had driven him towards more radical solutions to the increasing problem of poverty.[140]

At the time of the publication of her second article on dock labour in 1887, Beatrice was still emphasizing the character of the labour force as a primary cause of casual work and underemployment, but no longer focusing on the individual as the key to any solution. While recognizing that the irregularity of the wage made thrifty household management impossible for the casually employed, she characterized the men who became casuals as 'loafers' with a 'constitutional hatred of regularity', for whom the docks were but a gigantic form of outdoor relief. Her characterization of the problems of dock labour as 'the difficulty of living by regular work and the ease of living without it' was again in line with COS thinking. Recording in her diary a walk along the docks, Beatrice described a mass of 'loafers . . . bestial content or hopeless discontent on their faces', smoking and gambling, 'the lowest form of leisure'.[141] Such men were not only economically worthless but morally worse than worthless, for they dragged any who came to live among them down to their own low level. Beatrice's solution was true to the COS in that she was firmly set against any kind of doles that would give encouragement to an 'irregular' existence, and yet was antithetical to COS principles in that she also recommended state organization of dock work.

Not until her article on sweated labour, also prepared for Booth and published in 1890, did Beatrice achieve an analysis of causes that depended on more than individual character. As in her investigation of dock labour, she relied heavily on interview data, but also employed the method of observation while in disguise, something she had first tried out on her visits to Bacup. Just as she had achieved a powerful understanding of the moral underpinnings of the world of the Lancashire mill operatives by this method, so she also managed to analyse what she came to call the 'sweating system' incorporating the trouser hands' point of view.

Her visits to Bacup had already convinced her of the beneficial effects of factory legislation:

> It is here that one sees the benefits of the Factory Acts and consequent inspection. *Laissez-faire* breaks down when one watches these things from the inside. The individual worker cannot refuse to work overtime – if he does he loses his employment. Neither does he always *wish* to refuse – for many are ignorant of the meaning of constant strain in future life.[142]

First-hand observation of the tailoring trade pushed Beatrice's analysis of sweating beyond the knowledge of both her informants on the conditions of sweated workers, including low wages, excessive hours and insanitary conditions (which definition was accepted by the House of Lord's Committee on the subject),[143] and the sweated workers themselves, who talked in terms of the evils of middlemen, machinery, the subdivision of labour and foreign immigration. In her analysis the sweater was not a middleman but rather the whole nation. In effect she used the perceptions of all the actors to understand sweating as the product of bad conditions, the absence of responsible employers and of unskilled workers with a low standard of life. Unlike her first piece on the unemployed, the personal characteristics of the immigrant to the city passed into insignificance, while the 'low standard of life' of the sweated worker, usually a woman, became but one of many variables. Beatrice concluded that public opinion was not ripe for the logical solution to the problem, municipal workshops, but that it was possible to act to improve the conditions characterizing sweated labour, initially by extending factory inspection to workshops and later by also campaigning for a minimum wage for the sweated trades.[144]

In some key respects the nature of Beatrice's analysis and the language she used in her arguments remained in tune with that of philanthropists, social investigators and equalitarian feminists. Beatrice was congratulated by the conservative Mary Ward on her work to extend the Factory Acts, even though the latter believed that such legislation would promote greater individual freedom rather than collectivism.[145] Beatrice also cooperated with Louise Creighton and Helen Bosanquet in writing an article published in 1897 on the importance of extending factory inspection to laundries.[146] But while all agreed on the importance of extending factory legislation, Beatrice parted company from her fellow progressives over her advocacy of a national minimum wage. The primary aim of all groups was to create a better quality and more efficient workforce. As Beatrice put it in 1896:

> Let us accede to the opponents of factory legislation that we must do nothing to impair or limit the growing sense of personal responsibility in women; that we must seek, in every way, to increase their economic independence, and their efficiency as workers and citizens, not less than as wives and mothers; and that the best and only real means of attaining these ends is the safeguarding and promoting of women's freedom.

However, it should be realized, she argued, that the freedom of the poor widow to work in her own bedroom 'all the hours that God made', or of the wife to supplement a drunken husband's wage by working at home were 'being purchased at the exclusion from regular factory employment of thousands of "independent women" '.[147] Given that the aim was the creation of an efficient labour force, Beatrice argued that the nailmaker working 16 or 17 hours a day could not hope 'to develop that high level of moral and intellectual character necessary to effective work and profitable leisure'.[148] Beatrice's intention in respect of sweated women workers was similar to that respecting casual dock labourers: to eliminate them.

Beatrice's sophisticated understanding of all the elements of the sweating system allowed her to dismiss crisply the arguments of those who opposed her while continuing to claim the high political ground associated with the aim of creating a more 'efficient citizenship' and industry, and of fostering 'the social forces which make for industrial righteousness', identified as regularity, self-control, trustworthiness and technical skill. In brief her main objection to sweating was 'that the quality of the effort deteriorates and ultimately the worker degrades as an instrument of production'.[149] Indeed, she failed to give adequate attention to the future position of the woman worker herself and here we can discern the beginnings of Beatrice's growing enthusiasm for administrative solutions, developed in this instance out of a real understanding of the position of the worker but without due considera-tion of the effects of reform on the recipient. Beatrice argued for state legislation in order to check the parasitism of the sweated trades. At stake was the efficiency of the workforce and the fact that genuinely independent trades in which workers did not work in sweated conditions were being undercut by those employing sweated labour.

Sweated trades were unfair competitors in Beatrice's analysis. Under minimum-wage legislation the least effective women workers, who might be incapable of earning the minimum wage, would have to go to the poor law. To that degree the costs of securing fair industrial competition and an efficient labour force were to be allowed to fall on the workers themselves. Feminists (including Helen Bosanquet) anxious to preserve the right of women to 'a fair field and no favour' in terms of their capacity to compete in the labour market called for education of workers, employers and consumers as the major solution to the problem of women's sweated work.[150] But Beatrice did not advocate measures designed to improve women's training and educa-tion, seeing in inspection and minimum-wage legislation all that was necessary to eliminate the problem. To Beatrice (and to Sidney), patterns of sexual segregation in the labour force which meant that women tended to end up in the lowest-paid, lowest-status work were largely a product of essential sexual difference;[151] she never demonstrated any awareness or understanding of the kind of obstacles women faced in the labour market. Furthermore, she continued to use arguments that appealed to the promotion of national efficiency when, during World War I, she advocated a specific form of equal pay for equal work: the setting of a uniform 'rate for the job'. She anticipated once again that such a measure would result in 'inefficient women' being expelled from the workforce.[152]

The tendency to seek administrative solutions to social problems was also evident in Beatrice's Minority Report to the Royal Commission on the Poor Laws. Beatrice and Sidney believed firmly that the answer to the problems of pauperism and unemployment addressed by the commission rested in breaking up the poor law. There is no evidence that they thought beyond this essentially administrative solution. Beatrice felt that her opponents were narrowly concerned with the issue of preventing pauperism while she was proposing a solution to the causes of destitution, but the Webbs' scheme presented a comprehensive solution only in terms of machinery. In this respect the 1909 Minority Report represented the first of many subsequent efforts to construct a technical fix. It exhibited the same touching faith in the idea that with the right administrative structure the actors would behave correctly that was the main feature of so much local-government and health-service reform in the post-World War II decades. In just the same way, Beatrice believed that discrimination against women in the workplace would disappear once the right measures, such as uniform occupational rates, were implemented. Leonard Woolf got it more or less right when he suggested that the Webbs thought that

> if the machinery of society was properly constructed and controlled efficiently by intelligent people, if the functions of the various parts of the organisation were scientifically determined and the structure scientifically adapted to the function . . . then we should get an adequately civilised society. . . .[153]

Beatrice's faith in administrative machinery ran precisely counter to Octavia Hill's contempt for it and also proved one of the fundamental sources of disagreement with Helen Bosanquet. Beatrice had no faith in the efficacy of personal social work and no time for the piecemeal nature of voluntary effort. In her view and in Sidney's, the voluntary work of the future had to be subordinated to the expert direction of a well-organized state bureaucracy. Beatrice's diary entries during the 1890s also made plain on a number of occasions her lack of faith in democratic institutions to achieve meaningful social reform: 'Personally I think more is to be done by administrative experiment on the one hand and educating the constituencies on the other than by entering into the political game carried on in Parliament'.[154] She was preoccupied by the problem of how to use democratic machinery but had little intrinsic regard for it, which in part explains both her lack of interest in women's suffrage (even after she had withdrawn her formal opposition to it) and her relative indifference to Sidney's inter-war parliamentary career.

Beatrice had great admiration for the respectable working class but little regard for 'the average sensual man' and the ill-informed voter.[155] Indeed, the Minority Report exhibited remarkably little regard for the poor themselves. Putting the case of the minority, Beatrice defended the report as a rational document acceptable to all-party opinion:

> The Minority scheme is not Socialistic, however, in the sense in which Socialism is usually interpreted; that is, it does not involve or even lead to the nationalisation of production, distribution and exchange. On the contrary, it is just as applicable and just as necessary to an individualist as to a Socialist State – it is a sort of mains drainage system.

Apart from confirming that the report had little in the way of any theoretical underpinnings, Beatrice's use of the drainage metaphor was telling. In the same article she wrote of the unemployed in a similar way: 'The only way of dealing with this problem is to drain off any surplus'.[156] In her autobiography, she had recorded critically that her earliest recollection of any reference to the position of labour was her father's reference to workers as an abstraction, 'like water'.[157] In her work of social investigation in the late 1880s, Beatrice moved right away from such a conception that was at once unsympathetic and in danger of misjudging the situation through lack of any rigorous appraisal of it. But by the time of the Minority Report, her position was different. Lack of social observation and, at best, hurried analysis of documentary material resulted in a grand scheme that showed little commitment to the poor themselves and in which Beatrice's old contempt for the residuum shone through in the draconian proposals that she and Sidney believed were necessary in order to force recalcitrant labour into a useful life.

Beatrice remained preoccupied with the problem of unconditionality in social security systems throughout the inter-war period. Finishing the chapter on the Royal Commission on the Poor Laws for the Webbs' *History of the Poor Law* in 1927, she expressed the problem as one of devising 'some treatment of the unemployed which will be "less eligible" than wage labour without being blatantly inequitable to the men and their families who are out of work through no fault of their own'.[158] She remained convinced that the maintenance of the able-bodied in idleness was an 'ultra dangerous business' and in her 1931 evidence to the Royal Commission on Unemployment she advocated a programme not dissimilar to modern workfare schemes in the USA, whereby the recipient of a subsistence allowance should place his working time at the disposal of a Ministry of Employment.[159]

Identity: social investigation versus marriage

Beatrice met Sidney Webb in 1890 when she was still working on her study of the cooperative movement. The story of the courtship between the lower-middle-class, unprepossessing Fabian socialist and the wealthy, beautiful Beatrice Potter is well known. Within the relationship the balance of power was tipped in favour of Beatrice whose desire for Sidney was distinctly less strong than his for her, and whose independent income provided her with considerable autonomy. Bella Fisher was more sympathetic to the marriage than many of Beatrice's friends but worried about the fact that Beatrice rather than Sidney 'would be the leader' when in her view Beatrice needed a steadying and strong partner.[160] However, the nature of the imbalance in the relationship was crucial in view of the risks Beatrice took in deciding to marry Sidney.

Beatrice derived pride, sense of purpose and identity from her work as a social investigator. Yet she continued to fear that female inferiority would tell against her in her endeavours and she believed women were happier if married. Only a year before meeting Sidney, Beatrice had written in her diary of the unhappy late marriage of her friend Carey Darling and recorded her own heartfelt reactions: 'God preserve me from a lover between 35 and 45: no woman can resist a man's importunity during the last years of her unrealised womanhood. That to me is the moral of Carey's story'.[161] Sidney proved his worth in the two years before their marriage in 1892 by greatly assisting her work. Yet she worried that marriage might erode her painfully constructed identity as an investigator. She also risked losing support from her other friends, for example Herbert Spencer and Mary Booth, as well as from her family, who did not approve of the marriage. Beatrice struggled to achieve the kind of *modus vivendi* that would justify marriage in such circumstances. From the first, she spoke of the importance of seeing marriage as a duty and a means by which they might both make a bigger contribution to society than would have been the case had they remained single. On the whole, her hopes were justified. The Webb partnership was remarkably productive and viewed as a model by many contemporaries, the Coles perhaps coming closest to emulating it. But the tensions perceived by Beatrice at the beginning remained a ready source of anxiety that not infrequently bubbled to the surface. Beatrice also had to come to terms with the fact that while her feelings for Sidney were deeply affectionate and their relationship was often playful, it bore no comparison to the sexual desire she had felt for Chamberlain. Nor did Sidney share her more spiritual approach, which strengthened as she got older, to the larger problems of human existence.

As early as 1884, Margaret Harkness wrote to Beatrice remarking that she wished Beatrice would marry so 'as to satisfy first your ambition, secondly your affections, for so I read your necessity'.[162] The judgement was a shrewd one and predicted effectively the nature of Beatrice's marriage. During 1891, Beatrice argued with herself in her diary as to the pros and cons of marriage to Sidney. She recorded her fear that she would become absorbed in the details of domestic life:

> I do not despise these details, but it is no use forging a fine instrument with exceptional effort and then discarding it for a rough tool. It may have been misdirected effort to make the instrument – it may be a mistake to transform the Woman into a Thinker – but if the mistake has been paid for, one may hardly throw away the result.[163]

Beatrice's simultaneous faith in her own capacities and her belief in female inferiority were brought into even sharper relief by the prospect of her marriage. She felt strongly the need to defend and protect her identity as a social investigator, while at the same time wondering whether it was worth the effort.

Sidney assured her that he had no 'desire for possession' and that his greatest hope was to 'be as great an adjunct to your intellectual life as you are to my moral being'.[164] He added that he stood to gain doubly because he would also profit from her intellectual abilities, but he clearly valued Beatrice most for the way in which she nursed his ambitions and encouraged him to undertake work, most notably on the London County Council, that he lacked the confidence (as well as the income) to do by himself. Notwithstanding his oft-repeated and genuine commitment to furthering Beatrice's career as a social investigator, he saw no tension in also reflecting comfortably that Comte was surely right 'in making women the inspirers and guardians of morality'.[165] But Beatrice's insecurities were in part responsible for Sidney's views in this respect. Sidney's comments on Comte came in response to a letter from Beatrice in which she declared that she had nothing but 'moral maxims' to offer him.[166] Yet she made it clear that above all she sought Sidney's help in her work of social investigation. Early in the autumn of 1891, she was planning a study of trade unions, following on from her work on cooperation. But she was very anxious as to whether it was at all feasible to combine marriage and social research:

> To make a really good book of this [trade unions] I ought to spend much more than a year at the simple investigation. That is the simple truth. I ought first to get the official history of the unions. That will take perhaps a year. Then I ought to go and live among the miners and other operatives and observe them carefully and the place Unionism takes in their lives. How can I combine that with marriage in a year's time? Every now and then I feel I have got into a hole out of which I can't struggle. I love you but I love my work better! Unless I have my work I shall make a bad wife to you. You cannot follow me about the country and I cannot stay with you. How do you solve this problem?[167]

This was the critical issue for Beatrice, and if Sidney had not been both convincing and persistent in replying to it it is unlikely that the marriage would have taken place. As it was Sidney struck exactly the right note: 'You know, that I know, and I know that you know, that with each of us duty is imperative'.[168] Once Beatrice was convinced that they might accomplish more together than apart and that Sidney was ready 'to subordinate even our affection for each other to one single purpose to serve our people',[169] then the way was cleared. By October of 1891, Beatrice was 'much more confident that our marriage will not interfere with our work'.[170] But she warned Sidney that if the trade union book were not to be finished, she would never recover her confidence in married life.[171] She had rationalized marriage to a man she did not feel physically attracted to as a means of better accomplishing her work as a social investigator, which she believed to be a more meaningful form of social service than marriage. Ella Pycroft was shocked at Beatrice's approach to marriage, considering that it was far too calculating to be womanly. Beatrice explained to Sidney that Ella 'thought it horribly deliberate – to think of work as a cause, to think of anything but personal attraction in its best sense'.[172] But the compromise was one that Beatrice could live with. August 1892 found her reading Mary Ward's translation of the Swiss, Henri Frederic Amiel's *Journal Intime* (1882), as a means of relieving the preoccupations of the first days of married life.

Beatrice's fear of subordination within her marriage and her deep-seated belief in the inferiority of her intellect in comparison to Sidney's continued to perturb her throughout her married life. In tune with her failure either to recognize or to give herself credit for her particular strengths as an observer and interviewer, she feared that she tended to live in a world of persons rather than of ideas. She frequently worried as to whether she was not parasitic on Sidney, who could work longer hours than she; whose capacity to deal with documentary evidence was greater than hers; and who undertook most of the writing of their joint work, albeit only after Beatrice performed the crucial task of 'scheming out' the chapters.[173] (This picture of their way of working is confirmed by the observations of their first research assistant and secretary, Frank Wallis Galton, in his autobiography.)[174] Yet she clung firmly to her identity as a social investigator. Almost all the Webbs' joint work came out in both their names, which was important to Beatrice as she made clear when she explained in her diary how a short article on the policy of a 'national minimum' came to be signed by Sidney alone: 'I thought it better for Sidney to sign the article singly – the double signature overloads so slight a thing and it is too political in its tone to warrant the intervention of the female partner. I believe in mere "wife's politics" – only in research do I claim equality of recognition'.[175]

Beatrice did achieve recognition as a social investigator, as her appointment to the Royal Commission showed. On the whole, she managed to accomplish her goal of undertaking socially useful and publicly recognized work within a relationship that provided her with companionship and guarded her against isolation. Had she not married Sidney, Beatrice might have developed her particular talents as an investigator more fully but it is doubtful that she would have found as secure a base from which to examine subjects that interested her and which were dominated by men. Nevertheless, Beatrice certainly experienced periods of profound depression. In 1900–1901, she mourned the might-have-beens of her infatuation with Chamberlain, wondering whether she would have married the same man if her aim had been to have children and whether the books were worth the babies she might have had.[176] She applauded Sidney's simplicity and his apparent lack of a subconscious, but found no answering chord in him to match her own increasing preoccupation with the need for communion with a 'higher life'. Sidney felt her religious sensibilities to be neurotic.[177] These tensions, together with her ever-present fears as to her own abilities, must have been all the more intense because of Sidney's lack of emotional support other than Beatrice and because of their identity in public and among friends as a couple. Beatrice sacrificed one of her greatest friendships, with Mary Booth, when she married Sidney and she wrote often of the breaking of this friendship, which had supported her through the Chamberlain affair, through her years of nursing her father and looking after Rosie, and through her early efforts to write, as a 'great sorrow'.[178]

Even when she ceased to share interests in common with the friends who had supported her through her late girlhood and early womanhood she was reluctant to drop them; to drop a friend or be dropped 'degraded life'.[179] Beatrice often paused in her diary to take what amounted to an inventory of her acquaintances and friends, but these often merely reflected who was pro and who anti the Webbs.[180] Her sisters were important to her but, as she remarked on the eve of her marriage, they were absolutely ignorant of her life.[181] Her sister Kate, who had shared Beatrice's experience as a rent collector, bored Beatrice, who described her as a woman of 'great intelligence but no intellect'.[182] In 1934, she wrote that neither she nor Sidney desired emotional relationships and it seems that Beatrice did experience difficulty after her marriage in developing friendships of her own divorced from her persona as Sidney's wife.[183] This meant that the load carried by the marriage in terms of providing a focus for work and emotional support was huge.

Identity: private research versus public work

Beatrice wanted to use her marriage to consolidate her identity as a social investigator, which involved her in the essentially lonely and private work of research and writing. But after 1900 she was increasingly drawn into the public domain largely because of the Webbs' involvement with the LSE and the blossoming of their tactics of Fabian permeation, which involved increasing numbers of 'useful' dinners and more public speaking. Beatrice was very drawn to the world of political manipulation and to Society, but she worried that this sort of activity was less worthy a contribution than writing books and found it extremely exhausting. She also experienced considerable difficulty in knowing how to behave in the public world beyond the dinner party. Her experience as a member of the Royal Commission on the Poor Laws was a particularly sobering experience in this regard. During the four-year period of the commission's work (from 1905–1909) Beatrice and Sidney switched roles, with Beatrice playing the more public part. Both were active in the propaganda campaign following the publication of the commission's reports, and this Beatrice rather relished. But her relationship to public work was always ambivalent because of first, guilt that it did not represent the proper course of duty, second, her inability to handle particular kinds of public work, especially committee work, and third, the difficulties it posed in her relationship with Sidney. Beatrice was seemingly happiest when both she and Sidney were working on their books in the country. She profoundly disliked the years Sidney spent as an MP, in part because of the role of political wife she felt obliged to play out of a wifely sense of duty, and possibly in part also out of unacknowledged jealousy. Beatrice's attitute to the public world of work and citizenship was complicated. She was fascinated by it but, as a woman, found it very difficult to manage.

During the 1890s Beatrice researched the trade union movement and fought shy of public work. At the outset of her marriage she anticipated that 'our life will be – or rather my life will be that of a recluse, with Sidney as an open window onto the world'.[184] In large measure this was not so inaccurate a picture of her life during this period, notwithstanding her frequent research trips and long hours in the British Library. In particular she experienced considerable difficulty speaking in public, although at least one working-class woman recorded in her diary that she had been quite charmed by the 'winsome, sweet-faced' Beatrice on a public platform.[185] In 1888 she had referred to her appearance in front of the House of Lords Committee on Sweating as 'disagreeable'; the year before she had refused to speak at a meeting of dock labourers; and on another occasion wrote of being 'induced to speak [at Toynbee Hall] in spite of my dreadful nervousness'.[186] In typical style she added, 'I *must* conquer it'. However, her ambivalence about the extent to which women could or should play a public role also played a major part in fuelling her anxieties about taking the platform. Recording her admiration for Annie Besant as an orator, she added: 'But to *see* her speaking made me shudder. It is not womanly, to thrust yourself before the world. A woman, in all relations, should be sought'.[187] In 1891, she was horrified to find out that her name had been mentioned as a possible member of the Royal Commission on Labour. Furthermore, as she confessed to Edward Pease, Sidney also had a 'decided objection to seeing women speak in public',[188] although she may have merely been invoking Sidney to legitimize her own feelings. Certainly, in 1890, Sidney had expressed a wish that she would take part in the women's movement in politics.[189]

Beatrice channelled her ambitions for a public presence into Sidney, planning first his entry onto the London County Council and repeatedly assessing his strengths and possible career moves. In 1894, she decided that while he had not the personality for real 'direction' or 'mediation', his intelligence and lack of vanity rendered 'him an admirable instrument' and she set herself the task of finding him material to work upon.[190] In 1903, she recorded that Charles Booth's public standing was 'the sort of thing I aim at for Sidney'.[191] In fact, Sidney achieved much more and possibly a greater public exposure than Beatrice really cared for. Beatrice's plans to live vicariously through Sidney's career were not dissimilar to the role she would have had as Chamberlain's wife, except of course she was able to conjure with making something of Sidney – Chamberlain was already made – and with Sidney she could share the private work of writing and research. Beatrice frequently referred to her happiness when they were closeted in a country house reading and writing, protected from the world of the LCC and, later, the LSE and Parliamentary politics: 'It is so much pleasanter to investigate and write rather than organize and speak. Just now our life is so perfect: it might easily become strained and dissipated in mere manipulation'.[192]

The work of 'mere manipulation' increased rapidly after 1900. As Beatrice remarked, they were 'drifting up the social scale' as their (particularly Beatrice's) friendship with the Balfours showed, and in 1903, after dinner at the Asquiths, she confided to her diary that they were regarded as people with 'a special kind of chic'.[193] In 1905, unlike 1891, Beatrice welcomed the chance to join the Royal Commission on the Poor Laws. The commission brought Beatrice into the public arena for the first time since her appearance before the House of Lords Committee on Sweating in 1888. On that occasion she had suffered considerable anxiety not least because in the heat of the moment she had exaggerated the number of hours she had spent working as a trouser hand in a sweatshop and had subsequently had to alter her evidence. In her autobiography she commented: 'The Other One [Sidney] tells me that I might have put the correction in a footnote, but how was I to know that?'[194] The tone of angry frustration was genuine enough. It was very difficult for any woman to know the rules of behaviour governing a public forum.

The Royal Commission was to prove another extremely trying venture into the public sphere. Beatrice was unsure as to how to conduct herself and fell back with relentless vigour on her identity as an expert in social investigation. In this regard she felt superior to her fellow commissioners. Before the commission had even met she announced in her diary her plan to concentrate on three aspects of the poor law – the poor law and sweated trades, the workings of the boards of guardians and the policy of the central authority – leaving the rest to the other commissioners. A few months into the commission's work she again listed her own priorities, noting that she intended both to try and set the commission's agenda and to superintend the work on the issues closest to her heart. Early in 1906, declaring that she alone was interested in doing proper social investigation, she hired three assistants with her own money and set them to work on projects she considered appropriate.[195]

In fact, Beatrice completely mishandled the commission, in large measure because she continued to experience genuine difficulty in finding a suitable way to behave on it. To her fellow commissioners, she must have appeared arrogant and high-handed. Commenting on the lack of an agenda at the beginning of the commission's proceedings, Beatrice recorded that she had told them: ' "I don't want to make myself disagreeable", I ventured to add. It is extraordinarily unpleasant for a woman to do so in a Commission of men'.[196] She was not of course sitting on a 'Commission of men'; she merely failed to acknowledge her fellow women commissioners. Octavia Hill and Helen Bosanquet seemed to be invisible to her. The only time she referred at length to the latter in her diary was when Helen caused her some embarrassment by asking her to produce the correspondence she had conducted privately with medical officers of health as a means to formulating her policy on medical relief:

> A brilliant idea struck Mrs Bosanquet: why not ask Mrs Webb for her 'correspondence with medical officers of health' upon which she has manifestly based her report on the medical services. Can we not extract something from this correspondence which will discredit her? . . . Probably we shall find the MOHs [sic] were not predominantly in favour of the transfer [of poor law medical relief to the local authorities], thought the little woman.[197]

Beatrice's fellow commissioners were always described as little when Beatrice was displeased with them.

In part Beatrice was convinced of her own superiority and ability to manipulate the situation as if it were a dinner party, but in part she was self-confessedly unsure as to how to proceed. Early on she hit upon truculence as a possible way of securing the advantage: 'If one begins by being disagreeable, one may come in the end to a better bargain', although she confessed that it was a new experience to her to have to make herself disagreeable in order to gain her ends. In private life she was used to getting her way by being 'unusually pleasant'.[198] At the end of the commission's life, part of her was still convinced that she had outshone her fellow commissioners: 'If I ever sit again on a Royal Commission I hope my colleagues will be of a superior calibre – for really it is shockingly bad for one's character to be with such folk – it makes me feel intolerably superior'.[199]

Yet she was also often aware that she was hitting the wrong note. Early on she wrote that it would need all her 'self-command to keep myself from developing a foolish hostility and becoming *self-conscious* in my desire to get sound investigation'.[200] Nor was it just that she found herself failing to hit the right note in terms of presenting her argument. She quite literally did not know how to act on a committee. In part her high-handedness stemmed from an effort to behave as men did. Early in 1907 she recorded how she was trying to watch her fellow commissioners 'calmly' and to 'calculate' how much aggravation they would stand from her:

> With Sidney this attitude of indifference to his colleagues on public bodies is habitual – perhaps I am merely becoming masculine – losing the 'personal note' which is the characteristic of the woman in human intercourse. What is rather disconcerting is that I catch myself 'playing the personal note' when it suits my purpose – playing it without feeling it. Is that a characteristic of the woman on public bodies?[201]

Her difficulty in deciding whether to be impersonal, and if so how to achieve it, will be familiar to many women members of predominantly male committees today.

Beatrice had never been inclined to keep her counsel in the 'womanly' way of an Octavia Hill or a Helen Bosanquet. In 1906, she recorded that she found it extremely difficult to maintain 'a dignified silence': 'Ah! How hard it is for the quick-witted and somewhat vain woman to be discreet and accurate'.[202] Beatrice was often shrewd in perceiving the nature of her difficulties, but from an early stage she had been incapable of quelling her desire to shine in any particular situation. On the commission, however, she did not have a thick enough skin to deal with the hostility that she provoked by either her jaunty arrogance or truculence. She relished the excitement of the political gamesmanship played on the commission, retiring sick in 1907 with insomnia and indigestion when the intrigue got too much for her and when she had become literally exhausted by it. For she tended to try and manipulate matters outside the formal meetings of the commission in the only way she knew how and, as a woman, the only way open to her – she invited endless people to dinner. This was an additional reason for her collapse in 1907: 'my inveterate social instincts always mean that I lavish entertainment on my companions. I don't simply do my work'.[203]

Despite her attempts to manipulate the commission, Beatrice could not have misread the situation more badly. In late 1907, she was optimistic that as many as five commissioners might come down on her side. In early 1908, she was indeed puzzled by the apparent lack of activity on the part of her opponents, but read it as their incapacity to come to conclusions.[204] While she was right in her assessment of the incapacity and the indecision of many of her opponents, there is something pathetic about her account of the way in which she bullied the commission, bombarding it with memoranda, when it seems that she never fully understood the key role being played by Helen Bosanquet, in particular in the writing of the Majority Report.[205]

Beatrice and Sidney were determined from the end of 1907 to produce a separate report 'in the grandest style', in which they would present a comprehensive blueprint for reform. This made Beatrice a yet more difficult colleague on the commission and additionally blind to the purposes of her opponents. Sidney attributed the unity of opposition to Beatrice to the fact that the production of Beatrice's scheme for her own report (in December 1907) had driven them to drop their differences and unite behind 'a blurred outline'.[206] While there may be considerable truth in the idea of the majority achieving unity on the basis of opposition, this view, like Beatrice's own, attached too much importance to Beatrice. The work of the majority, while often diffuse, did rest on certain well-defined principles.

Beatrice enjoyed much more the propaganda campaign that followed the publication of the reports:

> Since we took up this propaganda we have had a straightforward job, with no problems of conduct, but with a great variety of active work . . . which absorbs all one's time without any severe strain on one's nerves. I enjoy it because I have the gift of personal intercourse and it is a gift I have never until now made full use of. I genuinely *like* my fellow mortals . . . I like to interest them, and inspire them, and even to order them, in a motherly sort of way. Also I enjoy leadership.[207]

The last comment was an honest one. In the campaign to promote the Minority Report, Beatrice, with Sidney at her side, was able to overcome her fear of public meetings and to orchestrate matters to suit herself, using the talents she had as a communicator to their best advantage. As usual, she experienced twinges of guilt as to whether the work of propaganda was as 'socially useful' as that of research.

After her work in connection with the Royal Commission on the Poor Laws, Beatrice was able to deal much more effectively with the numerous war-time committees she was appointed to: the Statutory Committee on Pensions in 1916, the Ministry of Reconstruction's Committee on the Machinery of Government in 1917 and the Women in Industry Committee in 1918. In the case of the last, she admitted that she found its subject-matter essentially boring, but perhaps because of this she was much more relaxed in regard to her behaviour on it while at the same time producing an effective Minority Report in which she refuted the assumption of the majority that paid employment was normally performed only by men. She suggested a formula for securing equal pay, albeit that she did not believe such a claim to be relevant to the majority of working women, because of the degree of sexual segregation in the labour market.[208]

In common with Helen Bosanquet and Mary Ward, Beatrice reacted strongly to the devastation of World War I, suffering another major depression in 1917. At the end of 1918, she decided to give up all her committee work in favour of research, some advisory work for Labour Party committees and typing up her diary. Her heart was only in the last of these and she wrote bitterly of the drudgery of social research:

> For long years I have contained my intellect, forced it to concentrate on one subject matter after another; in some of the dullest and least illuminating details of social organisation. I recall for instance the weeks of grinding toil spent on disentangling the various methods of recovering the cost of public maintenance from different classes of recipients of relief and their relatives. I vividly remember the nausea, with which, day after day I went on with this task. But I accomplished it. I think I am losing this power of grappling with new material, in any case I have lost all inclination to do it.[209]

This was Beatrice's most revealing and explosive outburst against the way in which her methods of social investigation had focused ever more narrowly on written documents in her work with Sidney on the evolution of social institutions. By 1919, she had somewhat recovered her faith, brooding 'in the old way' about the poor law material, but her attention remained firmly fixed on private work and most firmly of all on the writing of her autobiography.[210]

In part she retreated into the autobiography to escape the large issues of death and the meaning of life, raised by the war, which haunted her but which Sidney ignored. She repeatedly confessed herself pessimistic about everything, about capitalist profit-making, 'anarchy' abroad, the falling birth rate, the nationalist debates and, not least, the prospect that one of them might die soon.[211] In 1924 she felt great affinity to E. M. Forster's character in *A Passage to India*, Mrs Moore, and described herself as 'standing on a bare and bleak watershed of thought and feeling'.[212] In part also she gratefully retreated to her diary and autobiography when Sidney entered Parliament. In her diary she noted that she was responsible for encouraging him to stand but dreaded the disturbance to her daily routine and admitted that she could take little interest in his parliamentary career beyond what was required of wifely duty. Apart from anything else she now detested playing second fiddle, speaking as the candidate's wife to please the audience rather than presenting her own opinions.[213] When Sidney was elevated to the peerage in 1929, she refused to take the title of Lady Passfield, commenting that Sidney's obligations did not extend to his wife. She accounted for her decision in a perfectly rational manner: she objected to a House of Lords and her rejection of the title would make it a little harder for the Labour men 'to succumb to the temptation'.[214] But the gesture was interpreted by the press, not without some justice, as an assertion of personal identity, and indeed Beatrice ended up turning what had been a decision to eschew the public world of the peerage into an equally public personal campaign.

During the 1920s her main hope and source of identity was her autobiography, which an LSE professor referred to as her 'little book', but which she felt secretly was a 'big book in its high endeavour to explain my craft and my creed'.[215] Sidney, she admitted, did 'not quite like it', feeling it to be 'far too subjective, and at base the sentimental scribblings of a woman'.[216] As usual, Beatrice veered between great hopes and no hope for it. In retrospect she recognized that it was the 'personal element so long denied in her research work between 1892 and the end of World War I that gained me the prestige' and put her in great demand for BBC radio talks during the 1930s.[217] While her inclination was to pursue her own writing, she by no means turned her back on social investigation. In 1926, she noted that while research did not provide a livelihood 'what it does provide is a meaning to one's life'.[218] In 1928, at the age of seventy, with her right ear buzzing and suffering from symptoms of exhaustion, she was travelling across the country collecting documentary material for the Webbs' volumes on the poor law. But there is a sense in her diaries that such work seemed increasingly removed from the big social, political and spiritual questions that continued to haunt her throughout the 1930s and which she decided could best be answered by the model offered by the Soviet Union. Yet while writing a 'What I Believe' piece for the *Nation* in 1930, she once more exhibited all her old fears about relying on methods she considered to be subjective and of the way in which they might effectively dilute objective judgement based on facts derived from documentary evidence.[219]

Relationships between men and women

Beatrice never developed any real sympathy with the ambitions of feminists and was never very interested in their proposals for improving the position of women. Very early on she was shrewd enough to see a campaign for the endowment of motherhood as an attractive alternative to the 'fair field and no favour' goals of equalitarian feminists. She also welcomed the policy because she felt that it would elevate the 'generation and rearing of children into an art through the elaboration of a science'.[220] But she felt that socialists could not take up the 'woman's question' because it would prove too difficult to attack individualism in the family. Collective rule had first to be instigated in the workplace.

Nor did she pay much attention to the needs of the individual women who would be affected by her proposals for social reform, for example in the case of sweated trades. Her only committed involvement with working women took the form of the regular monthly, rather patronizing letters she wrote to the female voters in Sidney's mining constituency of Seaham between 1922 and 1926, which she believed served to raise their status in the eyes of their husbands and neighbours.[221] She never became involved in the organized feminist movement, joining only her friend Louise Creighton's National Union of Women Workers (NUWW), a non-political organization of middle-class women which aimed to help working women. She viewed it as a worthy if dull body and, rather optimistically, considered it promising 'virgin soil to Fabians'.[222] While Mary Ward was to leave the NUWW in 1912 when it broke asunder on the suffrage question, Beatrice resigned some fifteen years earlier over the issue of the executive's insistence on holding prayers before business meetings.

Nevertheless, the problem of relations between men and women at the individual level concerned her increasingly as time passed and comprised one of the most dominant themes in her diary after 1910. Like Mary Ward and Violet Markham, she strongly believed in the importance of a moral code as a means of controlling otherwise ungovernable sexual passions. But, unlike them, she moved in circles in which attitudes towards sex and marriage were being openly challenged. As a result, Beatrice spent some considerable time in an effort to re-examine her own views on these subjects in her diary. She concluded that she felt too unsure of her own traditional position to defend it publicly, but her revulsion from the new morality provided another spur towards what she perceived as the superior ascetic Soviet system.

For many Edwardian women social reformers (Mary Ward and Violet Markham included), H. G. Wells's affair with the young Amber Pember Reeves provided the occasion for intense debate about sexual morality. In 1906, three years before Amber's pregnancy made her relationship with Wells a matter of public scandal, Wells addressed the Fabian Society on the matter of personal relationships and, in Beatrice's view, used the occasion to attack the family and endorse promiscuity. Pondering the issues in her diary, Beatrice recorded her belief that friendship between men and women was not possible without physical intimacy; 'this, I believe, is true of our present rather gross state of body and mind'.[223] Furthermore, like her mentor Spencer, she clung to the thought that, in any case, 'man will only move upwards by the subordination of his physical desires and appetites to the intellectual and spiritual side of his nature'.[224] The apparent irrationality of desire horrified most female progressives, who were additionally aware that women were much more vulnerable than men when it came to illicit sexual relationships.

In the case of H. G. Wells and Amber Pember Reeves, Beatrice commented that the game was not played fairly, not 'even according to the rules of a game full of hazards – at any rate for the woman'. While she confessed that she was confused about the proper nature of a sexual code – 'approving of many things on paper which we violently object to when they are practised by those we care about' – she concluded that sexual experimentation inevitably involved deceit and secrecy and was therefore sordid and lowering.[225] In contrast to late-Victorian and Edwardian feminists who were anxious to promote a single moral standard, Beatrice further concluded that the only form of sexual experimentation possible remained the traditional recourse to prostitution. Her adherence to the double moral standard extended to making women the guardians of sexual purity. In cases of illicit sexual relationships, Beatrice always blamed the woman more than the man.[226]

She was more in tune with other progressive female opinion in terms of her views on the work of H. G. Wells (and to a lesser extent George Bernard Shaw) and, later, D. H. Lawrence, E. M. Forster, Aldous Huxley and C. S. Myers, who appeared to Beatrice to portray human nature as a one-sided caricature, emphasizing sexuality to the detriment of self-control and personal dignity. She profoundly disliked the way in which these writers divorced sexual relationships 'from conscious hygiene, personal affection, or social obligation'.[227] Writing of Shaw's *Mésalliance* and Granville Barker's *Madras House*, she was distressed by their apparent preoccupation with the 'rabbit-warren' aspect of human society and by their portrayal of women in particular as sex objects. Such a world bore no relation to her own:

> In the quiet area of respectable working class, middle class and professional life, and in much 'gentle' society there is not this over-sexed condition. The women are almost as intelligent as, and certainly a good deal more spiritual than, the men.[228]

The invitation to hedonism and abandonment to physical impulse sat ill with female social activists' commitment to serving others and to rational reform. Beatrice also spotted a strong element of cruelty towards the female characters in the work of Lawrence particularly, which she felt derived from the fulfilment of sexual desire without regard for loyalty.[229] Beatrice was inclined (albeit not to the same extent as Mary Ward) to see the quality of relationships between men and women in society as a microcosm of relationships in the wider society.[230] If faithfulness and loyalty were not features of private relationships how were these values to exist in the public sphere? In the final analysis, Beatrice was convinced that it was her and Sidney's 'insistence on the fulfilment of obligations', private and public, that caused Wells to dislike them.

During the inter-war years, Beatrice became increasingly perplexed in the face of changes in sexual morality. Observing the increasing number of divorces among those in her own social circle, she declared: 'old people like ourselves who have never thought out social morals find ourselves more and more troubled as to what line to take in the public interest'.[231] Beatrice had to reconcile herself to the fact that everyone seemed to put up with H. G. Wells's self-confessed promiscuity; with Bertrand and Dora Russell's extra-marital relationships; and, worse still, with William Beveridge's (the Director of the LSE) irregular relationship with the secretary of the school, Janet Mair. Worrying about the latter and its effect on the students, Beatrice reflected that

> there is today complete anarchy in opinion about sex relations. So far as I can make out from watching the behaviour of intelligent and well-intentioned men and women there is no objection to unfaithfulness in the marriage tie; no recognition that either husband or wife has any claim to the continual affection of the other; no insistence that legal marriage shall precede cohabitation.[232]

Beatrice was unwilling to turn away and leave such matters to be privately determined. She mourned the loss of a fixed sexual moral code, but did not feel sufficiently confident as to the rightness of her own beliefs to preach them (after all, science, as she admitted, was no guide):

> For my own part I instinctively believe in monogamy tempered by divorce and re-marriage in cases where both parties agree to part. But the ideal is faithfulness to one sex-relation during the life time of the persons concerned. But I do not know and therefore refuse to judge.[233]

However, the increase in the rate of divorce (which in fact did not extend beyond a minority of professionals and intellectuals until after World War II), together with the decline in the birth rate, conveyed to Beatrice a bleak 'vision of sterility as well as waste'.[234]

In her own household, the new morality caused her considerable difficulty in regard to the behaviour of her servants. But she was much more anxious about the effects on the behaviour of Labour Party MPs who might be tempted to succumb to the fleshpots of London Society.

Beatrice was very concerned to remodel official society 'on the basis of the simple hardworking life tempered by fastidiously chosen recreation and the good manners inherent in equality between man and man'.[235] Her effort to organize the wives of Labour MPs into the Half Circle Club was motivated in part by her desire to encourage them to steer clear of fashionable society and her understanding that they would need a sense of solidarity to do so. In 1927 she recorded her admiration for the Labour women MPs, Susan Lawrence, Margaret Bondfield and Ellen Wilkinson, for their respectability.[236] But in 1931 Ellen Wilkinson came to consult her as to the wisdom of seeing a man who was married (Frank Horabin). Beatrice replied that she remained a puritan on such matters but that she was not dogmatically opposed to extra-marital affairs as long as they were not promiscuous and not cruel to the other parties. She went on to reflect that Susan Lawrence and Margaret Bondfield represented 'the last of their class of celibate women in public life – a type of which there were many in my young days in the philanthropic world' and attributed the change in behaviour, as did most commentators, to the political emancipation of women and their entry into public life.[237] Women like Mary Ward and Violet Markham, who also entered the public world via philanthropy, had forecast that such a change in behaviour would follow women's political emancipation, and had argued that this alone proved sufficient reason for opposing female enfranchisement.

Beatrice found herself unable to suggest a form for a new sexual moral code, but she was encouraged by the nature of personal relationships in the Soviet Union. Communist puritanism in matters of health, sex, food and drink appealed to her enormously as the antithesis of the outlook of someone such as D. H. Lawrence. Indeed Soviet Communism represented to Beatrice a secular religion, approaching, she believed, a practical Comtian religion of humanity, that provided a framework for morals and beliefs as well as scientific materialism and which therefore proved the 'magnet' of her old age.[238]

Conclusion

Beatrice's faith in administrative machinery and in the beneficence of state bureaucracy made her ideas anathema to both Octavia Hill and Helen Bosanquet. Yet Beatrice shared with Octavia a strong belief in the importance of religion, and her emphasis on spirituality and goodness grew during the inter-war years. Nor were the ends she sought dissimilar from those of Octavia. During 1907, in the midst of working out the blueprint for the administration of poor relief, she wrote of the comfort she was deriving from Edward Carpenter's *Art of Creation*:

' "Love shining through knowledge" might be the summing up of his teaching . . . This little book has helped me much – has given me a lift up'.[239] She wrote happily to Sidney in the same vein: 'sooner or later the world has to be reorganised on love shining through knowledge. This is what you and I are striving or playing(?) for'.[240] While she heartily disliked the ideas of the COS, she and Sidney were of a COS caste of mind in terms of their commitment to working out a philosophy of social action. It was this shared commitment, albeit to very different philosophies, that made the Bosanquets and the Webbs implacable opponents.

But World War I shook Beatrice's faith that Webbian means were equal to the task. In 1925, when she was writing her autobiography and experiencing profound doubts as to the value of public political work and methods of social investigation, she wrote that looking back she realized 'how permanent are the evil impulses and instincts in man – how little you can count on changing some of these – for instance the appeal of wealth and power – by any change in machinery'.[241] Increasingly, it seemed to her that only the Soviet system could offer both a solution to material poverty and provide an external source of moral guidance to individuals. As the number of unemployed mounted, Beatrice was forced to admit that she had been 'seriously wrong' in her 1909 Minority Report when she suggested that she knew how to prevent unemployment.[242] In 1928 she described her own mental outlook as 'religious – a merging of self in a mystically beneficent spirit – alternating with complete scepticism' and recorded her strong sense of impending national decay unless a proper 'framework of prevention' was completed and unless the state took steps to 'manage' the birth rate, health standards, employment and the currency.[243] The Great Crash showed profit-making capitalism to be incapable of producing the goods and caused the Webbs to abandon their faith in the gradual evolution of socialism out of capitalism through progressive social service and rational administrative reform. Only a complete change of machinery would do.

The Soviet system promised to unite scientific rationalism and spirituality, the two major currents in Beatrice's thought: 'The religion of humanity foreseen by Auguste Comte and unwittingly accepted by Lenin and his followers, accepts science as its method and turns the thoughts and feelings of the individual man away from his own profit'.[244] Beatrice lauded the obligations the Soviet system placed on individuals to serve the community. She believed that such an emphasis on selflessness would secure the kind of personal responsibility that she desired quite as much as Octavia Hill. Soviet society seemed at last to be achieving the kind of mutuality and spirituality that she had first admired in Bacup. When she entertained a group of Soviet delegates at the International Cooperative Alliance in 1934, she remarked that they reminded her 'of my God-fearing Bacup relatives of 1884'.[245] As Nord has argued, Beatrice misread Soviet asceticism for ethical and spiritual power. She believed that communism offered a new code of conduct and a new religion, 'a higher standard of collective man'.[246] Beatrice shared Octavia Hill's vision of a loving and remoralized society, but ironically felt that she had found the means of achieving it in a political system whose approach to social problems was the fundamental anti-thesis to that advocated by Octavia Hill and the COS. Yet in large measure it was the inheritance that Beatrice Webb carried with her from her early work that inspired her enthusiasm for the Soviet system.

Despite having rejected the world of philanthropy, Beatrice never abandoned her commitment either to social service or to a self-denying morality that was inevitably tied to her sense of 'religious purpose – an ideal end – not for myself but for the world of men'.[247] But Beatrice was never willing to recognize the points of similarity between her ideas and those of other women social workers and investigators, in part because of fundamental disagreement as to methods, if not to ends, and in part because of her determination to reject the female world of social work. In her desire for useful work, her fears about absorption within her marriage and her difficulties in coping with the public world, Beatrice expressed clearly the classic problems of the late-Victorian and Edwardian woman. But her equally strong belief in the essential inferiority of women's intellect closed off any opportunity to come to grips with the true nature of gender inequality in her society and the insight such an understanding would have provided into her own situation. In the *angst* of Beatrice's early diary entries, with their detailed record of the battle to do her duty to her family versus the struggle to understand the social and political ideas which she also believed to be 'unnatural' for a woman to attempt; in her inability to find a suitable way of behaving on the Royal Commission on the Poor Laws; and in her desire to withdraw while writing her autobiography, Beatrice Webb captured precisely the nature of the female dilemma, which in her case was exacerbated by temperament. The tragedy was that she did not recognize it as such and often blamed herself severely for the difficulties she experienced. In many respects it is easier for the reader to sympathize with her struggles before her marriage than with those she experienced afterwards, chiefly because by the 1900s she was at once convinced of her status as an expert investigator and yet anxious about it, which led her to present herself in a manner that was often truculent and condescending and which only served to infuriate her opponents and often her friends. The twentieth-century Beatrice is less appealing in many respects than the nineteenth-century Beatrice. Yet her insecurity, her struggle to understand changes in sexual morality and her increasing preoccupation with an ideal society dominated and inspired by a vision of 'loving kindness' all contribute to making her thinking and behaviour more complicated than has often been acknowledged. Beatrice perceived her insistence on 'a purpose' for individuals and society as essentially Victorian.[248] More accurately, such a concern was characteristic of as many as three generations of late-Victorian and Edwardian women committed to social action.

Notes

1. B. Caine, *Destined to be Wives. The Sisters of Beatrice Webb* (Oxford: Clarendon, 1986).
2. F. Nightingale, 'Cassandra', in Ray Strachey, *The Cause* (Virago, 1978), 1st edn. 1928.
3. Brian Lee Crowley, *The Self, the Individual and the Community* (Oxford: Clarendon, 1987), in common with many political theorists misses this important strand in Beatrice's thinking because he treats 'the Webbs' as a single person. One of the few writers not to do this and also to credit Beatrice as 'the leading spirit' is Margaret Cole, 'The Webbs and Social Theory', *British Journal of Sociology* 12 (June 1961). David Nicholls, however, spots the link Beatrice made between 'the welfare god and the paternal state' in his *Deity and Domination* (Routledge, 1989), p. 34.
4. Deborah Epstein Nord, *The Apprenticeship of Beatrice Webb* (Macmillan, 1985).
5. Kitty Muggeridge and Ruth Adam, *Beatrice Webb: A Life, 1858–1943* (Secker & Warburg, 1967), p. 136.
6. Beatrice Webb, Diary TS (hereafter BWD), 18/5/83, f. 308, British Library of Political and Economic Science.
7. BWD, 30/4/83, f. 300.
8. Beatrice Webb, *My Apprenticeship* (Cambridge: Cambridge University Press, 1979), 1st edn 1926, chap. IV, p. 201; and BWD, 18/5/83, f. 308.
9. Webb, *Apprenticeship*, p. 97.
10. Ibid., 30/3/79, f. 104.
11. Webb, *Apprenticeship*, p. 296.
12. Ibid., p. 107.
13. BWD, 11/1/86, f. 482.
14. Ibid., 9/5/84, f. 379.
15. Ibid., 1/3/83, f. 274.
16. Norman Mackenzie (ed.), *The Letters of Sidney and Beatrice Webb*, Vol. I, *Apprenticeship, 1873–92* (Cambridge University Press, 1978), p. 40, Beatrice to Richard Potter, (?) Aug. 1885.
17. BWD, 13/8/82, f. 221.
18. Nord, *Apprenticeship of Beatrice Webb*, p. 251.
19. Cynthia Eagle Russett, *Sexual Science: The Victorian Construction of Womanhood* (Cambridge, Mass.: Harvard University Press, 1989); Carol Dyhouse, 'Social Darwinistic Ideas and the Development of Women's Education in England, 1870–1920', *History of Education* 5 (Feb. 1976); Jill Conway, 'Stereotypes of Femininity in a Theory of Sexual Evolution', in Martha Vicinus (ed.), *Suffer and be Still* (Bloomington: Indiana University Press, 1973).
20. BWD, 5/8/81, f. 172.

21. Ibid., 4/11/82, f. 246 and 23/3/83, f. 286.
22. Ibid., 23/3/83.
23. Webb, *Apprenticeship*, p. 101.
24. BWD, 10/12/86, p. 755.
25. Webb, *Apprenticeship*, p. 296.
26. Ibid., p. 119.
27. BWD, 27/12/83, f. 348.
28. Ibid., 2/2/81, f. 156.
29. Webb, *Apprenticeship*, pp. 265–6 and BWD, 7/11/86, f. 746.
30. BWD, 15/9/85, f. 429.
31. BWD, 5/9/85, f. 430 and 7/11/86, f. 743.
32. Ella Pycroft to Beatrice, 23/9/86, Item 161, Passfield Papers II (i) II, BLPES.
33. Ella to Beatrice, 4/9/86, Item 159, Passfield II (i) II.
34. Webb, *Apprenticeship*, p. 44.
35. Ella to Beatrice, 21/8/86, Item 158, Passfield II (i) II.
36. Ella to Beatrice, 6/7/86, Item 154, Passfield II (i) II.
37. BWD, 7/3/89, f. 1017 and 4/6/89, f. 1047. Comments on the importance of home and family for women are dotted throughout the Diary for the 1880s, eg. 5/11/83, f. 352.
38. Webb, *Apprenticeship*, p. 282.
39. BWD, 28/5/86, f. 669 and 9/10/86, f. 717.
40. Ella to Beatrice, 12/9/86, Item 160, Passfield II (i) II.
41. BWD, 7/8/85, f. 422–4.
42. Ella to Beatrice, 26/2/86, Item 150 and 4/32/86, Item 151, Passfield II (i) II.
43. Ella to Beatrice, 9/2/86, Item 148 and 14/8/86, Item 157, Passfield II (i) II.
44. Ella to Beatrice, 4/8/86, Item 156, Passfield II (i) II.
45. BWD, 28/5/86, f. 666.
46. Margaret Harkness to Beatrice, 1878, Item 46, Passfield Papers II (i) II. W. J. Fishman, *East End 1888* (Duckworth, 1988), makes extensive reference to Harkness's writings under her pseudonym.
47. BWD, 1/11/87, f. 887; 15/7/88, f. 944–5 and 21/2/89, f. 1009.
48. Ibid., Sept. 1888, f. 967.
49. Ibid., 30/7/86, f. 695 Arabella Fisher to Beatrice, 24/1/86, Item 139, Passfield II (i) II.
50. Herbert Spencer to Beatrice, 21/11/87, Item 22, II (i) II.
51. Webb, *Apprenticeship*, p. 351 and BWD, 6/3/89, f. 1012.
52. BWD, 21/11/80, f. 148.
53. Ibid., 18/10/87, f. 871.
54. Norman and Jeanne Mackenzie, *The First Fabians* (Weidenfeld & Nicolson, 1977), p. 133.
55. Nord, *The Apprenticeship of Beatrice Webb*, p. 115, and 'An Appeal Against Female Suffrage', *Nineteenth Century* XXV (June 1889), pp. 781–8.
56. Brian Harrison, *Separate Spheres. The Opposition to Women's Suffrage in Britain* (Croom Helm, 1978).
57. Webb, *Apprenticeship*, p. 354.
58. Beatrice Webb, *Our Partnership*, ed. B. Drake and M. I. Cole (Cambridge: Cambridge University Press, 1975), 1st edn 1948, pp. 362–3, letter from Beatrice to M. G. Fawcett which Beatrice allowed the latter to send to *The Times*, 5/11/06.
59. Webb, *Apprenticeship*, p. 373.
60. Ibid., p. 374; BWD, 28/5/86, f. 673.
61. Webb, *Apprenticeship*, p. 374.
62. BWD, 13/1/91, f. 1220.
63. Webb, *Apprenticeship*, p. 195.
64. Ibid., p. 200.
65. Ibid., p. 198.
66. Ella to Beatrice, 14/8/86, Item 157, Passfield II (i) II.

67. Ibid.
68. BWD, 20/5/83, f. 311.
69. Ella to Beatrice, 15/7/36, Item 155, Passfield II (i) II.
70. Ella to Beatrice, 4/3/86, Item 151, Passfield II (i) II.
71. BWD, 18/5/83, f. 308.
72. Webb, *Apprenticeship*, p. 202.
73. BWD, 26/11/84, f. 401, and Webb, *Apprenticeship*, pp. 277 and 261.
74. Mackenzie (ed.), *Letters of Sidney and Beatrice Webb*, Vol. I, p. 43, Beatrice to Richard Potter, Sept. 1885.
75. Ella Pycroft to Mr Bond, 1/1/86, Coll. Misc. 43, BLPES.
76. Ella to Beatrice, 15/7/86, Item 155 and 14/8/86, Item 157, Passfield II (i) II.
77. BWD, 7/11/86, f. 745.
78. Webb, *Apprenticeship*, pp. 151 and 157.
79. BWD, 12/8/85, f. 423, and Webb, *Apprenticeship*, p. 278.
80. Webb, *Apprenticeship*, p. 273.
81. BWD, 8/11/85, f. 461.
82. Webb, *Apprenticeship*, p. 27.
83. Ibid., p. 135.
84. BWD, 18/4/86, f. 652.
85. Ibid., 20/8/89, f. 1071.
86. Webb, *Apprenticeship*, p. 413.
87. Sidney and Beatrice Webb, *Methods of Social Study* (Cambridge: Cambridge University Press, 1975), 1st edn 1932, p. xxxv, T. H. Marshall discusses the fact that their research was not designed to test their beliefs. See also T. Simey, 'The Contribution of the Webbs to Sociology', *British Journal of Sociology* 12 (June 1961).
88. BWD, 10/7/94, f. 1317 and 10/8/94, f. 1332.
89. Ibid., 1/5/97, f. 1488.
90. Ibid., 22/5/1900, f. 2002.
91. Ibid., 11/5/20, f. 3750.
92. Ibid., 5/1/96, f. 1429.
93. Ibid., 25/2/03, f. 2191.
94. Norman Mackenzie (ed.), *The Letters of Sidney and Beatrice Webb*, Vol. II, *Partnership, 1892–1912* (Cambridge: Cambridge University Press, 1978), p. 313, Beatrice to Sidney, 2/5/08.
95. Mrs Sidney Webb, 'Methods of Social Investigation', *Sociological Papers* 1906 (Macmillan, 1907), p. 348.
96. BWD, 30/1/08, f. 2528.
97. Ibid., 15/5/06, f. 2406, and Parliamentary Papers, 1910, Cd. 4983, XLVI, Papers of the Royal Commission on the Poor Laws, 'Memoranda by Individual Commissioners on Various Subjects', p. 246.
98. Helen Bosanquet, 'The Historical Basis of English Poor Law Policy', *Economic Journal* 20 (June 1910), pp. 182–94.
99. Webb, *Partnership*, p. 348.
100. Ibid., p. 378.
101. BWD, 30/1/08, f. 257–8.
102. S. and B. Webb, *Methods of Social Study*.
103. B. Potter, *The Cooperative Movement in Great Britain* (Allen & Unwin, 1930), 1st edn 1891, Preface, p. xvi.
104. See T. H. Marshall's Preface to Webbs' *Methods of Social Study*, p. xvii.
105. BWD, 28/6/88, f. 942.
106. Webb, *Apprenticeship*, p. 270.
107. Particularly Marshall, Preface to Webbs' *Methods of Social Study*, p. xxxv.
108. Frank Wallis Galton, Autobiography, TS, Vol. I, Coll. Misc. 315, BLPES.
109. Norman and Jeanne Mackenzie, *The Diary of Beatrice Webb, 1873–1892*, Vol. I, *Glitter Around and Darkness Within* (Virago, 1982), p. 164, 17/4/86.

110. Webb, *Apprenticeship*, p. 358.
111. Webb, *Apprenticeship*, p. 420, Appendix A, 'Personal Observation and Statistical Enquiry', 27/9/87.
112. Webb, *Apprenticeship*, p. 230.
113. BWD, 2/1/83, f. 255.
114. Nord, *Apprenticeship of Beatrice Webb*, p. 169.
115. Webb, *Apprenticeship*, p. 317; BBC Radio talk on 'How to Study Social Questions', delivered on 20/3/29, Passfield VI, Item 80.
116. BWD, 28/4/99, f. 1958.
117. Webb, *Partnership*, p. 390, fn. 1. Her clever cross-questioning was acknowledged in the daily press.
118. Mackenzie (ed.), *Letters of Sidney and Beatrice Webb*, Vol. II, p. 287, Beatrice to Mary Playne, 22/2/08.
119. Webb, *Apprenticeship*, pp. 109 and 137.
120. BWD, 23/7/83, f. 323.
121. Ella Pycroft to Beatrice, 21/8/86, Item 158, Passfield II (i) II.
122. Charles Booth to Beatrice Webb, 31/7/86, Item 175, Passfield II (i) II.
123. Webb, *Apprenticeship*, p. 248.
124. J. Burrow, *Evolution and Society* (Cambridge: Cambridge University Press, 1966), p. 91.
125. BWD, 9/12/03, f. 2255.
126. Mrs Sidney Webb, 'Methods of Investigation', pp. 352–3.
127. Webb, *Apprenticeship*, pp. 437–46, Appendix D, 'On the Nature of Social Science'.
128. S. and B. Webb, *Industrial Democracy* (Longman, 1897), Preface, p. xiii.
129. BWD, 30/7/93, f. 1290.
130. 'How to Study Social Questions', 27/3/29, BBC Radio talk.
131. BWD, 6/10/85, f. 449.
132. Ella to Beatrice, 26/2/86, Item 150, Passfield II (i) II.
133. B. Webb, 'A Lady's View of the Unemployment at the East', *Pall Mall Gazette*, 18/2/86, Passfield VII, Item 4a.
134. Mackenzie (ed.), *Letters of Sidney and Beatrice Webb*, Vol. I, p. 53, Beatrice Potter to Joseph Chamberlain, March 1886.
135. Ella to Beatrice, 19/2/86, Item 149, Passfield II (i) II.
136. Ella to Beatrice, 15/7/86, Item 155, Passfield II (i) II.
137. Charles Mowat, *The Charity Organisation Society, 1869–1913* (Methuen, 1961), p. 127.
138. Canon Barnett to Beatrice, 3/3/86, Item 172, Passfield II (i) II; S. A. Barnett, *Practicable Socialism* (Longman, 1888).
139. Webb, *Apprenticeship*, p. 209.
140. S. A. Barnett, 'Distress in East London', *Nineteenth Century* 20 (Nov. 1886), pp. 678–92, and 'A Scheme for the Unemployed', *Nineteenth Century* 24 (Nov. 1888), pp. 753–63. In these articles, Barnett remained convinced as to the evils of out-relief, but advocated programmes for training and unionization of the unskilled.
141. Beatrice Webb, 'Dock Labour', *Nineteenth Century* (Oct. 1887), especially p. 495, Passfield VII, and BWD, 6/5/87, f. 814.
142. BWD, 31/10/86, f. 739.
143. PP, 1890, 257, XVII, Fifth Report of the Select Committee of the House of Lords on the Sweating System, p. xlii.
144. B. Potter, 'How Best To Do Away With The Sweating System', paper read at the 24th Annual Congress of Cooperative Societies, 1892 (Manchester Cooperative Union Ltd, 1892).
145. Mary Ward to Beatrice, 26/3/96, Item 49, Passfield II 4a 3.
146. Helen Bosanquet, Louise Creighton and Beatrice Webb, 'Law and the Laundry', *Nineteenth Century* 41 (Jan.–June 1897), pp. 224–35.

147. Beatrice Webb, *Women and the Factory Acts*, Fabian Tract No. 67, 1896, pp. 4–5 and 14.
148. Potter, 'How Best To Do Away With The Sweating System', p. 8.
149. Beatrice Webb (ed.), *The Case for the Factory Acts* (Grant Richards, 1901), p. 47, and BWD, 5/10/03, f. 2238.
150. Helen Bosanquet, 'The Outsider', Bosanquet Papers, Trunk III, pkt 13, nd, Newcastle University Library.
151. Webb, *Women and the Factory Acts*, p. 10; Sidney Webb, 'The Alleged Differences in Wages Paid to Men and to Women for Similar Work', *Economic Journal* 1 (Dec. 1891), pp. 635–62.
152. Beatrice Webb, 'Personal Rights and the Women's Movement', *New Statesman* 1/8/14, pp. 525–7, and PP, 1919, Cmd. 135, XXXI, Report of the War Cabinet Committee on Women in Industry, p. 241.
153. L. Woolf, 'Political Thought and the Webbs', in M. Cole (ed.), *The Webbs and their Work* (Frederick Muller Ltd, 1949), p. 21.
154. BWD, 10/3/93, f. 1279; see also 1/2/97, f. 1479. M. G. Tyldesley, 'The Political and Social Thought of Sidney and Beatrice Webb, 1884–1914. A Study in Democratic Socialism', unpublished PhD thesis, University of Manchester, 1985, has concluded that the Webbs were 'weak elitists': elections were needed to give a 'feeling' of consent, but voters could only indicate what results they wanted to see, not the projects they wanted carried out. Crowley, *The Self, the Individual and the Community*, has argued strongly that the Webbs were 'anti-political'.
155. BWD, 29/12/94, f. 1355 and 17/2/95, f. 1374.
156. Mrs Sidney Webb, 'The Prevention of Destitution', p. 17, and 'The Royal Commission on the Poor Laws and the Relief of Distress. A Course of Nine Lectures', *Sheffield Weekly News* reprints, 1909, Bosanquet Papers, Trunk II I (2). See also a reference in the Diary to 'a great social drainage scheme', 22/7/09, f. 2597.
157. Webb, *Apprenticeship*, p. 42.
158. BWD, 14/2/27, f. 4459.
159. Beatrice Webb's submission to the Royal Commission on Unemployment Insurance, 1931, paras 41–4, Passfield IV, Item 27.
160. Bella Fisher to Beatrice, 10/10/90, Item 145, Passfield II (i) II.
161. BWD, 30/9/89, f. 1104.
162. Margaret Harkness to Beatrice, 1184, Item 50, Passfield II (i) II.
163. BWD, 7/7/91, f. 1242.
164. Sidney to Beatrice, 30/5/90, Item 3, folder 1, Passfield II 3 (i).
165. Sidney to Beatrice, 24/6/90, Item 6, folder 1, Passfield II 3 (i).
166. Beatrice to Sidney, 16/5/90, Item 2, folder 1, Passfield II 3 (ii).
167. Beatrice to Sidney, 12/8/91, Item 49, folder 2, Passfield II 3 (ii).
168. Sidney to Beatrice, 14/9/91, Item 41, folder 4, Passfield II 2 (i).
169. Beatrice to Sidney, mid-Sept. 1891, Item 51, folder 2, Passfield II 3 (ii).
170. Beatrice to Sidney, mid-Oct. 1891, Item 63, folder 3, Passfield II 3 (ii).
171. Beatrice to Sidney, (?) early Jan. 1892, Item 9, folder 4, Passfield II 3 (ii).
172. Beatrice to Sidney, 8/12/91, Item 85, folder 3, Passfield II 3 (ii).
173. BWD, 30/7/93, f. 1289; 18/1/97, f. 1471; 17/1/04, f. 2267–8.
174. Galton, Autobiography TS.
175. BWD, 8/6/04, f. 2292/3.
176. Ibid., 24/4/01, f. 2076.
177. Ibid., 5/6/02, f. 2154; 1/12/03, f. 2249; 21/7/02, f. 2161.
178. Eg. 29/11/20, f. 3815, Mary Booth's letters in 1885–6 were especially important to Beatrice, see Passfield II (i) II, Items 121–8. She was also supportive in regard to Beatrice's encounter with Alfred Marshall in 1889, Mary Booth to Beatrice, 20/6/89, Item 132, Passfield II (i) II.
179. BWD, nd circa 1896, f. 1444.
180. BWD, 2/1/01, f. 2053 and 2/5/04, f. 2290.

181. Beatrice to Sidney, 1/11/91, Item 70, folder 3, Passfield II 3 (ii).
182. BWD, 12/8/23, f. 3976.
183. Ibid., 25/5/34, f. 5779.
184. Ibid., 1/12/92, f. 1273.
185. T. Thomson (ed.), *Dear Girl. The Diaries and Letters of Two Working Women, 1897–1917* (The Women's Press, 1987), p. 43.
186. Webb, *Apprenticeship*, p. 323; BWD, 13/11/87, f. 893.
187. BWD, 27/11/87, f. 894.
188. Mackenzie, *Letters of Sidney and Beatrice Webb*, Vol. II, p. 5, Beatrice to Edward Pease, 18/4/93.
189. Sidney to Beatrice, 30/11/90, Item 27, folder 3, Passfield II 3 (i).
190. BWD, 2/3/94, f. 1311.
191. Ibid., 20/12/03, f. 2263.
192. Ibid., 20/12/03, f. 2263. See also 11/10/94, f. 1346.
193. Ibid., 1/1/01, f. 2049 and 3/11/03, f. 2243.
194. Webb, *Apprenticeship*, p. 324.
195. BWD, 23/11/05, f. 2366; 5/2/06, f.2386; 1/3/06, f. 2395–9.
196. Ibid., 15/12/05, f. 2376.
197. Ibid., 29/10/07, f. 2512–14.
198. Ibid., 12/2/06, f. 2389 and 15/12/05, f. 2376.
199. Webb, *Partnership*, p. 420.
200. Ibid., p. 323.
201. Ibid., p. 377.
202. Webb, *Partnership*, p. 341.
203. Ibid., p. 371.
204. Mackenzie, *Letters of Sidney and Beatrice Webb*, Vol. II, p. 280, Beatrice to Mary Playne, 2/2/08.
205. BWD, 15/5/08, f. 2551. Beatrice refers briefly to Lord George Hamilton, William Smart and Helen Bosanquet writing the Majority Report.
206. Mackenzie, *Letters of Sidney and Beatrice Webb*, Vol. II, p. 276, Sidney Webb to Haldane, 12/12/07.
207. BWD, 31/12/09, f. 2621.
208. BWD, 8/12/18, f. 3652; Cmd. 135. Beatrice gave an account of her work on this Committee in the Diary, Sept. 1919, f. 3671.
209. BWD, 22/12/18, f. 3655.
210. Ibid., 12/3/19, f. 3685.
211. Ibid., 20/8/20, f. 3770 and 6/3/23, f. 3942.
212. Ibid., 10/7/24, f. 4092–4.
213. Ibid., 8/6/20, f. 4742 and 15/11/22, f. 3916.
214. Ibid., 20/6/29, f. 4742.
215. Ibid., 17/10/22, f. 3908 and 28/10/22, f. 3913.
216. Ibid., 19/3/25, f. 4164.
217. Ibid., 27/9/41, f. 7171.
218. Ibid., 31/12/26, f. 4438.
219. Ibid., 6/10/30, f. 4992.
220. Ibid., 25/7/94, f. 1325–8.
221. Ibid., 3/12/23, f. 3996. Beatrice claims the women of Seaham were very pleased with her letters. For the letters themselves, see Passfield IV, Item 15.
222. BWD, 18/10/95, f. 1418.
223. Ibid., 18/10/06, f. 2451.
224. Ibid., 30/11/06, f. 2461.
225. Ibid., 7/09, f. 2601.
226. For example in the case of Bertrand and Dora Russell, ibid., 21/4/31, f. 5102–3.
227. Ibid., 5/5/31, f. 5112 and 31/10/32, f. 5369.
228. Ibid., 13/3/10, f. 2631.
229. Ibid., 5/5/31, f. 5112 and 11/5/33, f. 5494.

230. Ibid., 29/11/20, f. 3815.
231. Ibid., 10/7/22, f. 3903.
232. Ibid., 20/8/25, f. 4194.
233. Ibid., 20/8/25, f. 4198.
234. Ibid., 2/5/28, f. 4592.
235. Ibid., 24/4/21, f. 3837.
236. Ibid., 17/8/27, f. 4515.
237. Ibid., 28/6/31, f. 5144.
238. Ibid., 4/1/32, f. 5236–7.
239. Ibid., 31/6/07, f. 2496.
240. Mackenzie, *Letters of Sidney and Beatrice Webb*, Vol. II, Beatrice to Sidney, 14/6/07, p. 260.
241. BWD, 5/12/25, f. 4232.
242. Ibid., 31/6/07, f. 2496–7.
243. Ibid., 24/7/28, f. 4615.
244. Ibid., 16/12/33, f. 5634.
245. Ibid., 9/9/34, f. 5839.
246. Ibid., 23/2/32, f. 5275.
247. Ibid., 17/9/20, f. 3803.
248. Ibid., 6/2/27, f. 4452.

3   Helen Bosanquet, 1860–1925

There is a certain symmetry about the lives of Helen Bosanquet and Beatrice Webb. Helen Bosanquet (née Dendy) was born two years after Beatrice Webb in 1860, the fifth child in a Manchester manufacturing family. Both Helen and Beatrice spent some time working for the Charity Organisation Society (COS) before they married. Helen married Bernard Bosanquet, the Idealist philosopher in 1895, three years after Beatrice married Sidney. Both the Bosanquets published extensively on the problem of poverty, albeit for the most part separately, and they remained childless. But there the symmetry ends.

Unlike Richard Potter, John Dendy's business failed and in the early 1880s the Dendy children, male and female, found that they had to support themselves. Helen's elder sister, Mary became first a lady companion and then, beginning in the late 1890s, made a name for herself as a pioneer in educating mentally disabled children. Helen initially kept house in Manchester for her two brothers and another sister who began work as a teacher. In 1886 she went to Newnham as a mature student, completing the Moral Sciences Tripos in 1889 and, in the manner of one of the heroines of Alice Stronach's novel about Newnham graduates, went to work as a paid district secretary for the COS in Shoreditch (albeit that few women reached the level of district secretary within the COS during the 1880s). During the five years she spent working for the society, Helen also showed a determination to write on poverty and the behaviour of the poor for the quarterly press and the *Charity Organisation Review*, but unlike Beatrice she never turned away from the ideals of active philanthropy and remained a pillar of the COS, albeit adopting a different approach to the poor from that of the 'hard and dry' element condemned by Octavia Hill. After her marriage, she gave up her work as a district secretary and published a series of major studies of poverty and the poor which were extremely influential in the training of early twentieth-century social workers. She also edited the *Charity Organisation Review* between 1909 and 1921. Both Helen Bosanquet and Beatrice Webb re-entered the public world in 1905, when they were appointed to the Royal Commission on the Poor Laws, where the gulf between their approaches to social investigation and their analyses of the problem of poverty resulted in a protracted propaganda battle in which they were supported by their respective spouses. A. M. McBriar[1] has depicted this accurately as a 'mixed doubles', while failing adequately to distinguish the roles played by the male and female players. However, this is easier to do for the Webbs, with the aid of Beatrice's diary, than for the Bosanquets for whom there are virtually no personal papers.

Helen Bosanquet developed her ideas about the problem of poverty and its solution within an Idealist framework. Undoubtedly her commitment to Idealist philosophy, which attributed to individual mind and will the key role in achieving social change, was strengthened by her relationship with Bernard Bosanquet, but her thinking was already following these lines before her marriage as the essays she published in the early 1890s show. Indeed, she and Bernard met at meetings of the Ethical Society. Nevertheless, Bernard's extensive writings on Idealist philosophy and social work are crucial for a full understanding of Helen's views. It was Idealism and its emphasis on the importance of self-development as much as ideas about Christian obligation and duty that convinced Helen of the importance of personal social work. Like Octavia Hill, Helen came from a Unitarian family, but she shared with a younger generation of social workers (including Violet Markham) a certain contempt for Christian ministers' admonitions to their congregations to love one another in charity, when sect warred against sect. Helen Bosanquet was as convinced as Octavia Hill that only by changing the behaviour of individuals would lasting social progress be achieved and was just as sceptical of what could be done by changing administrative machinery. But unlike Octavia Hill and like Beatrice Webb, she (and Bernard Bosanquet) believed strongly in the value of theory and consciously derived their ideas about social-work practice from Idealist principles rather than from the more nebulous Christian obligation to 'right action'. Theory sustained the faith of the social worker in his or her methods of practice; Bernard Bosanquet maintained that 'to philosophize was to vitalize'.[2] But theory without thought as to its application was as dangerous as practice without theory.

The task of the social worker, which was fleshed out in considerable detail by Helen Bosanquet, thus became one of changing the habits of the poor, strengthening their characters and enabling them to become independent and self-maintaining. Like Octavia Hill, Helen Bosanquet envisaged work with individuals as the key element in philanthropic endeavour and realized that it would be a long and slow process, requiring an army of people committed to personal social work. And, like Octavia, she was implacably opposed to state intervention because she believed that it threatened to undermine personal responsibility and character. Helen Bosanquet wrote her major texts on social problems during the late 1890s and early 1900s, at a time when the place of charity, the principles of charitable endeavour, and the convictions of philanthropists as to the rightness of their endeavours were all considerably more shaky than when Octavia Hill had begun to develop her ideas about the nature of 'right action'. Helen Bosanquet, together with Bernard, provided a well-worked out alternative of how to deal with the problem of poverty to that of Edwardian collectivists and the Webbs in particular. Their position relied heavily on Helen's effort to understand the poor. In this the Bosanquets' views were considerably more sophisticated than many members (probably a majority) of the COS. Rather than rehearsing COS principles, for example on the perils of outdoor relief and then describing those aspects of the behaviour of the poor that justified the principles, Helen's analysis began by attempting to understand the family dynamics and community relationships of the poor, before moving on to assess those aspects of their behaviour that required strengthening or modifying by social workers.

Helen Bosanquet was as committed as Beatrice Webb to developing a theory of society and social change. Her analysis of social institutions and social problems appears simplistic and monocausal compared to the subtlety achieved by Beatrice, but her prescriptions for social work training and practice were, as A. W. Vincent and R. Plant have recently argued, richly grounded in social and moral ideas that emphasized the integration and development of the individual and the moral demands exerted by membership of a community.[3] Helen Bosanquet's social theory effectively integrated the task of social work in a manner that has not since been achieved. Her emphasis on the importance of building character also gave the family a central place in her social theory, contrasting sharply with its relative neglect by both classical political economists and collectivists. Her commitment to individualism and to the family was profoundly conservative in its implications but she was not guilty, as Beatrice Webb charged, of taking a simplistic *laissez-faire* view. Her arguments were moral rather than economic and her vision of a moralized community had, paradoxically, much in common with that of Beatrice Webb's ideal society.

Unlike Beatrice, Helen left neither a diary nor personal letters. It is therefore impossible to know whether she experienced the same kind of personal conflicts between a perceived female duty to serve others, especially family members, and a desire to enter the male world of ideas. Probably her continuing commitment to a sphere of action that an earlier generation of workers under the guidance of women such as Octavia Hill had made the special province of women simplified matters. Her books on poverty and social action were intended as texts for COS workers and she had no ambitions to develop either a methodology for social studies or a science of society. She believed throughout her life that the proper subject for social investigation was the individual and that the solution to social problems was to be sought in voluntary effort mounted on a one-to-one basis. Beatrice Webb, on the other hand, moved away from this into what was at the end of the nineteenth century a no-man's-land for women in the belief that the proper subject for investigation was social structures and the only effective agent of social change, the state.

Paradoxically, in view of her own less controversial career, Helen Bosanquet exhibited more immediate sympathy with and understanding of women's position than did Beatrice Webb. In 1911 she came out openly in favour of votes for women, basing her arguments in large measure on the needs of working-class women for greater dignity and status. During her period as a district secretary for the COS in Shoreditch, she observed the conditions and constraints experienced by poor women and sympathized with their lot in a way that she never did with that of their husbands. Helen Bosanquet was the only one of the five women considered in this book to support votes for women from the first, notwithstanding her apparent conservatism as a pillar of the COS. The explanation lies in large part with her Idealist philosophy which encouraged each and every individual to develop his or her talents to the full and which therefore accepted the idea of active female participation in the political affairs of the community. Certainly, Bernard Bosanquet proved to have a greater commitment to sex equality in this respect than did Sidney Webb. However, Mary Ward, who like Bernard Bosanquet derived so much of her thinking from the Idealist thought of T. H. Green, proved a lifelong active opponent of votes for women. In her case, competing ideas as to the nature of women's duty, together with a commitment to imperialism and the concomitant need for a government backed by military force led to a conviction that national affairs should remain in the hands of men.

The Royal Commission on the Poor Laws provides a fascinating opportunity for a direct comparison of not only the ideas of Helen Bosanquet and Beatrice Webb but also their different ways of dealing with what proved for both to be a traumatic step into the public sphere; Beatrice Webb suffered a breakdown in 1907 and Helen severe heart trouble in 1908. (Octavia Hill was also a member of the Royal Commission, but whereas Beatrice and Helen were the leading protagonists, Helen writing the bulk of the Majority Report and Beatrice producing the Minority Report, Octavia, by then an elderly woman, played a lesser part.) Because of the paucity of personal papers on Helen's side, the tensions experienced by Beatrice are more easily analysed and, indeed, Helen's part is often glimpsed through Beatrice's record of the Royal Commission's work. Helen probably felt considerably more secure in both her public and private persona than did Beatrice. Both women were consulted as to how they wished their names to appear in the final Report of the Commission. Helen opted for Mrs Bosanquet while Beatrice, despite having mourned the loss of her name on marriage to Sidney, opted, as usual, for Mrs Sidney Webb.

The idea of social work

As the paid COS District Secretary for Shoreditch, Helen Bosanquet did what few middle-class women social workers could contemplate – she lived among the poor. Between 1890 and 1894, she stayed briefly at the Women's University Settlement but for the most part lived alone in Hoxton and in all probability as plainly as possible; her mother certainly made a point of sending her flowers and other gifts. She also had to weather verbal abuse from members of the local community and had the windows in her house broken by men whom C. S. Loch, the general secretary of the COS, called the local 'roughs'.[4] She paid the penalty of a necessarily restricted social life, and all for a salary which reached £150 a year by the time she resigned in 1895 (slightly more than could be expected by a good lady's maid). Throughout 1894, her mother urged her to leave the COS and to try to earn a living by a combination of writing and teaching. Helen's mother clearly felt the COS to be exploitative employers and worried about her daughter's isolation, but Helen resisted her plea that she should consider a more congenial occupation.[5] It is not clear whether she did so out of philosophical conviction as to the importance of the COS's approach to the problem of poverty or whether she shared Octavia Hill's love of the poor. Certainly her later writing showed a warmth of feeling about the 'sunny side' of East-End life and exhibited an optimistic faith, not unlike Octavia's, in the capacities and good qualities of the poor. When she reviewed Arthur Morrison's *A Child of the Jago* in the *Charity Organisation Review*, she praised the author's observation of working-class life but condemned the unrelievedly bleak picture he painted.[6]

Her job as district secretary was to deal with all the applicants for relief brought before the Shoreditch Committee to see that proper inquiries were made of the family, neighbours, employers and other 'respectable' members of the community in frequent contact with the applicant, so that the committee members could properly judge the applicant's eligibility for aid. She liaised with both the COS committee and the (voluntary) visitors to make sure that case histories were recorded. Clara Collet, who had already embarked on her career in the civil service, described the ideal district secretary as showing 'devotion to an ideal, unselfishness and personal attraction'.[7] Helen Bosanquet undoubtedly qualified in respect of the first two; of the third it is impossible to know. Very few women had sufficient training for such positions. Octavia Hill wrote to Helen Bosanquet in 1893 to ask her to train someone, commenting that she was 'never very hopeful of finding those rare ladies who are fit for district secretaryships', but hoped that with some help from Helen the person she had in mind might be able to find 'a humbler position'.[8]

From the first, Helen accepted the view of the COS as to the importance of investigating the cases of everyone who applied for relief. One of her fellow workers in Hoxton was Margaret Gladstone, who later married Ramsay McDonald and whose work Helen praised because it showed both a love of visiting people in their own homes and a capacity to file reports that were 'full of intimate detail and consideration for their welfare'.[9] One of Helen's influential early papers, published in 1893, was entitled 'Thorough Charity', the meaning of which was closely related to both Octavia Hill's use of the term 'wise charity' and the COS's own preference for 'scientific charity'.[10] In the minds of contemporaries and of historians since, the COS was irreparably associated with the repression of mendicity and the abolition of all forms of doles and out-relief to the poor. Indeed, scientific charity has been broadly equated with the doctrines of the classical economists, who believed that any relief given to the poor without fully testing whether the applicant was truly destitute would only serve to increase the evil of pauperism. In her history of the COS, Madeleine Rooff accepted that this described accurately the ideology of the organization but attempted to distinguish from it what she perceived as the COS's progressive ideas about social-work practice. However Gareth Stedman-Jones argued strongly in the mid-1970s that it was impossible to separate theory from practice; they must stand or fall together. Most recently A. W. Vincent has supported this judgement but has argued that later COS theory was by no means as crudely reactionary as has been suggested.[11] Helen Bosanquet's work shows the truth of this.

She and Bernard Bosanquet were two of the leading thinkers in the COS, and worked within a framework of ideas that both firmly rejected many of the tenets of classical political economy and tended to be contemptuous of the contribution of economists. In addition, because Helen Bosanquet wrote in order to inform early social-work practice, her work serves to support the view that theory and practice should not be separated in any assessment of late-Victorian charitable endeavour, although given the 'hard and dry' attitudes among many male rank and file committee members described by Octavia Hill, there was ample room for Helen Bosanquet's complex ideas to be reduced to a narrow, negative and distinctly unloving creed. The relationship between the various strands of thinking on charity, particularly the moral and economic, is enormously complicated. Stefan Collini has noted, without denying the originality of their contributions, that the language of Idealism used by Bernard and Helen Bosanquet fitted easily into existing Victorian attitudes about the importance of self-improvement, many of which were grounded in the *laissez-faire* ideas associated with classical economic thought.[12] But it is true that Helen Bosanquet's work in particular also built on an older strand of thinking within social work pioneered by Octavia Hill, as well as on political philosophy. Idealism provided additional support for Octavia's belief in the importance of individual work but also led to more detailed specification of the work. Social workers were offered more guidelines in their practice rather than being asked to rely on their capacity to get the poor to emulate their example.

Helen Bosanquet's idea of thorough charity built on Octavia's conviction that the middle-class worker desiring to do something about the condition of the poor must think through his or her actions from beginning to end. The conditions of every applicant had to be closely investigated and if it was decided to give money, then the social worker's task was to stay in touch with the case to see what effects it produced. Each worker had to take responsibility for actions taken in respect to an applicant for relief. Helen Bosanquet's work paid more attention than had that of Octavia Hill to theorizing the position of the applicant for relief. For only by understanding the mainsprings of human behaviour, and in particular the importance of character, could social workers develop a scientific rationale for their work. In a passage reminiscent of one of Octavia's favourite themes, Helen Bosanquet wrote: 'we want them to recognise that if they assume the heavy responsibility of intentionally influencing men's lives they must form some idea of what their influence is going to be'.[13]

Helen Bosanquet accepted the Idealist premise that the development of individual character was both the means and the ends of social change. By developing character, Idealists meant considerably more than an injunction to self-help. Bernard Bosanquet specifically rejected the idea of 'atomic individualism' that underpinned the idea of self-help, arguing instead for an ethical or 'higher individualism'.[14] Ethical individualism involved the development of a more complete human nature, part of which required individuals to fulfil their obligations to their fellow men. Idealists detested the Benthamite idea of rational individuals exclusively pursuing their own interests.

Idealism held individual character to be the most important determinant of the individual's circumstances but Bernard Bosanquet was at pains to emphasize that this did not entail attributing all blame for the person's position to that person and thereby leaving him to his fate:

> A moral point of view does not mean a point of view which holds a question as solved by apportioning blame to the unfortunate: it does mean a point of view which treats men not as economic abstractions, but as living selves with a history and ideas and a character of their own.[15]

In terms of seeking a practical solution to poverty, such a view emphasized above all the restorative power of character. To improve character would effect much more fundamental improvement than changing economic conditions, which could result in change for the better *only* if character was also improved. It followed that no misfortune, no matter how distressing, was irredeemable until the individual's will was broken. It became the task of social work to repair will and build character.

In a review of the Bosanquets' first book of essays, published in 1895, J. A. Hobson accused them, and through them the COS, of neglecting economic forces and of blaming the victim. In a joint reply the Bosanquets argued that while at any moment misfortune might make the individual's circumstances appear insuperable: 'given time, character – if not thwarted – will reassert itself, and mould circumstances to its own support'.[16] Helen Bosanquet put the case at length in *The Strength of the People* (1903) where she argued that a man's circumstances depended on what he himself was. It was therefore 'man himself' who must be changed if his 'circumstances are to be avoided'.[17] It was not clear, for example, that merely giving the poor more money would help unless the people were also educated to use it wisely. Her favourite example was the usual one for the COS: that of the drunkard who would merely spend more money on drink. Nor was it enough that doles be accompanied by instructions as to their use. The desire to spend money wisely, to seek higher pleasures, had to come from within, and the process of working with the people to strengthen their characters and thereby to get them to aspire to a 'higher standard' of life would in all likelihood prove a long one.[18] Only when the people were showing signs of aspiring to a higher standard would money help. The Bosanquets saw character 'as a name for life as it looks, when you take it as all connected together; circumstance is a name for life as it looks when you take it bit by bit'.[19] In practice, of course, it remained remarkably difficult to determine cause and effect in terms of character and circumstances. The Bosanquets' theoretical framework meant that their writings gave an even firmer priority to the importance of character as the causal factor than did those of Octavia Hill, although there was probably little difference between their practical approaches. At best the ideas of the Bosanquets amounted to empowering the individual, but at worst they resulted in the victim being blamed. Hobson was right to criticize them for a stubborn refusal to look at wholes above and beyond the level of the individual. The centrality of character in Idealist thought stemmed from the belief that the self-maintaining, independent citizen, possessed, in other words, of good character, was also the rational citizen, aware of common social purposes, and struggling to realize what T. H. Green called his 'best self' and what Bernard Bosanquet called the 'best life'.[20]

Anyone, rich or poor, could lack character; as Helen Bosanquet stressed in her early writings, the failings of the poor in this regard were merely more visible because they were more likely to become a charge on the public purse. The lives of the rich as much as those of the poor could be 'one incoherent jumble from beginning to end'.[21] And the rich as well as the poor could exhibit 'the same self-indulgence, the same eager devotion to trifles and absorption in the interests of the moment'. Helen Bosanquet's analysis provoked a number of personal responses. One woman, probably a fellow lady visitor, reflected that it made her feel 'a special compassion for the residuum, for perhaps I might (though I hope not) have been one myself, had it not been for accident of birth'.[22] Helen's brother confessed to being very struck by the idea that the idle rich and the idle poor might share the same characteristics.[23] Helen Bosanquet's analysis held considerable appeal for a middle-class audience that subscribed to the importance of duty. Furthermore her insistence that all were equally capable of developing, or failing to develop, character was essentially democratic. Indeed she argued that class prejudice stood in the way of social progress because it failed to recognize this.[24]

In the crucial process of the formation of character and purpose, mental struggle was considered the most important factor. It was, declared Helen Bosanquet, 'the first law of progress'.[25] Mind and will were the makings of character, for as Idealist logic had it, if circumstances were structured by actions, then actions were structured by mind. Changing mind thus became crucial to social progress. Finally, changing mind involved changing will. An understanding of how this was to be accomplished was vital for the potential social worker.

In 1886 C. S. Loch, the general secretary of the COS and close friend of the Bosanquets, wrote that pauperism consisted of

> not a poverty of possessions, but a poverty and degradation of life, an habitual reliance on others, due to want of self-control and foresight, and of the goodness that underlies these things. The man who in this sense is a pauper has lost some of his manhood, and will not or cannot, do a man's work in this world – and the woman has lost some of the influence of her womanhood on the home and the family.[26]

The first step to changing the individual's will and creating a purposeful and active citizen was to make an effort to understand the client's perceptions of his or her condition. The social worker had to be able to work out why it was that individuals saw things the way they did, to appreciate the values they held and then work with them to change their views and behaviour. It was not surprising that the Bosanquets, and Helen in particular, turned to the emerging discipline of psychology to assist in this difficult task. As Helen put it, a science of society had to be a science of mind. She argued that the individual had to be persuaded to raise his 'standard of life', something which was not thought about consciously, but rather manifested itself when someone said 'Oh, I could not live on x street'. In Bernard Bosanquet's account, the idea of a standard underpinned the struggle for a better life: 'the existence which any human being regards as tolerable is made what it is by ideas which depend on social conception – in short by a standard of life'.[27] Everyone, other than the members of the residuum, had a standard but each person's standard was different.

The crucial point was that standards were progressive. Helen Bosanquet deduced this from her reading of G. H. Stout's psychology (Stout was a colleague of Bernard Bosanquet at St Andrews University). She suggested that man could be distinguished from the lower animals by his progressive wants. In lower animals, the possession of instinct served to stop progressive development. Lacking instincts, man was left free to break the 'elementary cycle of appetites', by the recognition and pursuit of interests, particularly within the family unit; these enabled human beings to organize their minds purposively. However, some people failed to develop progressive wants, being satisfied to eat, drink and sleep. In such people, habit performed much the same function as instinct in animals. Helen argued that the question of habit was very much one of training and education. If a wrong habit were acquired then interests were not pursued.[28] The duty of the social worker was therefore to correct bad habits and develop the kind of interests that would enable the raising of individual standards. Helen maintained sternly that every class had the right and duty to fix its standards as high as it could; moral and economic well-being depended on its doing so. She deplored the Malthusian 'economics of despair' and believed that they reflected merely economic conditions at the end of the eighteenth century when the position of the majority of the people resembled that of the late-Victorian residuum. She dismissed the wage-fund theory of the classical economists, not out of deference to the late nineteenth-century theory of marginal utility but rather because it provided but a 'low spirited' view of the prospects of wage earners and because it gave insufficient recognition to the determination of the majority of working people to better themselves.[29]

Like most late-Victorian and Edwardian social reformers Helen Bosanquet maintained an essentially evolutionary and progressive view of social change. She was boundlessly optimistic about the capacities of working people, believing that it was their constant raising of their personal standards that had been the cause of social progress to date. She believed also that progressive wants, which made individuals raise their standards, led to constant emulation of social superiors, with the result that there was more basis for cooperation between classes than for struggle. While Helen deplored the enlarged role Edwardian liberalism gave the state, she was entirely sympathetic to the stress it placed on 'masses not classes'.

The family occupied a special place in the Bosanquets' arguments regarding human motivation and behaviour. In Idealist thought, social awareness was built up through the family. T. H. Green, Bernard Bosanquet's mentor, wrote in 1879:

> formation of family life supposes . . . that in the conception of his own good to which a man seeks to give reality there is included a conception of the well-being of others, connected with him by sexual relations . . . He must conceive of the well-being of these others as a permanent object bound up with his own.[30]

To the Bosanquets, the family was seen above all as the primary institution in which character was developed and in which cooperative individuals and rational citizens were produced. The Bosanquets were as convinced of the importance of the family as Octavia Hill, and shared her suspicions of the settlement movement because it was divorced from home life. In Helen's last major book, *The Family* (1906), which in many ways represented the culmination of her thinking, she argued that the Family (always capitalized) was the fundamental social unit. Its importance lay in the part it played in stimulating the interests of the individual. Because they conceptualized the family as a biological unit, the Bosanquets could in turn portray it as a natural building-block in the enlargement of self-awareness. 'Natural' affection between husband and wife, and between parent and child ensured that homes became 'nurseries of citizenship'.[31] As Bernard Bosanquet wrote in his most important treatise on the state: 'Beginning once more, within an ordered social sphere, at the ethical factor which stands nearest to the natural world, and has taken, so to speak, the minimum step into the realm of purpose and consciousness, we start from the family'.[32] The family was thus seen as the ethical root of a higher ethical state, a microcosm of the polis.

In *The Family*, Helen Bosanquet argued that the natural interest of family members in each other's welfare was a more powerful tie binding families together than economic considerations, patriarchal power or primitive maternal instinct. Through the altruistic love that naturally characterized family relations, individuals achieved consciousness of their unity with others. In *The Family*, Helen attributed more impor- tance to family tradition, and in particular to the links of affection between fathers and sons, than to property in perpetuating the family unit. The family stood as a 'half-way house', mediating between the individual and the community.[33] In Bernard Bosanquet's conception of the state as the embodiment of the wills of all people, it was impossible for the family to be 'anterior to the state', but it was seen as providing a private social sphere free of egoistic acquisitive tendencies.[34] A strong citizenry and a strong state depended on the strengthening of the bonds between the individual and the family and between the family and the wider community. Given the enormity of its role in developing charac- ter, the importance of protecting and strengthening the family became one of the most dominant themes in the work of both Helen and Bernard Bosanquet.

In many respects, the family was the key to the Bosanquets' analysis of social problems and their solutions. In a manner remarkably akin to structural functionalist theory of the 1950s, the family was seen as playing the crucial role in socializing the individual.[35] In fact, Helen Bosanquet drew heavily on the work of the French sociologist, Fred- erick le Play, who argued that 'good' family organization was an essential factor contributing to the prosperity and contentment of a people. Where family members developed their sense of responsibility one to the other, Helen argued, 'the Family presented itself as the medium by which the public interest is combined with private welfare'. In this analysis, social problems disappeared when the family was strong and effective; for example, old age pensions were unnecessary 'where the stable Family combines young and old in one strong bond of mutual helpfulness'.[36] Children also learned the meaning of responsibility and mutual service, trust and affection in their relationships with family members: because the interests of the child and its pleasures centred on the home, the child naturally wanted to contribute to it. The hallmark of the residuum was lack of family feeling and a failure to socialize the young into 'habits of labour and obedience'.

In many respects this analysis was superficially similar to that of Herbert Spencer who viewed the family as the seat of altruism, care and protection, while the public sphere was characterized by ruthless competition.[37] However while the Bosanquets envisaged a separate private sphere, they viewed public and private less as mutually exclusive, in the manner of Spencer, and more as points on a continuum. Helen Bosanquet listed the family's responsibilities as looking after people, sending them out to work and taking responsibility for ruling small communities beyond the family, in local government for example. The struggle for existence was in their view a struggle for a place in the community and, like L. T. Hobhouse, one of the leading exponents of New Liberalism, they believed that those places were reserved for those individuals who possessed the highest cooperative rather than competitive qualities. Cooperation was developed by virtue of family membership.[38] But despite the important theoretical differences between the Bosanquets and Spencer, in terms of practical policy the Bosanquets' views bore considerable resemblance to those of Spencerians. In practice there was very little material aid that could be offered to the family within the Bosanquets' framework without potentially damaging family responsibility and subverting character. And because the most likely agent to intervene in the family was the state, at the level of policy prescription state and family became effectively mutually exclusive spheres of interest. The Bosanquets would not, however, have gone so far as modern commentators like Ferdinand Mount in his hostility to any entry into the home.[39] Trained social workers were considered quite acceptable because they would educate those families in which interest in the welfare of each other was poorly developed. Ideally the work would consist of interaction between an applicant in the context of his family, and a *voluntary* social worker who would also strengthen his or her own character by undertaking the work and thus deepen the ties of obligation within the community.

Achieving social change by changing individual will was necessarily an inordinately slow business because the impetus for change (as for 'right action') had to come from within the individual. Successful change could only take place when the individual was ready for it; it was therefore unlikely that as crude an agent as the state could be effective in securing it. There was also the danger that the state would usurp the individual, in the pursuit of his interests, for example by providing school meals for his children, thereby setting back the whole process of true social reform which depended on the individual's struggle to achieve a better life. The relation between parent and child was based on 'instinctive love' but, argued Helen, 'unless instinctive love is strengthened by a growing sense of responsibility, it cannot develop'. In short nothing should be done that might hinder the development of a sense of responsibility between husband and wife and between parent and child, and in no circumstances should such responsibility be usurped by a third party: '[for if] interests are taken out of his hands, without the introduction of others equally powerful, he is simply left to drift without the possibility of development. The only way of really helping a man is to strengthen him by education'.[40] According to Bernard Bosanquet, state action to improve housing conditions, for example, would not necessarily stimulate mind and will unless there was a better life struggling 'to utter itself', and unless 'the dead-lift of interference just removed an obstacle, which bound it down, the good house will not be an element in a better life, and the encroachment on the ground of volition will have been made without compensation – a fact which may show itself in fatal ways'.[41]

The final test of any intervention in the life of an individual had to be whether it improved mind and character and it was unlikely that state action would ever be able to pass it. The Bosanquets were not opposed fundamentally to any and all state intervention but they believed that the danger it posed to character by subverting personal responsibility and thereby will and effort was too great. Some institutions crucial to the development of mind and purpose, the family, friendly societies or provident medical institutions, for example, were particularly liable to be weakened by state action. Bernard Bosanquet's theory of the state as the embodiment of individuals' wills should have rendered the very idea of interference with the individual meaningless, but the question remained as to how far and in what way the exercise of power by the state might hinder the very end for which it existed, viz, the pursuit of the 'best life' and a 'higher individuality'. State action to provide meals or medical inspection for schoolchildren would merely rob poor fathers of their natural 'interest' in providing for their offspring; old age pensions would forestall the natural impetus of children to care for their parents.

The Bosanquets were no more proponents of *laissez-faire* than of collectivism. Bernard Bosanquet saw no point in saying 'throw the people on their resources, don't interfere with them, and their responsibilities will see them through'. That species of nineteenth-century *laissez-faire* forgot 'that ever spiritual good must be social'.[42] He considered it a lazy approach to social problems. Rather, it was necessary to find a sure way of stimulating interests that would organize life and develop character. In an address to social workers in 1901, Bernard Bosanquet advocated social work and voluntary action as the only sure method: 'I know this sounds like moralizing, but it is not spoken in that sense, and it is the conclusion to which society has slowly and inevitably and with much reluctance been driven, and which sociology has upheld from its inception'.[43]

Individual social work was above all a form of education and had the additional advantage that it sprang from the self-development of middle-class individuals to the point where they responded to the noble impulse of fulfilling obligations to their fellow citizens. Charity would help develop character and raise the standard of the people; it would enhance the 'strength of the people'. Alfred Marshall wrote to Helen Bosanquet on the publication of her book with that title, endorsing her main argument:

> I have always held that poverty and pain, disease and death are evils of greatly less importance than they appear except in so far as they lead to weakness of life and character; and that true philanthropy aims at increasing strength more than at the direct and immediate relief of poverty.[44]

Despite dissenting from her rigid views on the role of the state, which many historians would view as the touchstone of late nineteenth- and early twentieth-century political debate, Marshall nevertheless considered himself to be in fundamental agreement with her identification of the mainsprings of human behaviour and the priority she attached to fostering active citizenship rather than material relief as the best way of achieving a self-maintaining society.

According to Helen Bosanquet the real work of charity was therefore 'not to afford facilities [such as outdoor relief] to the poor to lower their standard but to step in when calamity threatened and to prevent it from falling'.[45] Social workers also had a responsibility to encourage the poor to aspire to as high a personal standard in material and cultural terms as possible. In practice, however, social workers experienced some difficulty in integrating an analysis of the client's perceptions with work to change his will and cultivate higher aspirations. Helen Bosanquet stressed that minds had to be prepared for new ideas and that what minds saw depended in some measure on what they already were. This, as she observed, was what made 'intercourse between people of different "upbringings" ' so difficult, and she warned that this 'should make us especially careful in placing our ideas before minds less developed (or differently developed) than our own, without making sure how they are interpreted'.[46] One of the most important concerns of the late-Victorian middle class was the lack of communication between rich and poor, and both the COS in its individual casework and the settlement movement aimed to bring the social classes back into contact.[47] However the task was found to be extraordinarily difficult. One of the chief refrains running through the works of early twentieth-century social investigation, including that of Helen Bosanquet, was the lack of understanding between classes.[48] During the 1920s, Beatrice Webb also recognized this as a problem in regard to the way in which middle-class Labour politicians attempted to communicate with working-class voters: 'By continuously *talking to another class in the language they think that class speaks instead of in their own vernacular* they deceive themselves and create distrust in their audience'.[49] Inevitably, social workers and social investigators identified the perceptions of the poor in relation to their own understanding of what was conducive to good character, and to this extent work with the poor slipped, as it did in Octavia Hill's work of housing management, away from the ideal of empowerment and towards social control.

The Bosanquets believed that charitable work would increase the common good through mutual service based on reason and love. The idea of charity as love was of course the essentially Christian ideal that had inspired Octavia Hill. In 1898 Bernard Bosanquet went a stage further, grafting these ideas onto Idealism and characterizing COS work as a training in the logic of Idealism. He argued that Idealism combined faith in the world of facts with passion and wisdom because it had an idea, a principle, order and organization. Social work needed to combine careful investigation with love. Idealism also represented faith in reality as a whole. The social worker would strive for this through the 'completeness of casework'.[50] The material for social-work training was not to be found in economics texts:

> The idea of society as an embodied mind and character, on which recent sociology lays stress, and which the experiences of social workers had long previously established, seems to be approached by economic science so timidly as to give little guidance to the practical man.[51]

The aim of social work was moral improvement and prevention, in so far as it was the social worker's job to support an individual when misfortune threatened. As Helen Bosanquet put it in 1900, it was easy for potential COS workers to learn the categories 'not likely to benefit', 'left to the clergy', 'poor law case', but it was more difficult to learn how to keep a case out of one of these categories.[52] The key was to seek an understanding of the individual in relation to his environment and then work out the best method of promoting self-maintenance.

Methods of social investigation

When Helen Bosanquet turned to writing full-length studies about poverty and social work after her marriage, her Idealist framework meant that the elevation of the individual's character remained the goal and the individual himself remained the subject for social investigation. In short, the ends could not be separated from the means. Helen did not follow Beatrice in struggling to develop a new methodology for social science, although she did devote considerable attention to assessing the value of statistics, which she felt to be slight, and (in a more positive spirit) psychology; she certainly did not believe that theory would emerge from the facts.

Ross McKibbin has described Helen's analysis of social issues as being, like that of Margery Loane and Magdalen Stuart Pember Reeves, essentially anecdotal and episodic.[53] Helen's first book-length contribution, *Rich and Poor* (1896), relied heavily on the power of the single illustration using the speech patterns of the working class. For example, her argument regarding the evils of free hospital treatment and the possibilities it provided for 'shamming' was illustrated by a quotation from one such sinner's wife, who 'didn't see how he could bear all them poultices if he weren't really bad'.[54] Margery Loane used the same technique, drawing constantly on her experience as a district nurse and justifying it by reference to the ignorance of philanthropists about the realities of life among the poor.[55] Helen was presumably drawing on her memory as a COS worker. There is no reason to believe that the examples were anything but real, although their use has a certain music-hall quality which plays, patronizingly, on the mores of those whose behaviour she believed required correction.

Such a method of exposition proved extraordinarily popular in late-Victorian and Edwardian England. Those interested in poverty were more likely to learn their 'social point of view' from Helen Bosanquet or Margery Loane than from Bernard Bosanquet, whose writing one correspondent confessed to finding 'too stiff', or the equally dry works of political economy.[56] In a letter to Bernard Bosanquet's biographer (J. H. Muirhead), Margaret Frere, a manager of the Tower Street Board School in the late 1880s, wrote about how she had

> worked away as a Lady Bountiful and quite satisfied with my open-handed efforts. Then a book called 'Poverty and Riches' [actually *Rich and Poor*] by

a Mrs Helen Bosanquet fell into my hands and opened my eyes to the futility of the work I was doing.[57]

Miss Frere proceeded to start, in the words of Muirhead, 'constructive work' on COS lines, going on to become a coopted member of the London County Council and helping to establish the Children's Care Committees.

The use of direct quotation was designed to show the perceptions of the poor, which according to Helen Bosanquet had to be understood before workers could comprehend the possible consequences of the aid they offered. Her portrayal of working-class life was often acute and by no means unsympathetic. For example, the fortitude of the wife who reported 'Oh, I don't know what 'e gets, I only know what 'e gives me' was described in glowing terms.[58] But such data were then woven into a fabric of explanation dictated by Idealist philosophy. Thus the recipient of free medical treatment became a victim of the donor's misunderstanding of the world view of the poor, in which the status of invalid commanded a certain respect and in which free medical treatment might therefore be manipulated. Similarly, while the hard life of working-class women was shown to be primarily attributable to the unfair division of resources within the family, once this was understood, social workers' attention was drawn to the need to change the husband's behaviour rather than to relieving the immediate needs of wife and children.

Helen Bosanquet agreed with Beatrice Webb as to the importance of social observation. But what social observation confirmed, as Bernard Bosanquet wrote in the Preface to their book of essays published in 1895, was that circumstance was 'modifiable by character, and so far as the circumstance is a name for human action, by character alone'.[59] In other words, social observation could not afford to neglect mind and motive. Helen Bosanquet was highly critical of Booth and Rowntree's social surveys and of the Webbs' 'note-taking methods' because they ignored motivation. In the case of the Webbs, she suggested additionally that 'from the point of view of the historian the plan is open to the grave objection that the excerpts are very effectively separated from their context'.[60] This criticism was prescient, and remarkably close to that of Marshall in his 1975 introduction to the Webbs' text on methods.[61] Helen Bosanquet was certainly able effectively to destroy Beatrice Webb's dubious account of the development of the poor law, presented as a Memorandum to the 1909 Royal Commission, by paying more scrupulous attention to the historical context than had Beatrice.

In the case of the social-survey method, which caused Beatrice Webb to ponder the methods of social investigation at great length, Helen Bosanquet's objections were sustained primarily by the faith that the world of facts must have an idea, a principle and an order that had to be discovered first. Helen was opposed fundamentally to the notion that empirical facts could be reshuffled to produce a variety of causal explanatory frameworks. In respect of Booth and Rowntree's delineation of a poverty line, she was by no means convinced of the facts in the first place. While Ross McKibbin is undoubtedly correct to have faulted her rejection of Rowntree's argument that there was structural poverty in York as the result of low wages alone and quite independent of character, Andrew Vincent and Raymond Plant are also correct to have suggested that her criticisms of Rowntree's data collection and assumptions were valid.[62] As she pointed out, the poverty line of Booth and Rowntree had a 'false air of definiteness about it'.[63] It was based, in the case of Booth, on the opinion of school-board visitors and probably missed the income contributions of household members other than the male bread-winner (Margery Loane later made the same point).[64] Helen maintained in the manner of COS investigators that the true position of the family could only be ascertained after extensive interviews with family members, neighbours and employers. She also felt, less justifiably in the light of modern evidence, that Rowntree's dietetic standards were too high. She maintained that Booth and Rowntree appealed to the emotions on the basis of bad statistics, a criticism that could equally have been levelled at her own use of illustration. In this she was reversing Beatrice Webb's charge of 'sentimental philanthropy', which was directed at writers such as herself who relied on the emotional power of a single illustration. But her point that statistical material was not necessarily value-free, in the way that early practitioners, including Beatrice, assumed, has of course since been affirmed time and again by social scientists. It was a point taken up by other leading members of the COS. Loch, for example, criticized the Fabian Society's *Facts for Londoners* on the derivation of the statistical 'facts'.[65]

Helen Bosanquet was convinced that her own methods were beyond reproach. She began by asserting the importance of character and then used psychology as a science of mind to prop up a much larger moral and social theory than it had been intended to support. While her descriptions of working-class life were often both perceptive and sympathetic, the prescriptions following from her analysis again relied on the imposition of a pre-existing framework of moral and social philosophy which to all intents and purposes assumed the status of natural law. Beatrice Webb's criticism of Herbert Spencer's tendency to mix induction and deduction and to give hypothetical laws of behaviour the status of social facts could also have been levelled at Helen Bosanquet.

Understanding the poor

The intention of Helen Bosanquet's writing was to illustrate the application of Idealist thought to social-work practice. She therefore sought to show that the source of poverty was to be found in bad habits and the failure to develop interests, in other words in poor character. Second, she strove to help social workers understand the world view of the poor as a means to understanding why there were sections of society which failed to respond to appeals to 'rise'. In describing the lives of the poor, she felt that she would put social work on a sound empirical basis, using psychological principles as a guide to good practice. Like Octavia Hill, she was therefore concerned above all that those involved in charitable endeavour should 'know the poor'. She shared Octavia's preoccupation with the need to train social workers and became a strong supporter of Bedford College, whose social studies course was begun with the help of the COS in 1916 and was indeed largely controlled by the COS.[66] Helen believed it to be important that social workers had some notion of the values and lifestyle of the poor before they were loosed among them. She aimed to provide a realistic picture of the life of the poor, but was not content, as was Lady Bell, to leave it there.[67] For example, while both Helen Bosanquet and Lady Bell showed a sensitive understanding of the crucial role pawnbroking played in balancing the working-class wife's housekeeping budget, whereas Lady Bell refrained from either blame or prescription, Helen felt obliged to condemn the practice and to urge the social worker to encourage the practice of thrift.

Helen Bosanquet focused her attention on the family as the locus of social work, and within the family on its female members. In part this was because of her perception, in common with other Edwardian social investigators, male and female, that the woman's role in working-class families was pivotal. The welfare of the family rested in no small measure on her skills as a household manager. But Helen Bosanquet's interest in working-class wives and mothers sprang also partly from her feminism, which not only made her sympathetic to the difficulties they experienced but additionally led her to claim on their behalf the right to self-determination in the form of better educational opportunities and the exercise of the franchise. Her attitude towards the shortcomings of the working-class husband was less sympathetic.

Helen Bosanquet did not feel it necessary to conduct any rigorous investigation of the causes of poverty. It was sufficient to set out her theory of progressive wants, somehow short-circuited by want of character, and then to draw on illustrations of human behaviour derived from a 'thorough knowledge of the poor'. All her books, other than the first, which lacked reference to her explanatory framework and there-fore read as a more straightforward exercise in 'moralizing', followed this pattern. Asking why it was that a man was unemployed, she would reply that careful COS investigation as to circumstance and character taught that there was no such thing as being out of work 'through no fault of his own'. There was always a reason for unemployment. Assuming that the man neither drank, stole nor was wilfully idle, causes which accounted for a substantial number of the unemployed, the bulk of the remainder were, she asserted, incapable of work: 'Sheer incapa-city can never be helped, and all we can do with it in our charitable work is to be very careful that we do not put a premium on it'. Sometimes when the incapacity was accidental rather than congenital, the individual could be trained for useful work but, she warned, 'your incapable person is like a London garden, it takes a most extravagant amount of attention to get absurdly small results, but we are very proud of what we do get'.[68]

After unwilful incapacity, there were those who were unemployed because of changes in the manufacturing process, or because of a downturn in trade, or because of sickness. In the case of the first, it was the duty of the social worker to understand what was happening in the man's trade and recommend retraining or moving, including the pos-sibility of emigration. In regard to the second, because it was usual for many trades to have slack seasons, the proper course was to help the individual budget wisely in order to cover a period of under- or unemployment. The same was true in the case of sickness. Bernard Bosanquet quoted approvingly Beatrice Webb's description of the problems of dock labour as the 'difficulty of living by regular work and the ease of living without it', albeit that he attributed the phrase to Charles Booth.[69] Helen and Bernard Bosanquet were as keen as Beatrice to see the industrial residuum, described by Beatrice as a 'mass of social wreckage', disappear. In Helen's view the 'great problem' with the huge class of casual unskilled labourers was 'to bring them to regard life as anything but a huge chaos. The confusion which reigns in their minds is reflected in their worlds'.[70] These men had failed to develop the powers of purposive, rational thought that accompanied the pursuit of particular interests, and this made them neglectful of the future.[71] Thus Helen Bosanquet did not so much ignore the structural causes of unemployment as advocate the stock solutions of the neoclassical economist, albeit grounding them in what she considered to be a superior theory of human motivation and behaviour.

When Helen Bosanquet started from observations of poverty in the home rather than among the unemployed, she managed to reach similar conclusions. Inviting her readers to consider why a particular home exhibited signs of squalor, she again stressed the importance of careful investigation. Helen recognized and described in her own words the cycle of poverty within the lifespan of the individual, first identified by Rowntree, and also the way in which the family economy depended on the contributions of all family members. Taken together, she believed that these factors merely confirmed her strongly held view that 'the poverty line means so very little when measured in money income, and so very much when measured in essentials'.[72] She noted, as had Beatrice Webb in her work on dock labour, that families at the same stage of family-building and with similar total income often experienced very different levels of comfort, and she concluded that the crucial variable was the skill of the housewife in managing the family economy. Comparing five families she observed across the back garden of her Hoxton house in the early 1890s, she commented on the children of number 4: 'And yet their life might be almost as good as that of number 1; they live in exactly the same surroundings, and might go to the same school, it is wholesome home atmosphere which is wanting'.[73] Beatrice wrote similarly in her study of dock labour:

> In common with all other working men with a moderate but regular income, the permanent dock labourer is made by his wife. If she be a tidy woman and a good manager, decently versed in the rare art of cooking and sewing, the family life is independent, even comfortable, and the children may follow in the father's footsteps and rise to better things. If she be a gossip and a bungler – worse still a drunkard – the family sinks to the low level of the East London street, and the children are probably added to those who gain their livelihood by irregular work and by irregular means.[74]

Whereas Beatrice went on later to advocate a role for the state in eliminating the structural causes of poverty, Helen saw the solution in terms of social work that aimed to strengthen the character of family members, particularly the working-class wife. Perhaps the wife went out to work and failed to keep the home and children clean and tidy; perhaps she spent her day gossiping. Such differences between working-class women were, she contended, deeply seated and matters of mind and character.[75] Given this, moving the family living in squalor to better surroundings would have little positive effect but rather would serve only to bring out 'the wonderful similarity between their failings and those of the rich'.[76]

Helen Bosanquet also demonstrated considerable understanding of, and sympathy with, the position of working-class wives. This was inspired by the recognition that by dint of heroic effort wives often did make comfortable caring homes even when they were forced to cope with circumstances that were of their husbands', rather than their own, making; the woman who did not know what her husband earned, for example, laboured under a severe disadvantage. Unlike Beatrice Webb, Helen Bosanquet went on from her observation as to the importance of the working-class wife to comment and reflect at length on her situation and, in particular, to recognize the importance of her position as a consumer. In common with most late nineteenth-century social investigators, Helen felt the vast majority of working-class wives took their responsibilities for their children seriously. Only a minority could be considered wilfully neglectful because of drink or gossip. In her first book she spoke of their 'patient endurance, unceasing sacrifice and terrible devotion'.[77] Their role was crucial in that they were the most strategic figures in the process of developing character in the next generation: 'If the husband is the head of the Family, the wife is the centre'.[78] Helen's sympathy for working-class women's efforts to do well by their children sprang both from the belief that they were well-intentioned but ignorant and from a latent feminist understanding that they were by no means the arbiters of their own fate.

She recognized the difficulty of budgeting on an irregular income and of avoiding the temptation of credit. She demonstrated a thorough knowledge of the options of borrowing, pawning and delaying payment, and her estimate of the rates of interest involved – 24 per cent for pawnbrokers and up to 400 per cent for private money lenders – has been confirmed by a recent historical study.[79] She knew how it was that a costermonger's business practices forced him to use credit and how a housewife might use the pawnbroker as a way of equalizing income. She also appreciated the problems of cooking on an open fire and condemned the typical ignorance of the well-meaning philanthropist of the limitations that this imposed on the choice of menus.[80] And she realized how early marriage and frequent pregnancy could erode rather than develop maternal instinct. Watching a working-class wedding, she reflected on

> the light-hearted way in which they take this step. For the girls especially it means burdens which seem almost too heavy to be born – of care and sickness and poverty, of hopeless squalor or unceasing toil, leading to premature old age or death. By the time they are twenty-five all the elasticity and vigour of youth are crushed out of them, and those who maintain their self-respect have nothing to look forward to but drudgery.[81]

In writing of the working-class wife, Helen Bosanquet was often uncharacteristically bleak. But her admiration for the heroic struggle mounted by so many working women caused her to believe that wives could nevertheless be educated to aim at a higher standard for themselves and their families. 'Patient endurance' was also, she felt, accompanied all too often by 'patient unintelligence'. Where children were badly behaved she advised the social worker that 'the hard working mother of a large family is apt to lose sight of the fact that troublesomeness in children is often due to ill-health which a wise and sympathetic visitor may be able to detect and check'.[82] Significantly, in the case of women, Helen Bosanquet was prepared to extend her argument beyond the individual case to argue strongly for better educational opportunities. Noting that men complained of women's narrow-mindedness and lack of intelligent understanding of issues, she suggested that 'they have seldom realised that the discomfort they experience from these ill effects is, after all, only the natural consequence of their own ideas about women's education'.[83] Beatrice Webb twice commented on the ignorance of working-class wives in her diary, but showed no interest in the problem as a social issue. Helen Bosanquet additionally called attention to the need to train women for paid employment which, she argued, would make them wiser mothers and stand them in good stead in case of widowhood.

The depth of Helen Bosanquet's concern for the welfare of working-class women found its fullest expression in her support for votes for women. Her views on the suffrage were only hinted at in her book on the family,[84] but five years later she wrote a letter to *The Times* that was highly critical of the anti-suffrage position. In the main her argument rested on the need of working, rather than middle-class, women for the vote. First, she reiterated her faith in the good sense of working women: 'The more I see and know of our working sisters the more I am amazed at the sheer waste of practical wisdom in our country due to the exclusion of women from politics'. But the burden of her argument was based firmly on the belief that working women desired the vote and that this represented a genuine interest on their part that should under no circumstances be thwarted: 'even if I thought they were mistaken in their anticipation of all the vote might do for them I hope I should humbly stand aside and place no stumbling block in the way of their effort to raise their *status*'. In fact she felt that they were not mistaken, for while she did not believe that the vote would bring higher wages, shorter hours or good husbands, 'it will bring them at once something at least of the respect and consideration which forms the basis upon which we more fortunate women build our lives'.[85] Working women deserved encouragement in their desire to raise their standard. Moreover, political citizenship would bring them to take more interest in the world around them, which would enlarge their role as mothers and in turn give them additional leverage in their profoundly unequal relations with their husbands. Helen Bosanquet's Idealism was strongly touched by her feminism and it was the latter that allowed her to see a number of aspects of male/female relationships that remained hidden from both Beatrice Webb and male social investigators such as Booth and Rowntree. She was considerably less ambivalent than Beatrice about women taking an active part in public life. She had no difficulty in accommodating the idea that women, as rational creatures, should seize every opportunity to widen their interests: 'We all of us tread our daily round the better when there is at least one window through which we can look away to the hills'.[86]

Ideally the family was the natural focus of loving support and altruistic love, where the character of husbands and wives developed in relation to the interest they took in each other and their children, and where children learned their first lessons in responsibility to others. However, neither Helen nor Bernard Bosanquet were blind to the fact that wives and children did not often occupy a place of equal status within the family. In an early essay Bernard Bosanquet wrote of the need to deepen family sentiment:

> By remembering that the home is after all an element in the common good of the community; that the wife and children are not playthings, not animals to be fed, or instruments of social or industrial advancement, but are members of a great nation that has a past and a future, and relations of duty and participation in a common goal, binding together all its citizens.[87]

In her biography of Bernard, Helen Bosanquet paid tribute to her husband's 'high ideal of the dignity of womanhood' and in particular his enthusiasm for women's education.[88]

Helen Bosanquet regarded marriage as sacrosanct and was much opposed to the recommendation of the 1912 Royal Commission on Divorce that the grounds for divorce be liberalized.[89] But she felt strongly that the family could not perform its vital role if women did not achieve an equal dignity and status to their husbands: 'the noblest harmonies of life arise when two disciplined and independent wills combine'.[90] She did not envisage, any more than other feminists of the period, husbands and wives sharing the unpaid labour of housework and caring. Rather, she advocated a kind of companionate marriage, not unlike that favoured by Beatrice Webb in the course of her conversation with Alfred Marshall. Following the argument of Alice Clark in her classic history of women's work in pre-industrial England, she acknowledged that women had played a larger part in productive work before the industrial revolution. However, anticipating in no small measure Ivy Pinchbeck's analysis published in the 1930s, she welcomed the withdrawal of married women's labour from paid employment: 'for it has left the home more free for its highest function of all – proper care and nurture of the children'.[91] She accepted without question the wisdom of differentiating the roles of husbands and wives but believed that differentiation at the expense of women's development – 'arbitrarily narrowing the scope of women's activities' – did not serve to enrich family life.[92]

In particular she was concerned that women not be narrowly confined to the role of wife and mother. Working women who married young and had large families were likely to become demoralized and neglectful of their homes. In such circumstances the maternal instinct became degraded rather than developing into loving care. In an early article she used a mixture of Idealist philosophy and feminist ideas to justify an outspoken rejection of early marriage as a solution to what was seen as the problem of working-class immorality:

> Much of the evil is due to false ideas about life which are not peculiar to the people of whom we are speaking. It is only in the lower classes that girls are allowed to think, or even made to feel, that a woman's life has no legitimate interests outside of marriage, and that, therefore, to lose an opportunity of getting married may be to miss all of the good which life has to offer.

She went on to advocate that a higher standard than this be set for working women:

> To realise that the people have a capacity for rising as well as falling is the next step towards the social utopia in which no one will enter upon the responsibility of marriage without a fair prospect of being able to bring up a family in decency and comfort.[93]

Later, in her book on the family, she strongly advocated occupational training for women before marriage and, recognizing that this might make women less inclined to marry, she merely commented that better but fewer marriages would be no bad thing.[94]

Unlike male social investigators, Helen Bosanquet was not even convinced that domestic service was the best training for the future wives and mothers. The board schoolgirl who was sent to mind the neighbour's baby for a few pence a week and who graduated to become a slavey (general servant) in a lower middle-class household experienced hard work, small pay, poor food and sharp words. Helen's observation was acute enough to cause her to question the value of such 'training' for later life. Equally, a girl placed in a rich household might learn only the art of waste and self-indulgence.[95] On the whole, she favoured the discipline provided by learning a skilled trade under careful supervision.

Compared to Beatrice Webb, Helen Bosanquet was less constrained in her opinions by the ideas of male social scientists about sexual difference and women's inferior capacities. Idealist commitment to the development of character merged easily with the egalitarian feminist ideas of John Stuart Mill and Emily Davies, the pioneer of women's further education. Bosanquet echoed the former when she wrote: 'the minds of women have generally been artificial productions, based upon pre-conceived ideas of what was suitable to women'.[96] She did not, like Octavia Hill, adhere to the idea that womanly feeling found legitimate expression only in 'homelike' work, or wrestle with the issue like Beatrice Webb, finally spurning it altogether. She openly repudiated Ruskin's idea of perfect womanhood, preferring that of Mary Woll-stonecraft, and laid claim, like most pioneers of women's education, to the high moral ground in the debate by arguing that good mothers needed 'true knowledge'.

This did not mean that Helen favoured women engaging in paid employment during marriage. On the contrary, she was opposed to married women's work and believed that women should only be members of the labour force prior to marriage and during widowhood. Many parts of her analysis of married women's work were extremely simplistic, not least the idea that men's wages would rise if women withdrew from the workforce. But, because her analysis was focused so firmly on the family, she perceived an additional reason for the low wages accorded married women especially in the sweated trades: 'women's labour is then a by-product and not expected to repay its cost of production. In other words their earnings are merely subsidiary to those of men upon whom they are dependent'.[97] This analysis is remarkably similar to that of some contemporary feminists. She agreed with the importance Sidney Webb attached to custom in determining women's wages and believed that their marital dependency was one significant component.

In 1897 she cooperated with Beatrice Webb and Louise Creighton in the writing of a pamphlet on the need to extend factory and workshop legislation to the laundry trade.[98] She shared Beatrice's view that the sweated trades were essentially parasitic and this, together with her concern about the working conditions of young girls and working-class mothers, overrode her antipathy to state interference in this regard.

However, she could not go so far as to support minimum wage legislation which, as the Webbs acknowledged, might logically consign the weak to the ranks of the unemployed and, Helen Bosanquet feared above all, to the poor law. Rather she advocated rigorous training for women in new processes and techniques: 'They must be able to take their place as managers, not rivals of machinery, and then the starvation wage will disappear'.[99] She also exhibited a touching faith that what was well-made (by skilled labour using the latest technology) would be well-paid. Employers were to be moralized and consumers educated to pay more. But as Beatrice Webb commented acidly:

> Even if the consumer made the Quixotic rule of paying the old-fashioned price for everything, he has no ground for hoping or believing that the shopkeeper will pass his bounty on to the wholesale dealer, the wholesale dealer to the manufacturer and the manufacturer to the wage-earner.[100]

However, Helen Bosanquet did make the woman worker herself the focus of attention rather than, like Beatrice Webb, conceptualizing an efficient method of organizing industry designed to drag the worker with it.

Helen Bosanquet believed that a division of labour between husband and wife was 'natural and necessary': while women concentrated on the nurture of children, men were responsible for earning 'a family wage'. While she welcomed the decline of the patriarchal family and 'ancestor worship', as she called it, she accepted that men should be the heads of families, insisting only that paternal authority be based not on wifely submission but on loyalty born of mutual aid, something that recent research has suggested was part of working-class women's own view of marriage.[101] She was thus concerned both to delineate the conditions under which husbands could lay claim to their authority and to set firm limits to it. In her book on the family, her discussion of the role of husbands was rather less clear-cut and certainly less immediately sympathetic than that of wives. In the first historical section of the book, she focused implicitly on the middle-class family, the discussion revolving largely around property ownership, which Le Play considered crucial to the stability of the family as an institution. While Helen Bosanquet defended private property, she did so only as one manifestation of 'realised will', which meant that male authority and family stability had to be based on other foundations. She believed that the fundamental factor in family relationships was the care taken by family members each for the other. The 'equal but different' roles performed by husbands and wives constituted the active expression of such care and support. Thus at the beginning of the second part of *The Family*, which concentrated mainly on the working-class family, Bosanquet noted immediately that it was not true that families without property would not care for each other. But just as it was crucial that the wife exercise proper control over the family budget and the children, so the husband had to play his part and provide.

On the whole, Helen Bosanquet, in common with most commentators of the period, had less faith in, and therefore less sympathy with, the husband's good will in this respect. She wrote approvingly of Margery Loane's anecdote concerning a poor woman who

> allowed herself to be forced into the position of wage-earner: 'I'll regret it once, and that's all my life . . . there's only one rule for women who want a decent home for their children and themselves. If your husband comes home crying, and says he can't find any work, sit down on the other side of the fire and cry till he *does*'.[102]

'Natural' regard for his family's welfare was the primary impetus to the development of the adult male and his becoming a cooperative member of society:

> nothing but the considered rights and responsibilities of family life will ever rouse the average man to his full degree of efficiency, and induce him to continue working after he has earned sufficient to meet his own personal needs. The Family in short, is from this point of view, the only known way of ensuring, with any approach to success, that one generation will exert itself in the interests and for the sake of another, and its effect upon the economic efficiency of both generations is in this respect alone of paramount importance.[103]

The male's 'natural instinct' was, however, by no means so reliable as the maternal instinct. Whereas the mother's neglect was in Helen's estimation most likely to be due to ignorance, this was much less likely to be true of the father; a substantial number of the unemployed could after all be categorized as 'wilfully incapable of work'. Nevertheless, Helen Bosanquet was as anxious as Margery Loane to stress that working-class fathers should not be condemned out of hand. She deplored the 'vulgar assumption' that poor fathers had no natural family affection and, like Loane, emphasized the way working-class fathers demonstrated love for their very young children.[104]

It was on the question of men's role within the family that Helen Bosanquet's moral theory of human society, centred on the development of the ethical individual fulfilling his obligations to his fellow men, was allied most closely with the economist's preoccupation with securing male work incentives. The issue also raised something of a dilemma in respect of social-work practice. Theoretically, the individual could only be guided to an understanding that he had developed bad habits and towards the development of higher interests. According to Bernard Bosanquet, it was impossible to promote moral behaviour by force.[105] But in the matter of fulfilment of family obligations, the Bosanquets were more likely to favour the use of sticks than carrots. The line they drew between guidance and punishment was extremely fine. As they had pointed out, the development of family obligations was crucial to the formulation of progressive wants, which in turn were crucial to all human, including economic, progress. If a husband and father was not meeting his obligations towards his wife and children, serious questions were therefore raised about the kind of intervention that might be appropriate.

Remedies and tensions
In the view of the Bosanquets, any outdoor poor relief offered to the poor constituted a support to poverty. Out-relief, poor relief and the extension of credit merely perpetuated pauperism and encouraged the kinds of bad habits that characterized the residuum.[106] In short, any body or institution giving money to the poor ensured that wages would remain low and irregular because relief would act as a subsidy to them, and that the poor would not raise their standard because their attempt to struggle to earn more and push their way up the social ladder would be undermined.[107] It was in relation to the family that these prescriptions for action acquired their full force, forming the basis both for the COS's campaign against any measure of state intervention that threatened to erode the mutual responsibility of family members towards each other and for good social-work practice that would promote self-maintenance and independence among the poor.

Given that most parents could be expected to do their best by their children, it was important that they be left alone to develop and enjoy family feeling. If they failed in their responsibilities it was of cardinal importance that no one step in to relieve the parents of them. In particular it was important that no doles or relief be given to anyone as long as there were family members who might be called on to fulfil their natural obligation to maintain. While it was particularly important to make sure that parents took responsibility for children, it was also important that children assumed the care of elderly parents. In Helen Bosanquet's view the greatest threat to the integrity of the family was posed by the state. State intervention alone could subvert the real foundation of family strength and purpose, the bond of affection and obligation that existed between family members. Circumstances, such as bad housing, would not cause family breakdown, but if 'natural' family obligations were assumed by the state, selfishness and mutual indifference would result thereby ensuring the disappearance of the family and with it the ethical foundations of the state.[108] E. J. Urwick strongly condemned this dismissal of any relationship between environmental circumstance and family breakdown for, while equally devoted to a moral and indeed spiritual approach to social problems, he did not support Helen Bosanquet's rigid exclusion of the state from playing any part in solving those problems.[109] Helen firmly believed that neither charity nor state relief could ever replace family care.

In an early article she described the condition of some of her elderly poor: an old woman living in a garret, who clung to her last possession, an old beaver hat (once her brother's), and who ventured out only to buy bread, 'purchased at terrible cost'.[110] This woman had starved herself to pay the rent and then stayed her hunger only by the sacrifice of mementos. She was persuaded to go to the poor law guardians who gave her a pension of 5/9d a week, but apparently could not cope with such wealth and succumbed to mental infirmity. Helen used this example of an isolated old woman to condemn the lack of adequate relief at an early enough stage. Octavia Hill often did the same. To Helen's mind there was no more deserving case for charitable relief than the respectable, isolated old person. However where there were children, friends or neighbours, it behoved the social worker first 'to strengthen every tie, however slight, which still connects them with human sympathy and to guard against the thought, however kindly meant, that 5/- a week can by itself bring comfort into desolate lives'.[111] Of Fabian collectivists, Helen Bosanquet inquired sarcastically (as was her wont) whether 'under the Socialist regime there will be a special department for boiling kettles for poor old women, and so obviating the necessity for neighbourly kindness'.[112] Nevertheless, the understanding that care and attention as well as material relief were crucial to the welfare of the elderly had to be rediscovered by policymakers as late as the 1960s.

In the case of children, Helen Bosanquet pointed out long before the work of Anna Freud and John Bowlby during World War II that children taken into institutional care tended to do poorly. It was important both that children be given the chance to experience natural family affection, however uncertain it might be, and for parents to be 'forced' to fulfil their 'natural' obligations. This was true even in 'hard cases', for instance in respect of widows. One of the reasons for Helen Bosanquet's insistence on a high standard of industrial training for working-class women was in order that they might be able to sustain themselves in the event of widowhood. On the whole, her views were shared by the poor law authorities, which after 1871 tightened their regulations regarding outdoor relief for all women with children and without men.[113] Widows were usually expected to maintain one or two of their children and place the remainder in the workhouse. However, the authorities found it difficult to reach any absolute conclusion as to whether such women should be treated categorically as workers rather than as mothers, and practices in respect to outdoor relief varied widely. Helen Bosanquet had no such difficulties. It was part and parcel of parenthood to provide for children and, while every assistance should be given to parents by social workers to enable them to provide, if this proved impossible, it followed that parenthood should be foresworn and the shelter of the workhouse sought.

The prime importance accorded the fulfilment of family obligations serves to explain the otherwise incomprehensibly ferocious opposition mounted by Helen Bosanquet and the COS to the introduction of legislation permitting local authorities to provide school meals. To one COS member, school feeding represented the crucial issue for the organization: 'Outlying territory we can abandon, but here our citadel is reached. If we cannot defend this wall we might as well surrender'.[114] The Bosanquets insisted that if the trouble were taken to investigate each case a reason would be found for hunger in the child. It was impossible to treat the child without regard for the family context. To do so would be to subvert the role of the parents and to ignore the first principle of any intervention in the family: that it must further the development of the mind and character of the individual. Their position was ably summarized by Margery Loane in her many books on the poor, which received the approbation of Helen Bosanquet.[115] Octavia Hill also railed continuously against the practice of school feeding, considering it to be a subsidy to lazy parents. If the child were hungry because the father was unwilling to work or because the mother was lazy and slovenly, then these were problems to be tackled directly. If the family were passing through a temporary period of genuine distress, then it was unlikely that one meal a day would constitute adequate relief for the child and more relief should be offered. School meals threatened both to do irreparable damage to parental responsibility and citizenship and to thwart progress towards scientific charity by offering a kind of wholesale relief. Of the twin concerns it was the former that constituted the more fundamental threat. Loch stressed the temptation school meals posed to mothers to neglect their children's welfare,[116] but Helen Bosanquet and other women social investigators felt that the real danger was to the more fragile male incentive to provide. In *The Family*

Bosanquet quoted a woman who said that she was glad that there had been no school feeding when her children were at school because her husband spent too much on drink and would have cut her slender housekeeping money had state meals been available.[117] This view was confirmed by Anna Martin, a suffragist and settlement worker, who quoted the women she worked with as fearing not only that their husbands might not provide but also that an important source of their power and authority within the home might be usurped by the state.[118]

If school meals represented an entirely unacceptable extension of a system that was already too prone to offering doles and sapping character, true charity consisted of teaching people that fitting themselves for a positive function in society was the only avenue to life. Bernard Bosanquet maintained that the denial of relief was itself educational: 'people soon learn why you do and do not help. And it educates them'.[119] Both the Bosanquets were great advocates of a thorough system of casework that would carefully discern the true cause of distress and determine whether the case was helpable. In her 1893 article on 'thorough charity', Helen Bosanquet stressed the importance of investigating the applicants' circumstances: 'the main difficulty is to get understanding; when we have reached that, sympathy and experience will generally suggest the next step'. But she went on to talk about the difficulty of distinguishing deserving from undeserving applicants. In respect of the latter, she asked in a manner remarkably akin to that of Beatrice Webb when she had pondered the fate of the opium eater a decade before: 'after all, how many of us would have been more deserving under the circumstances?'[120] She feared that the use of the categories of deserving and undeserving turned COS workers into moral arbiters and encouraged applicants in the ways of 'hypocrisy and deceit'. She advocated instead that workers endeavour to establish whether an applicant was helpable, in other words, whether it was likely that he or she could become self-supporting. Helen acknowledged this term to be 'a barbarism', but she hoped that it would provide greater scientific neutrality in the classification of applicants. Her concern that the adjudication of applicants for relief should be affected neither by the subjective assessment of morals on the part of the COS worker nor by deceit on the part of the applicant did nothing to obviate Beatrice Webb's point that many of those in poverty through ill-fortune might not qualify as 'helpable' (see p. 102). And as Madeleine Rooff has observed, because judgement of character remained an essential factor in the assessment, the new classification remained as much a moral as a social one.[121] The debate between Bernard Bosanquet and Alfred Marshall over the issue of stigma arising from resort to the poor law bears out this point.[122] Bernard Bosanquet denied that there was any stigma involved because unhelpable cases were not necessarily disgraceful cases. There were hopeless conditions besides bad character, although no other was so hopeless. But the COS could not have it both ways; in so far as it judged the worst cases to lack character, the judgement was inevitably stigmatizing.

In 1898 Bernard Bosanquet reflected that

> the completeness of case work, and even the elaborate working of the special case system by application to individual donors, has in some degree put out of sight the direct campaign of organisation of charities or reform of poor law administration in the district. I do not know that this is to be regretted, supposing the Society now thoroughly considers the position, and brings itself to understand the task before it.[123]

The Bosanquets favoured casework above the original aim of the COS to organize all charitable endeavour in a particular district, such as was achieved by Octavia Hill in Marylebone, because it presented the surest way not only of weeding out the unhelpable but of establishing a more positive, cooperative relationship between rich and poor which would enable the latter to be guided towards better habits and a higher standard of life.

The problem of poverty could only be solved 'from a point of view which includes the whole mind and interests of the people in question'.[124] The social worker had to be prepared to attempt to understand all the influences affecting the lives of the individual seeking aid and in that sense to be a generalist. To Helen Bosanquet, specialization in social work involved adding deeper knowledge of a particular influence or condition to a general understanding of the whole, not concentrating on one aspect of the problem to the neglect of others. Only with such a complete understanding could social workers begin to stimulate the energies of the poor, inculcate responsibility and train their faculties.[125]

Workers had to be prepared to encourage the poor to expect the 'natural consequences' of sin and vice and to take responsibility for their 'natural duties'. Like Octavia Hill, Helen Bosanquet rejected the relationship of dependence between rich and poor, such as was fostered by the Lady Bountiful image. But Helen spelled out the content of correct social-work practice in considerably more detail than Octavia. The task of the social workers was primarily to foster self-maintenance. In practice this meant that visitors were advised to take a family a savings-bank card rather than a parish food-ticket. A crippled child should not be removed from its mother's care but rather the mother taught how to look after it, using whatever resources she had available. Those with sufficient earnings had to be encouraged to emigrate or to move to find better paid work; those who were suffering poverty because of sickness had to be introduced to a provident dispensary; those with a mentally disabled child had to be encouraged to seek appropriate education for it. None of this could be achieved overnight. 'Sprinkling charity' would achieve nothing; the worker had to be prepared to continue working with a case indefinitely. Helen Bosanquet used a homely analogy, one of her favourite devices, to make the point: 'I used to be taught as a child that I must not water my garden unless I were prepared to do it thoroughly'.[126] Workers were assured that their sympathy would carry them far. In the case of the troublesome child for example: 'the mere fact that someone is showing an interest in the child without being paid for it is apt to touch the parents in a way which will greatly strengthen your hand'.[127] It was incumbent on social workers to use the 'natural remedies' of family, neighbours and the individual's own resources of industry and thrift.

These principles of 'true charity' dominated the Majority Report of the Royal Commission on the Poor Laws, much of which was written by Helen. The chief desire of the Majority Report was to retain a single (albeit reformed) destitution authority that would investigate and treat the applicant for relief and his family as a unit. In her gloss on the 1909 Majority Report, Helen Bosanquet argued that the minority was wrong in its contention that the difference in applicants for relief was so great as to warrant breaking up the poor law. On the contrary: 'the common element is so important as to justify, indeed to necessitate – the existence of a special law to authorise and regulate the relief of these people, and of a special authority to apply and administer the law'.[128] Pauperism meant that the individual and his family were incapable of self-management. Its cure demanded individual treatment by social workers to find out first what powers of mind were lacking, and second an appropriate way of resuscitating them.

The Bosanquets argued that if a family had ceased to be self-sustaining it required help of a different order to that of the 'normal' family. The new public assistance (destitution) authorities would take full charge of a destitute family, insisting that it surrender to a programme of 'social therapeutics'. Bernard Bosanquet maintained that there must be a real difference between 'what we may call social therapeutics and the normal provision for health and education throughout the community'.[129] The public assistance authority would essentially become *in loco parentis* to the destitute family and assume total responsibility for its support and restoration to independence. It was, he argued, impossible for the state to take on the maintenance of an individual without assuming full responsibility for the reform of the family.[130] For example, it was hopeless for the state to give a child school meals without assessing the family situation and taking steps to correct the deficiencies in character of the mother and the father. One of the major criticisms levied by Loch against the Minority Report was that in proposing to break up the poor law and send each family member to a different place for relief, it ignored 'all the self-acting elements of society, all its springs of growth', whose main source was the family unit.[131]

In their extensive criticisms of the minority, Helen and Bernard Bosanquet also emphasized the confusion of responsibilities that would likely result from sending members of a family in need to a variety of different agencies for help, the unemployed to a Department of Labour and children to education authorities, for example, rather than treating the family as a unit and sending it to a single destitution authority.[132] The perception of the Webbs' report as administratively complicated was in the end extremely damaging, because in the lengthy debate following the publication of the 1909 report, the Webbs argued strongly for the administrative rationality of their proposals. But the proposals of the Majority Report were equally impractical. Individual work with all those applying for relief would have involved an army of social workers, as Bernard Bosanquet acknowledged:

> If the reforming movement of the COS could have had its way, every family in contact with the poor law, in the institutions and out, would have been under constant careful and friendly scrutiny with a view to its restoration to independent citizenship.[133]

He emphasized that in dealing with the destitute 'you offer *everything* – the whole matériel and guidance of life', which was why it was so important to make sure that the applicant had really failed to achieve self-maintenance in the first place. Once destitution was established, the social work to be done was described in terms resembling a religious crusade: 'there is as it were, an army of social healers to be trained and organised . . . disciplined and animated with a single spirit and purpose . . .'[134] The Bosanquets emphasized the importance of having specialists in the 'general problem of supervising family life' ready to deal with applicants for relief. It was not a case, they argued, of choosing between specialist agencies and a public assistance authority as the minority insisted, but rather of entrusting the care of non-self-supporting people to specialists within a special authority dedicated to case work.[135] In terms of numbers of social workers and their cost, the Bosanquets' scheme was as doubtful a starter politically as the Webbs' desire to abandon a public assistance authority altogether.

The proposals of the Majority Report regarding the destitute confirmed the movement within the COS towards a stronger emphasis on casework and away from the negative connotations associated with the early attempts to organize charity. In her extended gloss on the report, Helen took a most sympathetic view of the isolated elderly person in the workhouse: 'Everywhere there is the desire now to deal gently with the old people in the workhouses, but the success with which they are handled varies greatly'.[136] The Bosanquets' concern to keep the destitute as a separate category was not inspired, as Beatrice Webb inferred, by a simple desire to punish (in the sense of cause hardship to), as had so often been the result under the 1834 Poor Law. The only exception was the treatment envisaged for the recalcitrant:

> Your object is the restoration of the individual and the protection of society from temptation; your principle means primarily completeness of treatment and control of all who fail in self-maintenance, and where hardship is indicated as the remedy or preventative, you have the power and justification to apply it.[137]

On the last point the Bosanquets' view did not differ from that of the Webbs, who also envisaged the use of extremely severe punishment for those who proved unwilling to live a useful life.

Nevertheless, considerable tensions arose between the Majority Report's prescriptions for social-work practice and the theory that informed them. The Bosanquets insisted, in the Octavia Hill tradition, that casework represented an opportunity to develop relations between rich and poor based on love and sympathy. But the desire to promote interaction between rich and poor as freely associating individuals with the aim of raising the standards and level of happiness of the poor was hard to achieve in practice, and Helen's writing on social-work methods often revealed contradictions in her thinking about the way in which the rich were to approach and 'treat' the poor.

'Thorough charity' demanded scientific investigation of circumstances and character and inevitably represented a substantial intrusion into the privacy of the family, which Helen Bosanquet also insisted was crucial to the development of true family feeling. She urged social workers to think carefully before assuming the 'heavy responsibility' of intervening in the lives of others, but on the other hand, in an article published the same year as this advice was given, Bernard Bosanquet was ready to assure workers that respectable people would not mind inquiries being made of friends, neighbours and employers about their circumstances and character.[138] To Bernard Bosanquet charity was, as Vincent has pointed out, not a gift but the right of the individual citizen.[139] The Bosanquets also believed, however, that the poor had the responsibility of submitting to social scientific casework investigation.

Setting questions for discussion by trainee social workers in 1912, Helen Bosanquet posed two issues which remain relevant today:

> 1. What circumstances or conditions justify intervention in the private life of a family which has not offended against the law? 2. How far are we in danger of mistaking a mode of life which we should not take ourselves for one which must necessarily be put a stop to?[140]

In regard to the first issue, Helen Bosanquet advised social workers to 'see the head of the family before giving assistance (for instance in respect of a truant child) . . . he has the right to be consulted before we interfere with his duty of providing for his family. Often he will be found very much adverse to charity'.[141] In fact the evidence suggests that working-class men and women were anxious to receive non-stigmatizing, non-intrusive welfare.[142] Working women welcomed the advice offered by infant welfare clinics while continuing to be suspicious of the routine and uninvited visits by health visitors.[143] They were unlikely to have felt better disposed towards a voluntary worker whose job included 'scientific assessment', and who in all likelihood found Helen's second question either extremely difficult to answer or, worse, unworthy of serious attention.

In the Bosanquets' scheme of things, social workers were supposed to help the poor become self-maintaining by fostering whatever good habits they could find. Helen Bosanquet stated categorically that it was pointless to force benevolence and charity on the poor, for unless an effort was made to help people to raise their standards and meet their own needs they could not gain in progressive power. Such a method relied first on the capacity to recognize sources of strength that might not immediately be apparent to the middle-class observer and, second, on a willingness to work with the poor rather than dictate to them. Helen Bosanquet recognized both these points but there is evidence to suggest that, like Octavia Hill, she was inclined to contradict them when she considered it necessary. While she urged workers that legitimate sources of happiness existed among the working class that were alien to the experience of the middle-class observer (she cited, for example, the pleasure the working-class father took in the company of babies and small children), there were many other occasions on which she showed a propensity to ignore her own teaching that all social classes and all individuals had a standard which must be slowly and painfully improved, and preferred to impose standards of behaviour of her own. Thus meeting indoors was to be preferred to the tendency of working people to congregate on the street, and the female factory worker was to be 'taught' to buy warm underclothing rather than 'feathers and finery'.[144]

Because higher standards were inevitably associated with the middle class, the tendency was to teach social workers that the poor looked at things differently, and that while they should look for the 'sunnier side' of the poor's behaviour, they should then set about teaching more acceptable practices. The idea of working with the poor translated itself in practice, therefore, into something rather more didactic. Despite deploring the way in which philanthropists tended to treat the poor as dependent children, believing that this merely encouraged them to behave as such, Helen Bosanquet nevertheless described the state of mind of poor and uneducated wives as being akin to that of an untrained child and advised social workers that they should be prepared to develop the 'qualities of capacity and foresight for lack of which, more than for lack of money, so many make failures of their lives'.[145] In other words the social worker must be prepared to think for the poor on the assumption that the world view of the social worker would make inherently better sense than that of the poor.

It is important to recognize that both Helen and Bernard Bosanquet struggled to comprehend the issues at stake in any attempt to undertake social work. At the abstract level they conceptualized these well. George Orwell was to agonize over similar issues, using as an example the problem of diet and whether it was right for middle-class people to use their knowledge of nutrition to insist that working-class people eat brown bread, or whether they should rather show respect for working-class preferences and keep both their knowledge and their greater longevity to themselves.[146] The Bosanquets wanted to empower the poor but lacked a method of social work that would enable this to happen. Their thinking may have been confused at crucial points and they may have failed in their endeavour but they, like Octavia Hill, deserve credit for grasping the nettle. Beatrice Webb left the 'decaying masses' of St Katherine's Buildings behind in disgust, hoping that once a model for a socialist society had been derived from the respectable trade unionists and cooperators it could be successfully imposed on the rest.

Conclusion

Helen Bosanquet was not the kind of individualist that Beatrice Webb tried to make her out to be and historians critical of the COS have assumed her to be. Her analysis of the causes of poverty certainly gave firm priority to the importance of individual character over circumstances but the emphasis she placed on the importance of individual social work with families as a solution to the problem of poverty had little to do with the ideas of classical political economy for which the COS was accused of being the mouthpiece.

In an 1890 address to the Fabian Society, Bernard Bosanquet declared that, 'If I had before me an audience of plutocratic sympathies then I should have the pleasure of speaking much more than I shall tonight in the language of the Fabian essays'.[147] On this occasion, he argued that the real antithesis existed between economic individualism and moral socialism on the one hand, and moral individualism and economic socialism on the other, but that the moral antithesis dominated. Beatrice Webb was more intellectually in sympathy with the Bosanquets' search for moral principles to guide social action than was Sidney. It was above all the Bosanquets' resistance to the idea that social problems could be remedied by 'machinery' or 'mechanical support' that irrevocably separated them from the Webbs. The touchstone of their differences, notwithstanding the impossibility of labelling the Bosanquets as simple individualists, was their respective views as to the proper role of the state and state bureaucracy. The Bosanquets envisaged armies of social workers intervening in working-class family life but working as volunteers, not as part of a state bureaucracy. Helen Bosanquet attacked the Fabians strongly in the *Charity Organisation Review* during the 1890s and the Royal Commission on the Poor Laws showed the depth of antagonism between her and Beatrice. Yet she cooperated with Beatrice on the campaign against the sweated trades, as did both Mary Ward and Violet Markham.

The Bosanquets shared a transcendent commitment to social action as a means of tackling social problems common to Edwardians interested in social issues. They were not *laissez-faire* individualists. In many respects, Helen Bosanquet's commitment to 'understanding the poor', a necessary part of her Idealist approach to the problem of poverty, resulted in more sympathetic analysis than that of Beatrice Webb. Certainly the Bosanquets were more progressive in terms of the way they wanted to see the poor treated than most of the COS, as the society's reaction to the 1909 Majority Report showed. Octavia Hill, who failed to see how any change in machinery, including that advocated by the Majority Report (particularly the restructuring of the destitution authorities and the provision of public works for the unemployed) would achieve better results, apparently had a strong following. But the Bosanquets' tightly argued views on social questions became increasingly untenable in face of the growing perception of both liberals and conservatives (Mary Ward and Violet Markham among them) as to the necessity of invoking state assistance whether on grounds of social justice or national efficiency, or as a pragmatic response to the size of the problem to be solved.

Helen Bosanquet had great faith in women's capacities, which she demonstrated in her argument for more education and training for both working- and middle-class women. She was a recognized authority in the world of charity and social investigation but, until the Royal Commission on the Poor Laws, eschewed a public role. Indeed it seems that her work on the Royal Commission was unobtrusive. Possibly she consciously modelled her committee persona on that of her fellow commissioner, Octavia Hill. Yet she was responsible for influencing the whole direction of the Majority Report and wrote large sections of it. She may, like Beatrice Webb, have found the public work of the Royal Commission a strain. She suffered severe heart trouble in 1908 and in the autumn of that year attended meetings only with difficulty, sitting in an armchair in front of the fire rather than round the table.[148] Helen undoubtedly proved a shrewder tactician on the commission than did Beatrice but playing committee politics was probably not wholly to her taste, even though her writing, for example, her criticism of Fabian ideas, was often acerbic. Her fellow commissioner, Professor William Smart, an economist, wrote to her during her illness in 1908 in his usual amiable style: 'I hope you will follow your husband's example and confine yourself to writing books, you were never made to fight Mrs Webb – any more than she was made to write history' (Beatrice had just presented the commission with her version of the evolution of poor law principles).[149]

Helen Bosanquet seems largely to have avoided experiencing the kind of tensions between public and private in her own life that plagued Beatrice Webb. Conceivably, she avoided them deliberately. Helen's feminist consciousness may have alerted her to pitfalls which Beatrice experienced throughout her life but never fully comprehended. Helen was relatively immune to ideas about female inferiority and was seemingly secure in the niche she created for herself within the world of philanthropy. In addition her feminism made her considerably more sensitive to the position of working-class women in particular. Indeed, her work in this respect had much more in common with Florence Bell and Magdalen Stuart Pember Reeves, although she preferred to identify with that of Margery Loane, who was also a firm believer in COS principles.

World War I represented a crisis for Idealist thinkers. Bernard Bosanquet was accused of lauding a God-like state, notwithstanding his opposition to government intervention, because he rejected any antithesis between the individual and the state, the general will being embodied in the state.[150] Until his death in 1925, Bernard Bosanquet continued to believe the healthy state to be non-militant and to exist for the sake of promoting 'best selves'. But World War I inevitably caused both the Bosanquets seriously to doubt, probably for the first time, that progress towards a higher level of existence could be sustained. In 1917 Helen recognized that the task facing them was huge when she wrote that ideas as to what actions were right and wrong required reconstruction. She used the war-time campaign to bring down the infant mortality rate as an illustration, condemning the way in which campaigners were wont to count 'how many more divisions we should have been able to put in the field today if we had instituted schools for mothers twenty years ago'. While she granted that the method worked and that more babies were being kept alive, 'if they could be aware of the fate which awaits them they might well enter their feeble protest'.[151] She was one of a very few to protest the way in which this campaign was conducted.

Helen Bosanquet showed tenacity in her adherence to the idea that quality of mind and character were the crucial determinants of poverty. But behind this lay a commitment to fostering an active citizenship, a goal that never achieved prominence either in the Webbs' solutions to the problem of poverty or in the welfare-reform programme of the Liberal government of 1906–14. Her family-based sentiments were profoundly conservative but the importance of her concern to empower the poor was not accorded adequate recognition by comtemporaries (or most historians). Helen appeared more traditional than Beatrice Webb in terms of her place in the predominantly female world of charitable work yet her understanding of the lives of the poor, and especially of poor women, was in many ways more profound; her support for women's suffrage was more committed; and the voice she used in her published writing on social problems was unquestionably her own.

Notes

1. A. M. McBriar, *An Edwardian Mixed Doubles. The Bosanquets Versus the Webbs: A Study in British Social Policy, 1890–1929* (Oxford: Clarendon, 1987).
2. Bernard Bosanquet, 'The Philosophy of Casework', *Charity Organisation Review* (March 1916), p. 123.
3. Andrew Vincent and Raymond Plant, *Philosophy, Politics and Citizenship* (Oxford: Blackwell, 1984).
4. E. C. Price to Helen, 28/2/94, Bosanquet Papers, Newcastle University Archives, Trunk 2, B(i).

5. Sarah Dendy to Helen, 20/3/94, Bosanquet Papers, Trunk 2, Pkt C.
6. Helen Bosanquet, 'Review of *A Child of the Jago*', *Charity Organisation Review* (Jan. 1897), pp. 40–2.
7. C. E. Collet, 'Three Ideal COS Secretaries', *Charity Organisation Review* (March 1894), p. 120.
8. Octavia Hill to Helen, 9/10/93, Bosanquet Papers, Trunk 2, B(i).
9. Ramsay MacDonald, *Margaret Ethel MacDonald* (Allen & Unwin, 1912), p. 91.
10. Helen Dendy, 'Thorough Charity', *Charity Organisation Review* (June 1893), pp. 206–14.
11. Madeleine Rooff, *A Hundred Years of Family Welfare* (Michael Joseph, 1962); G. Stedman-Jones, *Outcast London* (Harmondsworth: Penguin, 1976), 1st edn 1971, Part III; and A. W. Vincent, 'The Poor Law Reports of 1909 and the Social Theory of the COS', *Victorian Studies* 27 (Spring 1984), pp. 343–63.
12. Stefan Collini, 'Hobhouse, Bosanquet and the State: Philosophical Idealism and Political Argument in England, 1880–1918', *Past and Present* 72 (Aug. 1976), p. 92.
13. Helen Dendy, 'The Meaning and Methods of True Charity', in Bernard Bosanquet (ed.), *Aspects of Social Reform* (Macmillan, 1895), p. 165.
14. Vincent and Plant, *Philosophy, Politics*, p. 100.
15. Bernard Bosanquet, 'Character in its bearing on Social Causation', in B. Bosanquet (ed.), *Aspects*, p. 105.
16. Helen and Bernard Bosanquet, 'Charity Organisation', *Contemporary Review* LXXI (1897), p. 115.
17. Helen Bosanquet, *Strength of the People. A Study in Social Economics* (Macmillan, 1903), 1st edn 1902, pp. 51 and 55.
18. Mrs Bernard Bosanquet, *The Standard of Life and Other Studies* (Macmillan, 1898), p. 31.
19. Bernard Bosanquet, 'The Meaning of Social Work', *International Journal of Ethics* XI (April 1901), p. 302.
20. Bernard Bosanquet, *The Philosophical Theory of the State* (Macmillan, 1899), p. 181.
21. Helen Dendy, 'The Industrial Residuum', in B. Bosanquet (ed.), *Aspects*, pp. 82–102; H. Bosanquet, *Strength of the People*, p. 51.
22. Henrietta Browne to Helen, 6/1/94, Bosanquet Papers, Trunk 2, B(i).
23. John Dendy to Helen, 28/1/94, Bosanquet Papers, Trunk 2, Pkt C.
24. H. Bosanquet, *Standard of Life*, p. 14.
25. Helen Bosanquet, 'The Psychology of Social Progress', *International Journal of Ethics* VII (April 1897) p. 271.
26. Charles Loch Mowat, *The Charity Organisation Society, 1869–1913* (Methuen, 1961), p. 68.
27. H. Bosanquet, *Standard of Life*, p. 3; Bernard Bosanquet, 'Socialism and Natural Selection', in B. Bosanquet (ed.), *Aspects*, p. 295.
28. H. Bosanquet, *Strength of the People*, pp. 11–35.
29. H. Bosanquet, *Standard of Life*, pp. 16 and 42.
30. Cited in Rodney Barker, *Political Ideas in Modern Britain* (Methuen, 1978), p. 114.
31. Bernard Bosanquet, 'The Duties of Citizenship', in B. Bosanquet (ed.), *Aspects*, p. 10.
32. B. Bosanquet, *Philosophical Theory of the State*, p. 269. This was an essentially Hegelian view; see Joan B. Landes, 'Hegel's Concept of the Family', in Jean B. Elshtain (ed.), *The Family in Political thought* (Amherst: University of Mass. Press, 1982).
33. Helen Bosanquet, *The Family* (Macmillan, 1906), pp. 204–6; see also Bernard Bosanquet, 'Duties of Citizenship', in B. Bosanquet (ed.), *Aspects*, p. 10.
34. B. Bosanquet, *Philosophical Theory of the State*, p. 300.

35. T. Parsons and R. F. Bales, *Family Socialization and Interaction Process* (Glencoe, Ill: Free Press, 1955).
36. H. Bosanquet, *Family*, pp. 95 and 99.
37. H. Spencer, *Man Versus the State* (Harmondsworth: Penguin, 1969), 1st edn 1884; Helen Bosanquet, 'Home and School in the Life of the Child', lecture under the auspices of the Carnegie Dunfermline Trust and School Board for the Borough of Dunfermline, Bosanquet Papers, Trunk 2, Box G.
38. H. Bosanquet, *Family*, p. 99; B. Bosanquet, 'Socialism and Natural Selection', p. 299.
39. Ferdinand Mount, *The Subversive Family. An Alternative History of Love and Marriage* (Allen & Unwin, 1983), 1st edn 1982.
40. H. Bosanquet, *Strength of the People*, p. 208; and *Standard of Life*, p. 130.
41. B. Bosanquet, *Philosophical Theory of the State*, pp. 198–9. See also H. Bosanquet, 'People and Houses', *Economic Journal* 10 (March 1900), pp. 47–59.
42. Bernard Bosanquet, 'The Social Criterion', paper read to the Edinburgh COS, 1907, Bosanquet Papers, Trunk 1, K6; see also Helen Bosanquet, 'Psychology of Social Progress', p. 277.
43. B. Bosanquet, 'The Meaning of Social Work', p. 296.
44. H. Bosanquet, *Strength of the People*, p. viii, preface to 2nd edn.
45. H. Bosanquet, *Standard of Life*, p. 52.
46. H. Bosanquet, 'Psychology of Social Progress', pp. 273–4.
47. Stedman-Jones, *Outcast London*, Pt II.
48. See also M. Loane, *The Queen's Poor* (Edward Arnold, 1910), chap. 4.
49. Beatrice Webb, Diary, TS, 14/5/26, f. 4303, BLPES.
50. B. Bosanquet, 'Idealism in Social Work', *Charity Organisation Review* (March 1898), pp. 122–33.
51. B. Bosanquet, 'Meaning of Social Work', p. 298.
52. H. Bosanquet, 'Methods of Training', *Charity Organisation Review* (Aug. 1900), pp. 103–9, reprinted in Marjorie Smith, *Professional Education for Social Work in Britain* (Allen & Unwin, 1953).
53. Ross McKibbin, 'Social Class and Social Observation in Edwardian England', *Transactions of the Royal Historical Society* 28 (1978), pp. 174–200.
54. Helen Bosanquet, *Rich and Poor* (Macmillan, 1896), p. 35.
55. Eg. M. Loane, *From their Point of View* (Edward Arnold, 1908), p. 184.
56. Anne de Selincourt to (?), nd, Bosanquet Papers, Trunk 2, Pkt E(i).
57. J. H. Muirhead (ed.), *Bernard Bosanquet and his Friends* (Allen & Unwin, 1935), p. 100.
58. H. Bosanquet, *Rich and Poor*, p. 106.
59. B. Bosanquet (ed.), *Aspects*, p. vi; see also C. S. Loch, *Charity and Social Life* (Macmillan, 1910), p. 377.
60. H. Bosanquet, 'The Historical Basis of English Poor Law Policy', *Economic Journal* 20 (June 1910), p. 193.
61. T. H. Marshall, Introduction to S. and B. Webb, *Methods of Social Study* (Cambridge: Cambridge University Press, 1975), 1st edn 1932.
62. McKibbin, 'Social Class and Social Observation', p. 276; Vincent and Plant, *Philosophy, Politics*, p. 98.
63. H. Bosanquet, 'The Poverty Line' (COS, 1903), p. 1.
64. M. Loane, *Queen's Poor*, p. 158.
65. C. S. Loch, 'Returns as an Instrument in Social Science', in B. Bosanquet (ed.), *Aspects*, p. 268.
66. 'Social Studies – COS', file AR 330/1, Bedford Archives.
67. Lady Bell, *At the Works. A Study of a Manufacturing Town* (Virago, 1985), 1st edn 1907, p. xxviii.
68. H. Bosanquet, 'Thorough Charity', p. 210; and *Rich and Poor*, p. 69.

69. B. Bosanquet, 'Character in its Bearing on Social Causation', in B. Bosanquet (ed.), *Aspects*, p. 113.
70. H. Bosanquet, *Rich and Poor*, p. 60.
71. H. Bosanquet, *Standard of Life*, pp. 128–9.
72. H. Bosanquet, *Strength of the People*, p. 102.
73. H. Dendy, 'The Children of Working London', in B. Bosanquet (ed.), *Aspects*, p. 32.
74. Beatrice Potter, 'Dock Labour', *Nineteenth Century* 128 (Oct. 1887), pp. 491–2, Passfield Papers VII, Item 7, BLPES.
75. H. Bosanquet, *Strength of the People*, p. 104.
76. H. Bosanquet, *Rich and Poor*, p. 75.
77. Ibid., pp. 102 and 107.
78. H. Bosanquet, *Family*, p. 279.
79. H. Bosanquet, *Standard of Life*, pp. 66–87; Melanie Tebbut, *Making Ends Meet. Pawnbroking and Working-Class Credit* (Leicester: Leicester University Press, 1983).
80. H. Bosanquet, *Rich and Poor*, p. 147.
81. Helen Dendy, 'Marriage in East London', in B. Bosanquet (ed.), *Aspects*, p. 76.
82. H. Bosanquet, *The Administration of Charitable Relief* (National Union of Women Workers, 1898), p. 15.
83. H. Bosanquet, *Family*, p. 284.
84. Ibid., pp. 271, 273, 286.
85. Helen Bosanquet to *The Times*, 21/12/11, Bosanquet Papers, Trunk 2, Pkt K(6).
86. Ibid.
87. B. Bosanquet (ed.), 'Duties of Citizenship', *Aspects*, p. 10.
88. H. Bosanquet, *Bernard Bosanquet: A Short Account of his Life* (Macmillan, 1924), p. 38.
89. H. Bosanquet, 'English Divorce Law and Report of the Royal Commission', *International Journal of Ethics* XXIII (July 1913), pp. 443–55.
90. H. Bosanquet, *Family*, p. 282.
91. H. Bosanquet, 'Home and School in the Life of the Child', 1905 lecture, p. 4; Alice Clark, *The Working Life of Women in the Seventeenth Century* (Routledge & Kegan Paul, 1982), 1st edn 1919; Ivy Pinchbeck, *Women Workers and the Industrial Revolution, 1750–1850* (Routledge & Kegan Paul, 1930).
92. H. Bosanquet, *Family*, p. 297.
93. H. Dendy, 'Marriage in East London', p. 81. Both Carol Dyhouse, *Feminism and the Family in England, 1880–1939* (Oxford: Blackwell, 1989) and P. Levine, ' "So Few Prizes and so Many Blanks": Marriage and Feminism in Late Nineteenth-Century England', *Journal of British Studies* 28 (April 1989), pp. 150–74, have stressed the importance of marriage and the family in late nineteenth- and early twentieth-century feminist debates. While Helen Bosanquet was not directly involved in these, they may well have affected her thinking about working-class family life.
94. H. Bosanquet, *Family*, p. 289.
95. H. Bosanquet, *Standard of Life*, p. 175; and *Family*, p. 294.
96. H. Bosanquet, *The Education of Women* (nd, circa 1900), p. 2, BLPES.
97. H. Bosanquet, *The Economics of Women's Work* (National Liberal Club, 1907), p. 6.
98. Helen Bosanquet, Louise Creighton and Beatrice Webb, 'Law and the Laundry', *Nineteenth Century* XLI (Jan.–June 1897), pp. 224–35.
99. H. Bosanquet, *Rich and Poor*, p. 115.
100. Ibid., p. 152; B. Webb (ed.), *The Case for the Factory Acts* (Grant Richards, 1901), p. 17.
101. H. Bosanquet, *Family*, pp. 15 and 273; Ellen Ross, ' "Fierce Questions and Taunts": Married Life in Working-Class London, 1870–1914', *Feminist Studies* 8 (1982).

102. Ibid., p. 200.
103. Ibid., p. 222.
104. Ibid., p. 276; M. Loane, *From their Point of View*, pp. 144–7.
105. B. Bosanquet, *Philosophical Theory of the State*, p. 192.
106. Bernard Bosanquet, 'The Limitations of the Poor Law', *Economic Journal* 2 (1892), p. 371.
107. H. Bosanquet, *Standard of Life*, p. 49.
108. H. Bosanquet, *Family*, p. 219; and *Strength of the People*, pp. 202 and 208.
109. E. J. Urwick, Review of Helen Bosanquet's *Strength of the People, Charity Organisation Review* (March 1903), pp. 142–53.
110. H. Dendy, 'Old Pensioners', in B. Bosanquet (ed.), *Aspects*, pp. 119–25.
111. Ibid., p. 225.
112. Helen Bosanquet, 'The Moral Aspects of Socialism', *International Journal of Ethics* 6 (1896), p. 509.
113. Pat Thane, 'Women and the Poor Law in Victorian and Edwardian England', *History Workshop Journal* 6 (1978), pp. 29–51.
114. Joseph Lee, 'The Integrity of the Family: A Vital Issue', COS Report (nd), Bosanquet Papers, Trunk II, Box H.
115. Especially M. Loane, *Queen's Poor*, chap. 6.
116. Loch, *Charity and Social Life*, p. 414.
117. H. Bosanquet, *Family*, p. 313.
118. Anna Martin, *Married Working Women* (National Union of Women Workers, 1911), pp. 29–30.
119. Bernard Bosanquet, 'The Principles and Chief Dangers of the Administration of Charity', in Jane Addams *et al.* (ed.), *Philanthropy and Social Progress. Seven Essays* (New York: Thomas Crowell & Co., 1893), p. 260.
120. H. Bosanquet, 'Thorough Charity', pp. 207–8.
121. Roof, *Hundred Years of Family Welfare*, p. 47.
122. B. Bosanquet, 'The Limitations of the Poor Law', pp. 369–71; A. Marshall, 'Poor Law Reform', *Economic Journal* 2 (June 1892), pp. 371–9.
123. B. Bosanquet, 'Idealism in Social Work', p. 129.
124. H. Bosanquet, *Strength of the People*, p. 109.
125. H. Bosanquet, 'Methods of Training'.
126. H. Bosanquet, *Rich and Poor*, pp. 137, 143, 144, 182; and 'Administration of Charitable Relief'.
127. H. Bosanquet, *Rich and Poor*, p. 156.
128. Helen Bosanquet, *The Poor Law Report of 1909* (Macmillan, 1909), p. 9.
129. Bernard Bosanquet, 'I. The Majority Report', *Sociological Review* 2 (April 1909), p. 112.
130. B. Bosanquet, 'Charity Organisation and the Majority', *International Journal of Ethics* 20 (July 1910), p. 406.
131. Loch, *Charity and Social Life*, p. 392.
132. Helen Bosanquet, 'A Reply to the Minority', *The School Child* 1 (April 1910), pp. 7–11.
133. B. Bosanquet, 'Charity Organisation and the Majority', p. 405.
134. B. Bosanquet, 'I. The Majority Report', p. 115.
135. Bernard Bosanquet, 'The Art of Public Assistance', pp. 50–51, Royal Commission on the Poor Laws and Relief of Distress, A Course of Nine Lectures, *Sheffield Weekly News* Reprints (1909), Bosanquet Papers, Trunk II, I(2).
136. H. Bosanquet, *The Poor Law Report of 1909*, p. 54.
137. B. Bosanquet, 'I. The Majority Report', p. 117; see also 'Charity Organisation anad the Majority', p. 403.
138. H. Bosanquet, *Family*, p. 325; 'Thorough Charity', p. 206; B. Bosanquet, 'The Principles and Chief Dangers of the Administration of Charity', p. 258.
139. Vincent, 'The Poor Law Reports of 1909', p. 350.

140. Helen Bosanquet, 'Some Problems of Social Relief: How to Help Cases of Distress', reprint from *General Course* (May 1912), Bosanquet Papers, Trunk III.
141. H. Bosanquet, *Administration of Charitable Relief*, p. 21.
142. Pat Thane, 'The Working Class State "Welfare" in Britain, 1880–1914', *Historical Journal* 27 (1984), pp. 877–900.
143. See, for example, the case of Hannah Mitchell, *The Hard Way Up*, edited by G. Mitchell (Faber, 1968).
144. H. Dendy, 'Children of Working London', p. 42.
145. H. Bosanquet, *Administration of Charitable Relief*, p. 7; *Rich and Poor*, p. 140.
146. George Orwell, *The Road to Wigan Pier* (Harmondsworth: Penguin, 1962), 1st edn 1937, pp. 89–90.
147. Bernard Bosanquet, 'The Antithesis between Individualism and Socialism Philosophically Considered', *Charity Organisation Review* (Sept. 1890), p. 357.
148. Lord George Hamilton (Chairman of the Royal Commission) to Helen, 18/9/08, Bosanquet Papers, Trunk II, Pkt 3.
149. W. Smart to Helen, 30/12/08, Bosanquet Papers, Trunk II, Pkt D(i).
150. Collini, 'Hobhouse, Bosanquet and the State'.
151. H. Bosanquet, 'Reconstruction of What?' *Hibbert Journal* (June 1917), p. 543.

4 Mary Ward, 1851–1920

Mary Ward was centrally placed within the Victorian intellectual aristocracy identified by Noel Annan.[1] Grand-daughter of Thomas Arnold of Rugby and niece of Matthew Arnold, she was also a niece of William Forster, responsible for education in Gladstone's first administration, sister-in-law to Leonard Huxley (T. H. Huxley's son) and mother-in-law to G. M. Trevelyan. Mary Ward spent her late teens and the first nine years of her married life in Oxford, whose intellectual debates and values exerted a most profound influence on her subsequent ideas. She saw herself following the strictures of the Liberal philosopher, T. H. Green, and combining a commitment to practical social action (in the form of first the University Hall and later the Passmore Edwards Settlement) with her work as a critic and novelist.

Mary Ward was a singularly successful novelist. *Robert Elsmere* (1888) was the best–selling novel of the 1880s and the income she derived from this and her twenty-two subsequent novels was of crucial importance in maintaining the family's country house at Stocks, supporting her son Arnold's political career (and later in paying his gambling debts) and in furthering her social work. Her husband Humphry's income as an art critic for *The Times* could not have supported the lifestyle to which Mary Ward rapidly became accustomed after *Elsmere's* success. In the early 1890s, out of an expenditure of £3–4000 a year, the Wards devoted £600 to philanthropic enterprises,[2] a proportion of income that was not unusual for middle-class Victorians. During the 1900s, Mary Ward's work in founding playcentres and for crippled children, carried out under the auspices of the settlement, threatened to absorb ever-increasing amounts of her own money. Indeed, her letters reveal an increasing obsession with money. Whereas her friend Louise Creighton (who had been an early object of Humphry's attentions in Oxford) was distressed by the rank materialism of early twentieth-century Canadian society, Mary Ward had rubbed her hands at the prospect of investing in land in Vancouver, apologizing to her husband for 'a mercenary letter' on the subject but adding happily: 'everybody here is so full of business and moneymaking'.[3]

Like Octavia Hill and Beatrice Webb, Mary Ward was 'driven' to work and like them she battled against nervous illness as well as bouts of extremely painful writer's cramp, rheumatism, eczema and a host of other ailments. In the summer of 1888 she was trying not to 'overexcite' herself working on her Greek and husbanding her resources for work on her next novel (*The History of David Grieve*, 1892), while also planning a new house.[4] She seems to have set herself a target of so many pages of writing for each morning, leaving the afternoons for her public work. She worked doggedly rather than with evident pleasure. Yet there was, as she wrote to her son Arnold, 'a certain quality of energy to be got out of rapid and continuous work' and as late as 1918 she told her sister Julia that she had just finished a novel and was as usual beginning another, for she would 'be lost without it'.[5] In *A Writer's Recollections* (1918), she wrote of the value of the mental discipline of a daily dose of Latin and Greek and the importance of the 'slight curb' of the 'physical toil' of writing;[6] she regretted that her friend Henry James took to dictating his novels, notwithstanding the evident physical relief this would have afforded her. She suffered doubts both as to her own capacities and as to whether writing novels was what she ought to be doing. Yet she certainly identified herself as first and foremost a novelist. When a novel was finished, she expressed enormous faith and a certain complacency about the result. She was also capable of exerting substantial demands on others in the course of her writing, whether it was for background books to be sent to her by her husband regardless of expense, or details of Roman Catholic doctrine to be supplied by her father by return of post.[7]

Looking at her in the context of her anti-suffrage work, Brian Harrison labelled Mary Ward as typically Victorian. Certainly G. B. Shaw felt that taking Mary Ward into dinner was a measure of middle-class respectability and Rebecca West delivered one of her swingeing attacks on Mary Ward's upright gospel and the 'solid Tottenham Court Road workmanship of her mental furniture'.[8] In her portraits, Mary Ward's pose looks remarkably like that of Queen Victoria, yet Mackenzie King, a future Liberal prime minister of Canada, who spent some months staying at the Passmore Edwards Settlement, described her as 'kind and motherly', albeit deeply earnest.[9] However, Virginia Woolf felt that few famous Victorian novelists had suffered as great a diminution in reputation as had Mary Ward by World War I, although in 1953 Violet Markham, who worked closely with Mary Ward in the National League for Opposing Women's Suffrage, wrote in *The Times* that she was 'rash enough to prophesy that within another 50 years Mrs Humphry Ward will know a come–back'.[10] (Mary's novels, but not her criticism, always appeared as the work of 'Mrs Humphry Ward'.)

Mary Ward certainly appeared serene, respectable and optimistic; an archetypical Victorian. Yet she was by no means an unbending, one-dimensional figure. In her late teens in Oxford she attended the Pattisons' tea parties and was entertained not only by Mark Pattison's (the Rector of Lincoln College) learning but by the daring tea-gowns (a new fashion) worn by his wife Emelia, who was later to marry Sir Charles Dilke after the divorce proceedings that wrecked his political career. Mary Ward also became a friend of Laura Lyttleton, née Tenant, a 'Soul', who was 'so golden', full of passion and poetry and to whom she dedicated *Elsmere*. When Laura died in childbirth, she wrote to her mother: 'I think I was simply in love with her from the first time I ever saw her'.[11] She acknowledged that she never was and never could be a part of the high society world the 'Souls' moved in, but it attracted her in much the same way that Beatrice Webb was endlessly drawn to it; both also shared an admiration for A. J. Balfour. But as Mary wrote to her Aunt Frances (Arnold) after a period in London: 'London has been very smart and when I have been through an outbreak of smartness I am apt to feel life is a foolish business'.[12] Mary Ward was unswerving in her belief that action should be inspired by moral purpose and was swift to condemn anyone who pursued amusement rather than self-culture or who demonstrated the love of self rather than making an effort to serve others. But there are strands in her novels, in her social work and in her views on women's position in society that makes her more of a transitional figure than most of her critics have been willing to acknowledge.

While her position on women's suffrage does appear well-grounded in Victorian beliefs and attitudes as to the importance of separate spheres, she was well-attuned to the changing position of women and made it a constant subject of discussion in her novels. In her own life she combined public work and private research and writing in a manner not dissimilar from Beatrice Webb. She probably undertook as much public speaking as Beatrice albeit, like Helen Bosanquet, in the more socially acceptable circles of philanthropy and, latterly, anti-suffrage. Like Beatrice, she experienced considerable tension in respect of the pressures of public life. London induced insomnia and, while she relished the excitement of its political life, she was always glad to retire to the Ward country house to write. As for her heroines, some contemporary critics claimed that the independent woman in her novels of the 1910s was little changed from her first such figure, Marcella Boyce, created some fifteen years before.[13] While their behaviour became somewhat more advanced (smoking was permitted and, by 1913, kissing on the lips)[14] the moral universe of the novels remained the same. This is broadly correct, but Mary Ward's strength lay in re-posing old moral dilemmas in a manner that accorded perfectly with contemporary preoccupations. During the late 1900s and 1910s, she managed this with great effect in respect of divorce and the double moral standard. She showed a perceptive awareness of the range of feminist positions on these issues (in *Eltham House*, 1915), as well as presenting a strongly polemical attack on divorce (in *Daphne or Marriage à la Mode*, 1909) which she grounded in a defence of the family that was broadly in tune not just with anti-suffrage opinion but with a broad spectrum of social investigators, commentators and policymakers during the Edwardian period.

Mary Ward's position in regard to her views on social action was also complicated. Like Octavia Hill, her inspiration was essentially religious. Again there were Unitarian connections, although Mary Ward's was a modernist Christianity, born of doubt; she was never a confirmed member of the Church of England. The emphasis she placed on the social significance of private actions, especially of the rich, should also be seen as part of what Stefan Collini and José Harris have identified as a hegemony of ideas as to the importance of social service, which crossed political and sectarian lines.[15] Indeed, many of Mary Ward's ideas were not out of sympathy with those of the Bosanquets, and on some matters of social reform she also managed to work with Beatrice Webb. Both Helen and Beatrice sat on the Council of the Passmore Edwards Settlement. But in its initial stages, Mary Ward's settlement was intended as a manifestation of a living faith and a practical Christianity. The most successful part of the settlement's work was that performed by Mary Ward, her daughters, Janet and Dorothy, and the Women's Work Committee for crippled children and playcentres for poor children. Mary Ward believed strongly in the contribution women could make to philanthropy and local government, if not to the national body politic, even though the settlement was not primarily intended as a vehicle for women's voluntary work. It was in the female-dominated activities of the settlement in the years before and during World War I that Mary Ward began to seek the kind of financial partnership with the state that would increasingly characterize post-war social service. Like Octavia Hill, Mary Ward had always proclaimed the importance of state regulation, particularly in respect of sanitation and housing, but her acceptance of state participation in work that both Octavia and Helen deemed the province of the voluntary sector was a new departure. Her appeal for state aid was not made out of any attachment to either socialist or New Liberal ideas; rather Mary Ward was a conservative (Liberal Unionist) and she countenanced state intervention primarily in the name of improving the welfare of race, nation and Empire. Her reverence for the land and a ruling aristocracy never abated. She saw action as a personal obligation of the privileged in the manner of Octavia Hill, but also recognized in a manner more in tune with pragmatic politicians such as Joseph Chamberlain that it was a 'ransom' property had to be prepared to pay. While Seth Koven has probably overdrawn the transition Mary Ward made to collectivism in his study of London settlements,[16] her brand of caring capitalism was significantly different from that of Octavia Hill a generation before, notwithstanding her continued commitment to personal service.

The meaning of social action

Novels of purpose

Mary Ward chose to identify herself as a novelist first and foremost. In 1892, she was glad to move from Russell Square to Grosvenor Place because she felt it better to be at a distance from the settlement in Bloomsbury, 'which ought not to absorb me too much. For my family life and my literary work ought to come before it'.[17] Her literary work was, in the main, novel-writing. She could have stuck to criticism and some of her Oxford mentors were keen for her to do so but, apart from its lesser financial rewards and its greater demands in terms of time away from her family, Mary Ward's examination of her own conscience and review of her capacities led her to write novels. She saw novel-writing as a kind of duty for there were certain issues she wished to discuss using this literary form. Given the didactic quality of much of her fiction, it is therefore not inappropriate to use the novels in an analysis of her thinking on social (and particularly on gender) issues. Most discussions of Mary Ward have focused either on her social work or her novels and many literary critics would look askance at the idea of the novels being used as source material. While Mary Ward's ideas were clearly influenced by much older patterns of literary thought, especially regarding ideas about sex and gender, as the most perceptive recent critic of her literary work has remarked, it is impossible to interpret Mary Ward outside her historical context.[18] She herself was, after all, overwhelmed by the power of the new German historical methodology and in her first novel sought to demonstrate its devastating effect on Biblical criticism. But it is also true that her literary work and social action intertwined in a way that makes the one an essential illumination of the other. For example, her concern about marriage and divorce in 1908 resulted in both a polemical novel on the subject[19] and the founding of the Women's National Anti-Suffrage League, which joined forces with the Men's Committee for Opposing Female Suffrage in 1910 to produce the National League for Opposing Women's Suffrage.

In her late teens, Mary Ward had embarked on serious scholarly work investigating the lives of early Spanish ecclesiastics (on behalf of Dr Wace, Canon of Canterbury) for the *Dictionary of Christian Biography*. Later she remembered this as her only real intellectual discipline and deplored the content of her formal education between the ages of nine and sixteen, first at Anne Clough's (the future principal of Newnham) school in Ambleside, then briefly and unhappily at Rock Terrace School for Young Ladies in Shropshire, and finally at a smaller and more expensive boarding school where she was happier but learned 'nothing thoroughly or accurately, and the German, French and Latin, which I soon discovered after my marriage to be essential to the kind of literary work I wanted to do, had all to be re-learnt before they could be of any real use to me'.[20] As a result of her research on early Spanish ecclesiastics, Mary Ward discovered for herself the power of '*sources – testimony*', in other words of historical methods, in questioning the orthodox faith in miracle.[21] It was this process that she would chronicle in *Elsmere*.

Both her religious novels and her social-reform novels were well-researched and read in large measure as a lengthy exposition of the issues that were perplexing contemporaries. Mary Ward held scholarship in the highest regard. When Gladstone criticized the modern faith adopted by Robert Elsmere, she took pleasure in writing a reply that demonstrated the depth of her reading and understanding of the issues. However, after the turn of the century, romances became her stock in trade. She argued that they too filled a social need and were in some measure vehicles for the presentation of social and moral issues but her defence was a touch defiant. Mary Ward reserved most respect for and felt most comfortable with herself when writing the intellectual novel.

After *Elsmere*, Benjamin Jowett, Master of Balliol, advised her to return to criticism. Mary Ward did not continue novel-writing without considerable self-questioning: what exactly was the nature of her gifts? *Elsmere*'s success could not just be enjoyed. It brought great moral strain and a great struggle to seek what Octavia Hill might have called 'right action'. Mary Ward felt obliged to redouble her efforts to 'look away from oneself' and to ensure that she was obeying Divine will in her work.[22] Writing her next novel, *David Grieve*, she wrote an uncharacteristically touching letter to her husband about coming to grips with the characters in the novel, ending with the hope that 'Perhaps after all I may believe in my métier and give myself up to it without qualms'.[23] But in 1897, writing what proved to be her best intellectual novel, *Helbeck of Bannisdale* (1898), she confessed that despite the occasional 'glow of pleasure' that seemed to say, 'this is my work after all and I am glad I can do it', often she was unable to 'see clearly what I *ought* to do [author's itals] – I want to be at Biblical criticism or something quite different – and then there are moments again when the gift for fiction seems quite clear'.[24] When her Preface to Emily Brontë's *Wuthering Heights* attracted criticism (Mary Ward was one of the first to suggest that it was superior to *Jane Eyre*), she again wondered whether she should not concentrate on Biblical criticism.[25]

The immediate cause of her abandoning scholarship and criticism was her marriage at the age of twenty-one (in 1872) to Humphry Ward, then a tutor at Brasenose College, Oxford. Dorothy was born in 1874, Arnold in 1876 and Janet in 1879. In addition Mary Ward faced considerable difficulties in coping with the problems of her parents. Indeed it is possible that her early marriage was related to what she referred to briefly as a rather bleak childhood;[26] her most recent biographer also believes that it was her search for a father-figure that explains her deferential relationships during her adult life, including with the leaders of the anti-suffrage movement. Certainly her letters from Rock Terrace frequently bewailed the lack of any communication from her parents, who were presumably at odds over her father's first experiment with Roman Catholicism. Her father went through one conversion to Catholicism, which lasted from 1854–65, and another (this time, life-long) in 1876 which meant that he had to leave Oxford. Mary Ward's Protestant mother refused to accompany him and they lived separately thereafter. Between 1873 and 1888 (when her mother died), Mary Ward's weekly letters to her mother and to her father (which she felt constituted a journal) chronicled not only her own struggles to juggle home, family and writing on a limited income but her constant efforts to mediate between her parents and to persuade her father (resident in Dublin) to provide an adequate income for her mother. The two major themes of her novels, religion and the meaning of marriage, were her daily concern in her relations with her parents. The demands of her family responsibilities were therefore heavy. In the summer of 1886 she apologized to her father for her erratic correspondence, explaining that she was trying to get on with *Elsmere* in the country but that she also had to write to Humphry and deal with the children.[27] To her mother, she apologized for not being able to spare the time for a weekly visit, but the remaining six chapters of *Elsmere* had to be written.[28] Late in 1887, she explained to her mother that she was spending six hours a day on revisions to *Elsmere*, was in great pain with her hand and arm, and taking both whisky and cocaine to relieve it.[29] When she was in London, Humphry's job with *The Times* demanded a degree of socializing which both attracted and repelled her but which certainly thwarted her efforts to establish a steady work routine. On the other hand, anything but novel-writing would have proved impossible to fit round such wide-ranging family commitments.

W. L. Courtney, writing on the 'feminine note in fiction' in 1904, felt that it was no criticism of Mary Ward to say that her novels were 'didactic, full of a serious and oppressive moral purpose'.[30] Mary Ward's didacticism was notorious and not everyone liked it. Beatrice Webb was pleased when it was used to argue in favour of extending protection to sweated workers (in *Sir George Tressady*, 1896) but otherwise found it dull and oppressive.[31] To Mary Ward, the opportunity for didacticism in large measure legitimated novel-writing. In her Preface to *David Grieve*, she strongly defended her desire to write novels with a purpose, notwithstanding the dismissive judgements of the quarterly magazines on the genre. She felt that such novels were justified in expressing ' "a criticism of life", which may advance, whether in the hearts of the many or the few, thoughts and causes dear to the writers'.[32] She insisted that art, like belief, had to be related to the realities of modern life. In many respects, she was not a defender of the modern novel. In a speech she gave at the opening of a Carnegie-funded library in Kendal in 1909, she warned that novels were merely the jam of literature and 'all properly conducted persons, as we know, should begin their meal with solid bread and butter'.[33] She feared that the pressure of modern life was making people's reading 'scrappy', lacking in both depth and discipline. In her own novels she was anxious to set out issues and dilemmas and usually did so in an even-handed fashion, notwithstanding their didactic purpose. The great attraction of her work lay in the fact that she chose to express the problems that her contemporaries were thinking about. Lady Florence Bell recalled a conversation with Mary Ward about the prospective *Elsmere*, during which Lady Bell doubted the appeal of a novel about religious doubt and belief. According to Bell, Mary Ward responded: 'But surely, there is nothing else so interesting in this world'.[34] In terms of sales her view proved justified. Jowett observed that the novel's success was due to Mary Ward having said what everyone was thinking, and Rowland Prothero in the *Edinburgh Review* remarked similarly that she succeeded in voicing widespread feelings that needed expression.[35]

Mary Ward also stressed that the novel writer's duty was to tell a story. Especially after 1900, she often referred to the novels she wrote alongside her growing commitments to the anti-suffrage campaign, and work for playcentres and crippled children, as 'tales'. In 1918, she referred to the special role of novels in war-time and to her desire to try her hand at a detective or mystery novel, which was the sort of thing the 'tired world' needed.[36] (Such a novel, *Harvest*, was published posthumously in 1920.) For the most part, her novels were carefully thought out, but even in the early ones she confessed sometimes to having been carried away by the characters and events she had created. As she recognized, these tended to be the most melodramatic and least successful parts of her books.[37] Her strength lay, even in the more romantic and less intellectual novels of the Edwardian period in carefully posing old dilemmas, particularly moral ones, in contemporary surroundings. In *Lady Rose's Daughter* (1903) and *The Marriage of William Ashe* (1905), she took old stories and reworked them in an up-to-date context. In *Lady Rose*, it was the relationship between Sainte-Beuve and Julie de Lespinasse; in *William Ashe*, the flirtation of William Lamb's (Lord Melbourne's) wife with Byron.

Both her intellectual and romantic novels addressed public and private concerns: the agony of personal doubt, its public acknowledgement and reworking into new faith, and the implications of private moral standards for public life where compromises reached in one sphere signalled compromises reached in the other. Private and public life remained separate. But Mary Ward believed that it was essential for women's moral guardianship of the private sphere to be used to raise the moral standard of the public world and that, prompted by 'true feeling', women would undertake work inspired by a 'social maternalism', thereby manifesting a claim to citizenship that was different but equal to that of men.

The importance of inner life

Not only, in Mary Ward's view, was there no more fascinating subject for a novel than belief and doubt, but thinking about the content of religion provided the framework for social action. Mary Ward acknowledged the two most important influences in her life as being Matthew Arnold and T. H. Green. In 1888 she wrote to her husband that she felt her 'main mission in life' to be the popularization of T. H. Green's thought.[38] Of all the various criticisms made of *Elsmere* it was probably the *Quarterly*'s attack on Balliol and hence on Green that offended her most. She followed Green in her rejection of Church of England theology and in his commitment to a modernized Christianity, in which it was important to express faith in action. In particular Mary Ward attached great importance to 'looking inward' and to the cultivation of 'true feeling', something that would make possible a remoralized public and private life.

Mary Ward was unable to accept religious dogma not because of Darwinian science but because of the rise of historical criticism, whose practice in Germany she referred to in the Preface to *Elsmere* and to which she had contributed in her own research on early Spanish ecclesiastics.[39] In 1884 she wrote to her father that her admiration for the Swiss writer Henri Frederic Amiel's *Journal Intime* (which she translated) derived from his rationality whereas her father revered St Theresa, with whose mysticism she could not sympathize.[40] By 1886 she wrote that 'everything from the critical and scientific standpoint seems to me continuous and natural – no sharp lines anywhere – one thing leading to another, event leading to event, belief to belief – and God unwrapping and unfolding all'.[41]

As early as 1881 she was upset when the Bampton lecturer in Oxford condemned those (such as Green) with unorthodox views as inherently sinful, for what historical criticism seemed to show was that there was no single way of seeing and no one truth.[42] Mark Pattison taught that history was a record of continuous unravelling and reweaving of systems of truth, the position adopted by Squire Wendover in *Elsmere*, although Mary Ward had no sympathy with either Pattison's or Wendover's acquisition of learning for learning's sake. New understanding, like the art of the novel, had to be put to practical use.[43] When Robert Elsmere leaves the church, he explains to his wife Catherine that while Christianity is not false, it is only an imperfect human reflection of a part of truth and truth cannot be contained in any one system or creed. The power of history is described by Richard Meynell (a later Elsmere-like character who chooses to stay within the church) as a 'magic lens within the mind which allows us to look deep into the past and see its life and colour and movement again'[44] and as a new discipline like science which is 'divine and authoritative'. The power Mary Ward attributed to historical criticism was not unlike that attributed by Beatrice Webb to social observation and social facts, although in common with Matthew Arnold and Helen Bosanquet, Mary Ward deplored any attempt to rely on mechanistic, abstract systems such as Utilitarianism or Fabian Socialism.[45]

T. H. Green's teaching was especially important for the way in which it managed to reconcile criticism and religion. In *Elsmere*, Grey, who was modelled on T. H. Green, differs from Wendover in his respect for established institutions and popular belief, and in his determination to make religion more real. In her 1892 address to the newly-founded University Hall settlement, Mary Ward spoke of the way in which, for Green, reason carried to its legitimate end issued in new faith.[46] Green reached the point where religion consisted of giving expression to the life of Jesus in our everyday lives. In this, the individual was not asked to imitate Christ but, rather, God became immanent in everyday duties and personal lives.[47] This idea was a source of enormous inspiration for many. For example, Mackenzie King read T. H. Green's essay on faith in the train, going to visit Mary Ward at her country house near Tring, and recorded that few things had ever pleased him more: 'we should seek to "die daily" and have the resurrection of life out of death a daily experience in our own lives, that in this way we can have and do have Christ in us'.[48] What this meant, as Mary Ward pointed out in her 1892 address, was that faith had daily to be expressed in action: 'ideas without the actions which belong to them profit nothing'.[49] It was incumbent on each person to undertake work that would further the common good. This kind of thinking inevitably privileged the individual work of personal service.

Thus a modern faith of the kind reached by Robert Elsmere and modelled on that of his teacher Grey (Green) was crucial both because learning and criticism were destructive and selfish if they were not linked to practical action, and because action was dangerous if not inspired by moral purpose. For Mary Ward, the link between criticism and practical work was as crucial as the link between theory and action for the Bosanquets. Mary Ward, however, followed Matthew Arnold in stressing that it was crucial to look inwards, to search for God in oneself and to rely on conscience, rather than on externally constructed systems as a guide to actions.[50] Mary Ward wrote of conscience as God's revelation in each of us and of the importance of constantly looking inward not for the purpose of self-analysis but to examine conscience in order to make sure that action was in accordance with the 'best self'.[51]

The emphasis on searching one's own conscience was not dissimilar from Octavia Hill's means of determining 'right action'. Mary Ward, however, went one stage further back in stressing the importance of first developing 'true feeling'. Ideally feeling amounted to more than heart and sentiment, although the more melodramatic episodes in her novels were characterized by feelings that were entirely sentimental.[52] Real feeling, however, could only be a product of a careful search of conscience which in turn depended on the development of character. In *Elsmere*, Squire Wendover 'knows', but does not 'feel'. Elsmere himself leaves the church not just because he is convinced by the factual testimony accumulated by the Squire (analogous to abstract systems of knowledge) but because he can no longer feel for church theology.[53] Not to be able to feel is portrayed as a terrible fate. Langham, the sceptic, is unable to allow himself to express his feelings for the artistic Rose, Elsmere's sister-in-law, and because he is unable fully to feel, he is unable to act. Finally, for Mary Ward, it was true feeling that enabled the unorthodox to be pure and good, something the Brampton lecturer refused to contemplate but which, by her portrayal of Laura Fountain in *Helbeck*, Mary Ward succeeded in persuading a Roman Catholic colleague of her father's was possible.[54] True feeling inspired forgetfulness of self and service to others and, like 'duty', was a gendered concept. The manifestation of true feeling in women was different from that in men. Ideally both were inspired by it to serve family and community and both were expected to put family first. But men's canvas was the larger and women's sense of service was expected to be complementary to that of men. Furthermore to achieve the depth of character necessary for the development of feeling, women were usually portrayed as needing to develop the crucial capacity to love a man and to become wives and mothers. Service to family thus occupied a greater place in the female universe than in that of the male.

Mary Ward's commitment to a modern, practical Christianity made her optimistic, despite the genuine pain of loss that she experienced in giving up the old faith.[55] As she said to her father, 'you will admit that as regards this life, my view is the more cheerful! To me at any given moment, in a certain broad sense "whatever is, is right" '.[56] Like Octavia Hill, she was convinced that social conscience was increasing and with it a sense of individual responsibility. Before she replied in print to Gladstone's criticism of *Elsmere*, she went to talk to him, and in her report of the conversation their difference turned on his preoccupation with sin and her more optimistic faith in progress: 'But I asked him, in spite of all drawbacks, do you see a gradual growth and diffusion of earnestness, of the social passion during the whole period?' Gladstone assented, but said that 'sin is the great fact in the world to me', to which Mary Ward replied that while she did not deny the existence of moral evil, 'the more one thought of it the more plain its connection with physical and social and therefore removable conditions'.[57] Gladstone could not agree. But it was this conclusion that was to make Mary Ward considerably more flexible in the range of interventions (including by the state) which she was prepared to consider appropriate in the solution of social problems. While she would never give priority to the social causes of poverty over those of individual failings of character, she was nevertheless prepared to join Beatrice Webb in looking beyond the individual to the state for a solution to problems such as sweated labour, the needs of crippled children and of poor children for play space.

In many respects, Mary Ward's faith in progress was derived from her concept of history which was, like that of Beatrice Webb, essentially evolutionary. In *Elsmere*, Squire Wendover was writing a 'History of Testimony' that he conceptualizes from the standpoint of evolution, something he feels no historian could afford to ignore.[58] As in the case of Beatrice, who followed Spencer in this respect, such a perspective logically induced a belief in progress. Mary Ward was additionally convinced that a modernized Christianity would make possible a remoralized public and private life that would be constructive, energetic and happy. It was crucial that all should learn, as Catherine Elsmere manages to do eventually, to dissociate moral judgement from religious dogma and to find truth within oneself. The comfort of a personal God and the knowledge that one was seeking to cultivate true feeling and to live in accordance with the dictates of one's best self resulted in a much more cheerful outlook than could be managed by Mary Ward's Roman Catholic father, by the evangelical Gladstone or by her fictional heroine, Catherine Elsmere. The last's constant lament, 'we're not here to be happy', is eschewed by her husband, Robert, in his new found faith.[59] Mary Ward envisaged modern, practical Christianity creating a buoyant and dynamic approach to life; it is significant that Robert Elsmere is first attracted by Grey's personality rather than his words. The task became, both for Elsmere and for Mary Ward, one of explaining the new ideas about the regenerated Christianity and how it was relevant to modern life. Robert Elsmere left the church to found the New Brotherhood of Christ, a kind of settlement, in which he sought with considerable success to explain the Bible anew to respectable working men. Mary Ward's first settlement, University Hall, began with similar aims and ambitions. While the settlement developed in practice along rather different lines, Mary Ward remained optimistic as to the possibilities for a revitalized faith. By 1911 when she published *The Case of Richard Meynell*, she no longer felt it necessary for a man believing in the new ideas she described in *Elsmere* to leave the church. Indeed, she had come around to Matthew Arnold's belief in the importance of an inclusive national church. In many respects, the repeated appeals made in *Richard Meynell* for a reformed Church of England used the same rationale as Mary Ward was to use in arguing for greater state intervention in social problems: the need of race and nation for social and spiritual leadership.[60]

Rich and poor in the work of the settlement
University Hall settlement was set up with explicitly religious objectives in view. As in other settlements, it was intended that an enlightened middle-class few would share their knowledge with working people.[61] Like Matthew Arnold's common culture, the new religious spirit which it was hoped would enfold all, was essentially a middle-class construct.

The press saw the settlement as the realization of Elsmere's vision, although from the first Mary Ward rejected the 'sentimental' association of the settlement with her novel.[62] In her opening address at the settlement, she reviewed the 'new synthesis in philosophy and Christian thought' and dedicated the work of the settlement to showing how the new faith might adapt itself 'to practical and social life'.[63] She wrote to her father of her hope both that the experiment would succeed in promoting the new religious teaching among working-class children and that the settlement would be constructive and helpful to all, rather than 'merely destructive and critical' of the established order.[64] She was, in the early 1890s, convinced that settlements would become increasingly religious and believed that it was the responsibility of the settlers to teach those 'perhaps of another class, whose starved education' meant that the more fortunate residents of the settlement had to take special pains in finding ways to kindle their imagination.[65]

Mary Ward consulted and negotiated with a large number of individuals before setting up University Hall. The settlement was often labelled theist or Unitarian – Elsmere had after all left the Church of England – but while admiring Unitarian values, Mary Ward shared her uncle's distrust of the provincial spirit that threatened to engulf a body of Dissenters such as the Unitarians, who deliberately cut themselves off from the mainstream of English spiritual life.[66] Mary Ward consulted James Martineau, a leading Unitarian, at length over the project and in particular over the settlement's lecture series, but she resisted explicit pleas, for example from Lord Carlisle, to include the word Unitarian in the name of the settlement. She also resisted J. H. Muirhead's proposals first, that the settlement should be associated only with the work of T. H. Green, disowning Unitarianism and, second, that it should merge with the Ethical Society which was dominated by Idealists including Bernard Bosanquet.[67] The first draft of the settlement's objectives stressed that it was designed to provide a rallying-point for those

> to whom Christianity, whether by inheritance or process of thought, has become a system of practical conduct, based on faith in God, and on the inspiring memory of a great teacher rather than a system of dogma based on a unique revelation.

However, Philip Wicksteed, a University of London professor of philosophy and an economist, who became the first warden of the settlement, insisted that this be softened so that residents were required to be 'in sympathy' with the hall's religious purpose but that no expression of religious belief was needed, and those not wishing to undertake religious teaching need not do so.[68] The governing board of the hall proved eclectic and included not only Helen Bosanquet and Beatrice Webb but also the politically Conservative, radical feminist, Frances Power Cobbe.

Mary Ward's ideas about the ways in which rich and poor would interact through the medium of the settlement and how the problem of poverty related to the settlement's aim of promoting a shared understanding of the new faith were extremely vague. Elsmere's New Brotherhood had provided a picture of a remoralized and inspirited community where the poor were respectable, the rich performed their duty of service to their fellow human beings and where collective organization in the form of the municipality could be called upon to make sure that the drains worked. The spirit of the new faith also promoted class conciliation. However, most reviewers of *Robert Elsmere* were convinced that any attempt to realize the ideals of the New Brotherhood in real life would prove unworkable.[69]

In her public addresses Mary Ward certainly appeared to place her hopes in a charismatic teacher of Elsmere's stature; as William Peterson has observed, she assumed that people naturally wanted to worship, but were somehow driven away by theology.[70] Mary Ward did not lecture or write explicitly on the problem of poverty and her thinking has to be derived for the most part from her social-reform novels of the mid- and late 1890s, particularly *Marcella* (1894) and its sequel, *Sir George Tressady*. Her position proves hard to classify in terms of simple individualism or collectivism.

Mary Ward realized that the settlement was likely to deal with only the respectable poor; Robert Elsmere concludes that the best chance of the religious reformer lay among the upper-working class and artisans, rather than the very poor, and those are the people he lectures to on the New Testament. Speaking at the new Liverpool Settlement at the turn of the century, Mary Ward said that while settlements did not influence Charles Booth's social classes A, B and C – the semi-criminal, semi-vicious and the casual poor – they did make contact with the poor but regularly employed (his classes D and E), and there was always the hope of making these people emissaries to the classes below them. Mary Ward felt that the hope of the settlement movement lay in 'a combination between the intelligence of those who mainly work with their brains and the intelligence of those who mainly work with their hands'.[71]

Like Octavia Hill, Beatrice Webb and the Charity Organisation Society (COS) generally, Mary Ward had great respect for the respectable working class. Research for *David Grieve* took her to Bacup in Lancashire where Beatrice Webb provided her with an introduction to the mill families she had stayed with some years previously. Mary Ward found them to be the salt of the earth, full of 'natural refinement and good feeling' and believed that Beatrice had been quite right in attributing their behaviour

> to their religion, to those hideous chapels, which develops in them the keenest individual sense of responsibility to God and man, and to their combination for a common education as in their cooperative societies, unions, and in their real sensitiveness to education and the things of the mind, up to a certain point of course.[72]

She was gratified that they were interested in grace and salvation, and in the struggle of the spirit against the flesh. When London filled her with despair, she told her father she thought of Bacup and felt comforted as to the future. These were the sort of people she could envisage making common cause with the settlers but they were also her model for a remoralized London poor.

Mary Ward's attitudes towards the poor were in fact somewhat confused. On the one hand she felt working people offered the simple practical discipline of life and in her opening speech to the new University Hall in 1891 she stressed that they already had more popular scientific training than did the middle classes, thanks to the education offered by the state elementary schools (since 1870), and that they had also managed to retain their religious sensibilities.[73] In other words the classes of poor that the settlement would reach were held up as 'equal but different'. And yet, of course, they were not equal in terms of their spiritual understanding and culture. In 1904 she wrote to a working-class member of the settlement's governing board, who was extremely critical of the direction of the settlement, of her 'deep Carlylian sense of debt to the working class', adding that it was this which would not let her 'rest 'till I had done something to brighten and help his [the working-class man's] path'.[74] Her respect for the respectable working poor was sincere and made her observation of the patronizing behaviour of both philanthropists and socialists acute in her novels, even if in practice she was never able to conquer her own *grande dame* approach. But her respect also made the assertion of what she as much as Matthew Arnold believed was a superior middle-class culture additionally problematic. In the end Mary Ward ducked the issue at the settlement, but in so doing left it without any rigorous *raison d'être*.

When it came to the problem of relieving the poor, Mary Ward roundly condemned the old philanthropy for reasons that had as much to do with the motives that inspired it as its demoralizing effects. In *Tressady*, a high-Tory lady expresses her sympathy for Letty Tressady as a wronged wife by saying: 'What can a woman do . . . A decent

woman, I mean . . . All she can do is to cry, and take a district'.[75] Time
and again good works were depicted by Mary Ward in her novels as a
selfish solace for the perpetrator rather than as a product of 'true
feeling' as to the needs of others. In *Fenwick's Career* (1906) 'doing
good' is described as a 'tempting dangerous pleasure' that 'leads astray
so many on whom Satan has no other hold!'[76] In *David Grieve*, Mary
Ward makes her commentary on the behaviour of David's wife, Lucy,
most explicit in this respect: 'Her Christianity had been originally of the
older High Church type, where the ideal of personal holiness had not
yet been fused with the ideal of social service'.[77] In this instance the
lady philanthropist is content to give 'doles and comforts', but cannot
understand the fuss about either insanitary houses and overcrowding,
or the need to provide personal service in teaching thrift, temperance
and education. Unlike so many of her contemporaries, Mary Ward was
not an active member of the COS. She had apparently read Edward
Denison's letters, to which her friend, Louise Creighton, attributed the
beginnings of the whole settlement movement,[78] and it is likely that her
acquaintance with the debates over poverty and its causes were for the
most part second hand. Nevertheless, her novels reveal a substantial
amount of reflection as to the difficulties of treating the problem of
poverty. She rejected both the doles of the old philanthropy and the
structural reform of the Fabians but without wholeheartedly espousing
the more rigid approach of many members of the COS. Her position
probably came closest to that of Helen Bosanquet but, because it was
much less systematic, allowed more room for a measure of collective
organization in addition to personal service.

In many respects, Mary Ward appeared to be judging and rejecting
both an unthinking individualist paternalism and thoroughgoing
collectivism in favour of, in her terms, a more middling ground, that
combined elements of both social work and collective provision. The
story of *Marcella* epitomized this process. Marcella Boyce moves, like
Beatrice Webb, from rent collection to Fabianism but in both guises is
shown to lack the true spirit of personal service to the poor. She is full
of great ideas as to how to increase the independence of the rural poor
by teaching them straw plaiting, 'But naturally they would be grateful;
they would let themselves be led'.[79] In part Mary Ward's shrewd
portrayal of relationships between rich and poor came from social
observation. The inspiration for the character of Mrs Jellison, one of
the candidates for the straw plait lessons, whose scepticism about
Marcella's motives proves justified, was drawn from the community
around Tring. Marcella is inspired not so much by the desire to serve
others but by the attraction of exerting power over others: 'It excited

her to say these things to these people, to these tottering old things . . .' Her passionate defence of Hurd, the poacher, and her protection of his widow is undertaken more for herself than out of a sincere appreciation of the needs of the Hurds. She is disappointed by the relationship she tries to form with Mrs Hurd after her husband's execution: 'It seemed to ask of her feelings that she [Mrs Hurd] could not have; Mrs Hurd could not really understand why a fine lady like Marcella should minister to her'.[80] As Marcella's mother reflects in regard to her daughter's persistent offer of sympathy to Mrs Hurd: '*Sympathy*! Who was ever yet fed, warmed, comforted by *sympathy*? Marcella robs that woman of the only thing the human being should want at such a moment – solitude. Why should we force on the poor what to us would be an outrage?'[81] To Marcella's disgust Mrs Hurd eventually remarries a charlatan elocution teacher. Not only were Marcella's actions essentially selfish but she sought to impose her sense of what was fitting on the poor. While Mary Ward accepted that middle-class culture was superior to that of working people, she agreed with Octavia Hill and Helen Bosanquet that the attitudes and beliefs of the poor warranted sympathetic understanding and deserved respect.

After a period spent as a district nurse in a poor area of London, Marcella sheds her impassioned socialist views and admits that she has learned the important role played by character in achieving lasting reform. As she explains to her Venturist (Fabian) friends; 'the emphasis – do what I will – comes to be less and less on possession and more and more on character'.[82] She goes on to provide an illustration which might have come straight from the writings of Helen Bosanquet: how else was it possible to explain the manner in which two families living on similar wages and in similar houses enjoyed comfort in the one case and descended into squalor in the other? This passage was cited as providing the last word on the subject in one of the two major books of essays on settlements that appeared in the 1890s.[83]

Mary Ward thus showed Marcella coming to the realization that the socialist's portrayal of one social class as the victim of another was false. In all probability, Mary Ward followed Green in his perception of the causes of poverty as two-fold: first as the product of individual moral failure, but second as the result of a failure on the part of the landed classes to ensure a more equal division of the property that was crucial to stimulating the development of character. This made a commitment to social service on the part of the rich more urgent. It may also explain why Mary Ward's novels were as preoccupied with exposing the ills of rural tenants on great estates as with urban problems, despite her commitment to the London settlement she founded.[84]

While the personal obligation of the rich to engage in individual social work with the poor, designed to change habits and character, was still the key in Mary Ward's solution to the problem of poverty, she recognized that social organization was also necessary. To use Peter Clarke's terminology, she was never a simple 'moral regenerationist' but was also a 'moral reformist'.[85] In the sequel to *Marcella*, *Sir George Tressady*, which was written to put the case for government legislation to regulate the sweated trades, the problems posed were those of individual lack of concern for community responsibility and collective theory that made too little of the rights and responsibilities of the individual.[86] For answers Mary Ward always looked for a conciliatory, inclusive rather than exclusive, middle way, hence the idea of the exercise of obligations between individuals that in no way excluded the possibility of state action.

In practice, personal service, while continuing to mean self-giving, was for Mary Ward a rather wider concept than that used by Octavia Hill. In *Tressady*, Marcella's friend Betty MacDonald decries social work as boring and 'so stupid, this "loving" everybody'; it transpires that she has disguised herself (in the manner of Beatrice Webb) so as to undertake an investigation of sweated work in the East End.[87] Marcella and her husband, Lord Maxwell, take a house in Mile End, East London, in order the better to get to 'know' sweated workers, while Lord Naseby, a follower of Marcella, also works on Booth's survey of London. In Mary Ward's novels the idea of personal help between social classes is stretched beyond purely one-to-one contact, for while recognizing that progress would inevitably be slow because modifying character was crucial, Mary Ward also acknowledged that the poor were impatient.[88] Something more wide-ranging and more inspiring than patient detailed individual work was therefore needed and she undoubtedly hoped that her settlement would provide a vehicle for other kinds of help.

From the first the settlement had two sides to its work: the teaching of the history and philosophy of religion and, in a separate building, what Dorothy Ward called 'the fraternisation between the brain and manual workers'.[89] The religious side of the work which Mary Ward saw as crucial to building a shared understanding between rich and poor rapidly proved a disaster. Her assumption that working people would become interested in religion if it was presented in an interesting way proved unfounded. Wicksteed had raised doubts in this respect in 1890 and had also questioned whether a body of settlers interested in Biblical criticism could be recruited.[90] In the event, both residents and working people preferred to meet in the social centre, which flourished. Mary

Ward accepted this turn of events and set about planning for the new, enlarged Passmore Edwards Settlement, opened in 1897, which emphasized the social side of the work. Adult education remained a major feature of the settlement's programme but only one lecture series specifically addressing religious issues remained. Speaking of Mary Ward after her death, Wicksteed referred to her 'magnanimity' in understanding that the residents were not prepared to carry out the Biblical-study project.[91] By the late 1890s, Mary Ward identified the aims of her ideal settlement in Arnoldian terms as developing good citizens and refined amusements. She explained to a Cambridge audience in the year the Passmore Edwards Settlement opened that the new settlement had no definite religious platform but had 'come to stand for an attitude not an opinion'.[92] She had come to accept, she told the Liverpool Settlement a year later, that the 'true and characteristic hope of the settlement movement' lay in the communication between hand and brain workers. Thus she emphasized the importance of class contact, using terminology that was also favoured by Fabian Socialists.[93]

However, Mary Ward remained a rather remote figure from both the settlers and the working people who came to the settlement. Early on one resident told her that the settlers did not really know her views and that she should make an effort to see more of them.[94] Similarly Frank Galton (the Webbs' secretary), who lived at the settlement from 1894 to 1899 on Beatrice's recommendation, described Mary Ward as 'very much the great lady', and remembered a mealtime conversation during which she had remarked: 'you know for my part I think no one can be said to be properly educated at all unless he has been to Eton or Harrow and Oxford or Cambridge'. According to Galton the table dissolved into laughter because no one present had been so privileged.[95]

Mary Ward preferred the role of fundraiser and publicist, and was happiest writing to officials at the Board of Education, sending her begging letters to *The Times* and negotiating with philanthropists like Passmore Edwards and the Duke of Bedford (who also contributed substantial sums to the building of the new settlement and to its running costs). She was less happy speaking publicly on behalf of the settlement – she apparently had a poor speaking voice – but nevertheless did so to considerable effect all over the country and to a variety of groups and organizations (for example the National League for Physical Education) which might be expected to lend either their financial or moral support to the settlement's endeavours. Her involvement in the day-to-day affairs of the settlement was chiefly confined to reading either Kipling or Stevenson to a group of boys once a week. The tone she employed in her Preface to the book published by St Pancras School for Mothers on the work of the 'pudding lady', who visited the homes of the poor on behalf of the school to teach cooking to working-class wives and mothers, indicated that she had little by way of the common touch. 'Knowing' the poor in the manner of an Octavia Hill, for example, would have proved impossible for her. Despite the understanding she demonstrated in her novels of the difficulties of relationships between rich and poor and in particular of the danger of middle-class women philanthropists being out of sympathy with the real needs of the poor, her appreciation of the work of the pudding lady was very much *de haute en bas* and was couched in the sentimental language of the philanthropy that she otherwise deplored:

> the Pudding Lady is doing what many of us have dreamed of doing – going into the actual homes of the poor and showing a young mother what astonishing things can be done with her own saucepan, on her own fire, with her own hands . . . [the object being] to show the helpless and ignorant that by a little teaching, a little kindness, a little sympathy, a little docility, this hard world can be made to yield its simple comforts and pleasure even to the very poor.[96]

Despite her recognition that the poor were impatient, Mary Ward was inclined to treat them, whether in fiction as members of Elsmere's New Brotherhood, or in her own settlement, as passive recipients of efforts made to enlighten them or to improve their welfare.

Nor did relations between Mary Ward and the residents show major improvement in the new settlement. In her address at the opening of the Passmore Edwards Settlement, she warned that 'what we want above all to avoid here, in the treatment of disputed questions, economic or social or religious, is the temper of mere partisanship, the temper of polemics'.[97] But both politics and the direction of the settlement's work became points of struggle that involved issues of class and of gender. Some residents and some members of the settlement's council wanted considerably more attention and recognition given to the social and educational work among adult working people. Mary Ward hastily wrote to her daughter, Dorothy, asking her to explain to visitors that this work was indeed at the core of the settlement's activities and was moreover its most difficult and important work.[98] She also sought to downplay the extent to which she controlled the running of the settlement and in particular the importance she attached to the work with children. This, she stressed, was the prerogative of the Women's Work Committee which was subordinate to the warden and council. It was comparatively easy work; women, being less occupied than men, were more readily available to do the work and the children were eager to learn. But her deprecatory remarks could not hide either her own absorbing interest in the crippled children and playcentre campaigns or their relative success compared to the work of the male settlers. The rivalries and bitterness simmered on. J. J. Dent, a council member nominated by the Working Men's Club and Institutional Union, and Percy Ashley, a resident and a representative of the London School of Economics (LSE) on the council, continued to object to the way in which the work with the children was made 'a subject of boasting'. J. J. Dent went on to make his desire to found a working-men's club (also a matter of conflict in many other London settlements) a matter on which he was prepared to resign. Mary Ward gave in, but replied angrily that

> sympathy for the workman's life and a desire to bring the resources of the richer and more educated classes to his aid has been one of the strongest feelings of my life. You will find it, I think, in all my books and for what other purpose should I have given up the leisure of a hard-worked profesional career to the foundation and growth of the Settlement?

She added her characteristic lament about the huge labour of writing fundraising letters with 'a lame hand, already bespoken for literary work'.[99]

Mackenzie King, who spent three months at Passmore Edwards at the end of 1899 and the beginning of 1900, felt that the Mansfield Settlement was doing much more for the poor despite its inferior club rooms, citing both its poor man's lawyer scheme and the greater involvement of the residents in local West Ham politics.[100] The latter was something that did not accord with either Mary Ward's desire to avoid partisan positions or with her financial sponsor, the Duke of Bedford's deep-seated suspicion of radicalism and socialism. Mary Ward had spoken in 1891 of the settlement providing something of a refuge for those who found themselves 'stranded and alone because of some irrevocable division which their reasoning power has wrought between them and the great traditional religions around them'.[101] But when the religious objective of the settlement faded, the rationale for both attracting and binding together a body of male residents also became less clear. Galton reported both the settlement's difficulty in getting enough residents to keep it going and the lack of success of its educational programme, which he attributed in large measure to the second warden, John Russell's (later Head of King Alfred School Hampstead) lack of managerial ability.[102] Certainly Mackenzie King's lectures were never attended by more than twenty people. The club nights were considerably more successful but their appeal lay as much in the sense of warmth and virtue they provided for residents as in the benefits they were perceived to bring the working people who attended. Mackenzie King delighted in the way contact with working people kept him 'human and rounded', although he confessed that he could no longer work up his former enthusiasm for playing draughts and rings (probably quoits) with the 30–40 boys who attended on boys' club nights. These evenings drained his stores of patience and he preferred conversation with the working men; helping with the parties for the crippled children, whose 'suffering bodies and bright and happy souls' elevated his thoughts; or attending the girls' club social evenings:

> I had a very pleasant dance with a young girl, Miss Gibb, who works in a drapery shop . . . Her cheeks and eyes blushed in a pure girl-like manner as I talked with her and treated her like a lady . . . To go there with a pure heart and help in word and act to elevate the thoughts and hopes of these girls must be good work.[103]

Mackenzie King was by no means a typical resident but he seems to have got on well with Mary Ward and his sense of *noblesse oblige* was probably not dissimilar to hers.

In a character sketch of Mary Ward, published in the *Daily News* in 1913, she was described as 'icily regular' and 'splendidly ineffectual'.[104] This may have been true both of some of her activities around the anti-suffrage movement, especially for the Women's Local Government Association, and of the religious programme of the settlement but it hardly described her work for children. While Mary Ward was a strong supporter of women's work at the local level, there was no special attention paid to the work women might do either in University Hall or in the Passmore Edwards Settlement. She may have avoided encouraging the kind of personal social work usually engaged in by women workers because of her distrust of what she perceived as the selfish motives of so many women philanthropists. But she herself had distributed a leaflet on infant feeding to poor mothers in Oxford early on in her married life and retained a strong interest in the problems working-class mothers experienced, especially during childbirth.[105] In University Hall the predominance of the religious objective in the work of the settlement would have ensured that men played the leading part, but this does not explain the continuing formal subordination of the Women's Work Committee to the male residents in the new settlement. By 1897, when Passmore Edwards opened, the most obvious model for a women's settlement was the Women's University Settlement (WUS), which was beginning to concentrate on social-work training, something Mary Ward did not aspire to do. But the WUS also ran a class for crippled children which certainly inspired Mary Ward's interest in this work.[106] The concentration of the Women's Work Committee on the needs of children, while pre-eminently women's work, was not typical within the settlement world, although the work for crippled children in particular was in line with the COS's new-found interest during the 1890s in making educational provision for 'mentally defective' children.[107] It was Mary Ward's own increasing interest in work with children and the time that she and her two daughters devoted to it that was responsible for raising the profile of the work; in so doing tensions were created between the women workers and the male residents.

The Passmore Edwards Settlement applied to the London School Board (LSB) to establish an Invalid Children's School in 1898, proposing to accommodate 15–18 children aged 5–14 years and to provide them with a hot lunch at 1½d per head. It asked the board to pay for a trained teacher and to furnish the schoolroom.[108] The Progressives on the board included two friends of Mary Ward, Lyulph Stanley and Graham Wallas, who helped to push the proposal through. Mrs Burgwin, the LSB's Superintendent of Special Schools (and a fellow anti-suffragist) helped to set up the schoolroom. Additional support came from the London hospitals and the Invalid Children's Aid Association. By 1906, the LSB had agreed to 23 such schools serving 1767 children.

Invalid children were an obviously deserving group whose welfare could be presented as a matter of national concern, in a similar manner to the arguments used by the COS to promote interest in mentally defective children. However, Mary Ward's concern to provide play-centres for children who were merely poor was harder to justify. She started her first Saturday morning playcentre in 1897 and the evening centres began in 1898, serving 250 children a week. By 1904 there were 1700 attendances at the Passmore Edwards Children's Recreational School.[109] From 1904 Mary Ward, together with her daughter Janet, promoted school playcentres at which attendances numbered 418,113 in 1907 and 1,752,173 in 1914. Mary Ward grounded her appeal for playcentres in first, the nation's need to do something about juvenile delinquency and hooliganism and second, in the Empire's need for a healthy strong race. As John Gillis and John Springhall have shown, the turn of the century saw the emergence of the adolescent as a social problem and a rising tide of convictions for juvenile delinquency that were as likely effect as cause.[110] In 1901 Mary Ward referred to the work of the Saturday morning play sessions and the settlement's cadet corps in curbing hooliganism in the neighbourhood.[111] In her advertisement for the settlement, she made clear that the playcentres were open to all, the children had only to be 'obedient, orderly, unselfish and happy'.[112] Janet Trevelyan noted that the first probation officer appointed under the 1908 Children's Act to supervise first offenders was drawn from the staff of the playcentres.[113]

The 1906 Education Act gave permission to local education authorities to provide playcentres, which reflected the power of the personal lobby mounted by Mary Ward. *The Times*, welcoming the 'Mary Ward clause', reported the motive behind it as being the desire to raise 'good citizens of the great Empire' and a concern 'that the burden of the Empire should not be put on rickety shoulders'.[114] Mary Ward herself pointed out that in the case of the public-school boy, play hours were as carefully supervised and 'thought for' as lesson hours: 'There is about him a constant atmosphere tending to good'.[115] Playcentres could help guard the development of the working-class child in a similar manner, imposing discipline in a healthy open-air environment. In common with so many of her contemporaries, Mary Ward shared a horror of urban degeneration that was brought into sharper focus by the report of the 1904 Interdepartmental Committee on Physical Deterioration.[116] She was a firm supporter of the Children's Country Holiday Association, of country outings for the children frequenting the settlement and, like Octavia Hill, was convinced as to the importance of introducing city children to plants and flowers. In a letter to *The Times* published in 1911, she appealed not for money but for flowers: 'The joy of the London child in flowers is well-known. It is pathetic and it is beautiful'.[117]

Mary Ward had no hesitation in invoking state aid for both her invalid schools and playcentres. In the case of playcentres, she redoubled her efforts after the permissive legislation of 1906. In a letter to *The Times* in 1908, she compared the situation in London unfavourably with that in New York which spent £50,000 per year on organizing and directing play for schoolchildren while London spent nothing and risked physical and moral damage to its children as a result: 'I am no friend to socialistic expenditure, but the economies the council is making in this direction are economies which London has no right to make'.[118] Her campaign to get the local authorities to make a financial commitment to playcentres encountered vehement opposition from another voluntary organization, the Children's Happy Evenings Association (CHEA), run by a fellow anti-suffragist, Lady Jersey. Mary Ward referred to the conflict in a letter to her friend, Louise Creighton, as 'harrowing and odious'.[119] The CHEA refused to countenance any state intervention and was determined to select the children for its playschemes by merit rather than need.[120] Mary Ward finally gained government financial support for her playcentres in 1916, subsequent to a Home Office

Circular which noted the rise of juvenile delinquency due, it was felt, to the absence of fathers on military service. As a war-time emergency measure, the Treasury agreed to a 75 per cent grant although, despite pressure from the Board of Education, it insisted on paying it in arrears, which forced Mary Ward to raise the money at the beginning of each financial year in the form of a bank loan. The regulations adopted by the Board of Education were modelled on Mary Ward's playcentres and the CHEA finally abandoned the struggle. In this conflict Mary Ward demonstrated considerable pragmatism and prescience in beginning a partnership between the voluntary sector and the state. Her playcentres were handed over to the London County Council in 1942.

Mary Ward campaigned similarly for greater state commitment to the welfare of crippled children and, using her newly formed Joint Parliamentary Advisory Council consisting of women social workers and MPs, lobbied hard for a clause obliging local education authorities to make provision to be inserted in the 1918 Education Act. The Board of Education did its best to avoid meeting Mary Ward and her supporters, fearing the cost of any compulsory extension of provision for physically disabled children.[121] But she was successful in getting her clause included in the 1918 Act. In this and in her playcentre campaign she saw clearly at a very early stage that settlements might play a part in experimental and volunteer work, 'which in preparing the way for the steady advance of the collective and legal methods of social reform, suit our English temper . . . These irregular and individualistic experiments are the necessary pioneers and accompaniments with us of all collective action'.[122] It is tempting to interpret this as a conversion to a kind of Fabian gradualism. However, Mary Ward never went so far as to welcome the idea of fully-fledged collectivism. At the turn of the century she depicted the type of development she had in mind as something of a compromise between the socialist's love of systems and piecemeal individual social work:

> The socialist dreams of attaining them [holidays, recreation etc] through the Collectivist organisation of the state. But at any rate he will admit that his goal is far, far distant; probably he feels it more distant now that [sic] he and his fellows thought it thirty years ago. Let him, let all of us reach meanwhile for something near our hands . . . for the spread [via settlements] that is, of knowledge of the higher pleasures, and of a true social power among the English working class.[123]

Her approach to local and central government for help in financing the work with children was pragmatic and must also be set within her interpretation of the 'citizen ideal' rather than as individualism or collectivism, an antithesis which she, like Bernard Bosanquet, was determined to reject. When she gave her speech at the opening of the new Passmore-Edwards Settlement, she made clear her own vision of a middle way: 'Certainly the Collectivist motive, or as I prefer to call it the citizen motive, will be here. It will take perhaps two forms – one more rigorous and dogmatic, one more pliant and opportunist – more Fabian in short'. Not that she was in sympathy with the Webbs' view of the role of the state for, she continued:

> Mrs Webb . . . writes an admirable little book to prove to us that Socialism of the rigorous sort has been stealing upon us from all quarters during the last half century. It may be so, and yet somehow the Individualists of any reasonable type see that they have very little to fear.[124]

When Mary Ward wrote a memoir of her brother, the historian and *Guardian* journalist, William Arnold, she quoted a letter he wrote to her approving of this address and in particular her view of collectivism. Believing the 'world of occupation' to be divided into two circles, that of 'collectivism' and that of 'individualism/enterprise', he wrote that

> it does not much matter whether the former gain here or there from the latter when reason and experience justify it. As long as there is the *alternative* circle, the socialistic tyranny will be impossible. What is to be resisted to the death is any *a priori* attempt to make the first circle cover all the ground.[125]

Mary Ward's philosophy was above all flexible and drew on a combination of Idealism, modern Christianity and the Edwardian cross-party concern about national efficiency.

She was not philosophically opposed to the state as were many hardliners within the COS and other voluntary organizations like the CHEA but she would not support any line of action explicitly designed to promote collectivism. The residents at the settlement never became involved in local working-class politics as did those at Mansfield for example, notwithstanding the Duke of Bedford's frequent complaints about their activities. The Duke fully supported Mary Ward's work with children but was very suspicious of any contacts the residents made with the adult (male) population of the neighbourhood. It was as much his pressure as the exigencies of war that transformed the settlement into a women's settlement under the direction of Hilda Oakley, former warden of King's College for Women, in 1915.[126] Nevertheless, the simple, intuitive conservatism of the Duke of Bedford, undiluted by ideas about the importance of developing the better selves of all citizens as in the case of Mary Ward, still found it possible to endorse state assistance in the provision of welfare for poor children. Mary Ward was able to appeal across a wide political spectrum as long as she grounded her arguments for voluntary and state cooperation in the need of race and nation, even when her opinions and actions ran counter to more traditional views on the proper apportionment of responsibilities in society. It is noteworthy that the settlement began by charging its crippled children for their hot dinners but soon provided meals free of charge in a large number of cases, despite the fact that this represented the COS's last-ditch stand for parental responsibility. Dorothy Ward recorded that she went with a friend to the Guildhall Conference on the issue of state feeding of children and 'found it so interesting and so burning that we went back after lunch . . . and I "testified" re cripples' dinners'.[127]

Mary Ward's support for the campaign against the sweated trades was also inspired by her commitment to improving the health and welfare of race and nation and in this her rhetoric was in perfect harmony with that of Beatrice Webb. *Tressady* argued for a piece of legislation that made it an offence to carry on particular trades in the home and which favoured the extension of the Factory Acts to small workshops, something the 1876 Factory Act had singularly failed to do.[128] The older Marcella explains the purpose of such an Act to George Tressady in very similar terms to those used by Beatrice Webb: it was incumbent on the state to tell some mothers that their sacrifice was too costly. Tressady objects that many will lose their livelihood and be driven into the workhouse, to which Marcella agrees, softening the blow only by her pious assertion that friends will help them. Beatrice congratulated Mary Ward on her clear exposition of the case for the Factory Acts, calling it the 'most useful bit of work that has been done for many a long day'.[129] She added that, while some of her friends would disagree, she was glad to see the argument for factory legislation disentangled from socialism, thereby acknowledging the case that could be made for such legislation on the basis of what was best 'for individuals and nations'. In her turn, Mary Ward explained in her Preface to Beatrice Webb's *Case for the Factory Acts* that factory legislation represented the kind of moral reformation that she perceived to be necessary for moral regeneration. Women workers needed protection in order to develop their 'better selves' and thereby to strengthen character. This in turn could only serve the cause of nation and Empire. An industrial race that was healthy, well fed and educated was a '*living* race . . . regulated by a body of law which represents the common conscience of England, intervening to protect the workers who are the true wealth of the nation from the tyranny of a non-moralised competition'.[130] Social reform thus became a matter of both moral and national necessity.

The call for national efficiency that became insistent in so many spheres of social and political life after the Boer War merely provided additional impetus to the views that Mary Ward believed to be a true reflection of the teaching of T. H. Green.[131] Other pupils of Green (C. S. Loch, the General Secretary of the COS, was one and L. T. Hobhouse, a major philosopher of New Liberalism, another) interpreted his ideas differently especially with regard to the proper role of the state, but the stress that all placed on ideals of service while using the rhetoric of either individualism or collectivism also deserves emphasis. In practice a variety of positions on different issues could be subsumed under the hegemonic idea of personal duty and contribution to the common good. Freeden has described New Liberalism in terms of an effort to re-establish a connection between ethics and politics,[132] but the remoralization of public life was also a major preoccupation of Mary Ward's and she was a firm Unionist. Her letters to her son Arnold constantly impressed on him the danger of sacrificing moral principle to practical political considerations.[133] She was also a very firm supporter of Graham Wallas, who was committed to moral reform, and she deeply regretted his defeat in the London County Council elections of 1907.[134] Interestingly, *Tressady* describes the way in which traditional political lines dissolved in face of the fight over the Factory Acts.

As an outsider, Mackenzie King observed first-hand the range of reformist political positions in late Victorian and early twentieth-century England and plumped firmly for Mary Ward's views. Fabian Socialists, he felt, were well-meaning, but lacked depth and too many were 'soreheaded' as a result of personal misfortune. Mrs Webb had too little faith in human nature and did not make enough allowance for the idealism in man. Alfred Marshall's injunction to be 'yourselves Idealists, but in thought realists' appealed to Mackenzie King as much as it did to Mary Ward.[135] Religious sensibility had to reach an accommodation with materialist thought. Moral regeneration within a framework of social reform seemed to him to strike the right balance and he saw it reflected in both Mary Ward's brand of conservatism and in his close friend Violet Markham's brand of (new) liberalism.

Mary Ward's conservatism and in particular her concern for the aristocratic interest, which she saw as the guardian of imperial tradition as well as of culture, injected an important additional note of pragmatic anxiety into her ideas about social action. If the privileged failed to understand that there were no private actions without social significance then the impatience of the poor would break its bounds and instead of the gradual social change that she endorsed, which was more Burkean in its regard for the established social order than Fabian, there would be a far more cataclysmic shift in social and political power. She saw the broad political framework in which she set her novel *Tressady* as more radical and potentially more damaging to the book's popularity than its message about the Factory Acts *per se*.[136] She intended that Tressady, initially uncaring about the poor and contemptuous of them, should be shown dying for them by accident (in a mine explosion) at the end of the novel. Tressady is shown moving from love of Empire towards social imperialism, and from the *laissez-faire* teachings of classical political economy to the beginnings of an appreciation of social service. But he remains politically ambivalent and the message of the novel is that his conversion is too slow and comes too late. In later novels a more utilitarian line of argument was used in respect of uncaring landowners, who were assured that bad citizenship (in the form of insanitary cottages) did not pay. But the sense of urgency Mary Ward felt about the need of the rich to recognize and realize their obligations as citizens if they were to retain their social position remained. At the end of a novel published on the eve of World War I, a minor socialist character bids landowners give the 'best of their souls' if they wish to remain in possession of their lands.[137]

The position of women

Ideal woman

Mary Ward's novels provide a wide spectrum of female characters whose histories make clear the limitations she perceived to exist on women's activities in terms of their relationships to men and, relatedly, to the public sphere. A majority of her heroines might be described as 'independent women' after the style of the 'new woman' beloved by so many novelists of the 1890s.[138] Mary Ward was sympathetic towards some of the new woman's thinking and behaviour but disapproved vehemently of her views on sex and marriage; the plots of many of her novels hinge on bringing the heroine to a truer appreciation of the proper range of possibilities open to her. A minority of her characters are good in the sense of saintly, but rarely without some qualifying tension, and a minority are rankly bad.

A few of the bad, like Louie Grieve (David Grieve's sister) or Kitty Bristol (in the *Marriage of William Ashe*), begin as independent women but prove unable to make the compromises and accommodations Mary Ward deemed necessary and thus enter a downward spiral that ends in death and destruction. Louie and Kitty are partially excused on grounds of genetic inheritance; both are described as having foreign blood. Julie Le Breton is similarly placed in *Lady Rose's Daughter* and Mary Ward later acknowledged her regret at not having had sufficient strength to give Julie the 'wretched end and degradation' that her immutable character and temperament demanded.[139] The straightforwardly and inexcusably bad women in Mary Ward's novels all have suffrage sympathies. Daphne has nothing to recommend her: she is a vulgar American; a product of new money; has a Spanish grandmother and therefore 'primitive blood'; and she reads American suffrage material which suggests that womanhood rather than wife and motherhood is the great fact of a woman's life.[140] As a result, she feels free to divorce her husband and afterwards devotes her time and money to the feminist movement. Characters of which Daphne is but the most extreme are portrayed as selfish, intolerant, rigid and authoritarian. Daphne's selfishness is the cause of her husband's misery and, even more darkly, the death of her child. Miss Fotheringham, a socialist and a suffragette in *The Testing of Diana Mallory* (1908), is also selfish to the point of inhumanity, fanatical, bigoted and hypocritical. When it is revealed that Diana's mother is a murderess, Miss Fotheringham writes to Diana to demand that she break her engagement to Miss Fotheringham's brother, because he will suffer politically. For Mary Ward, commitment to advancing a cause should never be allowed to override human sympathies. Gertrude Marvell in *Delia Blanchflower* (1914), a novel about the suffrage movement, is unrelievedly sinister and prepared to use and destroy other women in the name of the cause. She is well educated and has the ability to influence others, which makes her the more dangerous; she is ugly; and she has no personal openness or warmth. She plays on the vulnerability of Marion Andrew, the dull and dependent daughter of a family who live near Delia's estate and who, at 34 years of age, is described as never having had a penny of her own to spend or any experience of life beyond the home, and who is therefore protrayed as easy meat for the kind of excitement Gertrude can offer. Gertrude also demands total loyalty from Delia even when the latter's old servant is ill and needs careful nursing. Gertrude, in short, has no 'natural feeling'.

Mary Ward's 'good' women have if anything a surfeit of natural feeling. Catherine Elsmere is classically pure and saintly, such that Rebecca West felt that she would have failed to enjoy even 'the spiritual exhilaration of a meeting of the poor law guardians'.[141] Above all, Catherine is morally pure and it is this that secures her power within her own domestic sphere. Langham, the sceptic, perceives that Robert Elsmere was attracted to Catherine at a time when he was experiencing more difficulty being morally than intellectually clear. One of the reasons Mary Ward firmly rejected Comtist views on the position of women which superficially resembled her own (Frederic Harrison was also a firm anti-suffrage supporter) was because they denied wives and mothers this moral power. In *Robert Elsmere* we are told acerbically that the Comtist assumes the 'husband is the wife's Pope'.[142] This served to rob women of what Mary Ward felt was the true source of their legitimate social and political influence. Catherine Elsmere's daughter, Mary, exerts her moral power to persuade Richard Meynell to continue his fight for modernism within the church, even though such an open appeal made her wince: 'The primitive instinct of the woman, in this hour of painful victory, would have dearly liked to disavow her own power'.[143] The novels also contain a series of morally blameless women who exert powerful influence over their politically active husbands. William Ashe is brought low by the determination of the Liberal leader's wife and George Tressady's conservative political master is advised by a lady of High-Anglican conviction.

In the case of Catherine Elsmere, purity encompassed a knowledge of sin. The older Catherine (in *Richard Meynell*) helps to rescue 'fallen' girls, but how she ever found out about them is not clear. All Mary Ward's young heroines, including Richard Meynell's ward Hester and Delia Blanchflower, are protected by their male guardians from any knowledge of sexual 'sin' or 'disorder' even when, as in Hester's case, ignorance is plainly a contributory factor in her own downfall. However, the reader is given to understand that with a young and sullied mind she would in any case have stood no chance. Thus purity in women depended in large measure on male protection and in turn on a high moral standard among men.

However, like Octavia Hill, Mary Ward did not endorse the self-denial and renunciation that stereotypically good women habitually practised. Much as she admired Charlotte Brontë she would not have endorsed her efforts to deny herself the reading and writing she loved in order to do her perceived duty as a teacher and housekeeper/carer for her father, taking as her reward only her father's approbation.[144] The negative and repressive qualities inherent in such motivations to serve others did not appeal to Mary Ward, who preferred a sense of service grounded in a faith that did not insist on the price of self-fulfilment. Catherine Elsmere's rigidity in this respect meant that she was unable to appreciate all manner of God's other gifts, including her sister Rose's artistic talents. Dora, the high-church ascetic, in *David Grieve* is similarly full of feeling but with a tendency to renunciation that borders on spiritual arrogance. Dora is in love with David Grieve but feels that as a Christian she is obliged to give up anything she wants and therefore decides to help her friend Lucy marry him. It was this sense of thereby pressing 'the spikes into her flesh' and finding a 'numbing consolation in the pain' that Mary Ward found repellent.[145]

Furthermore, it was when such feelings motivated women to take up philanthropy that philanthropy stood condemned in Mary Ward's eyes. Catherine Elsmere is described as harbouring a tendency to 'devastating and depersonalizing charity'.[146] Other heroines are often portrayed as wanting to assuage personal grief, usually over a love affair, by taking up either district visiting or nursing. Susie Amberley in *Delia Blanch-flower*, lovesick for Delia's guardian, resolves 'to go away and scrub hospital floors and polish hospital taps. That would tame the anguish in her'.[147] Anxious to atone for her mother's guilt, Diana Mallory contemplates visiting the poor but then reflects that 'to use the poor as the means of spiritual "cure" seemed a dubious indecent thing'. Rather, she too turned to nursing:

> The scrubbing of hospital floors, the pacing of dreary streets on mechanical errands; the humblest obedience and routine; things that must be done, and in the doing of them deaden thought – these were what she turned to as the only means by which life could be lived.[148]

The young Marcella had, of course, done likewise and plunged into nursing, something that is referred to in *Tressady* as 'that common outlet for the woman at war with herself or society'.[149] But in the case of Marcella, an independent woman, a period of atonement is merely a stage in her development rather than an end in itself. The mature Marcella will be able to engage in philanthropy in the true spirit of self-giving which does not entail self-sacrifice.

Ella Pycroft had of course described the routine of rent collection as a way of deadening feeling rather than as a means of expressing it, and another friend of Beatrice Webb's, Margaret Harkness, also went nursing to get away from the unhappiness of her family situation. In her condemnation of this impetus to caring work, Mary Ward was probably drawing on the real-life example of her sister-in-law, Gertrude Ward, who spent most of the 1880s acting as Mary Ward's secretary and home help but whose high-church beliefs drove her away from the unconventional faith of Mary's household, towards district nursing for St Thomas's Hospital between 1891 and 1895 and then to missionary nursing in Africa. According to Gertrude, Mary Ward could not understand her position in the least and told her that she was wrong to desert her family.[150] It is difficult not to feel that Mary Ward's opposition to Gertrude's action was founded as much on her own self-interest as on principle. It seemed to Mary Ward that, unlike Gertrude, her daughter Dorothy did personify the genuinely good woman. Mackenzie King described Dorothy as earnest and as having 'deep sympathy'; and it was to Dorothy that Gertrude turned to explain her feelings about her position in the Ward household.[151] Mary Ward described Dorothy to Louise Creighton in 1905 as

> the angel in the house. What she gets through for everybody is really wonderful – but it *does* make her happy. Only more and more I think that people with such a marvellous unselfishness don't marry – and that troubles me.[152]

Again, Mary Ward apparently failed to see that her own demands might make it difficult for Dorothy, her eldest daughter, to marry. Even in war-time, when she was urging war service on other women, Mary Ward worried that in taking on the job of welfare supervisor Dorothy would overwork because she could not do with any less help from her at home.[153] Nor is it even clear that she was correct in her assessment that Dorothy undertook the work of serving others, principally her mother, in a true spirit of contentment rather than out of self-denial. Violet Markham found Dorothy to be a rather pathetic girl, who latched onto her friendship and support but for whom she found it impossible to do much.[154]

Mary Ward nevertheless had cause to be aware of the tensions generated by the changing position of women within her own family. Her younger daughter, Janet, to whom she wrote much more infrequently than to Dorothy, supported the idea of votes for women. All Mary Ward's novels demonstrate an awareness of gender issues, as Anne Bindslev has been one of the few modern critics to recognize.[155] For example, when Marcella tries to get Aldous Raeburn (later Lord Maxwell) and his grandfather to sign a petition for the release of Hurd the poacher, they refuse, but the old Lord Maxwell talks to her as an equal about the decision: 'an implied tribute, not only to Marcella, but perhaps to that altered position of the woman in our moving world which affects so many things and persons in unexpected ways'.[156] Twenty years later Lydia, more recognizably a modern heroine by her determination to earn her own living and by her smoking, is similarly described as a product of 'that remarkable change in the whole position and outlook of women which has marked this last half century',[157] even though it transpires that at heart Lydia is rather conservative. But it was part of Mary Ward's appeal that she managed to capture the tension between modern behaviour and traditional values. Mrs W. L. Courtney felt in 1913 that Mary Ward's touch in this respect was considerably more sure and accurate than that of H. G. Wells.[158] Looking back, Mary Ward attributed more importance to the railways in changing the position of women by increasing their mobility than to anything else.[159] This was very much a part of her determination to stress that women's position would improve gradually without the kind of radical change demanded by the suffragettes. But she was nevertheless aware of the range of variables making their differential impact on late Victorian and Edwardian middle-class women.

Mary Ward was not unsympathetic towards her independent women, of whom Marcella and Lydia were two. Possibly her regard for young, rebellious women had something to do with her own childhood behaviour, which was apparently far from demure.[160] To strive for self-development as Mary Ward's independent heroines do is not condemned. Catherine's sister, Rose, hates duty and is determined to be a musician. Robert Elsmere tries to persuade Catherine that music and art are not selfish indulgences to be denied and cites the efforts of the Kyrle Society, founded by Octavia Hill and her sister Miranda. In this novel and in others pity, as well as respect, is directed towards the women who, like Catherine, live in extraordinarily narrow worlds. Rebecca West condemned Mary Ward's ideal heroines as parasitic, but many are depicted as earning their own living. In *Delia Blanchflower*, Susie Amberly wails to her mother: 'I want to *know* something – to *do* something . . . It's such a big world, mother'.[161] Her mother reflects that *her* mother would have called her wicked to think of neglecting her duties at home but that it is now impossible not to let Susie take up nursing. In the same novel the reader is made to feel that a daughter who continues to live at home without a penny of her own is to be pitied; Marion Andrews is not blamed for following Gertrude Marvell. Again Mary Ward herself had personal cause to look favourably on women earning money of their own. Her income not only allowed her to pursue her charitable work but also permitted the family to keep the country house she loved so much.

Mary Ward consistently praised her heroines who sought a career and did well in it. This is more a feature of the later novels, but even in Marcella's case, her professionalism as a nurse is emphasized in the way in which she deals with a drunken general practitioner. The doctor swears he would rather have an 'old gamp' than the new lady nurses, whereupon Marcella uses her professional (but also her class) authority to call another doctor. Again, in *The Mating of Lydia* (1913), the quiet professionalism of the nurses who restore Faversham (who becomes Lydia's husband) to health is admired (and romanticized): 'Just a professional service for a professional fee. Yet his debt was measureless.

These are the things, he feebly understood, that women do for men'.[162] The capable Marion Vincent in *Diana Mallory* is described as 'self dependent' and 'self protected' and earns her living as a social investigator in the East End.

In the novels written during World War I the examples proliferate. Elizabeth, in *The War and Elizabeth* (1918) has a degree in Greek and not only helps her employer catalogue his collection of Greek artefacts but does his accounts and sorts out the affairs of his ill-managed estate. Nineteen-year-old Helena, in *Cousin Philip* (1919), comes into her own when she alone of all the men and women staying at a country house can drive a car: 'she was the professional, alert, cheerful, efficient – and handsomer than ever, thought French, in her close-fitting khaki . . . Here was the "new woman" indeed, in her best aspect'.[163] The hallmark of Mary Ward's successful working woman, as much as Octavia Hill's volunteer, is her quiet professionalism; to have drawn attention to herself (as did the suffragettes) would have been vulgar and unwomanly. But even in Mary Ward's novels of the 1890s, it was better to be engaged in useful work than to be vacuous and decorative like George Tressady's wife, Letty. While Mary Ward, like most late-Victorian women, feminist and non-feminist, agreed that wife and motherhood were supremely important, she was far from agreeing with the anti-feminist views of a writer such as Adèle Crepaz, who received Gladstone's approval and who felt that women should never venture into the public world of work.[164] Even in her very early stories, written as a teenager in the late 1860s, Mary Ward asserted:

> no one can say that to improve or cultivate the talents God has given us – to turn them to account in every possible way so far as is compatible with other duties – could ever be an action worthy of censure. Far from it – what *is* blameable, what *is* worthy of censure is the reckless indulgence of any one taste or inclination, be it intellectual or otherwise, to the utter oblivion of those obligations and responsibilities to the rest of the human race which no member of it can escape from.[165]

William Peterson has read this passage as exemplifying the extent to which Mary Ward was influenced by the mid-Victorian novelist, Charlotte Yonge, who preached female self-denial and submission.[166] But it may be read equally as an early vigorous endorsement of self-fulfilment, so long as it was not pursued at the expense of others.

In her novels, Mary Ward's independent women are, however, condemned and suffer if they pursue their own interests without due regard not just for their family duties but for the interests of the wider community. Elise, the French woman artist with whom David Grieve first falls in love, pursues art at the expense of human relationships: '*Art* breaks all chains, or accepts none. The woman that has art is free, and she alone; for she has sacked the men's heaven and stolen their sacred fire'.[167] But women's ties of connection to other human beings are in the end shown to be more powerful and also more productive of happiness. Elise marries a doctor admirer who then suffers a stroke and she relinquishes the artistic ambitions that caused her to be essentially uncaring of others. Marcella pursues the Hurds' cause out of her commitment to an abstract socialist theory, rather than out of consideration of the Hurds themselves, and in opposition to Aldous to whom she is engaged. Furthermore, she does so out of a desire to exert power: to protect Mrs Hurd and to re-order her life, and to assert her own independence of Aldous. Marcella has a passion for 'ruling and influencing' which extends, as she realizes by the novel's end, to ordering the lives of the poor rather than working to ensure that they have the wherewithal to grow and develop. Most damaging of all is the effort of any independent woman to exert power over men, whether as lover or competitor. Marcella also assumes that she will always 'take the lead and always be in the right' in her married life with Aldous.[168] Similarly Laura Fountain is tempted by the power she knows she can exert over her lover, Helbeck. These independent women survive and prosper as long as they are willing to learn to be self-giving. Laura Fountain cannot, and hers is a genuine and powerful tragedy because self-giving would require compromising her Protestant faith. Helbeck is a Catholic, and Laura is unable to yield her inner life to the Roman Catholic confession which would involve, she senses, a yielding of her personality and individuality. Laura therefore has to die, as do some other independent heroines. Mary Ward's independent women have to learn to search their consciences and to act in accordance with 'true feeling'; very few are lucky enough to be both independent and self-giving from the start.

The importance of the process by which an independent heroine learns to develop true feeling is best spelled out in the case of Marcella. In the wake of her unsuccessful attempt to persuade the Maxwells to petition for a reprieve for Hurd, sentenced to death for poaching, and her subsequently broken engagement to Aldous, she seeks self-forgetfulness in nursing in London. Undertaken for what are essentially selfish reasons, the experience of such personal service to others nevertheless serves to develop her character sufficiently so that she develops the capacity to love others and thus arrives at true feeling. Aldous's wise friend, Hallin, portrayed as someone who combines an appreciation of the importance of both moral regeneration and moral reform, comments that the young Marcella had been 'extraordinarily immature – much more immature than most girls of that age – as to feeling'.[169] Julie Le Breton's potential capacity to develop true feeling is signalled in her devotion to a crippled child although, as Mary Ward lamented, she does not undergo sufficient transformation of character to warrant the happy ending in which she is shown to be able to give of herself. Mary Ward's bad women, such as Daphne or Gertrude Marvell are, of course, characterized by an incapacity to love others. However, supporting votes for women need not in and of itself be irrevocably damaging so long as it does not result in such an incapacity. Marion Vincent, the social investigator in *Diana Mallory*, is portrayed sympathetically as a 'caring suffragist' who does not put the cause ahead of womanly feeling.

Mary Ward remained committed to the position she outlined in her earliest stories that all human beings, male and female, had to honour their obligation to serve others. But for women it was important that the development of true feeling, which signalled the capacity to love others unselfishly, manifest itself in both the public and private spheres. And for women, but not for men, greater importance was attached to personal than to social love. Thus Marcella learns the importance of personal service to others as the preferred form of social work, but she also learns that she will be able to exercise this best through marriage to Aldous who has at his command inherited wealth and political power. In *Tressady*, the older Marcella is first and foremost a devoted wife and mother even though the whole action of the novel is set around her social concerns.[170] In her marriage Marcella is able to exert as strong a moral influence as Catherine Elsmere and thus achieve power of a different kind. Independent women who seek to develop some artistic talent are also persuaded to put personal love first. Henry James, for one, found it impossible to understand why this was demanded of Catherine Elsmere's sister, Rose.[171] In many respects, the behaviour Mary Ward demanded of her heroines was similar to that demanded by Octavia Hill of her rent collectors – a premium being placed on marriage and family and after that on social maternalism. But the path of true feeling did not necessarily require self-denial. Rose could deplore the idea of duty and not be made to suffer for it so long as she loved unselfishly. Bindslev and Peterson agree that in the end Mary Ward's independent heroines are forced to submit, if they do not then they are destroyed, like Laura in *Helbeck*.[172] Certainly true feeling is only manifested once they have understood the importance of marriage, the antithesis of independence in feminist new-woman novels of the 1890s, as well as of social love. But marriage itself is not portrayed as an unequal relationship. Marcella remains her own woman. She learns to compromise in her relationship to Maxwell, rather than to submit. Mary Ward also held up a high standard of conduct for her male characters, which in turn profoundly affected the way in which she interpreted and defended the institution of marriage.

Ideal man

Federic Harrison wrote to Mary Ward on the publication of *Eleanor* in 1900, a novel chronicling Eleanor's efforts to retain the affections of an artistic but extremely egotistical man, Manisty, and asked whether she was not being too hard on men, for they were not all 'poseurs or fanatics'.[173] Rebecca West, on the other hand, felt that Mary Ward was prepared to endorse wholeheartedly the 'superman aristocrat class'.[174] In fact Mary consistently applied the test of true feeling to her male as well as to her female characters. Men also had to show care for others within the private sphere of the family and to demonstrate a sense of public service. Unlike women, they were permitted to keep their public careers entirely separate from their private lives. But, like women, they were expected to put the demands of the private sphere before those of the public. Donald Stone is thus correct to suggest that Victorian women writers called on both men and women to practise selflessness, although he fails to point out the way in which the expectation was gendered.[175]

It was as bad for men to seek power for selfish ends as for women to do so. Aldous Maxwell is ideal in his use of his extensive social and political power for the collective good rather than for his own interests. Maxwell is also portrayed as fulfilling a personal commitment to Mrs Allison, the pure-minded but high-Tory advisor to his political enemy, a commitment that overrides public, political considerations. Similarly, Richard Meynell puts his obligations as Hester's guardian ahead of his obligations to the Modernist movement within the Church of England, 'vowing that no public campaign must or should distract him from a private trust much older than it, and no less sacred'.[176] (Literary critics have condemned the space occupied in *Richard Meynell* by the Hester subplot, described by Peterson as 'hackneyed and old-fashioned', but, according to Mary Ward's moral tenets, it required an equal place.)[177]

Male artists are portrayed as being as handicapped as women in their development if they fail to develop the capacity to love. Like women, they are expected to marry; to concentrate wholly on art or on the acquisition of academic knowledge results in an incapacity to feel and to love which in turn rebounds on the intellectual endeavour. As one of Fenwick's artist friends puts it when he is dying: 'There are plenty of men like me . . . we are afraid of living – our art is our refuge. Then art takes its revenge – and we are bad artists, because we are poor and sterilized human beings'.[178] Similarly Langham, the dried-up intellectual and sceptic, cannot express his feeling for Rose because he is 'paralysed by habit and character' to the point where he cannot act.[179] But after love and marriage no further curbs are exerted on the male artist's ego. The aristocratic supermen are also depicted as having to develop the capacity to love but they are allowed more latitude than the women they marry to pursue their public lives separately because of their greater strength and the unbidden power of the racial inheritance they carry. Lady Connie's lover, Falloden, is described in terms of a Greek god, whose tendency to brutality is defended by an aunt of Connie's 'for the sake of the physique of our class – and it's the physique of our class that maintains the Empire'.[180] Falloden has to learn that he cannot subordinate love to his career, but equally it is acknowledged that his 'great brutal force' is unlikely to be subdued and, for the sake of nation and Empire should not be.

Relations between men and women

While Mary Ward set high ideals for her male characters and expected them to exhibit an active commitment to the private as well as to the public sphere, she felt that the scales would inevitably be tipped in men's favour in male/female relationships because of their superior strength and power. Independent women like Lady Connie learn that men's feelings are not to be trifled with. Men's greater strength meant that they occupied the most powerful political and social positions; women had always to operate from a position of weakness. It was therefore dangerous for independent women to try and exert power over men, additionally so because of the power of the male sex drive.

In Mary Ward's novels, illicit sex always takes place on foreign ground (usually France) and while, as Vineta Colby has observed, her heroes are often full of passion and her heroines of 'trembling yearnings', their code of behaviour means that nothing disreputable ever happens.[181] Like Beatrice Webb and Violet Markham, Mary Ward found H. G. Wells's *Ann Veronica* abhorrent. She wrote to her sister: 'I wish – vindictively! – that Wells didn't find it necessary to believe in God. It almost makes the belief itself . . . less beautiful'.[182] She probably also shared Louise Creighton's revulsion from E. M. Forster's *Howards End*.[183] She admired George Meredith's earthy quality, partly because he maintained good taste at all costs but partly because he considered the maintenance of a code of behaviour, or propriety, to be of material importance for women more than for men.[184] Men were expected to behave chivalrously and, like Delia Blanchflower's guardian, pity the female's weakness, admire female tenderness and offer protection. In the case of young women, the protection had to be both material and moral. Winnington protected Delia from knowledge of an incestuous relationship in a tenant's family and from the unsavoury particulars of a divorce case concerning a (male) fellow traveller in the suffragette cause. Meynell protected Hester from knowledge of her illegitimacy and Philip refused to tell his ward Helena why she should not see a particular young man other than to say that he was morally unsuitable.

Rebecca West charged that Mary Ward's morality depended on taboo rather than honesty, citing the example of *Daphne* which attacks divorce but not marrying for money.[185] But Mary Ward's approach was not untypical of the Victorian middle-class feminist's attack on the double moral standard whereby women had to remain pure and uncorrupted and enlist the help of like-minded men in order to raise the moral standard of all men. Mary's connection with the feminist Frances Power Cobbe derived in part from their shared commitment to promoting a higher moral standard for men.[186] Given men's greater strength and stronger sex drive all that could happen from women's point of view if the code of proprieties was abandoned was an increase in male brutality. In Mary Ward's view this was what the suffragettes invited by their wild, unfeminine behaviour and what they duly received at the hands of the police. Her reading of her own patriarchal society was not wholly inaccurate. Arnold Bennett certainly expressed the desire to see all her heroines raped *en masse* by an invading army and extreme male anti-suffragists were fond of contemplating the extent to which male brutality would extend if the 'wild women' forced them to abandon their hitherto selfless and chivalrous behaviour.[187]

Mary Ward also believed that the superior power and uncontrollability of the male sex drive made it impossible for mere friendship to exist between men and women. Her independent heroines often made errors in this respect. Lydia thinks that she can have two young men as her friends:

> Women who lived merely womanish lives, without knowledge of and comradeship with men, seemed to her limited and parochial creatures . . . 'we women are starved' – she thought, 'because men will only marry us – or make playthings of us. But the world is only just – these last years – open to us . . . Some of us would make such fratchy wives – and such excellent friends.'

Mary Ward tells us that Lydia was perfectly sincere in all this, 'but the comic spirit sitting aloft took note'.[188] Her sister, depicted as a rather humourless but otherwise harmless suffragist, warns her that men do not think and feel as women do, and finally, when both young men fall in love with her, the mother of one tells her flatly that men and women in middle life might manage to have intimate friendships, but not young people. The message that heterosexual attraction is natural, inevitable and uncontrollable (at least on the man's side) runs through many of the novels. It makes what Mary Ward perceived as 'sex antagonism' on the part of suffragettes unnatural. It also has implications for what women can hope to achieve in the public sphere because it makes entry into any occupation already occupied by men difficult (if it is impossible to be friends, it will also be very difficult to be colleagues). And it makes comprehensible the importance Mary Ward attached to maintaining strict proprieties (such as chaperonage) between young men and women. Finally, if sexual attraction was essentially irrational it needed to be contained within the rational bonds of the institution of marriage.

  Marriage was one of the themes Mary Ward treated most seriously in her novels and it was the theme she returned to most often. Furthermore, the ideas about the meaning of marriage and its importance that she worked out in some detail in the novels were used in her arguments against the suffrage. Mary Ward felt deeply and fiercely about marriage and the issue of divorce. Usually she presented dilemmas about relationships with care and a sense of fair play but, published in the year the British Royal Commission on Divorce began to sit, *Daphne* was essentially a polemic. Mary Ward acknowledged this when she referred to the book in a letter to Louise Creighton as 'my gruesome tale . . . which I am afraid has grown rather into a tract'.[189] *Daphne* was written on Mary's return from the United States, where she was shocked at the much more liberal grounds for, and higher incidence of, divorce. While *Daphne* was received as a diatribe against divorce, Mary Ward explained in the Preface she wrote later that what had really fascinated and appalled her in the USA was the transformation of the idea of marriage, rather than the incidence of divorce *per se*.[190] In a country with different marriage and divorce laws, Mary Ward was forced to think about why she believed it to be so important for two people to stay in a relationship that had apparently broken down. Her first instinct and the point she continued to make most often was that most of the relationships in which one partner sought divorce (usually the woman in the USA) had not irrevocably broken down.[191] The pursuit of divorce thus became one more symptom of modern restlessness and ill-discipline. But she was not merely eager to defend marriage as an institution. She also addressed the reasons why she felt the relationship was important and these again demonstrated the way in which her thinking eroded the existence of moral boundaries between public and private lives.

Her own experience in dealing with the problems faced by her parents meant that she was no stranger to marital stress and unhappiness. Her letters to her mother and father after the latter returned to Roman Catholicism and to Dublin, effectively separating from her mother, show an acute understanding of and sympathy with both their perspectives. While intellectually she had much more to share with her father, she was fully aware of the bitterness felt by her mother. Her letters were, as she described them to Louise Creighton, a record of the thinking that went into her novels,[192] but they were also practical letters of mediation and negotiation between both parents. She felt that her father was 'too hard on Mamma about money matters' and that returning her mother's bills annotated with questions was ridiculous: 'Mother's not a born economist, but she does her best and must be given her due'. Later she warned her father that 'you might just as well give her something deadly to drink as write letters to the tradesmen about her'.[193] But she also assured her father that she knew how difficult it was for such different temperaments to understand each other. To her mother she wrote of her doubts that her father could always have said what her mother reported: 'He is not a fiend'.[194] It was a difficult balancing act to perform and also a difficult situation to live with, for the separation was never publicly acknowledged. Yet when her mother died, she wrote to Humphry that her mother's feeling for her father had been the most absorbing part of her life and was clearly expressed just before she died.[195] Mary Ward was anxious to believe that to this extent their relationship had never ended.

Mary maintained a tender relationship with her parents despite what she (rarely) acknowledged to have been a rather unhappy childhood. Gertrude Ward's diary recorded that on being asked why she never talked of her girlhood, Mary Ward replied: 'I never feel as if I lived at all until my marriage'.[196] Humphry Ward remains a shadowy figure in Mary Ward's papers. He was obviously supportive in her dealings with her parents and, when either he was away or she stayed in the country to write, she sent him letters that occasionally asked his advice, often instructed him peremptorarily to pay a particular bill or purchase a particular item and almost never touched on her feelings for him or for her work. Yet ten years after her marriage when, as John Sutherland has noted, the balance of power was shifting very much towards her as the main breadwinner, she wrote that she hoped that every girl of twenty-one meeting her lover would be as happy as she was a decade hence, and then went on to assure him that the next ten years should be better still with fewer money worries and the children becoming more interesting.[197] Not unlike Beatrice Webb, Mary Ward saw her own marriage chiefly as a means of mutual support whereby each partner sought to enable the other to develop and offer to the wider community his or her God-given gifts.

There were, she felt, significant differences between women's and men's roles within marriage, but both sexes were expected to fulfil their obligation to be sexually faithful. The message of *Eltham House*, which reset the (early nineteenth-century) story of Lord and Lady Holland in the early twentieth century, was that moral standards were higher for men in the early twentieth century than they had been earlier.[198] Like Mary Ward's hero, Alec Wing, Lord Holland lived with a woman who left her husband and children for him. She set up a famous political salon to which only men came, and the women of the ruling class made sure that she was invited nowhere. Lord Holland's political career suffered no change. Alec Wing is sure that attitudes towards divorce have changed sufficiently that he too will suffer no harm, but his political career fails miserably. In Mary Ward's telling of the tale men are no longer permitted to divorce their standard of conduct in the private sphere from that in the public. This is the crucial corollary to her belief that the development of women's characters depended on their capacity for personal as well as social love.

Mary Ward expected wives ideally to be more than helpmeets and to exert their moral power within the home. In *Eleanor*, the reader cannot but have a modicum of anxiety about Lucy's future once Eleanor has decided to renounce her claim on the egotistical Manisty and do her best to bring him and Lucy together. But the Roman Catholic priest who is instrumental in persuading Eleanor to do this, and who also pauses to reflect on Lucy's fate, declares that women are born both to help men and to experience travail.[199] Women who desert their marriages consistently bear a greater portion of the blame in the novels than do men, in accordance with the greater responsibility they bear for upholding the moral fabric of relationships. Thus while it is Fenwick (in *Fenwick's Career*) who initially leaves his wife Phoebe to pursue his artistic education, more blame attaches to her when she decides to separate from him having, understandably but mistakenly, decided that he is in love with another: 'In so wrenching herself from him, she had perpetuated in him that excitable and unstable temper it should have been her first object to allay'.[200] Similarly, when Daphne's deserted husband Roger takes to drink, she is told by an American friend of Roger's that 'no one but a wife could save him'.[201] Falloden's only hope of curbing the brutal streak in his nature lies in the influence of Connie.

And even in her last novel, *Harvest* (1920), published posthumously, Mary Ward stuck to her conviction that women must exert their moral influence over men. Rachel had good reason for deserting her drunken, idle and abusive husband in Canada but is still wracked with guilt that she did not show more patience in dealing with him. Because women are obliged to invest more in marriage for the sake of their own development as well as for the moral welfare of men, they also have more to lose. While Alec Wing in *Eltham House* loses his political career, his wife Caroline dies, even though she is shown to have the stronger character and the truer feelings.

Husbands in their turn are, however, bound to protect the women they marry no matter what they do. The outstanding example from the novels is that of William Ashe, married to the incorrigible Kitty Bristol who cannot, despite her best efforts, control her wilful and headstrong passions. After a series of disasters, the modern reader is inclined to a certain sympathy with Ashe when he contemplates putting his public career before his commitment to Kitty. But Mary Ward quickly withdraws sympathy from Ashe as a churchman counsels him: 'Did you take your task seriously enough . . . she was so young, so undisciplined . . .'[202] Kitty loves Ashe and Ashe knew the kind of woman he was marrying. According to Mary Ward's code he was therefore obliged not only to stick it out but to make his marriage his most important commitment. While women are, first and foremost, obliged to live up to their obligations as moral guardians and are shown not to be able to exert power over men without dire consequences, men risk unhappiness if they either fail to take marriage and the choice of a marriage partner sufficiently seriously or if they neglect their obligations within the marital relationship.

Thus while the roles of men and women in marriage were unequal, Mary Ward did not portray marriage as a patriarchal relationship. Ashe does not attempt to coerce Kitty. Marcella continues to act as she feels best in her marriage to Aldous Maxwell, to the extent of speech-making at a meeting of sweated workers and political agitators in the East End. George Tressady's marriage is portrayed as inferior to that of the Maxwells because Letty is so patently lacking in any endeavours of her own. Not that Mary Ward believed that unequal marriage relationships like that of the Tressadys were unworkable, but men had to be alive to the kind of women they were contemplating spending their lives with. When Lydia (in *The Mating of Lydia*) decides to marry the Squire's agent, Faversham, Lord Tatham, who also loves her, decides to marry the fragile and disinherited daughter of the Squire, Felicia. Tatham tells Lydia that he feels he can 'take care of' Felicia and for a moment Lydia sees him 'as the truly tragic figure in their high-mingled comedy'. But later a wise socialist (after the manner of Hallin in *Marcella*) and a family friend reassures Tatham's mother: 'What does it matter . . . she is in love – head over ears . . . she will beat him if he looks at anybody else, but she will have ten children, and never have a thought or an interest that isn't his'.[203] Lydia's marriage might be superior but Tatham's will work just as well.

George Tressady laments that marriage 'makes or mars us all' and he is echoed by Daphne's Roger who reflects bitterly that if marriage 'doesn't make us it ruins us'.[204] Marriage was of crucial importance to Mary Ward because she believed husband and wife to be the unit of fundamental importance in society, as did Helen Bosanquet. If differences could not be worked out between husbands and wives, there was little chance of other social groupings reaching any accommodation. Much of the action in *Elsmere* revolves around Catherine coming to terms with Robert's loss of traditional faith. We are told that the issue is too grave to be worked out in 'bursts of feeling'; the 'ways of character' must take their course.[205] The process is long and painful and requires patience and understanding on both their parts. In *Helbeck* the strength of religious feeling is such that compromise proves impossible, which is the cause of the tragedy. When George Tressady realizes his marriage is a disaster, he reflects hopelessly 'no radical change was possible. It was character that makes circumstance and character is inexorable'.[206] But by the end of the novel, just before his death, there are signs that George and Letty are beginning painfully to reach a *modus vivendi*. For Mary Ward, marriage provided the important proof that in the majority of daily lives character could undergo change and, if character could change, feeling could develop. David Grieve explains to his wife that he has come to realize how important marriage is:

> I have come to think the most disappointing and hopeless marriage, nobly borne, to be better worth having than what people call an 'ideal passion' – if the ideal passion must be enjoyed at the expense of one of those fundamental rules which poor human nature has worked out, with such infinite difficulty and pain, for the protection and help of its own weakness.[207]

In other words, marriage was a discipline and an order. The institution imposed rational bonds on irrational (sexual) urges. Reckless divorce threatened to destroy an institution that acted as a civilizing force on base human instincts. Even one of the supporters of Alec and Caroline Wing in *Eltham House* agrees that marriage as an institution must be protected to prevent human beings turning into 'Barbary apes'. In the last letter she writes to Alec before she dies, Caroline admits that they did wrong and that the law is there to defend men and women from theselves and thereby to save nation and Empire.[208] As Mary Ward wrote in her Preface to *Daphne*, her aim was to show

> both the temptation and the cruelty of a lax marriage law [by which she meant a liberal divorce law] . . . Perhaps especially did I wish to illustrate what it means for the common place man, in whose life marriage and fatherhood represent often the only stays against temptations which are unintelligible to most women.[209]

Mary Ward was firmly of the opinion, like many nineteenth-century feminists (for example, Josephine Butler, Millicent Garret Fawcett and Frances Power Cobbe), that women's overwhelming need was for home and family, and men's for sex. A single high moral standard for both men and women, underpinned by a strict divorce law, therefore protected women's interests above all and could be justified to Victorian men as representing a higher form of civilized behaviour.

But Mary Ward was not unaware of the complex feminist and non-feminist positions on the issue of marriage and divorce. She wrote her Preface to *Daphne* in the same year that the Royal Commission on Divorce recommended more equal grounds for divorce, chiefly as a means of enabling the large numbers of working people living in common-law marriages to remarry.[210] Mary Ward commented:

> On the one hand I found myself upholding the equality of men and women in the matter of divorce, resenting what appeared to be the arrogant attitude of extreme opinion in the Anglican church towards the whole subject; and eager to give the same relief to the poor as to the rich; while on the other hand, to multiply the causes of divorce as they have been multiplied in some States of the American Union seemed to me the shortest and sharpest road to break down the sacredness, the ever-active discipline of marriage, that has ever yet been devised.[211]

In *Eltham House* the possible positions on the issue are cleverly delineated. Mary Ward understood that contemporary feminists might either support or condemn Caroline's action in leaving her husband and children for Alec Wing. It is important that Caroline is portrayed sympathetically from first to last and that both Alec and her first husband are not. Alec's political master, the Liberal leader, is powerfully influenced to Alec's detriment by his non-conformist, suffragist wife who cannot condone Alec and Caroline's relationship. Other feminists would like to see Caroline as a flagbearer. But ironically she is a 'womanly woman' rather than a rebel and full of strong emotions and weakness, despite a strong basis of true feeling; a similar combination to that found in Eleanor and one which Mary Ward found particularly attractive.[212] The wife of the Liberal leader, however, asks what a women's movement is worth if it cannot exclude people like the Wings, and her husband agrees that feminists who would espouse greater liberality in their relationships with men (a position Mary Ward falsely associated with the militant suffragettes) have no political clout: 'what we have to deal with is the general tightening up for *men* – of the connection between public service and private morals'.[213] Mary Ward agreed and clearly also saw this development as a victory for women that a militant feminism would destroy.

Anti-suffrage and public life
While the wife of the Liberal leader in *Eltham House* managed to combine support for a high moral standard in private and public life with support for the suffrage cause, Mary Ward did not. But her opposition to votes for women was not prompted by any simple anti-feminist desire to forbid women from entering public life. In her own early married life Mary Ward had fought to open up higher education to women at Oxford and she believed firmly that while women should not take part in 'imperial' politics they should play a large part in the affairs of local government. Her views on suffrage followed logically from her beliefs as to how true feeling manifested itself differently in men and in women.

Mary Ward formed the Committee for Women's Higher Education in 1873 with Louise Creighton and Mrs T. H. Green. It became the Association for the Education of Women in 1877 and worked successfully to found Somerville Hall (later College).[214] *Lady Connie* (1916) provides an idealized picture of the Oxford of the 1870s that Mary Ward had so loved. The 'pretty girl-graduates' are described as being watched by 'hostile eyes' but, with typical optimism and faith in progress, Mary Ward declares that 'all the generous forces in Oxford were behind them', thereby minimizing the achievement of her own committee.[215] In 1883 Mary Ward wrote proudly to her mother to tell her that she had been appointed the first female examiner of men at either Oxford or Cambridge.[216] Given her dissatisfaction and frustration with the quality of the education she had received and the determination with which she had pursued her self-education in Oxford it was a considerable achievement. Academic achievement and Oxford values were extremely important to Mary Ward; the fact that Caroline Wing's parents are Oxford academics is a clear signal that her character will prove stronger than that of her husband. In speeches she made throughout the Edwardian years, Mary Ward continued to stress the importance of education and training for women and often referred to the work she had put into the founding of Somerville.[217] When she was discussing with Louise Creighton possible signatories for the anti-suffrage petition, published in the *Nineteenth Century* in 1889, Mary Ward considered the possibility of making common cause with Comtists such as Frederic Harrison but, as she stated in *Elsmere*, felt she could not agree with their 'semi-religious beliefs as to the natural and necessary position of women'.[218]

In her novels the problems faced by many of both her 'good' and 'independent' heroines stem from a poor education. Catherine Elsmere replies harshly to Robert when he has been trying to explain why he is going to leave the church: 'I cannot follow all you have been saying . . . I know so little of books, I cannot give them the place you do'.[219] Lydia, striving to be a modern woman artist, is also described as full of feeling but lacking in education. Most strikingly, in *Helbeck*, lack of education is the key to Laura Fountain's tragedy. Laura is brought up by an Oxford academic father, who espouses a philosophy similar to that of T. H. Green. But being 'old fashioned' about women and their claims, he did not give Laura an education. Laura is brought up a 'modern' – she had always planned to travel and study music – but she knows nothing; she wails to Helbeck: 'Oh, I wish I was a new woman . . . But I'm not good enough – I don't know anything'. She is described as having personality but little character. At the height of her struggle with Helbeck and Catholicism she goes back to her father's old friend, Dr Friedland (another T. H. Green figure), who remarks to his wife:

> He [Laura's father] makes Laura a child of knowledge, a child of Freedom, a child of Revolution – without an ounce of training to fit her for the part . . . Then you put her to the test – surely – conspicuously. And she stands fast – she does not yield . . . But it is a blind instinct, carried through at what a cost! . . . But where is she to look for self-respect, for peace of mind?. . . If you believe, my good friend, Educate! And if you doubt, still more – Educate! Educate![220]

As Mary Ward herself realized, Friedland's speech was almost too revelatory of the cause of Laura's tragedy.[221]

Given the obvious importance Mary Ward attached to the education of women as well as men, her decisions with regard to the education of her daughters come as a surprise. There was no hesitation about Arnold's education. He went to Oxford, and Mary Ward's suffocatingly possessive letters to him chronicle in detail her anxieties over his various scholarship failures and successes. But neither Dorothy nor Janet went to university. There is little by which to judge their academic merit, but

Janet's subsequent writing would seem to indicate that she would have reached the required standard for entry. By the 1910s, Mary Ward had become deeply suspicious of the way in which feminism had permeated the world of women teachers in higher education. In *Delia Blanch-flower*, Gertrude Marvell, the suffragette, was depicted as being highly educated and thus all the more dangerous and, in 1912, Mary Ward wrote to *The Times*, deploring the fact that high schools and colleges for girls were staffed 'almost exclusively' by suffragists, arguing that this was 'unfair to the younger generation and unfair to parents'.[222] But it is unlikely that she had reached this position by the time a decision had to be made about Dorothy and Janet's futures.

In all probability her decision about what was appropriate for her daughters related to her complex feelings about the balance of public and private interests necessary for women to develop character and true feeling. After all, Mary Ward had herself married very young and had given up disciplined academic work to do so. The view that higher education could always be pursued later, but that women should never let the possibility of marriage and children slip away, is confirmed in some of the novels. For example, Lady Connie is portrayed as worldly and quick witted, but she is essentially uneducated and rather lazy. She is always intending to pursue some course of study because everybody in Oxford does (a paraphrase of the reply Mary Ward is reported to have given Taine when he inquired about her work in the Bodleian), but she never does.[223] Yet she is portrayed as a much more interesting and desirable figure than the solid Nora, her cousin, who works hard as a home student. Connie is in awe of Nora and the other women students but wonders, like some of the characters in Alice Stronach's novel about Newnham graduates: 'Do they never think about a *man*?'[224] The image of female university students as drab and spinsterish was widely shared. Beatrice Webb reflected after a visit to Somerville in 1896 that, while it offered the kind of education that she had longed for as a young woman, she felt that no woman should be a tutor without first living in the outside world.[225] Beatrice shared Mary Ward's fear that young women going straight from home to university would become unsexed.

The idea that marriage and family should take precedence over education, without necessarily becoming an alternative, is spelled out clearly in *Cousin Philip*. Helena's mother had been an intellectual but has 'no trust in any of the new professional and technical careers into which she saw women crowding'. She believes sex to be the dominating fact of life and she wished her daughter Helena first to fulfil herself sexually. As she is dying she says: 'If she goes to College, at once, as soon as I am gone, and her brain and ambition are appealed to before she has time to fall in love, she will develop on that side prematurely – marvellously – and the rest will atrophy'.[226] It is hard not to hear in this the voice, and, indeed, see reflected the experience, of Mary Ward herself. Janet Ward married at twenty-five and continued to play a major part in her mother's work for playcentres, writing a book about them (published in 1920) and a biography of her mother (published in 1923). Dorothy suffered the fate of so many eldest Victorian daughters, whose services to their parents were judged indispensable, even though in the letter Mary Ward wrote to Louise Creighton (see p. 226) there is some evidence that she was 'troubled' that Dorothy might be too 'unselfish' to marry. As it was, in all likelihood Mary Ward's own selfishness prevented her elder daughter from scaling the heights of either matrimony or intellectual success.

The same conviction as to the primary importance of home and family to women and the inevitability and uncontrollability of sexual attraction between men and women wherever they might meet underlay Mary Ward's views on the issue of the suffrage itself. She was a leading anti-suffragist and put together the anti-suffrage petition, which gave a public persona to the anti-suffrage movement, with James Knowles, editor of the *Nineteenth Century*, at a dinner party. She wrote to her father that she and Knowles had 'concocted a women's manifesto against women's suffrage which we mean to launch when the critical moment comes'.[227] The 'Appeal', published in June 1889, contained all the main themes Mary Ward stuck to until 1918 when the movement finally admitted defeat: that women's participation in the affairs of state was rendered impossible by the 'disabilities of sex' and 'by strong formations of custom and habit resting ultimately upon physical difference'; that women's 'natural sphere' of activity lay in the local community, for example in service on school boards and boards of guardians; and that women's participation in national politics could only undermine family life.[228] When Mary Ward wrote another article on this subject for the *Nineteenth Century* in 1908, she emphasized the same points, stressing additionally the progress women had made, for instance in the fight against the sweated trades, without the vote.[229]

Mary Ward had a firm and pragmatic grasp of what the issue of women's suffrage meant in terms of party politics. In an exchange in *Marcella*, voting on an eight-hour bill is compared to a vote on suffrage with the speaker expressing the view that MPs would vote for such a bill until there was a chance of getting it passed, whereupon they would smash it.[230] A similar analysis is offered by Marcella's friend, Betty MacDonald, in *Tressady*. Mary Ward roundly condemned the machinations surrounding the suffrage issue in 1912, when a 'conciliation bill' seemed possible, and in 1918, prior to the granting of the vote. She abhorred party manoeuvrings on an issue that was to her a matter of high principle as shameful.[231] Her strong feelings about the need for a high standard of public morality meant that the suffrage fight must be waged honourably. Delia Blanchflower's guardian tells her that if she must work for women's suffrage she should do so with honour.[232] In Mary Ward's view suffragists such as Millicent Garrett Fawcett, whom she much admired, behaved decently and suffragettes did not.

Mary Ward believed fundamentally that women could not, for reasons of both sex difference and sexual attraction, engage in party political life. She was herself intrigued by politics and the political dinner parties she and Humphry were obliged to give (in connection with his work for *The Times*) were as much a part and parcel of her love/hate relationship with London Society as they were for Beatrice Webb. In 1886 she wrote to her father that she was looking forward to dinner gossip with the Gosdens: 'politics are dreadfully exciting'.[233] She was also thrilled by the experience of speaking in public, although she always felt that she was not good at it and tended to avoid large and important gatherings. After a speech on behalf of University Hall in the Manchester Free Trade Hall, she wrote that she had had: 'a taste of what the exhilaration of public speaking must be to those who can really do it. But I can't'.[234] Indeed, in moving the adoption of the Annual Report of the National League for Opposing Women's Suffrage (NLOWS) in 1913, she began with the declaration that habitual public speaking had not in her case made a good speaker and that she wished heartily that someone would provide anti-suffragists with new arguments.[235]

Mary Ward played a leading public role in the anti-suffrage movement out of what she regarded as moral and national duty. But she also played a major part in influencing her son Arnold's political career: providing him with money; advising him on his speeches; persuading him to take up the anti-suffrage cause in parliament; and writing a series of pamphlets addressed to the 'plain village folk' among his constituents, explaining the Unionist position in the elections of 1910 on the People's Budget and the role of the House of Lords.[236] Mary Ward was especially eager to defend landlords, the majority of whom she felt were living up to their obligations towards their tenants (she assured Arnold's constituents that she had discovered this in the course of her research for *Marcella*).[237] Mrs Fawcett criticized her involvement in Arnold's political career as essentially hypocritical. But Mary Ward felt there was no inconsistency: 'a woman is perfectly free to express opinion and to exert influence if she can in ways most natural to her'.[238] The means of influencing men, she believed, ranged infinitely wider than the parliamentary vote. Women could and should exercise indirect influence over national affairs. Mary Ward was convinced that such influence could prove crucial because of her beliefs as to how the political system worked. She was also convinced that women had to be very careful not to cross the dividing line between indirect and direct political activity, notwithstanding that her role in the anti-suffrage movement was itself direct political intervention.

Mary Ward's novels make clear the way in which she believed political matters were decided among a few ruling-class families. She presented this as a matter of fact without commenting on its desirability, although it is unlikely that she would have wished to see any substantial change. She may have inclined to populism on religious matters, but not in politics. Aldous Maxwell spends much of his time socializing with other landed families because 'we have still, it seems, a "ruling class" '.[239] Julie Le Breton's success as a salon hostess was based on the same premise:

> The English aristocratic class, as we all know, is no longer exclusive. It mingles freely with the commoner world on apparently equal terms. But on the whole its personal and family cohesion is perhaps greater than ever.[240]

The family politics described in *Eltham House* represent the extreme of Mary Ward's views in this regard. Ernest Simon, the Manchester councillor and social reformer, felt that (in 1915) this view of politics was outdated. While he had enjoyed the novel, he did not believe that public life 'depends as much as some people think on social display and plotting and planning'.[241] While the social background of MPs, especially in the Liberal Party, had changed more than Mary Ward was prepared to credit, in fact her estimation of the power of the landed classes and their social world was not so inaccurate for the period before World War I.

On the assumption that ruling-class politics were essentially family politics, Mary Ward could also portray them as essentially civilized, for example Aldous Maxwell helps the advisor of his political opponent find her son. It was possible, not merely desirable, for private obligations to take precedence over political causes. It was also possible for women to exert a major influence: Marcella over Maxwell, the Liberal leader's wife over her husband and over the fate of Alec Wing, and similarly Lady Parham, another political wife, over William Ashe because of her dislike of his wife Kitty. The most instructive case is that of the older

Marcella Maxwell in *Tressady*. Early on in the novel the question of the nature of Marcella's influence is raised:

> Was her position an illustration of some new power in women's hands, or was it merely an example of something as well-known to the Pharaohs as to the nineteenth century – the ability of any woman with a certain physique to get her way?[242]

While the answer tends to the latter, Marcella's influence was based on her firm understanding of the issues surrounding the Factory Acts and sweated labour, as well as on her capacity to manipulate men. But it was her capacity to charm, her sexuality, that proved dangerous. Lord Naseby, a devoted follower of Marcella, discounted the influence of 'platform women':

> The women who matter just now – and you women are getting a terrible amount of influence – more than you've had any time this half-century – are the women who sit at home in their drawing rooms, wear beautiful gowns and attract the men who are governing the country to come and see them.[243]

This was in fact a more accurate portrait of Caroline Wing or Julie Le Breton than Marcella Maxwell, but it was nevertheless Marcella's beauty and charm that converted George Tressady to Maxwell's cause in the matter of the Factory Acts. Marcella is a devoted wife but as Tressady himself remarks:

> the very perfectness of the tie that bound them [Marcella and Maxwell] together weakened her somewhat as a woman in her dealing with the outside world. It withdrew from her some of a woman's ordinary intuitions with regard to the men around her. The heart had no wants, and therefore no fears.[244]

Marcella fails to spot that Tressady is falling in love with her. Thus while Marcella effectively, albeit unconsciously, uses feminine wiles to worthy political ends, her sex and sexuality prove a problem and, for Mary Ward, constituted the reason why women could never be successful in politics. After realizing her fatal mistake with Tressady, Marcella retreats to the private sphere. Mary Ward did not believe that women and men could mix as friends or colleagues; the male sexual instinct was too strong and complications were inevitable, which in matters of imperial politics could only prove disastrous to state and nation.

Allied to this deeply grounded fear as to the fragility of the moral code governing male/female relationships were Mary Ward's fears regarding the effect of the suffrage on the family. When she returned from the USA in 1908, deeply shocked about US rates of divorce, she set about first writing *Daphne* and then organizing a Women's National Anti-Suffrage League. The two projects were intimately linked, as she explained to Louise Creighton:

> The whole idea of marriage is becoming radically transformed in that strange nation [the USA] and part of the strong opposition to suffrage [not in fact as strong as Mary Ward liked to make out] comes there from the feeling that it is the suffragist women who are helping in the disintegration of the family.[245]

Mary Ward continued to reserve her most forthright condemnation for radical feminists, such as those writing in the *Freewoman*, who advocated free love as well as suffrage.[246] Louise Creighton also attacked votes for women on the grounds that they would endanger marriage and the family, arguing that to give married women the vote would make marriage a contract rather than a union, so changing the entire character of the family.[247]

At the end of the day imperial politics required the attention of, preferably, the best-educated men, who could also in the last resort use physical force to defend state and nation. The sexual difference argument thus comprised two parts: the issue of difficulties inherent in men and women working side by side, and the more commonly discussed issue of differences in physical strength. Mary Ward conceded that it might be possible for small countries (she gave the examples of Finland and New Zealand) to grant women's suffrage. But England was not a minor power, 'she is the "weary Titan" on whose shoulders lie the burdens that only men can lift'.[248] Given the argument that important nations could not afford to grant women votes, Mary Ward was particularly concerned to convince public opinion that the tide had turned against women's suffrage in the USA. This led to frequent exchanges on this subject between her and Mrs Fawcett.[249] Mary Ward never moved from the position that imperial politics required strong male leadership and preferably aristocratic male leadership.

When Janet Trevelyan wrote to Violet Markham in 1947 and speculated on the reasons for her mother's anti-suffragism, she stressed the importance of Mary Ward's academic elitism and anti-democratic instincts.[250] Certainly Mary Ward believed in the reality of a ruling class and confessed to her father in 1882 that the progress of democracy made her quail.[251] In particular she felt that working-class women did not have the education or public experience that would make them informed voters and lacked the time to read newspapers or to take an intelligent interest in politics.[252] Mary Ward explicitly refuted Helen

Bosanquet's views in this respect. Helen's sister, Mary Dendy, wrote bitterly of Mary Ward as being

> content to use all the force of a fluent and not very logical pen in violent vituperation of the more thoughtful and less selfish members of her sex . . . She writes as if the world was divided into two halves; one, comfortably furnished and pleasantly secluded, for the modest good and amiable, a kind of palace of the sleeping beauty, not ever doing anything so improper as opening her eyes until the Prince came, nor even then unless he be the right prince; and the other a wilderness into which if any woman stray, either of free will or necessity, it serves her right that howling wolves should come and devour her.[253]

Mary Dendy was a middle-class woman but wrote with all the feeling of one who knew what it was to live alone and to earn her own living.

Mary Ward's most pressing fear was of a link between suffragism and socialism. Some of the most undesirable characters in her novels worked for both causes; for example the idle, dishonest and cynical Paul Lathrop in *Delia Blanchflower* supports the women's suffrage movement, is a socialist and, for good measure, is divorced. In 1918 Mary Ward wrote to her sister of her fear that if women were granted the vote Labour might be elected with the result that the war would be lost.[254] She feared, above all, that the suffrage movement would provoke sudden radical change which might in turn produce a violent shift in politics towards socialism.[255] She contended that imperial politics required males of character, who tended in her thinking to be men of the aristocracy. Furthermore, men of character needs must move slowly. The few supporters of the suffrage who received sympathetic treatment in her novels understood this. For example, Lady Tonbridge in *Delia Blanchflower* declared that 'the difference between me and the Fury [Gertrude Marvell] is that she wants the vote this year – this month – this *minute* – and I don't care whether it comes in my time – or Nora's time [her daughter] – or my grandchildren's time'.[256]

Mary Ward never moved from the position she adopted in 1889: 'that citizenship is not dependent upon or identical with the possession of the suffrage. Citizenship lies in the participation of each individual in effort for the good of the community'.[257] It was a position that was developed logically from her belief as to what constituted true feeling for men and for women; Violet Markham would go on to elaborate this gendered concept of citizenship. Mary Ward argued that in the final analysis the issue of inequality in citizenship was irrelevant because women did not need the vote; first, social reform benefiting women was being enacted anyway, and second, women had a 'natural' place in which to participate directly in political life (albeit in a disinterested and sympathetic manner) at the local level.[258] In a public debate with Mrs Fawcett, Mary Ward used Beatrice Webb's idea of the Common Rule (consisting of a minimum standard for working conditions maintained on one side by trade unionism and on the other by the Factory Acts) to explain why women had gained so much in terms of better working conditions, shorter hours and higher wages without the vote, and in a 1913 speech she cited the 'organised forces of public opinion' to which women could contribute without the vote, as the campaign against the sweated trades had proved.[259] In *Delia Blanchflower*, Delia's guardian reflects that women 'have seized with the old faith on the confident cries of 60 years ago', but that the vote *per se* was no more likely to prove a cure-all for women's problems than it had for those of men.[260]

Mary Ward was prepared to fight passionately and to the end for the anti-suffrage cause as her troubled association with the National Union of Women Workers (NUWW) showed. She had hardly been an active member of this organization of middle-class, philanthropic women but, like Beatrice Webb and Louise Creighton, she regarded it as producing the kind of shift in public opinion that would result in social reform to benefit working women. However, in 1910, to Mary Ward's disgust, the NUWW sent representatives to a suffrage meeting in Trafalgar Square. This resulted in a lengthy correspondence with her friend Louise Creighton, president of the organization. Putting principle before friendship distressed both women. Louise Creighton declared that she hated controversy and said that she had always wondered whether anyone 'could engage in controversy and save their souls'.[261] After pleading for compromise, Mary Ward felt by 1912 that she had no option but to resign, warning Louise that there would be many who would feel they could not belong to an organization where 'there will be fear of suffrage or divorce revolution', but continued to express her sorrow over their differences and in 1914 wrote that the friendship was too 'old and dear' for them ever to differ again.[262] While the suffrage issue did drive deep wedges between members of the same family and between friends, the extent to which women suffragists (if not suffragettes) and anti-suffragists retained their respect and even liking for one another is also remarkable. Mary Ward went on to found the Joint Parliamentary Advisory Council out of the anti-suffragist members of the NUWW, and it was this body of women philanthropists and MPs that helped in her campaign to gain state funding for playcentres and crippled children.

Mary Ward never failed to stress the worth of such philanthropic work and the natural alternative it provided to national politics. In her debate with Mrs Fawcett she said that she wished that Frances Power Cobbe's suggestion of the 1880s, that standing local committees of women should be established, had been followed.[263] Then the interests of education and of women and children could have been effectively monitored. But even as things were, her settlement desperately needed workers to come forward to help with crippled children and with playcentres; care committees needed volunteers; and local councils and boards of guardians needed women members. In *Delia Blanchflower*, Delia's guardian has a pet project in the form of a county school for crippled children for which he cannot find enough women of the right sort to help. Delia is accused of finding school and poor law work unimportant compared to the vote. She understands what is meant and replies: 'I suppose that means, that if we did all the work we might do – we needn't bother about the vote'; she nevertheless refuses to accept the argument.[264]

After 1908, Mary Ward actively promoted the work of women in local government by setting up the Women's Local Government Association as an affiliate of the NLOWS. In the *Anti-Suffrage Review* of 1911 she made it clear that she could not agree with those 'Antis' who felt that women had no role beyond the home. She said that she refused 'to allow the devil to have all the best tunes'. To women engaged in work of caring for the poor, for children and for the sick, 'to those women who have the time and the feeling to give to them, they become the most absorbing form of human service; they are steeped in the pathos and tenderness of human life, they speak to the heart, and they train the mind'.[265] Women's call to social maternalism was equal, albeit different to men's call to public service at the behest of empire.

War and the reiteration of belief in a world turned upside down
Mary Ward struggled against suffrage until it was granted (to women of 30 and over) in 1918. She wrote to Louise Creighton that 'as a patriot' she was obliged to fight to the end.[266] Conservative commitment to Empire overrode Idealist commitment to the development of 'best selves' when it came to the issue of women and the vote. Indeed, she drafted the last anti-suffrage amendment on which the House of Lords voted, having agreed in December 1917 to chair the Executive Committee of the NLOWS because of the looming crisis over suffrage in the House of Lords and the role that Lord Curzon, hitherto the League's leader, would have to play. By this time not only had Louise Creighton deserted the anti-suffrage cause, but so had the other major female voice within the League, Violet Markham. Mary Ward could only hope that they were right in their views; for herself, she remained 'full of

anxiety', fearing that female suffrage would produce a socialist takeover and the end of Empire. To the very last she continued to urge that a referendum be held on the question of women's suffrage and to appeal to patriotic feeling over that of party.[267]

Mary Ward had a strong feeling that war would indeed prove the 'locomotive of change' and succeed, where pre-war militant suffragism and trade unions had failed, in producing the kind of radical social change she feared so much. William Peterson believes that she was 'tormented and obsessed by the spectacle of war', which threatened her belief in progress, and so 'retreated' into patriotism.[268] It is logical that given her system of ideas she should have felt the impact of war as much as Beatrice Webb or Helen Bosanquet but unlike them she revealed no written sign of distress regarding her framework of beliefs. Nor is it likely that she retreated into patriotism; war merely exacerbated her feelings about nation and Empire. When Roosevelt wrote to ask her to explain the British case to the American public, she took up the task of helping Americans to visualize the effort 'of the soldier, the working woman and the capitalist' with huge energy and commitment.[269]

She also completed five novels during the war, largely to compensate for a sharp decrease in her income (due to falling royalties, rising taxation and the gambling debts incurred by her son Arnold). The novels dealing with the war emphasized the new burden of taxation falling on the middle class and on the landowner, and the onerous nature of war-time state regulation, while also depicting them as temporary measures of patriotic necessity. Both *Missing* (1917) and *The War and Elizabeth* (1918) have characters with old (and, we are given to understand, worthy) liberal values, who are not pacifists but who refuse to be dictated to by government. Elizabeth ponders her employer's (the local squire) reluctance to obey the County War Agricultural Committee: 'No-one ought to be free to ruin his land as he pleases! It concerns the *state*'.[270] A working-class townsman also explains to the recalcitrant squire that young men such as himself may have resisted the demands of war-time production, but they also support government regulation. Given the slum conditions in which men like himself have been brought up, they will not countenance profiteering. He declares himself to be for England, for DORA (the Defence of the Realm Act) and for socialism, in that order. The novels also stress the disappearance of any remnant of deferential behaviour on the part of rural workers. The squire's employees threaten to leave him, saying that there is plenty of work for everyone in war-time. The social exclusiveness of landed ruling-class families is also shown to be breaking down dramatically. Whereas in *The Mating of Lydia*, Lord Tatham's mother had difficulty contemplating that her son might marry a commoner, in *Missing* and *The War and Elizabeth* members of old families comment that the 'old lines were being rubbed', or more prosaically that there seemed to be too many other things to worry about.[271]

As Mary Ward wrote to Louise Creighton: 'War is producing great effect moral and social'.[272] While she was prepared to accept certain aspects of the changes that appeared to be necessary for military victory, hoping that they would be but temporary (especially the increasing role of the state, notwithstanding the benefits it conferred on her own projects for crippled children and playcentres), she viewed with more anxiety the changes that were taking place in social relations, particularly as they affected landowners.[273] Her own country house represented to her 'that kind of inheritance from the past to shelter one's own later life'.[274] She dreaded that war might result in the kind of cataclysmic shift that would bring the Labour Party, which she referred to as the 'extreme party', to power and with it the transfer of all land and capital.[275] Mary Ward's recognition of the changes that were taking place led her to defend ever more vehemently the old ways that she felt had served England so well. On no issue was her reaction so marked as in regard to the position of women.

Mary Ward toured munitions factories in pursuit of material to put in her letters to the American people on *England's Effort* (1916). She was delighted at the response of women to the demands of war-time production. To her the war offered women an opportunity for honourable service to their county: 'What an honour for women – and they know it!'[276] War-time employment represented merely another, albeit extraordinary, opportunity for women to serve the community. As Anne Summers has shown, this was exactly the way in which women serving as nurses saw their work; in other words, war work served to reinforce, rather than change, the gendered idea of citizenship.[277] Mary Ward had no patience with the efforts of women trade unionists to secure better working conditions for munitions workers, which she regarded as merely mischievous and unpatriotic and, contrary even to the findings of contemporary government inquiries, declared that she never saw healthier women than in the munitions factories.[278] Her flattering descriptions of women in uniform, khaki caps 'shewing the many pretty heads, and slender necks', found their way into her novels as well as into her letters to Americans.[279] War service was exceptional; she hoped and worked hard to convince her readers that nothing had changed the women beneath the caps. They still required protection and that, in the last instance, provided sufficient reason for not giving them votes. In *Cousin Philip* the heroine, Helena, who proved herself by stepping to the breach and driving the men in the household to the local town where demobbed soldiers were rioting, is portrayed as vulnerable and still needing chaperonage, albeit against her will. Helena is also told forcefully and bluntly by her guardian to marry and bring up children – 'that's the chief duty of Englishwomen just now'.[280] And in *Harvest*, the eligible American army captain says that while women are claiming that they do not need protection, they do. Mary Ward feared the effects of the vote on nation and Empire; she would also have been horrified to have witnessed the long-term effects of war on social mores. For while the vast majority of women returned, after the war, to the home and to traditional occupations such as domestic service in just the manner she would have approved of, chaperonage did not revive and, from middle-class women's diaries, it would seem that one of the greatest effects of the war was on sexual mores and on the nature of relationships between men and women.[281] During the inter-war years the ideal of marriage became more companionate, but divorce became easier. Moral standards levelled down rather than up and Mary Ward's dream of women's moral purity raising the standards of men both domestically and publicly disappeared.

Notes

1. Noel Annan, 'The Intellectual Aristocracy', in J. H. Plumb, *Studies in Social History* (Longmans, 1955), p. 73.
2. Enid Huws Jones, *Mrs Humphry Ward* (New York: St Martin's Press, 1973), p. 103.
3. Mary Ward (hereafter MW) to Humphry Ward, 31/5/08, Ward Papers 2/5, Pusey House, Oxford (hereafter Ward Papers).
4. MW to Humphry, 16/8/88, Ward Papers 2/5.
5. MW to Arnold, 28/2/02, Ward Papers 2/9; MW to Julia, 30/4/18, Huxley Papers 2/3, Pusey House, Oxford.
6. Mrs Humphry Ward, *A Writer's Recollections* (Collins, 1918), p. 345.
7. MW to father, 21/9/91, Ward Papers 2/2; MW to Humphry, 7/4/99, Ward Papers 2/5.
8. Brian Harrison, *Separate Spheres: The Opposition to Women's Suffrage in Britain* (Croom Helm, 1978), p. 21; Vineta Colby, *The Singular Anomaly: Women Novelists of the Nineteenth Century* (New York: New York University Press, 1970), p. 165; Rebecca West, 'The Gospel According to Mrs Humphry Ward', *The Freewoman*, 15/2/12, reprinted in Jane Marcus (ed.), *The Young Rebecca. Writings of Rebecca West, 1911–17* (Virago, 1983), p. 14.
9. Diary of Mackenzie King, 13/11/99, Trans. 13, Microfilm University of Toronto Press.
10. Jones, *Mrs Humphry Ward*, p. 169.
11. MW to mother, 26/4/86, Ward Papers 2/2. Pat Jalland, *Women, Marriage and Politics, 1860–1914* (Oxford: Clarendon Press, 1986) has described the world of the 'Souls', see especially pp. 103–4.
12. MW to Frances Arnold, 28/6/89, Ward Papers 2/4.
13. W. L. Courtney, 'The English Girl in Fiction', *North American Review* 198 (November 1913), pp. 664–74; Mrs Humphry Ward, *Marcella* (Thomas Nelson, 1894). All references to the text are to this edn.

14. Mrs Humphry Ward, *The Coryston Family* (Smith Elder, 1913).
15. Stefan Collini, *Liberalism and Sociology* (Cambridge: Cambridge University Press, 1979), pp. 49–50; José Harris, 'The Webbs, the COS and the Ratan Tata Foundation: Social Policy from the Perspective of 1912', in Martin Bulmer, Jane Lewis and David Piachaud (eds), *The Goals of Social Policy* (Unwin Hyman, 1989), pp. 27–63.
16. Seth Koven, 'Culture and Poverty: The London Settlement House Movement, 1870–1914', unpublished PhD thesis, Harvard University, 1987.
17. MW to father 9/11/90, Ward Papers 2/2.
18. Anne M. Bindslev, *Mrs Humphry Ward. A Study in Late Victorian Feminine Consciousness and Creative Expression*, Stockholm Studies in English LXIII (Stockholm: Almqvist & Wiksell International, 1985).
19. Mrs Humphry Ward, *Daphne or Marriage à la Mode* (Cassell, 1909). All references to the text are to this edn.
20. Ward, *Writer's Recollections*, pp. 96, 102–6; Janet Penrose Trevelyan, *The Life of Mrs Humphry Ward* (Constable, 1923), pp. 8–10.
21. Ward, *Writer's Recollections*, p. 165.
22. MW to father, 3/12/88, Ward Papers 2/2.
23. MW to Humphry, 3/6/90, Ward Papers 2/5.
24. MW to Humphry, 26/3/97, ibid.
25. MW to Arnold, 1/3/1900, Ward Papers 2/9.
26. Ward, *Writer's Recollections*, p. 100; John Sutherland, *Mrs Humphry Ward, Eminent Victorian, Pre–eminent Edwardian* (Oxford: Oxford University Press, 1990).
27. MW to father, 4/8/86, Ward Papers 2/2.
28. MW to mother, 28/12/86, ibid.
29. MW to mother, 25/10/87, ibid.
30. W. L. Courtney, *The Feminine Note in Fiction* (Chapman Hall, 1904), p. 24.
31. Beatrice Webb's Diary, 26/10/28, f. 4690, TS, BLPES.
32. Mrs Humphry Ward, *The History of David Grieve* (Smith Elder, 1892), Preface, pp. xii and xv. All references to text and Preface to this edn. The prefaces to the novels were prepared for the Westmoreland edn of Mary Ward's works, published by Smith Elder in 1911, and provided Mary Ward with an opportunity to justify her work at a time when it was clearly coming to be regarded as old-fashioned. Hereafter, editions used for textual references and for the prefaces will be clearly indicated. Dates of first editions are indicated in the text.
33. Mary Ward, Speech at the opening of the Carnegie Library in Kendal, 1909, TS, Mary Ward Centre Archives (hereafter MWC), Box 25.
34. Lady Bell, 'Mrs Humphry Ward', in *Landmarks. A Reprint of Some Essays and Other Pieces Published between 1894 and 1922* (Ernest Benn, 1929), p. 98. I am grateful to Angela V. John for this reference.
35. William S. Peterson, *Victorian Heretic. Mrs Humphry Ward's Robert Elsmere* (Leicester: Leicester University Press, 1976), p. 160; Colby, *Singular Anomaly*, p. 115.
36. MW to Julia, 30/4/18, Huxley Papers 2/3.
37. Ward, *Marcella* (Smith Elder, 1911), Preface, p. xii; *Sir George Tressady* (Smith Elder, 1911), Preface, p. x. All references to these prefaces are to these edns.
38. MW to Humphry, 18/10/88, Ward Papers 2/5.
39. Mrs Humphry Ward, *Robert Elsmere* (Smith Elder, 1911), 1st edn. 1888, Preface, xiv; see also Walter E. Houghton, *The Victorian Frame of Mind, 1830–1870* (New Haven: Yale University Press, 14–17).
40. MW to father, 5/3/84, Ward Papers 2/2.
41. MW to father, 3/10/86, ibid.
42. Ward, *Elsmere*, Preface, p. xxv.
43. Mrs Humphry Ward, *Robert Elsmere* (George Newnes, 1899), p. 266. All references to the text are to this edn.

44. Mrs Humphry Ward, *The Case of Richard Meynell* (Smith Elder, 1911), p. 518. All references to text and preface are to this edn.
45. Mrs Humphry Ward, *New Forms of Christian Education* (Smith Elder, 1892). This work was signed 'Mary Ward'.
46. Mrs Humphry Ward, *The Future of University Hall. An Address* (Smith Elder, 1892), p. 24.
47. Andrew Vincent (ed.), *The Philosophy of T. H. Green* (Gower, 1986), Introduction, p. 4.
48. Mackenzie King Diary, 12/11/99, Trans. 13.
49. Ward, *Future of University Hall*, p. 24.
50. Matthew Arnold, *Culture and Anarchy* (Smith Elder, 1889), 1st edn 1869, pp. xxxv, 21, 27, 89.
51. MW to Humphry, 19/7/81, Ward Papers 2/5; Ward, *Writer's Recollections*, p. 261.
52. See Houghton, *Victorian Frame of Mind*, pp. 272–8 on the degeneration of benevolence into sentimentality.
53. Ward, *Elsmere*, pp. 308 and 181.
54. Mrs Humphry Ward, *Helbeck of Bannisdale* (Harmondsworth: Penguin, 1983) 1st edn. 1898, Preface, pp. xviii–xix. All references to text and Preface are to this edn.
55. MW to Mandell Creighton, 13/3/88, Ward Papers 3/4.
56. MW to father, 5/9/88, Ward Papers 2/2.
57. MW to Humphry, 9/4/88, Ward Papers 2/5.
58. Ward, *Elsmere*, p. 168.
59. Ibid., p. 67.
60. Ward, *Meynell*, pp. 73, 158, 248, 256.
61. Koven, 'Culture and Poverty'; Standish Meacham, *Toynbee Hall and Social Reform, 1880–1914* (New Haven: Yale University Press, 1988).
62. 'The Passmore Edwards Settlement', *The Times*, 11/2/98, Ward Papers, University College (hereafter Ward Papers UC), MS ADD. 202.
63. Mrs Humphry Ward, *University Hall: Opening Address* (Smith Elder, 1891), p. 33.
64. MW to father, 1/2/90 and 26/2/90, Ward Papers 2/2.
65. Ward, *New Forms of Christian Education*, pp. 13–15; *Future of University Hall*, p. 7.
66. Arnold, *Culture and Anarchy*, p. xiv; Mrs Humphry Ward, *Unitarians and the Future*, Essex Hall Lecture (Philip Green, 1894), pp. 47, 60–1.
67. James Martineau to MW, 9/12/89, MWC Box 8; Lord Carlisle to MW, 9/12/89; J. H. Muirhead to MW, 4/3/90; P. Wicksteed to MW, 6/10/90, MWC Box 28.
68. Committee of University Hall, 'University Hall: Objects', March 1890, MWC; M. A. Ward and Philip H. Wicksteed, 'Words to Residents', November 1890, MWC.
69. Basil Willey, 'How Robert Elsmere Struck Some Contemporaries', *Essays and Studies* 10 (1957), pp. 53–68.
70. Peterson, *Victorian Heretic*, p. 202.
71. Mrs Humphry Ward, Speech to Liverpool Settlement 1899/1900, TS, MWC, Box 25.
72. MW to father, 22/11/89 and 20//9/90, Ward Papers 2/2.
73. Ward, *University Hall: Opening Adddress*, pp. 36–7.
74. MW to J. J. Dent, 28/10/04, MWC Scrapbook.
75. Mrs Humphry Ward, *Sir George Tressady* (Smith Elder, 1896), p. 411. All references to the text are to this edn.
76. Mrs Humphry Ward, *Fenwick's Career* (Harper & Bros, 1906), p. 167. All references to the text are to this edn.
77. Ward, *David Grieve*, p. 459.
78. Peterson, *Victorian Heretic*, p. 153; Edward Denison, *A Brief Record: Being Selections from Letters and other Writings of the Late Edward Denison, MP for Newark*, ed. Baldwin Leighton (privately printed, 1871). Denison lived in Stepney

during 1867, was elected a Liberal MP in 1868, served on early COS committees and died at the age of 30 in 1870; Louise Creighton, 'Women's Settlements', *Nineteenth Century* LXIII (April 1908), pp. 607–13.

79. Ward, *Marcella*, p. 75.
80. Ibid., p. 352.
81. Ibid., p. 302.
82. Ibid., p. 384. David Grieve, who harboured rather advanced ideas about profit-sharing, states firmly that he does not subscribe to socialist ideas because of his belief that the best life must 'grow from within'. Human progress depends on 'the spring of will and conscience in the individual', which mechanical socialist systems strike down (Ward, *David Grieve*, p. 521).
83. W. A. Bailward, 'The Oxford House and the Organisation of Charity', in J. M. Knapp (ed.), *The Universities and the Social Problem. An Account of Settlements in East London* (Rivington Percival & Co., 1895), p. 167.
84. Social investigation into rural poverty was rare. The classic Edwardian account is B. Seebohm Rowntree and May Kendall, *How the Labourer Lives. A Study of the Rural Labour Problem* (Thomas Nelson, 1913).
85. Peter Clarke, *Liberals and Social Democrats* (Cambridge: Cambridge University Press, 1978), p. 14.
86. Ward, *Tressady*, Preface, p. xii.
87. Ward, *Tressady*, p. 106.
88. Ward, *Marcella*, Preface, p. xvii.
89. Dorothy Ward, 'The Origins of the Mary Ward Settlement', TS (1947), MWC.
90. Philip Wicksteed to MW, 17/9/90, MWC Box 28.
91. Philip Wicksteed, 'In Memoriam. Mrs Humphry Ward and the Passmore Edwards Settlement' (June 1921), p. 22, MWC Box 3.
92. Mrs Humphry Ward, Draft of a Cambridge Speech on Settlements, circa 1897/8, TS, MWC, Box 25.
93. Ward, Speech to Liverpool Settlement.
94. Blake Odgers to MW, 12/4/91, MWC Box 28.
95. Frank Wallis Galton, Autobiography, TS, Coll. Misc. 315, BLPES.
96. 'Letter from Mrs Humphry Ward', in Miss Bibby, Miss Colles, Miss Petty and Dr Sykes, *The Pudding Lady. A New Departure in Social Work* (Stead's Publishing House, circa 1910), p. vi.
97. Mrs Humphry Ward, 'Social Ideals', Address at the opening of Passmore Edwards Settlement, 1897, MWC, Box 25.
98. MW to Dorothy, 12/2/99, Ward Papers 2/10.
99. Dent's and Ashley's letters were quoted by Mary Ward in her reply addressed to Dent, 28/10/04, MWC Scrapbook.
100. Mackenzie King Diary, 13/2/1900, Trans. 14; Koven, 'Culture and Poverty', p. 547.
101. Ward, *University Hall: Opening Address*, p. 33.
102. Galton, Autobiography.
103. Mackenzie King Diary, 16/10/90, Trans. 13; 13/10/99, 20/10/99, 27/10/99, 21/12/99, Trans. 14.
104. A. G. Gardner, 'Woman of the Week. Mrs Humphry Ward', *Daily News*, 23/3/13, MWC Clippings Box.
105. For example, Speech to Dinner in aid of Queen's Jubilee Nurses, 23/6/08, Ward Papers, Box 1/2/4.
106. Trevelyan, *Life of Mrs Humphry Ward*, p. 132.
107. For example, Charity Organisation Society, *The Epileptic and Crippled Child and Adult* (Swann Sonnenschein, 1893); *The Feeble Minded Child and Adult* (Swann Sonnenschein, 1893).
108. PRO, ED 14/43, Application from the Passmore Edwards Settlement for the Establishment of an Invalid Children's School to Chairman of Special Schools Sub-Committee of the London School Board, 30/12/98.

109. Janet Penrose Trevelyan, *Evening Play Centres for Children* (Methuen, 1920), p. 4.
110. John Gillis, *Youth and History* (New York: Academic Press, 1974), and 'Evolution of Juvenile Delinquency in England, 1890–1914', *Past and Present* 67 (1975), pp. 96–126; John Springhall, *Youth, Empire and Society, 1883–1940* (Croom Helm, 1977).
111. Mrs Humphry Ward, *The Passmore Edwards Settlement* (np, 1901), p. 8.
112. Mrs Humphry Ward to the Children of the Board and Voluntary Schools around the Settlement, July 1902, MWC Clippings Book.
113. Trevelyan, *Evening Play Centres*, pp. 28–9.
114. 'Vacation School at the Passmore Edwards Settlement', *The Times*, 2/8/06, p. 15, col. 6.
115. Mrs Humphry Ward, 'Playcentres', nd, TS, Ward Papers, 1/2/18.
116. PP, 1904, Cd. 2175, Report of the Interdepartmental Committee on Physical Deterioration.
117. M. A. Ward to *The Times*, 31/7/11, p. 11, col. 5. See also, Mrs Humphry Ward, 'Children's Country Holidays', MS, 21/5/06, Ward Papers 1/2/2.
118. M. A. Ward to *The Times*, 1/10/08, p. 4, col. 1.
119. MW to Louise Creighton, 16/12/09, Ward Papers 3/3.
120. PRO, ED 65/34, 5/1/17, Minute, and ED 65/13, 4/3/19, Minute.
121. PRO, ED 50/152, Ainsworth to Newman, 6/3/18.
122. Ward, Speech to Liverpool Settlement.
123. Ward, *The Passmore Edwards Settlement*, p. 20.
124. Ward, 'Social Ideals'.
125. W. T. Arnold, *Studies of Roman Imperialism. A Memoir by Mrs Humphry Ward* (Manchester: Manchester University Press, 1906), pp. li–liii.
126. Bedford to MW, 15/1/07, MWC, Box 14, and 1/5/14, 17/5/14, MWC, Box 28.
127. Dorothy Ward's Diary, 1906, Ward Papers UC, Item 43.
128. See Jenny Morris, *Women Workers and the Sweated Trades* (Gower, 1986), pp. 173–4. The 1895 Factory Act gave greater powers to inspectors to enter domestic workshops.
129. Beatrice Webb to MW, circa 1896, Ward Papers 5/6.
130. Mrs Sidney Webb (ed.), *The Case for the Factory Acts* (Grant Richards, 1901), Preface by Mrs Humphry Ward, p. lx.
131. On national efficiency, see Bernard Semmel, *Imperialism and Social Reform* (Allen & Unwin, 1960).
132. M. Freeden, *The New Liberalism. An Ideology of Social Reform* (Oxford: Clarendon, 1978), pp. 10–15.
133. MW to Arnold, 9/1/06 and 19/1/06, Ward Papers 2/9.
134. Clarke, *Liberals and Social Democrats*, p. 54.
135. Mackenzie King Diaries, 3/1/1900 and 4–8/11/99, Trans. 14. Mary Ward also saw this in Marshall, see *David Grieve*, Preface, p. xviii.
136. MW to Mandell Creighton, 2/7/98, Ward Papers 3/4.
137. Mrs Humphry Ward, *The Mating of Lydia* (Garden City New York: Doubleday Page & Co.), p. 512. All references to the text are to this edn.
138. Lucy Bland, 'Marrage Laid Bare: Middle-Class Women and Marital Sex, 1880–1914', in J. Lewis (ed.), *Labour and Love: Women's Experience of Home and Family, 1850–1940* (Oxford: Blackwell, 1986), pp. 123–48, and 'The Married Woman, the "New Woman" and the Feminist: Sexual Politics of the 1890s', in Jane Rendall (ed.), *Equal or Different? Women's Politics 1800–1914* (Oxford: Blackwell, 1987); Gail Cunningham, *The New Woman and the Victorian Novel* (Macmillan, 1978).
139. Mrs Humphry Ward, *Lady Rose's Daughter* (Smith Elder, 1911), Preface, p. ix. All references to the Preface are to this edn. Sutherland, *Mrs Humphry Ward*, pp. 240–41, also suggests that her failure to kill off her heroine was prompted by the fact that unhappy endings did not go down well with readers.

140.   *Daphne*, pp. 63, 83, 136, 184–5, 252.
141.   West, 'The Gospel According to Mrs Humphry Ward', p. 16.
142.   Ibid., p. 268.
143.   Ward, *Richard Meynell*, p. 511.
144.   Sandra M. Gilbert and Susan Gubar, *The Madwoman in the Attic. The Woman Writer and the Nineteenth-Century Literary Imagination* (New Haven: Yale University Press, 1979), p. 64.
145.   Ward, *David Grieve*, pp. 207 and 177.
146.   Ward, *Richard Meynell*, p. 158.
147.   Mrs Humphry Ward, *Delia Blanchflower* (Ward Lock, 1915), p. 135. All references to the text are to this edn.
148.   Mrs Humphry Ward, *The Testing of Diana Mallory* (Harper Brothers, 1908), pp. 379 and 502. All references to the text are to this edn.
149.   Ward, *Tressady*, p. 119.
150.   Gertrude Ward's Diary, 20/3/90, Ward Papers 10/4.
151.   Mackenzie King Diaries, 21/11/99, Trans. 13; Gertrude Ward to Dorothy, 17/11/95, Ward Papers 13/5.
152.   MW to Louise Creighton, (?)1905, Ward Papers, 3/3.
153.   MW to Dorothy, 12/6/17, Ward Papers 2/10.
154.   Violet Markham to Hilda Cashmore, 3/7/(?)12, f. 228, Violet Markham Papers 25/12, BLPES.
155.   Bindslev, *Mrs Humphry Ward*.
156.   Ward, *Marcella*, p. 293.
157.   Ward, *Lydia*, p. 165.
158.   Courtney, 'The English Girl in Fiction', p. 673.
159.   Ward, *Writer's Recollections*, p. 98.
160.   Trevelyan, *Life of Mrs Humphry Ward*, p. 12.
161.   Ward, *Delia Blanchflower*, p.134.
162.   Ward, *Lydia*, p. 133.
163.   Mrs Humphry Ward, *Cousin Philip* (Collins, 1919), pp. 108 and 113. All references to the text are to this edn.
164.   Adèle Crepaz, *The Emancipation of Women and its Probable Consequences* (Swann Sonnenschein, 1893).
165.   Peterson, *Victorian Heretic*, p. 51.
166.   Ibid. On Charlotte Yonge, see Catherine Sandbach Dahlström, *Be Good Sweet Maid. Charlotte's Yonge's Domestic Fiction. A Study in Dogmatic Purpose and Fictional Form*, Stockholm Studies in English LIX (Stockholm: Almqvist & Wiksell, 1984).
167.   Ward, *David Grieve*, p. 317.
168.   Ward, *Marcella*, pp. 124, 182, 212, 385, 573.
169.   Ibid., p. 521.
170.   Bindslev, *Mrs Humphry Ward*, chapter 3, explores the 'competing centres of consciousness' in the novel in more detail.
171.   Ward, *Elsmere*, 1911 edn, Preface, p. xxxix.
172.   Bindslev, *Mrs Humphry Ward*, pp. 28, 42, 44; Peterson, *Victorian Heretic*, p. 8.
173.   Frederic Harrison to MW, circa 1900, Ward Papers 6/3.
174.   Rebecca West, 'The Gospel According to Mrs Humphry Ward', p. 16.
175.   Donald Stone, 'Victorian Feminism in the Nineteenth Century Novel', *Women's Studies* 1 (Fall 1972), pp. 65–91.
176.   Ward, *Richard Meynell*, p. 117.
177.   Peterson, *Victorian Heretic*, p. 198.
178.   Ward, *Fenwick's Career*, p. 277.
179.   Ward, *Elsmere*, p. 236.
180.   Mrs Humphry Ward, *Lady Connie* (Smith Elder, 1916), p. 249. All references to the text are to this edn.
181.   Colby, *The Singular Anomaly*, p. 122.

182. MW to Julia, 1/7/13, Huxley Papers 2/3.
183. Louise Creighton to MW, 17/11/10, Ward Papers 6/1.
184. Mary Poovey, *The Proper Lady and the Woman Writer* (Chicago: University of Chicago Press, 1984), especially p. 242, explores the parameters of propriety.
185. West, 'Gospel According to Mrs Humphry Ward', p. 15.
186. Frances Power Cobbe was particularly noted for her campaign to end wife-battering, which she called 'wife torture'. See *The Life of Frances Power Cobbe by Herself*, 2 vols (R. Bentley & Son, 1894).
187. Peterson, *Victorian Heretic*, p. 4; Harold Owen, *Women Adrift: The Menace of Suffragism* (Stanley Paul & Co., 1912); Belfort Bax, The Fraud of Feminism (Grant Richards, 1913). Martha Vicinus, *Independent Women: Work and Community for Single Women, 1850–1920* (Virago, 1987), chapter 7, has provided the most sensitive interpretation of the suffragette struggle, setting it in the context of male as well as female violence.
188. Ward, *Lydia*, pp. 165–6 and 256.
189. MW to Louise Creighton, 31/1/09, Ward Papers 3/3.
190. Mrs Humphry Ward, *Daphne* (Smith Elder, 1911), Preface, p. xiv. All references to the Preface are to this edn.
191. In Britain, it was not until the introduction of legal aid in 1946 that a majority of petitioners for divorce became women.
192. MW to Louise Creighton, 3/11/18, Ward Papers 3/3.
193. MW to father, 24/5/80 and 11/3/85, Ward Papers 2/2.
194. MW to mother, 5/10/86, Ward Papers 2/2.
195. MW to Humphry, 6/4/88, Ward Papers 2/5.
196. Gertrude Ward's Diary, April 1884, Ward Papers 10/4.
197. Sutherland, *Mrs Humphry Ward*, p. 87; MW to Humphry, 12/6/81, Ward Papers 2/5.
198. Mrs Humphry Ward, *Eltham House* (Cassell, 1915). All references to the text are to this edn. Esther Marion Greenwell Smith, *Mrs Humphry Ward* (Twayne Publishers, 1980), p. 75, misses the point when she concludes that divorce did not worry Mary Ward in this novel.
199. Mrs Humphry Ward, *Eleanor* (Macmillan, 1900), p. 486.
200. Ward, *Fenwick's Career*, p. 210.
201. Ward, *Daphne*, p. 272.
202. Mrs Humphry Ward, *Marriage of William Ashe* (Nelson, 1907), p. 439. All references to the text are to this edn.
203. Ward, *Lydia*, pp. 509 and 511.
204. Ward, *Tressady*, p. 195 and *Daphne*, p. 290.
205. Ward, *Elsmere*, p. 198.
206. Ward, *Tressady*, p. 343.
207. Ward, *David Grieve*, p. 524.
208. Ward, *Eltham House*, pp. 234–5 and 335.
209. Ward, *Daphne*, Preface, pp. xiv–v.
210. PP, 1912–13, Cd. 6487, XVIII, Report of the Royal Commission on Divorce and Matrimonial Causes. See also Iris Minor, 'Working-Class Women and Matrimonial Law Reform, 1890–1914', in David E. Martin and David Rubinstein (eds), *Ideology and the Labour Movement* (Croom Helm, 1979), pp. 103–24.
211. Ward, *Daphne*, Preface, p. xiv.
212. MW to Mandell Creighton, circa 1900, Ward Papers 3/4.
213. Ward, *Eltham House*, p. 134.
214. Trevelyan, *Life of Mrs Humphry Ward*, p. 30.
215. Ward, *Lady Connie*, p. 396.
216. MW to mother, 22/2/83, Ward Papers 2/2.
217. Mrs Humphry Ward, Speech to the Irish Central Bureau for the Employment of Women, Dublin, 1905, Ward Papers 1/2/1; and TS on women's work, fragment, Ward Papers 1/2/19.

218. MW to Louise Creighton, 18/4/89, Ward Papers 3/3.
219. Ward, *Elsmere*, p. 193.
220. Ward, *Helbeck*, pp. 145 and 315–16.
221. MW to Humphry, 3/5/98, Ward Papers 2/5.
222. Mary A. Ward to *The Times*, 12/4/12, p. 15, col. 1.
223. Ward, *Lady Connie*, pp. 111, 358; Trevelyan, *Life of Mrs Humphry Ward*, p. 24.
224. Ward, *Lady Connie*, p. 396; Alice Stronach, *A Newnham Friendship* (Blackie & Son, 1901).
225. Beatrice Webb's Diary, 1/3/96, f. 1446, BPLES; see also Gwen Raverat, *Period Piece. A Cambridge Childhood* (Faber & Faber, 1952), p. 45, on Newnham students.
226. Ward, *Cousin Philip*, p. 47.
227. MW to father, 21/1/89, Ward Papers 2/2.
228. 'An Appeal against Female Suffrage', *Nineteenth Century* XXV (June 1889), pp. 781–8.
229. Mary A. Ward, 'The Women's Anti-Suffrage Movement', *Nineteenth Century* LXIV (Aug. 1908), pp. 343–52.
230. Ward, *Marcella*, p. 322.
231. Mary A. Ward, 'Rhetoric and Revolution', letter to *The Times* 27/11/11, reprinted in *The Anti-Suffrage Review* (Jan. 1912), pp. 13–14; 'The Enfranchisement of Women', letter, *The Anti-Suffrage Review* (Jan. 1918), pp. 5–6.
232. Ward, *Delia Blanchflower*, p. 285.
233. MW to father, 29/3/86, Ward Papers 2/2.
234. MW to father, 22/11/92, Ward Papers 2/2.
235. Report of Annual Council Meeting for 1913, *The Anti-Suffrage Review* (July 1913), p. 146.
236. Mrs Humphry Ward, *Letters to My Neighbours on the Present Election* (Smith Elder, 1910).
237. Ward, *Letters to My Neighbours*, Letter 5, Nov. 1910.
238. Mary A. Ward to *The Times*, 20/6/10, p. 10, col. 3.
239. Ward, *Tressady*, p. 131.
240. Mrs Humphry Ward, *Lady Rose's Daughter* (Nelson, 1907), pp. 212–13. All references to the text are to this edn.
241. Sir John Simon to MW, 5/11/15, Ward Papers 5/14.
242. Ward, *Tressady*, p. 86.
243. Ibid., p. 369.
244. Ibid., p. 430.
245. MW to Louise Creighton, 23/8/08, Ward Papers 3/3.
246. Mary A. Ward, 'Religion and the Suffrage', letter to *The Times*, 19/6/12, p. 14, col. 2.
247. Louise Creighton, 'The Appeal Against Female Suffrage: A Rejoinder', *Nineteenth Century* XXVI (July–Dec. 1889), p. 352.
248. 'Local Government Advancement Committee. Report of Meeting', *The Anti-Suffrage Review* (Dec. 1912), p. 286.
249. Mary A. Ward to *The Times*, 6/7/08, p. 9, col. 4, and 19/10/11, p. 7, col. 4, both replies to M. G. Fawcett.
250. Janet Trevelyan to Violet Markham, 29/6/47, f. 6, Violet Markham Papers 25/83, BLPES.
251. MW to father, 12/6/82, Ward Papers 2/2.
252. Mary A. Ward to *The Times* 19/12/11, p. 8, col. 3; Text of a Debate with Mrs Fawcett on Suffrage, Feb. 1909, TS, Ward Papers, 1/1/06.
253. H. MacLachlan, *Records of a Family, 1800–1933* (Manchester: Manchester University Press, 1935), p. 146.
254. MW to Julia, 20/3/18, Huxley Papers 2/3.
255. Mary A. Ward to *The Times*, 6/7/08, p. 9, col. 4.
256. Ward, *Delia Blanchflower*, p. 111.

257. 'An Appeal against Female Suffrage', p. 783.

258. Mary A. Ward to *The Times*, 1/8/08, p. 11, col. 4.

259. Text of a Debate with Mrs Fawcett on Suffrage (1909); 'Adoption of the Annual Report', *Anti-Suffrage Review* (July 1913), p. 147.

260. Ward, *Delia Blanchflower*, p. 340.

261. Louise Creighton to MW, 21/9/10 and 23/12/13, Ward Papers 6/1. I could find little of the 'wariness' between the two women referred to by Harrison, *Separate Spheres*, p. 132.

262. MW to Louise Creighton, 13/2/14, Ward Papers 3/3.

263. Text of a Debate with Mrs Fawcett on Suffrage (1909), p. 33.

264. Ward, *Delia Blanchflower*, pp. 24, 79, 269.

265. 'Third Annual Meeting. Report', *Anti-Suffrage Review* (Aug. 1911), p. 167.

266. MW to Louise Creighton, 14/3/18, Ward Papers 3/3.

267. 'The Case for the Referendum', *The Anti-Suffrage Review* (Dec. 1917), p. 91; 'The Enfranchisement of Women', *Anti-Suffrage Review* (Jan. 1918), pp. 5–6.

268. Peterson, *Victorian Heretic*, p. 208.

269. Theodore Roosevelt to Mrs Humphry Ward, 27/12/15, Ward Papers 6/4. The product was Mrs Humphry Ward, *England's Effort. Six Letters to An American Friend* (Smith Elder, 1916).

270. Mrs Humphry Ward, *The War and Elizabeth* (Collins, 1918), p. 106. All references to the text are to this edn.

271. Mrs Humphry Ward, *Missing* (Collins, 1917), p. 189. All references to the text are to this edn; Ward, *War and Elizabeth*, p. 68.

272. MW to Louise Creighton, 28/10/16, Ward Papers 3/3.

273. Bernard Waites looks in more detail at changes in the relationships between social classes in *A Class Society at War, Britain 1914–1918* (Leamington Spa: Berg, 1987).

274. MW to father, 24/7/90, Ward Papers 2/2.

275. 'The Enfranchisement of Women', *The Anti-Suffrage Review* (Jan. 1918), p. 5.

276. MW to Louise Creighton, 6/2/16, Ward Papers 3/3.

277. Anne Summers, *Angels and Citizens, British Women as Military Nurses, 1854–1914* (Routledge & Kegan Paul, 1988), especially chapter 10.

278. MW to Louise Creighton, 23/6/16, Ward Papers 3/3; for a more accurate assessment of women munition workers' health, see Deborah Thom and Antonia Ineson, 'Women Workers and TNT Poisoning', in P. Weindling (ed.), *A Social History of Occupational Health* (Croom Helm, 1985).

279. Ward, *England's Effort*, p. 43; *Cousin Philip*, p. 108.

280. Ward, *Cousin Philip*, p. 145.

281. Vera Brittain, *Testament of Youth. An Autobiographical Study of the Years 1900–25* (Gollancz, 1938).

5   Violet Markham, 1872–1959

Violet Markham was the younger daughter and fifth child of a solid nineteenth-century liberal family of Chesterfield mineowners. In her autobiography she described her mother as agnostic,[1] certainly she was keen to read the work of new thinkers including T. H. Green, but the family attended church regularly and Violet's early diary frequently recorded her opinion (usually extremely critical) of the sermons. These early diaries lack the *angst* of those of Beatrice Webb but there is a similar dissatisfaction with the philanthropic work that Violet began in 1897, visiting poor law workhouses and sitting on the committees of the local school board, and an ambition to move on to bigger things. This she contrived to do after 1901 when an inheritance provided her with the means to take a house in London as well as to expand her voluntary work in Chesterfield. Violet proceeded to found a settlement in her home town, which enabled her to push forward her own ideas on social questions. She also became a pillar of the campaign against women's suffrage and played the most public role of those few women at the forefront of its affairs. Indeed, her anti-suffrage work formed something of a bridge from what were her broadening social-work interests of the 1900s to the very public career of government committee member and public servant which she began during World War I and which fully occupied her until she died in 1959.

Even though she renounced her anti-suffrage views in 1916, she did not fundamentally change her position on women's role and place in society, which rested on a profound belief in sexual difference that was both biologically and culturally based. Her easy move into a highly successful public career was unusual and raised the anger of many suffrage activists. Sylvia Pankhurst spoke of her in 1954 as a 'foul traitor' who, while women were hunger striking, appeared on anti-suffrage platforms in the company of men like Lord Curzon and Lord Cromer, the chief organizers of the National League for Opposing Women's Suffrage.[2] It was of course in large measure the ease that she experienced in working with such men in the anti-suffrage world that stood her in good stead later in public life. Violet Markham experienced none of Beatrice Webb's difficulties in knowing how to behave on committees but nor did she feel like Octavia Hill and Helen Bosanquet that she had to be reticent. Unlike the other women considered in this book, she was both confident about and adept at committee work. Her sense of identity came from neither 'quiet detailed' personal social work nor the private work of research and/or writing, but rather from public service. While she experienced some doubts as to her own capacities (confined mainly to the 1890s) she did not experience any extreme conflict in respect of her choice of work outside the home. Family responsibilities there were, and while Violet took these seriously and unquestioningly, she also sought ways of reconciling them with her public work rather than, in Octavia Hill fashion, insisting that they take first place. Her belief in the importance of domestic service, which she expressed strongly during World War I in the course of her work as a member for the Central Committee on Women's Training and Employment (which trained nearly 100,000 women chiefly as servants) and during the Second World War in the report of an inquiry on the subject that she carried out for the government in 1944, showed that she was also convinced as to the importance of middle-class women's contribution to the wider society. Her views foreshadowed the more systematic claim of feminists during the 1950s for middle-class women's right to both a family life and a career, albeit that they wished this to be sustained primarily by flexible work patterns rather than by domestic help.[3]

Violet Markham saw no contradiction between her anti-suffragism and her public career. The crucial connecting principle was her idea of citizenship. This remained as deeply gendered as Octavia Hill's idea of duty but, like that of Mary Ward, permitted women fully to participate in appropriate areas of public life, especially in the work of local government and administration. Violet shared Mary Ward's belief both in the fundamental importance of sexual difference and in policymaking on the basis of national needs. While not denying the importance of the individual, she did not share Helen Bosanquet's view that all active citizens, male and female, should be free to cultivate their talents. She saw the individual's development primarily as a means to furthering the national health and welfare; it was not in the national interest that women should vote but it was that (middle-class) women should involve themselves in useful and appropriate public work. In her public activities during the inter-war years, she was happy to take on responsibility for the 'women's issues'; for example, as the only woman appointed to the Unemployment Assistance Board in 1934 she made it her business to pay special attention to the situation of unemployed women. In this way, a belief in sexual difference was reconciled with a commitment to public service.

It was this understanding of citizenship that also structured Violet's attitudes towards the issues of poverty and social work, the central concerns in her work, and made them significantly different from those of the Charity Organisation Society (COS), from which she publicly parted company in 1911. Violet Markham did not move neatly from 'individualism' to 'collectivism' any more than did any New Liberal, but she was anxious to see the state participate as an equal partner in the all-important task of improving the welfare of its citizens. She drew the line of demarcation between the state and the voluntary sector less strictly in this respect, just as she loosened strict late nineteenth-century ideas about the boundary between male and female spheres. But she continued to believe that both the voluntary sector and the state, and male and female activities, should maintain separate existences.

In many respects, Violet Markham is the most clearly twentieth-century figure of the five women considered in this book, as at home in the 1950s as the 1900s. Her views were founded more on a secular morality, although she did return to the church under the influence of the liberal churchman Hensley Henson, rector of St Margaret's Westminster, and shared the concern to pursue a larger truth that was common among many late nineteenth- and early twentieth-century social reformers. Still, she was probably less spiritual than, say, Beatrice Webb. She was also rather more worldly than many, not in the sense of any great capacity to move in Society, to which she was probably rather less attracted than either Beatrice or Mary Ward, but in terms of personal morality. She did not like H. G. Wells's determination to 'tell it how it was' in *Ann Veronica*[4] any better than Beatrice or Mary, and she too feared that an extension of the grounds for divorce would lead to couples treating marriage more casually, which she deplored. But, possibly because so many of her family members were involved in disastrous marriages, she was prepared to be more accepting of such personal failings just as she was not so keen as many members of the COS to dwell on individual moral failure as a cause of poverty. This is not to say that family and 'character' had no importance for her, but because her concern was more with the national interest than with either moral absolutes (as in the case of Octavia Hill) or carefully built ideas as to how best to achieve social change (as in the case of Beatrice Webb and Helen Bosanquet), she was able to inject considerably more pragmatism into her work.

From local duty to the affairs of nation, 1890–1918

Chesterfield in the 1890s

On Christmas Day 1896, Violet Markham and her mother paid their usual visit to the workhouse. Violet's thoughts were far from cheery:

I dread these occasional visits to the Union. The faces of those old men and women haunt me for days; they look like people who have gone out of life and have nothing left to hope or to fear. They wished me a Merry Christmas and I felt half-choked in replying. All the Christmas decorations on the walls seemed to be mockery. Merriment and happiness in the New Year can scarcely be their lot. It was intensely pathetic.[5]

On 29 December she attended the 'workhouse entertainment': 'a dreary mortification of the flesh, which is probably wholesome, but is certainly exceedingly depressing'. It was at this point that she recorded the fact that

daily I feel more compelled to take some active part in the work of this town. Life up here is pleasant, intellectual and selfish. I ought to be up and doing as a member of the community and help if I can in the public business of the place I live in. Poor Law work would suit me best. I can't be mixed up with church concerns. I hate the whole thing and yet I feel duty points that way.[6]

Violet's attitude towards the philanthropic work of visiting the work-house and monitoring the welfare of its inhabitants was not substantially to change. She embarked on it more out of a vague 'class consciousness of sin' than out of love for the poor and, unlike Beatrice Webb, did not have any expectations as to the possible spin-offs from such work in terms of the opportunities for social observation or as a stepping-stone to other things.

At this point (she was 24), Violet's life lacked purpose. She had received more formal education than Beatrice, and while she was later to compare it unfavourably to that received by a child educated in a state elementary school, especially in terms of mathematics, her diary entries indicate that examinations were frequent and taken very seriously at the time. Certainly her mother felt education to be important for girls as well as boys and once remarked that the 'modern girl without education is the odious product of the age'.[7] But Violet only spent a matter of some eighteen months, from the age of sixteen, at school. Before that governesses played a significant role in her develop-ment, and her attempts at self-education were distinctly unsystematic compared with those of Beatrice Webb. Violet worried about the apparent lack of direction in her life and, albeit much less frequently than either Octavia Hill or Beatrice, reproached herself for her faults and prayed for additional strength to do her duty, even though she was by no means clear as to what this should be. In the late 1890s, she spent long hours playing the piano and for the rest tried rather unsuccessfully to write. In June 1897 she started a novel, but recorded that her 'physical difficulty in setting down ideas' made it hard for her to finish anything and she concluded, out of a sense of deep discontent as to her creative powers, that 'philanthropy will perhaps find an outlet for efforts which seem wasted at present on literature'.[8] She did not wholly give up her efforts at journalism but did not meet with any real success until a trip to South Africa in 1899 fired her enthusiasm for the British cause sufficiently to prompt her to write a book on the subject.

Violet's sense of duty, which she always referred to as the chief motivating force behind her entry into the world of philanthropic social work, did not originate in the Christian faith. Like Beatrice Webb, she found the doctrine of atonement impossible to come to terms with: 'It is monstrous to think of a just and all-good God demanding the sacrifice of an innocent man as a propitiation for those sins of human beings for whom God himself is responsible'.[9] She tended to be scathing about the performance of clergy in her own parish and could not have contemplated work as a parish visitor. While she often deplored ritualistic practice in the Church of England, she was impatient of the kind of debates that Mary Ward found so enthralling. Commenting on a dinner party discussion of Gladstone's book on Anglican Orders, she found it impossible to understand how, in the late nineteenth century, people could argue about whether or not bishops of the Church of England had received the Holy Ghost in direct apostolic succession.[10] Her impatience with the squabbles of organized religion was later deepened by her experiences as a member of the Chesterfield School Board. Furthermore, she found 'good women' doing good works rather boring.[11] Nevertheless, late in 1896 she found herself very much inspired by Mary Ward's call to faith, beauty and enthusiasm when she opened a local bazaar and wrote that she felt doubt to be a debilitating force operating in her own generation:

> we analyse everything, doubt everything and think a vast lot of our Darwin and scientific education and yet how poor and unsatisfactory are the results as testified by a generation without faith and without enthusiasms.[12]

Certainly her entry into social work was as wearily resigned as Octavia Hill's had been spirited: 'I feel very tired and have caught a cold again. But one must help people when one can. Among many doubts and perplexities I feel sure of that. One offers a good deal of self-sacrifice as a sort of propitiation to the Gods'.[13]

The desire to do something useful was linked in part, as it was in the case of Beatrice Webb, to the problems facing an unmarried young woman in late-Victorian society. In mid-1897 Violet took comfort in Benjamin Jowett's advice to young women in Oxford that it mattered not if they married as long as they lived useful and dignified lives.[14] Her early diary is much more discreet on the subject of her personal life than that of Beatrice. She pondered her feelings about men rarely and in a rather matter-of-fact manner, wondering whether they bored her or whether she put them off. Later in 1897, her comments on family weddings contained a veiled sarcasm that might indicate either further disillusionment with men or, more probably, a disappointed love affair.

As or more important a motivating factor was Violet's sense of obligation stemming from her social-class position. In her autobiography she commented on the sense of social responsibility shown by many Edwardian women: 'the social order was given, but so was social service'.[15] She added that she personally found it harder to go into Society than to engage in social work, although there was almost certainly an element, albeit not nearly as strong, of the same ambivalence about Society that Beatrice experienced. Violet's early diary often commented on the local balls, the clothes and who among the women looked the best. There is certainly no suggestion that she found herself ill-at-ease or awkward socially, although like Beatrice, she was probably happiest attending gatherings of her (not inconsiderable) circle of intimates. In all probability her feelings about social work were similar to those of another Edwardian social worker and social investigator, Violet Butler, who described her motives to Brian Harrison in a 1974 interview as having been 'a form of paying your rent, do you see, . . . we felt quite guilty'.[16]

These were certainly the kind of sentiments Violet expressed at Christmas 1896, when she felt that the memories of happy days and family gatherings that crowded in at such times would have been 'intolerable if not accompanied by service for others'.[17] Her sister Geraldine, however, seems to have experienced no such injunction to serve. Her letters to Violet (mainly from the inter-war years) show her to have been much more preoccupied with social gossip. Even during World War II she had to be pushed by Violet into taking evacuee children.[18] Violet's eldest brother Arthur shared her sense of social responsibility and tried both to improve conditions in his colliery villages and later fought, as MP for Mansfield, for the eight-hour day. Indeed in some respects, Violet's social position and ideas can usefully be compared to those of Lady Bell, the wife of the Middlesbrough ironmaster. Lady Bell painted a very sympathetic portrait of working people in Middlesbrough and yet, as Angela John has commented, in her work of social observation she must have used the natural class authority that flowed from her position in the town.[19] Violet thought consciously about such matters and decided (much later) that it was impossible to achieve equal social relations in social work and that it was better for her to visit the Brodsworth colliery people 'frankly as the Chairman's sister'.[20] Human and personal relations were, she felt, the better for it. While the befriending of working-class women in the manner advocated by Octavia Hill and an earlier generation was not ruled out, class differences were openly recognized. Possibly a similar realism enabled Lady Bell to maintain some distance from her subjects and yet to reach an understanding of their lives that was remarkably sympathetic and balanced.

Nevertheless, Violet began her work as a poor-law visitor with little of the enthusiasm that characterized Octavia Hill in her desire to know, love and befriend the poor. Immediately following her Christmas reflections on the need to do something to serve her community and the poor in particular, she received an invitation from the ladies' board (attached to the Board of Guardians) to join them. She accepted dutifully: 'I shall be glad to do what is wanted not because I like it but because I think I ought'. A few days later she was thinking seriously about 'a few weeks' training with the COS in the East End of London in order to set about charitable work in the right way, but thought that perhaps she should feel her way gently with the ladies' board before attempting 'more ambitious flights'.[21] She also thought that she would like to take up work as a member of the school board, but felt this would be far in the future; in fact within a year she was engaged in this as well as poor-law work in Chesterfield without ever having pursued the COS training she initially believed to be desirable.

Like Beatrice Webb, Mary Ward and the COS more generally, Violet Markham held the respectable working poor in high esteem. She said that she much preferred having the state elementary school teachers to tea (most of whom would have been the daughters of skilled men) than members of her own class, and relished listening to an argument between a moulder and a fitter at the party she held to reward her school-board election helpers in 1898.[22] Like Beatrice Webb, she found it much harder to love 'the residuum'. She was embarrassed by the 'garrulous sorrow' of the poor in times of adversity and sarcastic about the heartfelt response of working-class audiences to melodrama, when at home they 'bang their wives and kick their children'.[23] She often commented negatively on the workhouse inhabitants she visited. Above all, they lacked 'moral sense', she was particularly appalled by the apparent lack of shame on the part of the unmarried mothers. Nor did she have any firm answers to the problem of poverty and pauperism. She remonstrated with her mother about the latter's habit of letting very poor tenants pay only a small portion of their rent, knowing that according to the tenets of 'scientific charity', 'such behaviour is hope-lessly wrong and demoralizing'.[24] However, like so many women visiting the poor, she felt that COS principles were hard to follow in practice and knew that she would want to do the same as her mother because of feelings of guilt about her own wealth. Not surprisingly, she found poor-law work very depressing. Visits of inspection to the workhouse merely became somewhat less distasteful as time passed. On Christmas Day 1897, she felt much less miserable after her visit, confining her comments to the amount of beef and pudding the 'poor wretches' managed to eat.[25]

Regular workhouse visiting at least made her feel virtuous, even if she found the ladies' board singularly inefficient and incompetent. From her exhaustive treatment of women's work in local government, Pat Hollis has concluded that in respect of their poor-law work 'women remade the workhouse'.[26] Violet Markham's ladies' board in Chester-field was typical in undertaking work of inspection and in recommend-ing measures to improve comfort and cleanliness, but it is also revealing for the spirit in which it went about its business. Violet came to share her fellow board members' sense of virtue at doing something for the poor, which was not dissimilar from the feelings that had characterized the despised Lady Bountiful. However, she also deplored the narrow-ness of the concerns of the ladies' board and the long-windedness of its proceedings. At her first meeting she found their proceedings 'vacuous to a point which was really comical . . . They talked for twenty minutes and dissolved'.[27] Six months later she recorded that the only sensible resolution at the ladies' board meeting was her own to adjourn the proceedings over the summer months. Many late nineteenth-century female participants in social work were as lost when it came to running a meeting as they were in keeping account books. In some, this provoked a desire to broaden women's education and opportunities, but Violet Markham seems above all to have developed a profound contempt for women's ignorance of such matters, which she carried with her into her anti-suffrage work.

Violet got on rather better with her education work, which was more unusual for a woman in that it involved male-dominated committee work rather than the visiting associated with a ladies' committee. There is little evidence that she ever gained any more sympathetic an under-standing of the families of the children attending the state elementary schools in her district than she had of the workhouse inmates. At her first meeting of the committee of the board dealing with school attendance, she was greatly astonished and somewhat amused by the excuses that the mothers brought before the committee, even though these were well known to social investigators at the time and had been summarized frequently as falling mainly under one of three headings: 'the baby difficulty' whereby an elder child, usually a girl, was required to stay at home from school to mind a younger one; 'the boots difficulty', meaning that the child in question lacked suitable footwear (sometimes so widespread that in 1875 a donor provided the COS with money to remedy the situation in deserving cases); and the 'out of control difficulty', referring to truancy problems among young boys.[28] While not inclined to be hard in her treatment of those who came before the committee, Violet nevertheless almost certainly would have ranked among those committee members (the majority of whom were men) condemned by Octavia Hill as acting in ignorance of the daily lives of the people of whom they stood in judgement.

Initially, Violet took up work as a school manager and from her first tour of the schools in her care she found the children rather more pleasant than she had expected and the teachers glad to have a woman on the management board. She warmed to the proceedings of the male management board rather more than to the ladies' board of the poor-law union. The management board dealt with larger issues, although she soon found that again she became impatient of its inefficiency and, in her view, its carelessness of ratepayers' money. Again, in keeping with Hollis's picture of women's work in the administration of late nineteenth-century state elementary-school education, she made a special effort to keep in touch with the women teachers and to investigate the conditions of the children, especially in respect of the number of hours they worked outside school time in the local potteries and factories.[29] But Violet was more unusual in the interest she took in the finance of education and the relish with which she pursued committee politics. Like Beatrice Webb, she was quite prepared to use any social occasion to lobby for her point of view and, unlike many similarly active women described by Hollis, she tended to act as much as a guardian of the ratepayers' purses as a champion of the children's welfare. She lined up firmly, for example, with those determined to retain school fees. While Helen Taylor and Annie Besant had successfully led the fight to ensure that the London School Board would abolish school fees as soon as the 1891 Fees Act made it possible for them to do so, Violet was instrumental in securing the vote to retain fees in Chesterfield and indeed took some pleasure in being told that her tactics in so doing bore comparison to those of the Star Chamber.

In 1898, she stood for election to the Chesterfield School Board, appealing to the electors as someone whose first concern was to secure efficient and economical expenditure. She also stressed the desirability of a woman member 'who would devote particular attention to the needs and welfare of her own sex'.[30] But the strong attraction of education work for her rested primarily on the important role she felt it could play in training future citizens. Her election manifesto spoke of adapting primary education to the practical needs of the children and of fitting them for their working lives, but also ensuring that it might 'worthily sustain their rights and duties as English citizens'.[31] In many respects her own election experience served to confirm her belief that there was an urgent need for a more educated and informed electorate:

> Liberal though I am, there are times when the ignorance, the apathy, the utter lack of discrimination in the class to whom we have handed over the governing power fill me with despair. There is of course only one remedy and that is education and plenty of it. And by education I don't mean only more reading and writing, but the developing of a sense of responsibility and the knowledge of the practical duties which devolve from the possession of the franchise.[32]

She regarded state elementary schools as crucial vehicles for imparting the values of restraint, duty and obedience. Once, she confessed, she had agreed with those who had blamed the flightiness of the post-1870 servant on elementary education. But as a result of her first-hand contact with the state elementary schools she had changed her mind. Like Mary Ward, she remained somewhat pessimistic about the capacity of the majority of the poor, male and female, for political citizenship, but she also shared Booth's faith in the board schools as beacons of civilization in an otherwise depressing and often anxiety-producing urban environment.[33] Violet therefore approached her school-board work with a much firmer sense of purpose than her poor-law work.

By 1898 Violet had discovered the satisfaction that could come from a good day's work, just as Beatrice Webb had done a decade and a half before. Early in 1898 she recorded in her diary that it had been a quiet week 'but satisfactory because I have got through a good deal of steady work and after all that is the only satisfactory thing in life, I think'. Four months later she remarked positively on her busy week: 'I am happiest when this is the case. I can't bear myself when I have nothing to do'.[34] But in the end, the brain-numbing quality of much of her work in local administration proved no more satisfying to Violet than had the details of rent collection to Beatrice. Violet was disturbed to find that her voluntary work proved unconducive to 'mental activity of any kind'.[35] She remained haunted by the thought that her life continued to lack any firm direction and, in her worse moments, also questioned how far such small-scale work at the local level could make any impact on larger social problems.[36]

At the same time, her home duties bored her, and this was made worse by the feeling of guilt that arose from her perception that she performed them in an 'indifferent' and 'perfunctory' manner.[37] Her mother shared her aversion to paying the calls their social standing in the neighbourhood demanded, but these had nevertheless to be accomplished and, worse still, from Violet's point of view, Tapton House's large staff had to be organized and monitored. She shared the unquestioning sense of obligation to care for home and parents common to virtually all late nineteenth-century women (and a large number of their late twentieth-century sisters), but the pull of a more independent life, open to but a few middle-class women of independent means, was a constant source of tension in her life as it was in Beatrice's.

Violet was incapable of elevating deeply felt family obligations into the kind of ideal women's work Octavia Hill believed them to be. She undertook to run Tapton for seven years following her mother's death in 1912 and commented in her autobiography on the problems she experienced in managing a staff of seven servants and a household budget of some £2,500–3,000 a year.[38] At the forefront of her difficulties was the time such an undertaking consumed. But Violet was also well aware that the existence of servants crucially underpinned the work outside the home that she was able to do, and to the end of her days she staunchly defended domestic service as an institution that both permitted civilized social gatherings in the home and liberated middle-class women for the important contribution they could make to the wider community. Much of her inter-war correspondence with her sister Geraldine was on the 'servant problem' and the importance of understanding servant psychology, something that beset many middle-class women employing one or two servants in the smaller villa dwellings of those years.[39] Not unlike some early twentieth-century feminist theorists, she argued that it was perfectly appropriate for women to specialize, some in domestic work, some in public work.[40] The problem lay in the lack of status attaching to the former. As late as World War II she was advocating a system of formal qualifications for domestic service and the promotion of a scheme to provide home help for women of all social classes who might need it.[41] Such universalism was in keeping with both the spirit of post-war reconstruction and Markham's own desire to promote equal citizenship. However, it was clear from her autobiography that she was also particularly anxious to ensure that middle-class women be able to continue to make what she felt had been their uniquely valuable contribution to the communities in which they lived.[42] Violet was sure that middle-class women should be freed to make such a contribution. She commented frankly of R. B. Haldane's sister, Elizabeth, for example, that while she had been made a Companion of Honour and had received an honorary degree from Edinburgh, 'I often wished that her life had been less wholly devoted to the service of others and had belonged more to herself'.[43]

Violet herself faced some conflict with her mother as she tried to create more of a life of her own, and she had some doubts during the late 1890s not only about whether the work she was set on doing was worthwhile but also whether she was capable of doing it: 'Nature has treated me unkindly in the matter of brains. She has given me enough capacity to desire great things, but she has not given me enough to achieve them'.[44] Frustrated by the kind of work she found herself doing locally, confused as to its significance and her own capacity, and guilty as well as impatient at the demands exerted by home and family, Violet was diagnosed neurasthenic late in 1898 and a major health breakdown followed. The solution, as was usual in such cases, was deemed to lie in travel abroad, and Violet spent 1899 in South Africa. This trip, during which she met Alfred Milner and Cecil Rhodes, fuelled her already strong commitment to Empire. With war looming, she wrote that she would 'go and break windows in Downing Street if they fail Sir Alfred [Milner]'.[45] Violet Markham adopted a strongly anti-Boer position and her diary reveals the extent to which she found the larger imperial debates she engaged with in South Africa revitalizing. Even her writing block disappeared. When she returned, her inheritance enabled her to construct an existence independent of Chesterfield in her London house and to pursue a much wider range of social and political issues in both cities.

Citizenship and social work, 1900–1918
Like Octavia Hill, Violet Markham described herself as a doer rather than a thinker. She was not impatient with thinkers as was Octavia, and was indeed profoundly influenced by Hilda Cashmore, who helped run the Chesterfield Settlement between 1903 and 1911 and whose position on social questions was far more developed than Violet's own. But the general direction of Violet's work was nevertheless derived more from her personal experience (especially of committee work and travel), set within the broad liberal political principles she carried with her through her adult life. The key to understanding her approach to social work and to social problems in the Edwardian period lies in the strength of her commitment to the national interest, which she interpreted, in the manner of a large number of politicians, civil servants and

commentators, as the pursuit of a substantially improved level of national health and welfare. When Violet used, as she often did, the concept of citizenship to argue for social action and social reform, she meant that working people were to be enabled to become healthy and well-educated members of an imperial nation and that the better-off were to fulfil their duties of public service that would both promote social reform and wise government. Needless to say, such a concept of citizenship was profoundly gendered and, as in the case of Mary Ward, this helps to explain the position Violet adopted on the issue of suffrage.

In 1903, Violet started the Chesterfield Settlement with the help of Hilda Cashmore, who went on to become warden of the Bristol Settlement in 1911 and of the Manchester Settlement from 1926 to 1933, and Elsie Wright who left Chesterfield fairly soon to get married. Violet acknowledged Hilda Cashmore as the most important influence on her thinking. They differed profoundly on what Violet referred to as the big questions, for Hilda's politics were socialist. But Hilda undoubtedly reinforced Violet's New Liberal views as to the desirability of a more equal role for the state in solving social problems and also helped shape Violet's personal values. While there is no direct evidence, it is likely that it was Hilda's example (she was a devout Quaker) that enabled Violet to find a new peace within the church. Many of the moral principles that informed Hilda Cashmore's social work recall those of Octavia Hill and F. D. Maurice, but her ideas as to the solution of the problem of poverty looked beyond the individual employer, philanthropist and pauper to the modification of society's structures. She was, as Elsie Wright commented, devoted to practical, personal social work but also had a vision of a better ordered world.[46] During the Edwardian period, some settlements, in London at least, continued to approach their work out of religious belief and eschewed politics (as in the case of Mary Ward's Passmore Edwards Settlement), while others such as Mansfield Hall became more consciously involved in supporting working-class political action in their districts and were more inclined to radical and socialist beliefs. It seems that Hilda Cashmore combined elements of both these approaches.

Hilda was also greatly concerned to look inward and to search through prayer for guidance as to 'right action'. Violet was very impressed by Hilda Cashmore's stress on the importance of the 'quiet regulation of our minds'.[47] Elsie Wright wrote in a similar vein after her marriage:

> Again and again one's personal individual greedy self rises up and clamours for its desires to be gratified – and I have come to think (mostly through

Hilda) that it is enormously a matter of getting one's centre fixed in the right plane, of really forgetting to think how things affect oneself.[48]

Self-giving was still very much part of Hilda Cashmore's code and, unlike Octavia Hill, she insisted on living among the poor and in as frugal a fashion as possible, something Violet admired but found impossible to contemplate. She had, as Violet put it, a 'passion for the poor'.[49]

Most important perhaps was the way in which Hilda Cashmore reinforced in Violet the idea that all social action had to be principled. Violet Markham was in many respects more pragmatic in her approach to social questions, especially in her later career as a public servant, than were most late nineteenth- and early twentieth-century women social workers, but she never acted without reference to a basic framework of moral principles which were the common currency of so many of her fellow social activists, feminist and non-feminist, socialist, liberal and conservative. Like Beatrice Webb and Mary Ward and probably, although there is no direct evidence, Helen Bosanquet, she deplored the kind of thinking embodied in the work of H. G. Wells, not just because of its sexual explicitness but because she saw in it an essential selfishness, an underlying cruelty and destructiveness and a lust for power in the desire to strip away hypocrisy. She liked Hilda Cashmore's penetrating analysis of Wells's *The New Machiavelli*: 'his antithesis too between the training of character and the training of creative power [is] curiously misleading. The pursuit of one divorced from the other is just what the Wells type of person is after'.[50] Wells stood condemned because at the end of the day he was not very bothered about 'right action', 'feeling', or 'character'.

The Chesterfield Settlement started schools for mothers and crippled children along the lines of Mary Ward's Passmore Edwards experiment. It also gave birth to the Chesterfield Civic Guild, which like the other Guilds of Help and Civic Leagues that came into existence during the 1900s, aimed to deepen the sense of civic responsibility for the care of the poor through the provision of personal service to anyone (not just the 'helpable') who needed it, and to work as closely as possible with local government authorities while maintaining the COS's opposition to direct almsgiving. Advocates of the guilds acknowledged that the COS was also committed to personal social work and to the organization of charity but criticized it for not putting sufficient effort into the organization of voluntary helpers/visitors; for using very narrow criteria in assessing whom it could help; for setting itself apart from other organizations and authorities in the field and for adopting a 'superior person' attitude; and, allied to this last point, for failing enthusiastically to cooperate with other relief agencies.[51] In his 1912 review of the progress of the guilds for the COS, Mr L. V. Shairp (who also wrote a manual on visiting for the Chesterfield Guild) stated that in 1911 there were some 70 guilds in existence and that two-thirds of these were in the North of England.[52] In Bradford, where the first guild was set up, the COS was apparently particularly 'hard and dry'. But for the most part the COS's influence was significantly weaker outside London. The guilds were incorporated nationally in 1911 with 8000 members. Shef-field had enlisted 1000 helpers, Birmingham 700 and Bradford 400.[53]

Violet, together with Mrs D. D. Lyttleton (the author of a play showing the evils of sweated work), also acted as organizing secretary to the London-based Personal Service Association (PSA), which was formed in 1908 (with its headquarters in the Passmore Edwards Settlement) to visit the unemployed. Volunteers worked alongside both the Distress Committees of the Central Unemployment Body (part of the administrative machinery set up by the Unemployed Workmen's Act of 1905) and COS committees.[54] The PSA represented the extension of the most important part of the work of the Guilds of Help to London and was supported by a wide spectrum of social activists and politicians, including Mary Ward, Millicent Garrett Fawcett, Margot Asquith and Arthur Henderson. In terms of its practical aim to bring helper and receiver into a friendly relationship it was indistinguishable from the principles of visiting espoused by Octavia Hill and the COS, but its client group, the unemployed, and its willingness to work with the statutory authorities set it apart from more traditional elements within the COS and made clear its roots in the Guilds of Help movement. The PSA was anxious that its volunteers should come to realize that a large percentage of the unemployed were not work-shy but rather patient, decent people, 'not first class in the labour market, but a good second class, and beyond reproach in personal character', and thereby to feel a greater sense of civic responsibility towards them.[55] The aim of both the PSA and the guilds was to build corporate life. The idea of civic responsibility was linked intimately to that of strengthening the social fabric and thereby creating a greater sense of national solidarity and consensus. The emphasis, in the manner of New Liberalism, was on masses rather than classes. However, the achievements of the PSA appear to have been limited; Russell Wakefield (a signatory of the Minority Report of the 1909 Royal Commission on the Poor Laws and a founder member of the Hampstead Civic Guild) was an early supporter, but in 1909 he refused to join the PSA general committee because he felt it was too poorly managed.[56]

By 1909, Violet was advising others on setting up Guilds of Help in provincial towns. However, the record of the Chesterfield Guild was, like the PSA, somewhat mixed and certainly far from the picture of harmonious positive cooperation between volunteers and between agencies beloved of spokesmen for the guild movement. In 1907, the Chesterfield Guild was experiencing both serious financial difficulties and friction on its executive committee between different religious denominations, and in 1910 Violet had to defend herself from criticism that she had played too dominant a role in its management. The guild was also to experience considerable conflict with other agencies, notably the Women's Cooperative Guild, in its effort to work with the local authority's public-health department in developing maternity clinics during and after World War I.[57]

Regardless of the difficulties she experienced in the Chesterfield Guild and in the PSA (which remained largely hidden from public view), by 1911 Violet felt that there was sufficient difference between this movement and the COS to warrant public criticism of the latter. She wrote to the *Spectator* arguing that the causes of poverty were not always the same and certainly not always due to individual moral failure. Furthermore, it was difficult to accept the rigid boundary the COS insisted on drawing between state relief for the 'unhelpable' and voluntary relief for the 'helpable':

> Is it not increasingly difficult to accept the view that the great forces of the state are only to be at the service of the pauper, the lunatic, and the criminal, and that the honest and deserving citizen, if he falls on evil days, should be handed over to what Malthus wrily called 'the uncertain support of private charity'?[58]

Violet was not alone in reaching this conclusion or in publicly expressing her views. As Brian Harrison has pointed out, Violet Butler's study of Oxford, published in 1912, showed considerably more appreciation of the work that could be achieved by the voluntary and state sectors working together than had a study of Cambridge published some six years before.[59] Violet's own letter to the *Spectator* was followed by a lengthy correspondence in the *Charity Organisation Review* in which she restated her belief that the COS stood for 'extreme individualism'. She suggested that the COS's insistence on rigid lines of demarcation between its work and that of the state effectively robbed the latter of its best source of advice: 'The state cannot do its work unless it is moralised and vitalised by the individual'. She stressed that the aim should be to 'evolve a state the functions of which shall be *creative* rather than *oppressive*'.[60]

She denied both publicly and in private correspondence any desire to disparage the COS to which she felt she owed so much. Nor did she question the nature of its casework practice.[61] Rather, she sought above all to introduce greater flexibility into the COS and to encourage a more positive view of its relationship with state relief agencies as one of equal partnership. W. A. Bailward, who promoted cooperation between the Oxford House Settlement and the COS, replied that the COS had nothing against state intervention to secure, for example, the regulation of building codes and sanitary standards, but it would continue to resist a greater role for it in the direct provision of relief, which could only serve to undermine personal responsibility. All too often state officials acted merely out of personal ambition with 'one eye on the electorate'.[62] This left Violet the opening to reiterate that this was why local authorities needed the wise advice of COS people. Environmental circumstances and character were equally to blame in the creation of poverty and it was therefore crucial that the state and voluntary sector work together.

> I am satisfied it is not the organisation of charity we want so much today as the stimulation of a higher sense of citizenship . . . We do not want to be taught our duties as individuals, we want to be taught to live worthily as members of a community – a point on which the COS lays relatively little stress. If we could get members of public bodies from Parliament downwards to take Aristotle's view that 'the end of the State is the production of virtuous action', would not the whole of our national life wear a different aspect?[63]

The Bosanquets had in fact taught something very similar, but here Violet was placing as much emphasis on the importance of fulfilling mutual obligations within the community, that is on the means, as on the development of individual self-maintenance, which remained the goal and the main practical focus of most COS workers.

In many respects it is not too hard to understand the COS's lament that it had been misunderstood. The problem was, as Octavia Hill had perceived as early as the 1870s, that the work of local COS committees turned out in practice to be considerably 'harder and dryer' than was necessarily dictated by the organization's principles. Faced also by losses in the propaganda war following the publication of the Majority and Minority Reports of the Royal Commission on the Poor Laws, the COS sought in 1913 to minimize its differences with the guilds and, stressing their common admiration for the Elberfield scheme of visiting which had so inspired Octavia Hill, called a joint conference of the two organizations. But Violet's perception that there were real differences between them was correct.

The tone adopted by advocates of the Guilds of Help was above all positive and enabling. Mr P. S. Grundy, the General Secretary of the Manchester League of Help, referred to the difficulty of reconciling the guilds' 'new spirit of local patriotism' with the work of the COS, which was so often characterized by a meanness of spirit reminiscent of its original aim to repress mendicity and its concern to eradicate pauperism by stopping almsgiving and outdoor poor-law relief.[64] Supporters of the Guilds of Help like Violet Markham in no way dissented from the essential belief of the COS in the importance of self-maintenance; much later in the 1930s, as a member of the Unemployment Assistance Board, Violet admitted that she was probably more anxious than her fellow board members to root out young women who preferred to draw relief than look for work, reserving her sympathy, not unlike Octavia Hill, for the elderly unemployed widow.[65] However, she was also committed to a more universalist interpretation of personal service that was more in keeping with her emphasis on common citizenship. Inevitably the rich would continue to 'serve' the poor, but anyone in poverty would be helped and as a result both rich and poor would develop greater civic responsibility. The state should also help both the deserving and the undeserving poor. As early as 1897, Violet had recorded her approbation of a sermon which had asked legislators to fill up their water pots 'with honest work and pure intentions, which might turn into wine for the poor'.[66] Unlike the COS, Violet Markham and the Guilds of Help did not fear that state welfare would undermine personal responsibility and prove demoralizing to the individual or the family. Like E. J. Urwick, whom she found personally impressive, she believed that if the state did more, for example by providing school meals, this would enable the family better to fulfil its ethical role in socializing its young.[67] Meeting the family's material needs would provide greater impetus to internal enrichment.

Violet described herself as a Radical, meaning a radical liberal. Her close friend, Mackenzie King, the future Liberal Prime Minister of Canada and a close friend of both Violet and Mary Ward, reported with great satisfaction in his diary for 1919 that Violet's ideas about the evolution of industry and about political development, 'indeed on all those questions of what real Liberalism seems to involve' were similar to his own.[68] On her side, Violet recorded her appreciation of Mackenzie King's rejection of *laissez-faire*, and by World War II she had even come to share his view of Empire as more a Commonwealth than an imperial federation.[69] Violet was in fact part of a circle of Edwardian progressives whose female members probably spanned an even wider spectrum of political opinion than did the men.[70] They shared a principled commitment to social action. As José Harris has remarked when commenting on the philosophy of E. J. Urwick, a belief in religious truth and in the importance of the idea of the conscious pursuit of the good life (in the sense of best selves) were themes transcending collectivism and individualism in the Edwardian period.[71] In the fight against the sweated trades, for example, Violet worked closely with May Tennant and Lucy Deane Streatfeild, both former women factory inspectors and Liberals; Lady Dilke, Gertrude Tuckwell and Mary Macarthur (founder of the National Federation of Working Women) from the women's trade union movement; as well as Mary Ward and Beatrice Webb. Just as in the case of school meals or national insurance, Violet believed that direct state intervention to regulate the labour market, such that (predominantly married) women's sweated labour was abolished, could only improve national welfare and national efficiency. By 1918, she tended to see the Webbs as the people who had really come into their own and, like Eleanor Rathbone, she experienced considerable difficulty in opposing Labour on election platforms.[72]

Notwithstanding the COS's decision to cooperate as best it could with the Guilds of Help in the years before World War I, there still remained a gulf between the kind of approach to social problems espoused by someone like Violet Markham and that of a mainstream member of the COS, such as Octavia Hill's old associate, Margaret Sewell. In a consideration of 'changing social ideals' in 1917, Sewell remained convinced that state welfare would merely resuscitate the ills of paternalist benevolence and indiscriminate almsgiving. Nor could she readily accept more democratic ideas of personal service. She was prepared to contemplate a day when ' "social work" will no longer carry the meaning it does today – the work of one class as such for another as such', but that day had most certainly not come; the poor were still largely uneducated and education remained a major responsibility of the middle-class social worker.[73]

One of the few real points of contact between the like of Violet Markham and Margaret Sewell was their common insistence on the importance of training for the work of personal service. Social-work education made large strides during World War I because of vastly increased interest on the part of industry and government in the relationship between personal welfare and rates of production, particularly in munitions.[74] Violet wrote approvingly to Hilda Cashmore of May Tennant's call for more war-time industrial welfare workers on the basis not of philanthropy but rather as an indication of the employers' commitment to a common notion of citizenship.[75] In 1916, Violet Markham together with Elizabeth Macadam (who lived with Eleanor

Rathbone) and the PSA were instrumental in setting up both a Joint Social Studies Committee, to consider the best method of training voluntary social workers, and a Provisional Committee on Social Service. From these beginnings emerged the Joint Universities Council for Social Studies.[76] Violet preferred to negotiate a scheme of professional training with Urwick at the London School of Economics (LSE), rather than with Bedford College, fearing the strength of COS influence within the latter.[77]

Despite Elizabeth Macadam's insistence on asking Sewell to join the Joint Social Studies Committee in recognition of her pioneering work in the training of social workers, her comments showed how the ascendancy in thinking on this subject had passed from the COS to those who shared Violet Markham's views on what Macadam was to call in 1934 'the new philanthropy': 'a unique partnership between the voluntary sector and the state'.[78] Commenting specifically on the role of voluntary workers in a 1918 letter to Violet, Macadam explicitly adopted the views of the Webbs on the relationship between these and the state:

> The state through its officials is responsible . . . and voluntary effort must learn to confine itself on the one hand at its best, to pioneer or experimental work or . . . to supplementary state or municipal effort as in Care Committee Work, prison visiting and after-care *ad infinitum*.[79]

In this Macadam was referring only to the position of unpaid workers in the voluntary sector. Neither she nor Violet Markham were any more ready than Helen Bosanquet to welcome the idea of a voluntary sector subordinated to the bureaucracy of a welfare state.

Citizenship and suffrage

Violet was by far the most publicly active woman in the anti-suffrage movement. Her speech at an anti-suffrage meeting in the Albert Hall in 1912 received widespread coverage and involved addressing a huge audience, something Mary Ward never did. Like Beatrice Webb and Mary Ward, she was very concerned about speaking in public, learning to do so chiefly in the course of her work for the Chesterfield School Board. By the late 1900s, she was besieged by requests to speak against suffrage. Not surprisingly, given that most believed that public platforms were not the place for women, there was a singular lack of women who were prepared to speak in public for the Antis; Octavia Hill had found it difficult enough to write a letter to *The Times* on the subject of suffrage.

Just as Mary Ward also played an active political role in support of her son Arnold, Violet also extended her political activities to the support of her brother Arthur, elected Liberal MP for Mansfield in 1900. Like Mary Ward she prepared an address on the House of Lords during the elections of 1910 but she delivered it at a public meeting rather than circulating a pamphlet and as a Liberal, she also proposed reform of the Upper Chamber rather than defence of the *status quo*. She also spoke in support of the 'labour and progressive' candidate, Mr Barnett Kenyon, in the Chesterfield by-election of 1913.[80]

Anti-suffrage work was very much part and parcel of Violet's expanding world and proved a stepping-stone on the path to a highly successful public career. Brian Harrison has suggested that it was the strength of the ideas held by the anti-suffragists in the wider society that accounts for the subsequent success of women like Violet Markham.[81] This is undoubtedly an important part of the explanation. But it is as important to consider the 'supply side', the way in which Violet Markham's views on women's position in society and in particular her ideas on sexual difference made it relatively easy for her to enter the public sphere; her behaviour on committees was infinitely more effective than that of Beatrice Webb, for example, although part of this was undoubtedly due to a difference in temperament. For while she changed her attitude towards votes for women in 1916, Violet never changed her views on sexual difference which were the crucial underpinning of the anti-suffrage position.

Paradoxically, Violet Markham's antipathy towards the idea of votes for women began with her election to the Chesterfield School Board. Suffrage not only split the world of philanthropy, but the experience of philanthropy would seem to have been a powerful determinant of attitudes towards suffrage for the women involved in it. Shortly after her election experience, Violet recorded in her diary her first reference to the 'absurd women's suffrage Bill'.[82] She spent her election day in 1898 driving about the town in a cart decked out with violets and mauve ribbon: 'This fetched the mob vastly though inwardly I was writhing with shame at such clap trap'.[83] She was disgusted not only by parading in front of an ill-informed electorate but also by the role she played in the subsequent politickings of the board itself. She found that she held the balance of power between four churchmen and four dissenters, but she deplored her power as kingmaker: 'I really do think it is humiliating for my masculine colleagues to feel they are at the mercy of one girl'.[84] She spent the week before the chairmanship was decided feeling harassed and battered:

> I have never spent a more wretched week . . . It has convinced me more fully than years of mere thought would have done what folly it is for women to

engage in public life. One of two evils must overtake them. Either they become more or less unsexed and callous in their dealings with men, or else they remain women and at the same time do their work properly but with a mental wear and tear in the latter case which is a tremendous strain on their endurance. Certain women can do men's work perhaps, but *always* with double the fatigue and double the exertion both mental and physical.[85]

In many respects this is reminiscent of Beatrice Webb's puzzled musings about how she should behave on the Royal Commission on the Poor Laws. But whereas Beatrice never did reach a *modus vivendi* in such a forum, Violet very soon became a most effective school-board member and seems to have enjoyed 'hatching plots' with her colleagues on the board. But the conviction that there was a line to be drawn in respect of women's sphere of operations, and that it excluded voting, remained.

Violet Markham's own *ex-post facto* explanation of her position on suffrage was four-fold: the influence of her mother who was also an Anti; her conviction that women would prove an exceptionally ignorant electorate; the excesses of those claiming the vote (that is, of the suffragettes); and the fact that while women possessed the local suffrage they made little use of it. These seem a fair representation of the elements influencing her thinking but they require rather more elaboration, some modification and a shading in terms of emphasis. In fact, the divide between Violet and many suffrage sympathizers was not so wide in terms of their underlying assumptions and this in turn helps additionally to explain why Violet found it relatively easy to embark upon a career as a public servant after the suffrage campaign was over.

Violet's mother was certainly opposed to suffrage and so were many family friends, for example Gertrude Bell, whose family, like the Markhams, were coal-owners and iron manufacturers. Many people Violet had a great admiration for, such as Beatrice Webb, Louise Creighton, Mrs J. R. Green, Mrs T. H. Green and Mrs Arnold Toynbee, were also anti-suffragists. But equally, many people whom Violet was extremely close to could not understand her position. Most notable was Hilda Cashmore, who wrote frankly to Violet in a vein not dissimilar to that used by the male cooperators to Beatrice Webb some two decades earlier: '[you] have all that most women are fighting to get and so do not quite realise the worth of the issues to those who have not got this'.[86] Constance Smith, an inspector of factories with whom Violet had campaigned to reduce the number of hours that could be worked by schoolchildren, also dissented from her views but in so doing revealed the way in which Violet Markham as a 'good Anti' was able to remain close to at least many of the constitutional suffragists who, on many other issues, shared her Progressive opinions and who also shared a common class-background. Smith had wanted to go and hear Violet speak at the Albert Hall in 1912 but she could not quite bring herself to do so: 'As you know, I am heartily in agreement with a great deal that you said, but not with your conclusions. I do not quite see how you arrive at them, since you are, if you will let me say so, much too big a person to confound principles and persons'.[87]

Many suffragists deplored suffrage militancy as much as the Antis and Violet Markham and, more fundamental still, they also shared many of her underlying assumptions about the nature of sexual difference and the importance of women's home and family responsibilities. It was possible to believe that women were equal but different and argue either a suffragist position (like Mrs Fawcett, on occasion),[88] or an anti-suffrage view. When Maude Selborne, a suffragist, wrote to Violet to ask her to contribute to a book of essays on the vote representing both sides in the debate, she stressed that they both sought similar ends in the form of progressive legislation to give widows pensions and additional protection to children and to women at work; that they agreed that too many suffragists overplayed the potential benefits of the vote in respect of women's ability to secure such legislation, just as too many Antis were prone to dismiss them altogether; that she felt voting would merely force the 'best home-loving women' to think more about politics and that would raise the quality of home life to the good of the nation; and that she, too, abhorred the notion of women active in political life: 'But voting is such a nice quiet ladylike way of saying which man you prefer'.[89] Just like Mary Ward, Selborne refused to let differences of opinion prevent civilized friendship, something that was easier given the large tracts of common ground she was able to outline. St Loe Strachey, editor of the *Spectator* and a firm and vehement Anti, deplored the suffrage inclinations of his aunt yet insisted that there had been no family quarrel over it.[90] It would be wrong to underestimate the profound split within families and between friends and acquaintances that was occasioned by the suffrage struggle, but it is also wrong not to recognize that views could be polarized on the suffrage itself without there being any division in the underlying beliefs that were broadly shared by many women and between families in the middle and upper classes.

Violet Markham shared Mary Ward's detestation of suffrage militancy and the threat that it seemed to pose to her deeply-rooted ideas as to the proper form for relations between men and women. This 'hatred of excess' that she identified as the principal cause of her anti-suffrage activities was intimately linked to her ideas about what it was proper for men to do and for women to do in society, which were in turn derived from notions of sexual difference that were as much culturally and class specific as biologically based. She engaged in a long correspondence with St Loe Strachey who was willing to publish her ideas on both suffrage and social work in the *Spectator* in the 1910s. In a strangely twisted letter about Almroth Wright's notorious letter to *The Times* (in which he described suffragettes as man-haters and as sexually abnormal and which was followed by a public disclaimer signed by both Violet Markham and Mary Ward), Strachey said that Wright's letter had strengthened his anti-suffrage feelings: 'It shows to what lengths we should get if we once engaged in anything approaching a sex-war'.[91] Strachey blamed the militants for having brought matters to the point where 'such things can be said and are openly said'. There was in this a fear that the civilized trappings of relations between the sexes, the small courtesies, the male protective impulse, would break down, leaving a vacuum in which what Herbert Spencer called the lower passions would hold sway. Mary Ward was beset by the same fear. While, like other anti-suffrage men, such as Harold Owens and Belfort Bax, Strachey felt that such a situation would serve women right, he dreaded the consequences for the comfortable, carefully-constructed upper middle-class society in which he moved. So did Violet Markham and Mary Ward, and undoubtedly many other middle- and upper middle-class women suffragists did too. Violet was horrified not just by the public behaviour of the suffragettes but by their apparent lack of regard for customary standards of etiquette to be observed in male/ female interaction. The *Freewoman*, a radical feminist paper in which Rebecca West frequently denounced Mary Ward and also attacked Violet Markham on the subject of charity and social work, particularly upset her by its freethinking approach to sexual relationships.[92]

Violet believed that relations between men and women should be characterized by male chivalry and protection. Indeed she felt very comfortable when visiting families such as that of General Botha in South Africa, which she herself described as patriarchal.[93] Hilda Cashmore deplored the practice of chivalry, which she felt destroyed the possibility of comradeship between men and women.[94] But Violet, like Mary Ward, felt that the traditional courtesies, such as door-opening and hat-doffing that were extended by men to women were a necessary veneer covering brute passions, and she also doubted the possibility of genuine comradeship between the sexes although she seems not to have shared Mary Ward's view that this would impede women from entering public life. Presumably, she felt that ritualized forms of social interaction between men and women would provide sufficient protection there too. Violet also accepted that male protection was crucial to women in the family and at work. The free-love ideas expressed in the *Freewoman* and the sexual radicalism of H. G. Wells's *Ann Veronica* appeared to her, to St Loe Strachey and to many others to threaten to make women more vulnerable by destroying the marriage contract whereby men provided for women and stood between them and a predatory outside world in return for sexual fidelity and household services.

The woman of a lower social class who had to engage in paid labour also required protection. Violet fought with Beatrice Webb, Mary Macarthur, Emilia Dilke and Gertrude Tuckwell among others against sweated labour and for the Trade Boards Act of 1909, which set up a minimum wage for (primarily women) workers in a restricted number of trades. While Macarthur looked on the demand for minimum wage legislation as a recognition of women's right to work, Webb, Tuckwell, Dilke and Markham argued for the legislation first on the grounds that it would raise male wage rates and make women's work unnecessary, and second that 'inefficient' women workers would be squeezed out of the labour market.[95] All agreed that women's primary responsibility was to home and family and that legislation against the sweated trades would improve the health and welfare of mothers and thus the health of an imperial race. Like Beatrice Webb, Violet associated the suffragist position with opposition to all protective legislation for women. This was not entirely correct, but some late nineteenth-century liberal equalitarian feminists, such as Millicent Garrett Fawcett, had certainly claimed the right of women to work on the same terms as men; protective legislation at work has continued to prove a touchstone of equalitarian versus equal-but-different schools of thought within feminism.[96] Even though attitudes towards protective legislation did not provide an absolute dividing line between suffragists and Antis, Violet Markham, Beatrice Webb and Mary Ward and their allies were able to make much of the apparent indifference of those in favour of the vote towards the welfare of wives and mothers working in industry.[97]

Violet Markham felt that ideas regarding a biological basis for sexual difference were 'eminently plausible'. She was, for example, attracted to Patrick Geddes and J. Arthur Thompson's influential ideas, which grounded sexual difference in physiology but which stressed that women were equal although entirely different. Geddes and Thompson wrote at length on the possibilities of civic or social motherhood, lauding women 'as eupsychic inspirer and eugenic mother, as instructive synthesist, as educationalist, as orderly home planner and citizen'.[98] In all probability Violet was much attached to the view that, within the carefully constructed fabric of marriage and family, women had the opportunity and the responsibility of acting as the civilizers. Like late-Victorian social scientists and leading literary figures (Violet was fond of quoting Tennyson), she believed that middle-class women in western society were the most 'civilised' (Spencer would have said 'most highly evolved'). Within a framework of male chivalry, protection and respect, women were able to provide an enviable standard of peace and culture and to act as guardians of society's moral virtues.

As a young girl, Violet had lived up to the later Victorian prescriptions that required girls to act as the moral guardians of their male family members.[99] Writing to Arthur at Rugby, Violet urged him to behave like a true Markham, to be a man of honour and not to do anything to cause his family 'a blush of shame'.[100] She also seems to have been genuinely convinced of masculine superiority, despite her recognition of the incompetence of many of her early male school-board colleagues, for example. In large measure this belief was grounded, as was the case with most anti-suffragists, in the recognition of superior male strength. If women were the civilizers, men were the imperial protectors. Like Mary Ward, Violet Markham had reacted strongly first to the Irish Question in the 1880s (although she was too young to make the break from Liberalism over it), then to the Fashoda crisis and to the Boer War. Keeping the vote in the hands of men came down to a question of patriotism. To take power out of male hands and to give it to what was a majority of women, all of whom required male protection, would be 'an intolerable situation for a great nation and a great empire'.[101] A dividing line had to be drawn, she felt, between the administrative and the legislative functions of the state in respect to female participation, because 'a woman's citizenship is different in kind and in quality from that of a man'. E. J. Urwick also argued that the basis of women's citizenship was different from that of men but, like Helen Bosanquet, he did not feel that the different nature of male/female duties in and of itself warranted differential treatment in respect of the vote. He argued that all duties were public in that they took the individual an unlimited distance beyond the ordinary self and that women's duty as citizens to promote the good of the community was as important to the commonweal as men's duty to protect family and nation.[102]

Violet Markham could not agree. She believed that the differential quality of women's citizenship found just and proper reflection in their political representation at the local, but not the national level. As St Loe Strachey summarized her position:

I think your distinction between local government and the central government is a perfectly sound one, and for this reason: county councils do not make peace or war nor do they legislate, that is say the supreme word as to how the country is governed.[103]

Violet had obviously put to one side her early discontented musings as to whether work at the local level was in the end of any great significance. Violet Markham and Mary Ward were both committed to promoting a positive anti-suffrage policy that stressed the importance of securing greater opportunities for women in local government. But from the first days of the anti-suffrage movement the question of such a 'forward policy' had been a bone of contention, first between the women in the Women's National Anti-Suffrage League and later between the women activists and the men in the National League for Opposing Woman Suffrage, founded in 1910. Mary Ward had soon become disheartened about the possibility of pushing a positive local government plank into the aims and objectives of the anti-suffrage movement and Violet Markham's support for so doing came at a critical juncture.[104] Initially, Violet favoured a fully-fledged women's council at the national level as well but, while Gertrude Bell was enthusiastic, Mary Ward felt that this would prove 'too big and too vague and have no more practical effect than the National Union of Women Workers'.[105] St Loe Strachey counselled that the suffrage movement had shown that it was too dangerous to allow women to act together in any forum; the result would inevitably be some form of mass hysteria.[106]

Nor were the male leaders of the Antis at all anxious to promote women's position in local government. Matters came to a head over the extent to which the League would adopt a positive position on women in local government in 1912, when Mary Ward's Local Government Advancement Committee (LGAC) sent a letter of support to Dr Sophia Jevons, a non-active suffragist who was standing for election in West Marylebone. The LGAC had supported Dr Jevons both as a Progressive and as a female candidate. Captain Percy Creed, the league's director and Lord Cromer, its president (until 1912), were angry above all that a pro-suffrage candidate should receive any endorsement. Mary Ward felt that Creed was 'wholly illiberal and bigoted . . . and simply believes that the local government movement is doing harm'.[107] Cromer explained to Violet Markham that both she and Mary Ward were extremists 'although I do not doubt that you are quite unaware of the fact – who invite the ratepayers to vote for a woman merely on account of her sex'. Furthermore, he, together with Lords Curzon (the League's president after 1912) and Northcote, was firmly opposed to any attempt to link the question of anti-suffrage to the enlarging of women's role in local government.[108] Violet Markham replied cheerfully that she was an unrepentant extremist in this regard. But she denied supporting women *qua* women candidates, referring again to Dr Jevons's excellent qualifications for election. Furthermore, women anxious to serve locally had been dismayed to see a section of the male reformers in West Marylebone prepared to fill one of the few seats held by a woman on the local council with a man. Quite apart from Dr Jevons, there were other excellent female candidates:

> All women interested in women's work must feel badly treated by West Marylebone and this is not good at a time of so much feeling . . . I cannot but feel it would be a real disaster for our cause if we give even the least impression, however unjustified, of being anti-woman.[109]

Cromer was nevertheless successful in forcing the LGAC to end its official connection with the League. All Mary Ward and Violet Markham could do was to seek excuses for the men's behaviour in Cromer's ill-health.[110] The LGAC was supported by Gertrude Bell, Mrs Burgwin, the Superintendent of Special Schools with the London County Council, Mrs Frederic Harrison and Mrs Dunn Garner, the COS member who had promoted the training of social workers in the 1890s. It continued to appeal to Antis who, 'while believing with us that the suffrage agitation is in reality an unpatriotic agitation, the success of which would weaken and hamper the English state', desired to support women's public service at the local level.[111] Violet Markham stated additionally to Mary Ward that she could not agree to any harassment of good suffragist candidates at the local level, nor would she be able to support a bad female candidate over a good suffragist one. As an individual she would also wish to support her suffragist friends, such as May Tennant and Constance Smith, another testimony to the power that shared values and friendship had in surmounting suffrage divisions.[112] Violet also anticipated real difficulty in finding sufficient numbers of progressive Antis to stand.

In her major anti-suffrage speech at the Albert Hall in 1912, Violet used what she regarded as women's apathy towards, and ignorance of, the work to be done locally as her trump card in arguing against the suffrage. She accused women of not taking advantage of the opportunities they already possessed locally and of not performing their natural duties: 'We hold that it is through the faithful fulfilment of duty, through service, not self-assertion, that woman will arrive at a true conception of her place in the body politic'.[113] She also believed firmly that women would prove a singularly ill-informed electorate at the national level. Mass democracy and the ignorance of working-class male electors perturbed both her and Mary Ward; Violet had first registered her opinions on this issue during her 1898 school-board election. Even in 1916, when she wrote to Cromer to explain that she had changed her mind on votes for women, she confessed that she wanted 'to see the franchise altered and women brought in but not only by any measure of wholesale extension'.[114] She went on to ask him, somewhat rhetorically, if he thought it 'chimerical' to press for a complete revision of the basis of the franchise such that it would be exercised in respect of 'service, citizenship and education' rather than property and age. Violet Markham had no great hopes of the mass of voters male or female, and she felt that enfranchising all women over twenty-one would merely exacerbate an already worrying situation. Indeed in 1919 she was still advocating local government as the preferred outlet for women's talents, chiefly because it was crucial for them to obtain a grounding in the principles of public service and citizenship.[115]

In Patricia Hollis's estimation, Mary Ward and Violet Markham's LGAC proved singularly incapable of finding and running candidates in winnable seats, and she has questioned whether it sincerely tried to do so.[116] Brian Harrison feels that Markham and Ward's local government strategy was fundamentally misconceived because they ignored the realities of politics at the local level and because the distinction between local and national politics was unrealistic.[117] The first point is certainly correct. In accordance with her construction of local government work as part and parcel of women's work of service to the local community, Violet Markham argued that it should be non-party political, but in reality women failed to be nominated by political parties at the local level as the West Marylebone case showed.[118] Violet confused the 'ought' with the 'is' in offering local government as an alternative to national political activity for women. The Women's Local Government Society took her severely to task for her 1912 Albert Hall speech, pointing out quite correctly how hard it was for women to be adopted as candidates and how full of anomalies the local suffrage was.[119] Violet's reply that the local suffrage was full of anomalies for men too was weak indeed.[120] Harrison's second point is undoubtedly correct given the advantages of hindsight, but many people interested in social reform felt local government to be the focal point for their activities in the early 1900s. Violet Markham argued that local government was where administration as opposed to legislation took place and it was with administration that women citizens should be primarily concerned. The dawning realization that local government was increasingly not so critical in the achievement of social reform was given by Beatrice Webb as one of her reasons for changing her mind on the suffrage in 1906.

Harrison does not address the point that Mary Ward and Violet Markham made most of: the importance they attached to the anti-suffrage movement adopting a line that was not entirely negative. Violet insisted to Lord Cromer that to detach the moderates they had to be positive about women's contribution and 'not meet the whole feminist movement with a blunt *non possimus*'.[121]

She was probably right, but this raises the more complex issue of gender relations within the anti-suffrage movement. The few women activists were on the periphery of the League. Yet Curzon and Cromer took care to ensure a façade of equal participation. In 1913, 1005 of the subscribing members of the central League office were males and 2375 females.[122] Male Antis needed women supporters if they were to avoid the charge of a sex war, which they so greatly deplored. Lord Cromer might have found Mary Ward 'tiresome' but her support was invaluable, just as Violet Markham's 1912 Albert Hall speech gave one of the biggest boosts to the Antis' propaganda war. Mary Ward reported that Violet had held her 'vast audience in a grip of feeling'.[123] Yet these female activists wanted support for women's public work at the local level that the Cromers, Curzons and Creeds were not prepared to give. The gender conflict at the heart of the anti-suffrage movement was profound and, when World War I made the local/national division in public life finally redundant, Violet Markham was quick to leave the Anti-Suffrage League.

A successful public career
During World War I, Violet Markham made three dramatic moves: in 1915 she married a soldier and racehorse owner, Colonel James Carruthers; in 1916 she renounced the anti-suffrage movement; and she then began a series of public appointments, with the Central Committee on Women's Training and Employment, the National Relief Fund and the National Registration Committee, before standing unsuccessfully for election in 1918. During the 1920s she returned to Chesterfield politics, becoming a councillor in 1925 and Lady Mayor in 1927. For much of the 1930s she served as a member of the Unemployment Assistance Board before being swept into another flurry of war-time committees.

World War I seems to have been a less traumatic event for her than for Helen Bosanquet, Beatrice Webb or Mary Ward. Her simple and fervent patriotism seemed to mute the horrors of war. Like Mary Ward, she could not understand any obstruction on the part of the workforce to war-time conditions of production, for example over the issue of dilution: 'For me only one thing exists today – England and her need'.[124]

She was constitutionally more inclined to look for work to do than to reflect on the implications of war for the future of civilization. Because of her political leanings, she was much less perturbed than Mary Ward either by the enlarged role of the state or by the apparent changes in the social structure and in particular the fortunes of the landed aristocracy. Finally, her position was additionally eased by the novelty of engaging in government committee work. Without attempting a full analysis of her public career during the period 1914–50, the rest of this chapter will explore briefly how it was possible for her to achieve the kind of public success that so angered the likes of Sylvia Pankhurst.

Violet Markham was undoubtedly good at committee work and probably had a natural talent for it. But unlike Beatrice Webb, she also had the assurance necessary to develop that talent. There were two important sources of this: the way in which she had managed to achieve for herself an independent persona; and the extent to which she was able to fit in with male committee members' ideas as to how a woman should behave and with what she should concern herself. Unlike Beatrice Webb, she did not seek to establish an identity as an expert that in turn made it difficult to behave in a 'womanly' fashion. She was quite content to be consigned the responsibility for 'women's issues', on which, because of her acceptance of women's traditional role in society, her views as to the treatment of women clients were often conservative. Her belief in the value of middle-class women's public service meant, however, that she often used her position to argue for an expanded role on their behalf.

An independent income had allowed Violet Markham considerable freedom of action in her work in both London and Chesterfield and she established a firm identity of her own, which her relatively late marriage at the age of forty-three did not impinge upon in any way; Cromer asked her to continue to use her maiden name for the purposes of anti-suffrage work because it was better known.[125] In her autobiography, she remembered a cousin reminding her widowed mother that life offered considerable advantages to a woman left alone with an adequate income and property.[126] So it proved in her own case. She found herself free to pursue whichever lines of work suited her best and was not subjected to the kinds of frustrations experienced by one of the early career women, Clara Collet, who frequently felt that her talents were undervalued at the Board of Trade.[127] Having successfully constructed a public life of her own choosing, Violet Markham had considerable qualms about the threat marriage might pose to her work and to her freedom of manoeuvre. When she confided in Hilda Cashmore her intention to marry she worried that to search for personal happiness seemed 'utterly wrong and selfish', and on those grounds alone she felt that she might be better advised to stick to the responsibilities of her own work. She also 'feared running up against his [James's] strong will and character', but she was relieved to find that her new husband did not try to interfere with her work: 'I come and go exactly as I like and am in London half the week'. Marriage, she reported with relief, was fun and seemed simple; little had changed in terms of the organization of her life.[128] James Carruthers pursued his own interests, chiefly in horse racing, and they seem to have led companionable, mutually supportive and fairly separate lives until his death in 1936. The only point at which her husband seems to have objected to her public career was on the occasion of her decision to stand in the general election of 1918, causing Violet to write to her election agent saying that because of his opposition it was important that she not undertake election work that might interrupt his leave.[129] For this reason and because, like many Progressive Liberals (Eleanor Rathbone was another) she was not sure about standing against a Progressive Labour candidate,[130] Violet's election efforts seem to have been somewhat less than wholehearted. But in this as in all other aspects of the work she undertook during her adult life Violet Markham remained very much her own person. Her sturdy self-assurance meant that in her correspondence she was far more often to be found giving practical help and advice than seeking it.

Violet enjoyed committee work and from her earliest days on the Chesterfield School Board relished a certain amount of politicking. In many respects she was a man's woman, not least because she accepted men's ideas about women's position. When she wrote to Cromer to say that she had changed her mind about the suffrage, she stressed that given women's service during the war, she no longer felt that she could stand on a public platform and say 'the things we said in the old days'. Anti-suffrage was no longer 'practical politics'. But, she assured him:

> I do not think my opinions have changed very fundamentally. The man as worker, the woman as homemaker remains my ideal of society. But in this difficult world one has to take facts as they are. The conditions of modern life are thoroughly artificial.[131]

Violet's decision to support the suffrage in 1916 was therefore largely taken on pragmatic grounds; her idea of men as protectors and women as civilizers and servers did not change and she embarked on her committee work with the idea of contributing as a woman, in much the same manner as nineteenth-century female social workers had asked to be permitted to extend their domestic work of caring to workhouses, hospitals and the homes of the poor. Not only did Violet Markham feel entirely comfortable with this understanding of her public work, but it also proved non-threatening to her male colleagues. In fact, during World War I, she worked largely with women, such as Mary Macarthur on the Central Committee on Women's Employment and May Tennant on the National Registration Committee, drawing on various male mentors (chiefly Robert Morant and J. H. Thomas) for help and advice on procedure. Nevertheless, she was a shrewd and quick assessor of political intrigues and in her work with the Women's Section of the National Service Department it was she who took care to cover both herself and May Tennant in face of the manoeuvrings of the War Office on the one side and the Employment Department on the other.[132]

Violet Markham was usually appointed to a committee with the explicit task of looking after women's interests, for example in regard to women's employment and the women's services during World War I. She felt this responsibility deeply, in the same way that she had been concerned to represent women teachers in her work on the Chesterfield School Board. However, just as nineteenth-century women philanthropists ended in large measure inculcating their own ideas as to domestic order into working-class wives and mothers, so Violet Markham took her strong notions of women's place with her into her work of policy-making. In her autobiography she stated that because they were in any case 'birds of passage', unemployed women workers did not present the same kind of problem as men.[133] She also accepted that women's lower wages were justified because she believed that the economic value of their work was lower. As a member of the Unemployment Assistance Board, she argued for more discretionary payments for older women claimants and, after hesitation, for equal allowances for men and women on the grounds that these were related to food and subsistence needs rather than wages, but she did not feel that female unemployment represented as serious a problem as male unemployment and was inclined to adopt a particularly hard line in regard to the young female unemployed.[134] She felt that it was imperative to impose greater discipline on young women claimants, whom she felt were mostly of a 'very poor type', with little value either as homemakers or industrial wokers, and who often had an 'unreasoning hatred' of domestic work. Violet Markham did not take the extreme view that all unemployed women should be forced into domestic service (adopted by much of the press and many policymakers in the inter-war years), but she certainly favoured compulsory training for young women, much of which would have inevitably been domestic.

However, in her position on the Departmental Committee on Factory Inspection, Violet was quite prepared to fight for (middle-class) women to be accorded the same status as men. She also advised the Lord Chancellor on the appointment of women magistrates (of whom Mary Ward was one) in the wake of the Sex Disqualification (Removal) Act of 1919. And in Chesterfield, during the 1920s, she took up the cudgels on behalf of a woman property manager who had been trained in the Octavia Hill system and whom the council's Housing Committee wanted to sack in order to give over the job of rent collecting to a man, who would do just that and no personal social work. While Violet Markham believed that women's primary responsibility was to home and family, she was also entirely convinced of the importance of middle-class women's civilizing mission beyond the home, which she felt constituted part of their duties as citizens.

Conclusion

Work was enormously important to Violet. First, it was essential to be busy. In the 1890s she bemoaned the idle Sunday 'with nothing to do and too much time to think'.[135] (As for Ella Pycroft, work filled the gaps and there was no sign that this substantially changed even after her marriage.) Second, work had to be both satisfying and purposeful. Detailed work at the local level did not fulfil Violet's ambitions. But her work on a much-expanded canvas remained largely voluntary; she strenuously denied reports of a large salary during the 1930s and was in fact unpaid other than for her Unemployment Assistance Board work for which she was paid on a part-time basis.[136] At a time when women in most professions were obliged to resign on marriage she had to tread carefully, but it was one of her beliefs that women should volunteer their services. Her own public career fitted her expanding definition of women's citizenship as service in the national interest.

Violet Markham took family duties seriously too, although these often provided unwelcome competition with her public career. In 1912, she thanked Hilda Cashmore for holding her to looking after her mother prior to the latter's death: 'I never let go the duty and I do bless you my friend for your example which was solely responsible for my sticking to my post to the last . . . I wish I had done it better, but at least I didn't run away'.[137] During the inter-war years she became something of a family matriarch, advising on the domestic crises of her sisters and on the numerous personal problems of her nephews and nieces. Both her brothers divorced, as did two of her nephews. Violet took marriage seriously, although possibly because of the family experience of her relatives she did not pontificate on the subject. In her autobiography she remarked that divorce was not the end of the world and what she deplored was not the individual case of divorce but the casual attitude towards marriage as a relationship.[138] This was a rather more flexible and worldly view than that of Mary Ward and one that emphasized the importance of the private relational aspect of marriage, as much as its significance as a public institution. Violet Markham's view of male and female roles within marriage was nevertheless traditional. She criticized her mother for having insisted on reading her mail at breakfast instead of attending to the pouring of her father's tea and she advised Elsie Wright, whose marriage did not turn out well, not to lecture her husband but 'to pet him and be feminine'.[139] Elsie's experience, together with the example of her friend May Tennant who had to leave her civil service job and scale down her public commitments on her marriage in 1896, may have influenced Violet in her decision, if such it was, to delay marriage. Late marriage enabled her to avoid the danger of submerging her own identity in that of her husband, something she was still aware of as a risk even in 1915, when her own public persona was firmly established. Very few women were able to do as Mary Ward, marry young and still establish a separate public identity.

Violet Markham's ideas about women's position in society were very different from those of Octavia Hill and yet they were in many respects but a greatly expanded version of Octavia's notions of duty and service to others. Under this expanded definition, the line between public and private was not so rigidly drawn and in the end could encompass suffrage as well, but Violet continued to believe that the activities of men and women in society should be fundamentally different. She was willing to fight for middle-class women's right to serve as magistrates but at the end of her life she would not have considered it any more appropriate for a woman to become Chancellor of the Exchequer than when she had ridiculed the idea in her anti-suffrage speech of 1912. She concerned herself with working-class women's welfare and middle-class women's right to an expanded field of service within a firmly-held framework of beliefs as to the proper social and economic relationships between men and women. Her approach allowed her to work both in the men's world of government committees and with a close network of like-minded women, many of whom opposed her views on suffrage but who shared her commitment to progressive social reform that dated from the days of the campaign for the extension of the Factory Acts.

Violet Markham was, like Octavia Hill, a doer and like Octavia she was concerned that her actions be principled. Her main reference point was more likely to be the national interest than Christianity, which meant that there was considerably more room for pragmatic considerations to enter. But the sincerity of the settlement worker's quest for something more than the facts, in the form of at least a quasi-religious truth such as Violet admired so much in Hilda Cashmore and which attracted her to E. J. Urwick, was also apparent. Violet felt that her husband shared these qualities: 'He's not intellectual, but he has the most true instincts and the soundest values', she wrote.[140] If Orwell had met them in the 1930s, he may well have thought them 'decent'.

Notes

1. Violet Markham, *Return Passage* (Oxford: Oxford University Press, 1953), p. 21.
2. Brian Harrison, *Separate Spheres. The Opposition to Women's Suffrage in Britain* (Croom Helm, 1978), p. 13.
3. PP, 1944–5, Cmd. 6650, *Report on the Post-War Organization of Private Domestic Employment*. Typical of the approach of 1950s feminists was that of Alva Myrdal and Viola Klein, *Women's Two Roles* (Routledge & Kegan Paul, 1957).
4. H. G. Wells, *Ann Veronica* (Virago, 1980), 1st edn 1909.
5. Violet Markham's Diary (hereafter VMD), 17/3, 25/12/96, Markham Personal Papers, Pt II, BLPES.
6. Ibid., 17/3, 29/12/96.
7. Ibid., 17/3, 6/5/97; 17/2, 12/1/89; 17/3, 25/11/96.
8. Ibid., 17/3, 14/1/97 and 16/1/97.
9. Ibid., 17/4, 8/4/98.
10. Ibid., 17/3, 9/2/97.
11. Ibid., 17/3, 25/11/96.
12. Ibid., 17/3, 20/10/96 and 7/12/96.
13. Ibid., 17/4, 24/12/97.
14. Ibid., 17/3, 29/5/97.
15. Markham, *Return Passage*, p. 137.
16. Brian Harrison, 'Miss Butler's Oxford Survey', in A. H. Halsey (ed.), *Traditions of Social Policy. Essays in Honour of Violet Butler* (Oxford: Blackwell, 1976), p. 67.
17. VMD, 17/3, 24/12/96.
18. Violet to Geraldine, 26/8/39, Markham Papers Pt II, 19/30.
19. Lady Bell, *At the Works. A Study of a Manufacturing Town* (Virago, 1985), 1st edn 1907, Introduction by Angela V. John.
20. Violet to Hilda Cashmore, 1/10/11, f. 130, Markham Papers Pt II, 25/12.
21. VMD, 17/3, 7/1/97.
22. Ibid., 17/3, 17/7/97, and 17/4, 3/2/98. On board school-teachers, see Frances Widdowson, *Going up into the Next Class* (Hutchinson, 1981).
23. VMD, 17/3, 5/6/97, and 17/4, 16/11/97.
24. Ibid., 17/3, 2/11/96.
25. Ibid., 17/4, 25/12/97.
26. Patricia Hollis, *Ladies Elect. Women in English Local Government, 1865–1914* (Oxford: Clarendon, 1987), p. 285.
27. VMD, 17/3, 2/1/97.
28. Ibid., 17/4, 26/7/98. On the issue of school attendance see also J. Lewis, 'Parents, Children, School Fees and the London School Board, 1870–90', *History of Education* 11 (1982), pp. 291–312.
29. VMD, 17/3, 25/2/97; 17/4, 3/8/97 and 18/10/97.
30. Ibid., 17/4, 11/1/98 and 14/1/98.
31. Ibid., 17/4, 11/1/98.
32. Ibid., 17/4, 24/1/98.
33. Charles Booth, *London Life and Labour*, Vol. I (Williams & Norgate, 1889), p. 129.
34. VMD, 17/4, 26/6/98 and 24/6/97.
35. Ibid., 17/3, 11/8/97.

36. Ibid., 17/3, 9/4/98.
37. Ibid., 17/3, 7/3/97.
38. Markham, *Return Passage*, pp. 25–6.
39. Markham Papers Pt II, 19/31, contains the letters between Violet and Geraldine in which they discuss 'the servant problem'. See also Nicola Beauman, *A Very Great Profession. The Woman's Novel, 1914–39* (Virago, 1983), for insights into the domestic worlds of women during the inter-war years.
40. Eg. C. P. Gilman, *Women and Economics* (NY: Harper Torch Books, 1966), 1st edn 1898.
41. Cmd. 6650.
42. Markham, *Return Passage*, p. 226.
43. Violet Markham, *Friendship's Harvest* (Max Reinhardt, 1956), p. 48.
44. VMD, 17/3, 27/2/97.
45. Ibid., 17/5, 30/7/99.
46. Elsie Wallis (née Wright) to Violet, 28/5/(?)44, Markham Papers Pt II, 28/68.
47. Violet to Hilda Cashmore, 5/2/12, f. 111, Markham Papers Pt II, 25/12.
48. Elsie Wallis to Violet, nd (circa 1906), Markham Papers P II, 26/9.
49. Memoir to Hilda Cashmore, 1876–1943, printed for private circulation by Miss M. F. Pearse, March 1944, Part III by Violet Markham, Markham Papers Pt II, 28/68.
50. Hilda to Violet, nd, f. 81, Markham Papers Pt II, 25/12.
51. J. W. Milledge (Bradford City Guild of Help), 'Guilds of Help', *Charity Organisation Review* (July 1906), pp. 46–57; N. Masterman, 'The Guild of Help Movement', *Charity Organisation Review* (Sept. 1906), pp. 139–50.
52. L. V. Shairp, 'The COS and the Guilds of Help', *Charity Organisation Review* (July 1912), p. 78.
53. M. Cahill and T. Jowett, 'The New Philanthropy: The Emergence of Bradford City Guild of Help', *Journal of Social Policy* 9 (July 1980); and Michael J. Moore, 'Social Work and Social Welfare: The Organisation of Philanthropic Resources in Britain, 1900–14', *Journal of British Studies* XVI (Spring 1977), p. 93.
54. 'Association in Charity and Personal Service', *Charity Organisation Review* (Dec. 1908), pp. 336–8, reprint of a letter to *The Times* signed by D. D. Lyttleton, Violet Markham, Margot Asquith, Millicent Garrett Fawcett and Mary Ward.
55. Reprint of a letter to *The Times* from H. Russell Wakefield, *Charity Organisation Review* (Dec. 1908), p. 340.
56. R. Wakefield to Violet Markham, 17/3/09, Markham Papers Pt II, 26/38.
57. Jessie Smith (Women's Cooperative Guild) to Violet, 9/9/14, Markham Papers Pt II, 26/9.
58. Letter from Violet Markham to the *Spectator*, 'The Problem of Poverty', 26/8/11, Markham Papers Pt II, 28/55.
59. 'Miss Markham on the COS', *Charity Organisation Review* (March 1912), p. 129.
60. Ibid., p. 132.
61. Ibid., p. 133; Violet to Hilda, 13/2/12, Markham Papers Pt II, 25/12.
62. 'Miss Markham on the COS', p. 136.
63. Ibid., p. 138.
64. Mr S. P. Grundy, 'The Relations of the COS and the Guilds of Help', *Charity Organisation Review* (July 1912), p. 87.
65. Violet to Mr G. T. Reid, 25/1/39, Markham Papers Pt I, 7/27; Violet Markham, 'Training and Unemployment among Women and Young People', Memo 261, May 1937, Markham Papers Pt I, 6/12.
66. VMD, 17/3, 17/1/97.
67. E. J. Urwick, *A Philosophy of Social Progress* (Methuen, 1912), pp. 200 and 212; Violet to Elizabeth Macadam, 21/3/18, Markham Papers Pt I, 2/3.
68. William Lyon Mackenzie King, Diary, 28/7/19, Trans. 41, University of Toronto Microfilm.
69. Markham, *Friendship's Harvest*, pp. 147–56.

70. On Progressives, see Peter Clarke, 'The Progressive Movement in England', *Transactions of the Royal Historical Society* 24 (1974), pp. 159–81.
71. José Harris, 'The Webbs, the COS and the Ratan Tata Foundation: Social Policy from the Perspective of 1912', in Martin Bulmer, Jane Lewis, and David Piachaud (eds), *The Goals of Social Policy* (Unwin Hyman, 1989), pp. 27–63.
72. Eleanor Rathbone to Violet, 30/12/18, Markham Papers Pt II, 26/23; Violet to Hilda, 25/11/18, Markham Papers Pt II, 26/18.
73. M. Sewell, 'Changing Social Ideals', *Charity Organisation Review* (April 1917), pp. 136–54.
74. Noel Whiteside, 'Industrial Welfare and Labour Regulation in Britain in the Time of the First World War', *International Review of Social History* 25 (1980), Pt 3, pp. 307–31.
75. Violet to Hilda, 1918, f. 296, Markham Papers Pt II, 25/12.
76. Elizabeth Macadam, *The Equipment of the Social Worker* (Allen & Unwin, 1925), p. 31. Bedford College Archives AR 330/2 traces this development through 1916–18.
77. Violet to Elizabeth Macadam, 21/3/18, Markham Papers Pt I, 2/3.
78. Elizabeth Macadam, *The New Philanthropy. A Study of the Relationships between the Statutory and Voluntary Social Services* (Allen & Unwin, 1934), p. 18.
79. Elizabeth Macadam to Violet, 19/2/18, Markham Papers Pt II, 2/3.
80. 'The Great Struggle. Peers Versus People. Defence of the Peoples' Rights', speech delivered by Miss Violet Markham, Drill Hall, Chesterfield, 7/12/10, Markham Papers Pt II, 28/91; 'Chesterfield Parliamentary By-Election. Candidature of Mr Barret Kenyon. Inspiring Speech by Miss Violet Markham', reprinted from the *Derbyshire Courier*, 16/8/13, Markham Papers Pt II, 28/93.
81. Harrison, *Separate Spheres*, p. 19.
82. VMD, 17/4, 8/2/98.
83. Ibid., 17/4, 24/1/98.
84. Ibid., 17/4, 26/1/98.
85. Ibid., 17/4, 1/2/98.
86. Hilda to Violet, 24/8/10, f. 9, Markham Papers Pt II, 25/12.
87. Constance Smith to Violet, 29/2/12, f. 43, Markham Papers Pt II, 25/74.
88. Mrs Henry Fawcett, *Home and Politics* (Women's Printing Society, 1894).
89. Maud Selborne to Violet, 23/2/(?), 27/2/(?), 1/3/(?), Markham Papers Pt II, 26/30.
90. St Loe Strachey to Violet, 11/4/12, Markham Papers Pt II, 26/30.
91. Almroth E. Wright, *The Unexpurgated Case Against Women's Suffrage* (Constable, 1913), develops his argument. St Loe Strachey to Violet, 9/4/12, Markham Papers Pt II, 26/30.
92. Rebecca West, 'The Personal Service Association: Work for Idle Hands To Do', the *Clarion*, 13/12/12, reprinted in Jane Marcus (ed.), *The Young Rebecca. Writings of Rebecca West, 1911–17* (Virago, 1983), pp. 127–30.
93. Violet to Captain Jim Carruthers, 25/12/12, Markham Papers Pt II, 19/24.
94. Hilda to Violet, 24/8/10, Markham Papers Pt II, 25/12.
95. J. Morris, *Women Workers and the Sweated Trades. The Origins of Minimum Wage Legislation* (Gower, 1986), pp. 143–4; Deborah Thom, 'The Ideology of Women's Work, 1914–24, with special reference to the National Federation of Women Workers and other Trade Unions', unpublished PhD thesis, Thames Polytechnic, 1982.
96. Celia Davies and Jane Lewis, 'The Strategy of Protective Legislation in Britain, 1870–1990', forthcoming in *Policy and Politics* (1991). For the nineteenth-century equalitarian position see, J. Boucherette and H. Blackburn, *The Condition of Working Women and the Factory Acts* (Elliot Stock, 1896).
97. Eg. Mary Ward's Debate with Mrs Fawcett, Feb. 1909, TS, Ward Papers, 1/1/6, Pusey House, Oxford.
98. VMD, 17/4, 25/5/98; Patrick Geddes and J. Arthur Thompson, *Sex* (Williams & Norgate, 1914), p. 244.

99.   Joan N. Burstyn, *Victorian Education and the Ideal of Womanhood* (Croom Helm, 1980); Deborah Gorham, *The Victorian Girl and the Feminine Ideal* (Croom Helm, 1982), p. 8.
100. Violet to Arthur, nd, f. 29, Markham Papers Pt II, 19/24.
101. 'Speakers in the Franchise Debate', *The Anti-Suffrage Review* (Aug. 1910), p. 18.
102. Urwick, *Philosophy of Social Progress*, p. 194.
103. St Loe Strachey to Violet, 11/10/09, Markham Papers Pt II, 26/30.
104. Lady Jersey to Violet, 23/9/(?)08, ibid.
105. Mary Ward to Violet, 29/9/09, ibid.
106. St Loe Strachey to Violet, 11/10/09, ibid.
107. Mary Ward to Violet, 11/2/12; see also 7/2/12, ibid.
108. Cromer to Violet, 9/2/12, ibid.
109. Violet to Cromer, 10/2/12, ibid.
110. Mary Ward to Violet, 14/2/12, ibid.
111. Local Government Advancement Committee, publicity letter to editors, nd (circa 1912), ibid.
112. Violet to Mary Ward, March 1912, ibid.
113. 'Miss Violet Markham's Great Speech in the Albert Hall, February 28th 1912' (National League for Opposing Women's Suffrage, 1912), Markham Papers Pt II, 28/92i.
114. Violet to Cromer, 2/11/16, Markham Papers Pt II, 26/30.
115. Violet to Hilda, 15/1/19, f. 398, Markham Papers Pt II, 25/12.
116. Hollis, *Ladies Elect*, p. 472.
117. Harrison, *Separate Spheres*, pp. 135–6.
118. Violet to Cromer, 10/2/12, Markham Papers Pt II, 26/30; Dorothy Ward, 'Running a Woman Candidate for the LCC in Hoxton', *The Anti-Suffrage Review* (April 1913), pp. 78–9, provided a frank and bitter account of the difficulties in getting women candidates accepted by the established political parties.
119. Letter from Lady Jane M. Strachey and others of the Women's Local Government Society to the *Guardian*, 22/3/12; and Mrs Elinor Rendel, letter to the *Spectator*, 6/4/12, ibid.
120. Violet to Lady Strachey, 6/4/12, ibid.
121. Violet to Cromer, 10/2/12, ibid.
122. Harrison, *Separate Spheres*, pp. 97 and 128.
123. Mary Ward to Julia Arnold (her father's second wife), 3/3/12, Ward Papers, 2/3, Pusey House, Oxford.
124. Violet to Hilda, 1/2/(?)15, f. 236, Markham Papers Pt II, 25/12.
125. Cromer to Violet, 31/10/16, Markham Papers Pt II, 26/30.
126. Markham, *Return Passage*, p. 15.
127. Clara Collet's Diary, 20/8/04–67, 10/8/10–137, MS, Warwick University Modern Archives.
128. Violet to Hilda, 20/5/13, f. 197 and 10/3/15, f. 283–4, Markham Papers Pt II, 25/12.
129. Violet to J. E. Alcock, 13/11/18, Markham Papers Pt II, 26/18.
130. Violet to Hilda, 25/11/18, 26/18; Eleanor Rathbone to Violet, 30/12/18, 26/23.
131. Violet to Cromer, 2/11/16, Markham Papers Pt II, 26/30.
132. Violet to May Tennant, 7/6/17, Markham Papers Pt I, 4/5; 10/8/17, 4/6.
133. Markham, *Return Passage*, p. 205.
134. Violet Markham, 'Allowances for Women', Memo 80, 19/3/35, Markham Papers Pt I, 6/8; 'Training and Unemployment Among Women and Young People'.
135. VMD, 26/6/98, 17/4.
136. Letter from Violet Markham to the *Sheffield Telegram*, 27/11/37, Markham Papers Pt I, 9/2.
137. Violet to Hilda, 27/4/12, f. 216, Markham Papers Pt II, 25/12.
138. Markham, *Return Passage*, p. 239.
139. Ibid., p. 8; Violet to Hilda, 12/9/09, f. 83, Markham Papers Pt II, 25/12.

140.   Violet to Hilda, 2/8/14, f. 227, ibid.

Conclusion
Women's social action: possibilities and limitations

Unlike the great majority of women involved in philanthropy and local government, the five women subjects of this book were articulate and sought by their writing, speeches and by their projects both to promote a particular approach to social problems and to establish what they considered to be an appropriate place for women in solving them. They insisted that women's contribution be made without any fanfare. Octavia Hill referred constantly in the 1860s and 1870s to the importance of quiet detailed work, while as late as World War I, Mary Ward similarly insisted upon 'quiet professionalism'. They achieved considerable influence and authority, although most denied seeking it. Even Beatrice Webb sought recognition only for her work in research.

The dimensions of their influence are not easy to measure. It is not the case, for example, that Octavia Hill's example in housing management was either widely imitated during the nineteenth century or adopted by the large numbers of new local authority landlords in the early twentieth. But her views were sought and recognized by government to be important. This was true for all five women. Indeed, Octavia Hill, Helen Bosanquet and Beatrice Webb in particular may be considered the first of many 'token women' in their positions as members of the Royal Commission on the Poor Laws. After the vote was granted in 1918, most government committees had a woman member. Violet Markham was one, although few were as independent minded as she. However, the real significance of the work of these women does not lie in the extent to which their ideas were adopted by government. Most histories of the welfare state have chosen to stress the way in which the prescriptions of Beatrice Webb's Minority Report to the Royal Commission on the Poor Laws were eventually followed, whereas the 'individualism' of Octavia Hill and Helen Bosanquet was rejected.[1] But this is to miss the point that at the turn of the century those female advocates of, above all, personal social work were proponents (together with male members of agencies such as the Charity Organisation Society) of a powerfully argued alternative approach to social problems. The views of the Webbs and other social investigators committed to the study of aggregates and to solutions involving government bureaucracy were by no means dominant. In a somewhat modified form, the more holistic solutions to social problems based on the individual remained influential into the inter-war period, as the work of Mary Ward and Violet Markham shows. Furthermore, this approach – centred as it was on the importance of family and community – was particularly conducive to women's participation. As Beatrice Webb found, the world of social investigation and of solutions that relied on what Octavia Hill termed government 'machinery' was more difficult for women to penetrate.

A number of factors may be identified that when taken together serve to explain the central position women achieved as social activists at the turn of the century. First, the size and influence of the voluntary sector in both the making of policies towards the poor and in the delivery of welfare was extensive. The amount of money passing through the hands of late nineteenth-century philanthropic agencies was larger than that distributed via the poor law, and the influence of the world of philanthropy was evidenced by the representation the Charity Organisation Society (COS) achieved on a body such as the Royal Commission on the Poor Laws. Women had a place in the philanthropic world, albeit that they were for the most part excluded from the executive and policy-making committees of major voluntary organizations and were largely confined to 'frontline' work among the poor.

Nevertheless, the philanthropic world was an acceptable and a comfortable place for women to be and exceptional women, like Octavia Hill, could even carve out a small empire of their own, or like Helen Bosanquet, establish a reputation as a writer whose contributions were acknowledged to set the direction of the work performed by volunteer visitors. Women undertook philanthropic work for a variety of reasons, ranging from the conviction that it was part and parcel of women's 'duty', as in the case of Octavia Hill, to the more self-interested motives of a Beatrice Potter, who hoped that it might help develop her skills in social observation. Some, like Octavia Hill, welcomed the chance to work among the poor, seeing it as an opportunity for the self-giving that gave meaning to life. Others, like Violet Markham, saw it as a duty on a par with the rituals of calling and card-leaving among social peers. She perceived both as duties to the wider society and undertook them with a distinct lack of enthusiasm. It was probably rare for a late nineteenth-century, young, middle-class woman to reject voluntary work entirely, even if it amounted to no more than a yearly visit to the local workhouse. Mary Ward did not commit herself to regular philanthropic work, but she wrote a manual on infant care addressed to working-class mothers in Oxford, and turned towards voluntary effort in the form of the settlement movement and her campaign for playcentres when, in London, she came to address the 'social question' more thoroughly. The extent to which philanthropic work was considered a natural and normal part of the lives of middle-class women cannot be underestimated, and while it was work that was usually conceived of as a duty, women also felt that they had a right to participate in it. A substantial number justified their social activism in terms of women's 'natural' right to exert moral and social authority within the family, which was the site of so much philanthropic endeavour. Such a belief resulted in a strong commitment to the work and a high level of earnestness.

Second, and closely linked to the importance of the voluntary sector in nineteenth-century social welfare provision, was the fact that social problems were dealt with locally. When Violet Markham came to feel as an adolescent that she should get involved in philanthropic work, she conceived of it as fulfilling her social obligations within her own community. The administration of both the poor law and of voluntary organizations was determined locally; it was to be 1934 before government introduced a national scale of relief. From the point of view of the middle-class woman voluntary worker, this again was fortunate. While the new philanthropy of the COS consciously rejected the Lady Bountiful image of bourgeois beneficence distributed to poor neighbours, it was nevertheless this tradition that continued to make it natural for women to offer their services as visitors to the COS, to their local parishes, and to locally elected bodies such as boards of guardians. The links between family and community were embedded in the practice of social administration within both the state and voluntary sectors; in the way in which women were encouraged to view their obligations to their own families as stretching out to encompass the families of the poor within their reach; and in late nineteenth-century social theory, which saw family and community as the crucial mediators of the relationship between the individual and the state. At the local level, women could hope to exert real influence over social administration, if not over social policymaking, as social workers and as members of boards of guardians, school boards and local councils. Such locally-based work was largely acceptable to and for women, although as Mary Ward and Violet Markham found, efforts to get more women into local government were not always actively encouraged by male colleagues.

As the work of social administration moved more firmly into the orbit of national government, then women social activists were faced with a decision as to whether to move with it and to claim the right to fulfil their citizenship obligations at a different level. It is possible to see the split among women philanthropists over the vote as a battle about whether to redraw the boundary between public and private spheres such as to push it substantially beyond the local community. When she realized the extent to which social questions were becoming national questions, Beatrice Webb changed her mind about votes for women. In the end, Violet Markham also accepted the inevitable. But this did not mean that either woman made any substantial change in her belief as to the existence of fundamental sexual difference. While the boundary between public and private was shifted, the contributions of men and women to the solution of social problems continued to be profoundly gendered. Violet Markham reconciled her enlarged role on inter-war public bodies with her unchanged belief in a pre-war gender order by concerning herself with questions pertaining to the welfare of women and children, much as she had done when a member of a local school board.

Third, the dominant strand in late nineteenth-century social theory made the work performed by such large numbers of women philanthropists – personal social work – central to the achievement of social progress. At the turn of the century, social work was as integrated with social theory as it has become remote from it today. Both strongly held notions of Christian obligation and, later, of Idealism inspired a belief in the importance of helping individuals to achieve self-maintenance such that they might become fully participating citizens. The social worker was perceived as the person responsible for forging the crucial links between individual, family and community, and hence to the wider society and state. The fulfilment of (gendered) family obligations on the part of all social classes was viewed as the crucial first step to the building of a higher ethical state. The language of family feeling, duty and responsibility was common to all three generations of women and the special role of women in fostering all these was generally accepted. Even when she rejected the work of the COS as ineffectual, Beatrice Webb did not reject the importance of the mutual obligations of husband and wife, which were held by women philanthropists more generally to be pivotal in building a healthy society. Nor did Beatrice Webb ever eschew the spiritual component of her vision for society, something Sidney found difficult to comprehend, but which was shared by the other women subjects of this book, all of whom believed that the solution to the problem of poverty involved achieving more than an adequate level of material welfare. The role of the social worker was also to foster active participation in society by the poor. In this way, the solution to social problems that relied on an all-encompassing personal social work, rather than on government machinery and a more fragmented treatment of the problems of individuals according to the diagnosis of their cause, made the private sphere of the family and the promotion of a high level of private morality and responsibility the essence of social policy. Women were therefore able to claim a right to a special place in the work of social administration and to assert the importance of men's as well as of women's family obligations, something that Mary Ward made a major theme in her novels. But, as Denise Riley has shown, women thus became wholly identified with the world of the social in a manner that was hard to break away from and which left them high and dry when the family no longer occupied a large place within social theory and social work was no longer accepted as providing the principal solution to social problems.[2]

Women entering voluntary work did so as amateurs. Those like Octavia Hill and Helen Bosanquet were strongly convinced that they should be prepared to undergo training and that voluntary work should not be equated with inefficient amateurism. But it is nonetheless a fourth factor explaining late nineteenth-century women's position as social activists that they did not have to deal with the apparatus of professionalism, which tended both to confine women to the lower reaches of the professions and to deny them control over their own professional education.[3] Women dominated early social work training at the Women's University Settlement, the COS's School of Sociology, and, from the 1900s at first the London School of Economics (LSE) and later Bedford College, although within the universities in particular lecturers were often male. Violet Markham continued to play an important role in the decisions that were taken about social work training in the universities during and after World War I, but as social work training became formalized, it also became impossible to sustain the close female control exerted, for example, by Octavia Hill, Helen Bosanquet and Margaret Sewell at the Women's University Settlement. In addition, as social work became a more residual activity so its status fell, which was in turn probably exacerbated by the fact that it was an occupation dominated by women. Within British universities, social work became subordinated to social policy and work with individuals to that focusing on social investigation and the machinery of government.[4]

As important as these external factors are those associated with women social activists' perceptions of themselves and of their work. The women in this book shared above all a commitment to social action that transcended party and feminist politics. Friendship networks based on this commitment often sustained particular campaigns, for example that to extend the Factory Acts, and were able to survive substantial disagreement, especially over the vote. The passion for social action was inspired by varying degrees of self-interest and duty, but all believed that women could make a contribution to the wider society. Octavia Hill, Helen Bosanquet and Mary Ward believed that women were obliged as citizens to give of themselves to the community as well as to their own families. Furthermore, they stressed the importance of improved education if women were to do this effectively. All five women believed in the existence of fundamental sexual difference and in men and women performing different tasks, although they did not agree as to which ones. But they all, again in very different ways, sought to enlarge the space for women's participation in society as far as their notions of female propriety would permit.

Most have been considered to be anti-feminist, which if the vote is taken as the touchstone is certainly the case. But as the picture of nineteenth-century feminism becomes more complicated, so it becomes harder to use such crude measures. None of the women in this book believed in boundless possibilities for women. Rather they were careful to delineate particular territories as appropriate for women and to stress that their rights depended entirely on the proper fulfilment of their obligations, which were different from those of men. But all were anxious that women's contribution be valued, albeit not necessarily in monetary terms, and many, Helen Bosanquet particularly, exhibited sensitivity in their discussion of the position of working-class women. All were conscious to some extent of operating within the bounds of the gender order of their social class which decreed that there was something that could be defined as 'proper behaviour' for women and that if they were not to call forth male antagonism then they should keep to their 'place'. Mary Ward was particularly aware of the hazards of crossing boundaries, but at the same time she, like the other four women, were convinced that some sort of boundary had to be preserved in the interest of society and, in both her view and that of Violet Markham, the nation.

The work they claimed for their own was often far from pleasant. Beatrice Potter was honest about her revulsion from the everyday lives of the poor. Many must have felt similarly to some degree and yet continued to do the work. Obviously these women were not entirely altruistic and must have gained considerable satisfaction from it. Some historians would argue that they enlarged the scope of their own activities at the expense of the poor, who suffered class condescension and treatment that was incapable of providing an adequate solution to their difficulties.[5] This may be a not wholly inaccurate depiction of the outcomes of much of the work of personal service. Certainly women like Octavia Hill wielded considerable class authority and personal social workers were in the end dedicated to changing the habits of working people. In addition, her ideas could all too easily be interpreted meanly by others. However, the motives of female proponents of individual social work did not include the achievement of conspicuous social control over the poor, but rather aimed to encourage their full participation as citizens, albeit in accordance with a script that prescribed clear responsibilities specific to both class and gender. Both Helen Bosanquet and Mary Ward were explicit in applying their thinking about the proper ordering of family relations to middle- as well as to working-class families. Mary Ward saw women's domestic and social work as fundamental to maintaining the social order, both at the individual level of ensuring civilized relations between men and women and in the wider society. Only if women fulfilled their obligations to family would men support women. The maintenance of the gender order assumed a moral as well as a social significance. The fulfilment of responsibilities on the part of husbands and wives in the first instance was designed to do more than ensure material self-sufficiency; it was also anticipated that well-ordered families would build an ethical state. The vision of women social activists, Beatrice Webb included, was above all of a remoralized, respectable working class and a morally and socially decent middle class. Their differences were over means rather than ends. For women like these, the desire to bolster proper family relationships was therefore larger than the urge to do something useful with their spare time. Their earnestness was due to their conviction that the future of state and nation depended on their success.

Thus, at the turn of the century, ideas as to the kind of work that was appropriate for women to do outside the home – voluntary and local – coalesced with the kind of social intervention – social work with individuals – that was believed by many to be the key to securing social change and social progress. While women were successful in claiming this particular territory of social intervention, the long-term implications were less appealing. Women became identified with a specific form of social intervention which made them both the agents and the objects of reform. The notion of 'women's mission to women' relied on the idea that women were both cause and cure of social ills. The attention of the female social worker inevitably focused more sternly on the working-class wife in the home than on the working-class husband. It was possible both to look on her with more sympathy and to exercise greater authority over her. Indeed the belief that pressing social problems, for example, juvenile delinquency, could be solved by better mothering, enjoyed a life long beyond the desire of philanthropic women to promote the fulfilment of family responsibilities and in particular was reinforced by mid twentieth-century professionals and academic psychologists.[6]

From the perspective of the women agents of social intervention, the dictates of family propriety, which made voluntary social work suitable and possible, also imposed considerable limitations. In practice, women social activists often faced a series of conflicting responsibilities around the central axis of family and community. The basis of social action – in the form of the importance of bolstering family feeling and responsibilities – made it easy to justify women's participation, but in practice women social activists often experienced considerable conflicts between their public and private lives. While service to family was crucially construed as service to society and was agreed by all the women in this book to take priority in their concerns, many felt resentment and, close on its heels, guilt at the way in which close family duties impeded their work in the wider community. Beatrice Potter felt this in respect of caring for her father and Violet Markham in respect of her mother. Thus in the lived life, personal family responsibilities did not meld so easily with work to promote the family responsibilities of others. Octavia Hill stated firmly that she experienced no such conflict and gladly put caring for her sister first, but she had reached a stage in her affairs when she could both delegate to others and demand them to be accountable to her. For Beatrice Potter and Violet Markham, family duties interrupted the difficult task of constructing a public persona. In addition, women social activists experienced conflicting pulls between society in the sense of service to their communities, and Society in the sense of social obligations to their peer group. The pressures exerted by the need to maintain the social rituals of their own class were also broadly accepted as a duty falling on women. Mary Ward was attracted to the world of dinner parties and political conversation (both of which were necessary to her husband's work as a journalist) and yet found them a distraction from her work as a writer. Beatrice Webb reconciled the 'useful dinner party' with the work of political manipulation, but she nevertheless felt this to be morally and socially inferior to her work of social investigation and research with Sidney.

The firm conviction that work outside the confines of their own homes should be out of sight, together with the fear of self-advertisement, which was felt as much by Beatrice Webb as by Octavia Hill, meant that it was never likely that these women would slide easily into positions of decision and policymaking. Beatrice Webb made the transition painfully: her experience on the Royal Commission on the Poor Laws showed the extent to which even influential women knew little about the workings of government machinery or how to behave in a forum of that kind. Influential women philanthropists remained by definition outside the machinery of central government and the granting of the vote was too little and probably too late to bring them in and give them a central place in the making of new welfare policies. The importance attached to the work of women philanthropists derived fundamentally from an acceptance that personal service to one's own family and to those of others constituted vital public service.

By the end of World War I, this idea was no longer so powerful. The Liberal government of 1906–1914 had implicitly accepted the impossibility of an individual solution to the problem of poverty. After all, the social surveys of Charles Booth in London and of Benjamin Seebohm Rowntree in York had shown the dimensions of the problem to be vast; one third of the populations of both cities were found to be 'in poverty'.[7] After 1906, the Liberal government acted to take more 'deserving' groups outside the poor law. Children, the elderly and (mainly) regularly employed male workers were offered school meals, pensions and national unemployment and health insurance respectively. During the War, someone like Mary Ward struggled to hold onto her ideas as to the proper ordering of the social and moral fabric in face of the upheavals of war, which appeared to change the world of middle-class women perhaps more than any other social group. Mary Ward feared the possibility that the gender order, which in her view provided the sociological underpinnings to a 'civilized' society, was crumbling. She reacted against women achieving greater autonomy in terms of paid employment and freedom of movement, and against the vote, which she believed would destroy the basis of women's moral authority within the family and put an end to the possibility of securing a higher level of personal and public behaviour from men. The War also caused anguish to Beatrice Webb and Helen Bosanquet, for it not only cast doubt on the validity of social and political principles, but also raised questions about the worth of social action. Only Violet Markham, whose approach was more pragmatic, flourished unambiguously during the war, carrying her new found place on government committees into the post-war world.

Most women did not make the transition as successfully as Violet Markham. As Sylvia Pankhurst remarked bitterly, most of those who had actually fought to secure the vote for women were excluded from government bodies. Women exerted very little influence on the making of the national welfare state. It may be argued that groups such as the Women's Labour League and the Women's Cooperative Guild lobbied hard (although in the case of the latter more often at the local than the national level), but as Susan Pedersen has shown, the major feminist campaign of the 1920s for a level of family allowance that would both reward women's (unpaid) caring work in the home and restructure the wage so as to secure equal pay failed in the face of opposition from the labour movement, the civil service and from male social investigators.[8] The tradition of female philanthropy had little to contribute to such debates. The likes of Octavia Hill and Helen Bosanquet could not have countenanced such a role for the state in reallocating resources, while Violet Markham continued to express anxiety that the post-World War II welfare legislation, which included a measure of family allowances (passed in 1945), would undermine family responsibility.

Nevertheless, the changing relationship between the state and voluntary sectors was increasingly accepted by those, like Violet Markham and Elizabeth Macadam, who were concerned about both voluntary work and the professional training of social workers. But the shift in balance in favour of the state meant that women social workers no longer had such an important platform from which to speak. When professionally trained social workers entered the state machinery of welfare provision, they did so as 'front-line' workers with little influence over policymaking. This is not to say that the ideas of turn of the century women philanthropists, especially those of Helen Bosanquet, disappeared overnight. A belief in individualism in the sense of holistic treatment of an individual's problems, together with the conviction that welfare amounted to more than material provision, was promoted in particular by E. J. Urwick at the LSE, which was why Violet Markham favoured his Department as a site for social work training in the discussions that took place during World War I. It was also true that government policy remained as determined to promote the traditional family with its gendered responsibilities as any nineteenth-century woman philanthropist, and made assumptions as to its existence the basis of social security provision.[9] But just as the welfare state failed to integrate women as decision makers, so it also failed to recognize the importance of some of the goals that late nineteenth-century women social activists had set greatest store by, such as participative citizenship. Personal social work might not have succeeded in achieving this, but the recognition of its significance remains one of the most important contributions of women philanthropists, which, had it been pursued, would have changed the shape and perhaps influenced the fate of the post-war welfare state.

Notes
1. The 'linear' perspective of earlier, standard histories of the welfare state is examined

in Pat Thane's review essay, 'The Historiography of the British Welfare State', *Social History Society Newsletter* 15 (Spring 1990), pp. 12–15.

2. Denise Riley, *Am I that Name? Feminism and the Category of 'Women'* (Macmillan, 1989), especially chapter 3.

3. Harold Perkin's analysis of the gains made by the professions in his *The Rise of Professional Society: England since 1880* (Routledge, 1989) is largely ungendered and ignores recent sociological work that highlights both the way in which organizations are gendered and how the process of professionalization has often disadvantaged women in particular. See for example, Jeff Hearn, *'Sex' at 'Work': The Power and Paradox of Organization Sexuality* (Brighton: Wheatsheaf, 1987).

4. For a futher commentary on the development of social science more generally, see Kevin Bales, Martin Bulmer and Katherine Shish Sklar (eds), *The Social Survey in Historical Perspective, 1880–1940* (Cambridge: Cambridge University Press, 1991).

5. This is the view of Eileen Yeo, *The Contest for the Social Sciences in Britain, 1789–1914: Representations of Gender and Class* (Virago, forthcoming).

6. See Jane Lewis, 'Anxieties about the Family and Relationships between Parents, Children and the State in Twentieth Century England', in *Children in Social Worlds*, ed. M. P. M. Richards (Oxford: Blackwell, 1986).

7. On the problem of the meaning of the poverty line, see E. P. Hennock, 'Poverty and Social Theory in England: the experience of the eighteen-eighties', *Social History* 1 (Jan. 1976), and 'The Concept of Poverty in the British Social Surveys from Charles Booth to Arthur Bowley', in Bales, Bulmer and Sklar (eds), *The Social Survey in Historical Perspective, 1880–1940*.

8. Susan Pedersen, 'The Failure of Feminism in the Making of the British Welfare State', *Radical History Review* 43 (Winter 1989), pp. 86–110.

9. See for example the essays in Jane Lewis (ed.), *Women's Welfare/Women's Rights* (Croom Helm, 1983).

Select bibliography

This bibliography contains only published books and articles and is intended as a guide to some of contemporary and more recent historical work that was particularly important in the writing of this book. Place of publication is London (as in Notes) unless otherwise stated.

Books published post–1960

Barker, Rodney (1978) *Political Ideas in Modern Britain*, Methuen.

Bindslev, Anne M. (1985) *Mrs Humphry Ward. A Study in Late-Victorian Feminine Consciousness and Creative Expression*, Stockholm: Almqvist & Wiksell International.

Boyd, Nancy (1982) *Josephine Butler, Octavia Hill and Florence Nightingale*, Macmillan.

Brodzski, Bella and Schenck, Celeste (eds) (1988) *Life/Lives. Theorizing Women's Autobiography*, Ithaca: Cornell University Press.

Burrow, J. (1966) *Evolution and Society*, Cambridge: Cambridge University Press.

Burstyn, Joan N. (1980) *Victorian Education and the Ideal of Womanhood*, Croom Helm.

Caine, Barbara (1986) *Destined to be Wives. The Sisters of Beatrice Webb*, Oxford: Clarendon.

Clarke, Peter (1978) *Liberals and Social Democrats*, Cambridge: Cambridge University Press.

Colby, Vineta (1970) *The Singular Anomaly: Women Novelists of the Nineteenth Century*, New York: New York University Press.

Collini, Stefan (1979) *Liberalism and Sociology. L. T. Hobhouse and Political Argument in England, 1880–1914*, Cambridge: Cambridge University Press.

Crowley, Brian Lee (1987) *The Self, the Individual and the Community*, Oxford: Clarendon Press.

Cunningham, Gail (1978) *The New Woman and the Victorian Novel*, Macmillan.

Darley, Gillian (1990) *Octavia Hill. A Life*, Constable.

Davidoff, Leonore (1975) *The Best Circles*, Croom Helm.

Davidoff, Leonore and Hall, Catherine (1987) *Family Fortunes. Men and Women of the English Middle Class, 1780–1850*, Hutchinson.

Dennis, Norman and Halsey, A. H. (1988) *English Ethical Socialism: Thomas More to R. H. Tawney*, Oxford: Clarendon.

Dyhouse, Carol (1981) *Girls Growing up in Late Victorian and Edwardian England*, Routledge & Kegan Paul.

Elshtain, Jean B. (ed.) (1982) *The Family in Political Thought*, Amherst: University of Mass. Press.

Fraser, Derek (1973) *The Evolution of the Welfare State*, Macmillan.

Freeden, M. (1978) *The New Liberalism. An Ideology of Social Reform*, Oxford: Clarendon.

Gordon, Linda (1988) *Heroes of Their Own Lives. The Politics and History of Family Violence in Boston, 1880–1960*, New York: Viking.

Gorham, Deborah (1982) *The Victorian Girl and the Feminine Ideal*, Croom Helm.

Greenleaf, W. H. (1983) *The British Political Tradition*, Vol. 2, Methuen.

Guest, Revel and John, Angela V. (1989) *Lady Charlotte. A Biography of the Nineteenth Century*, Weidenfeld & Nicolson.

Harrison, Brian (1978) *Separate Spheres. The Opposition to Women's Suffrage in Britain*, Croom Helm.

Hollis, Patricia (1987) *Ladies Elect. Women in English Local Government, 1865–1914*, Oxford: Clarendon.

Holton, Sandra Stanley (1986) *Feminism and Democracy. Women's Suffrage and Reform Politics in Britain, 1900–1918*, Cambridge: Cambridge University Press.

Jalland, Pat (1986) *Women, Marriage and Politics, 1860–1914*, Oxford: Clarendon.

Johnson, Paul (1985) *Saving and Spending: The Working Class Economy in Britain, 1870–1939*, Oxford: Clarendon.

Jones, Edith Huws (1973) *Mrs Humphry Ward*, New York: St Martin's Press.

Kent, Christopher (1978) *Brains and Numbers, Elitism, Comtism and Democracy in Mid-Victorian England*, Toronto: University of Toronto Press.

Lewis, Jane (1980) *The Politics of Motherhood. Child and Maternal Welfare in England, 1900–1939*, Croom Helm.

Lewis, Jane (1984) *Women in England, 1870–1950*, Brighton: Wheatsheaf.

Lewis, Jane (ed.) (1986) *Labour and Love: Women's Experience of Home and Family, 1850–1940*, Oxford: Blackwell.

Lown, Judy (1989) *Women and Industrialisation. Gender at Work in Nineteenth-Century England*, Cambridge: Polity Press.

McBriar, A. M. (1987) *An Edwardian Mixed Doubles: The Bosanquets versus the Webbs. A Study in British Social Policy, 1890–1929*, Oxford: Clarendon.

McClain, Frank, Norris, Richard and Orens, John (1982) *F. D. Maurice: A Study*, Cowley Pubs.

Mackenzie, Norman (ed.) (1978) *The Letters of Sidney and Beatrice Webb*, Vols I and II, Cambridge: Cambridge University Press.

Mackenzie, Norman and Mackenzie, Jeanne (1982) *The Diary of Beatrice Webb, 1873–1892*, Vol. I, Virago.

Marcus, Jane (ed.) (1983) *The Young Rebecca. Writings of Rebecca West, 1911–17*, Virago.

Meacham, Standish (1988) *Toynbee Hall and Social Reform, 1880–1914*, New Haven: Yale University Press.

Mitchell, Hannah (1968) *The Hard Way Up*, Faber & Faber.

Morris, Jenny (1986) *Women Workers and the Sweated Trades*, Gower.

Mount, Ferdinand (1983) *The Subversive Family: An Alternative History of Love and Marriage*, Allen & Unwin.

Mowat, Charles Loch (1961) *The Charity Organisation Society, 1869–1913*, Methuen.

Muggeridge, Kitty and Adam, Ruth (1967) *Beatrice Webb: A Life, 1858–1943*, Secker & Warburg.

Nead, Lynda (1988) *Myths of Sexuality. Representations of Women in Victorian Britain*, Oxford: Blackwell.

Nord, Deborah Epstein (1985) *The Apprenticeship of Beatrice Webb*, Macmillan.

Oldfield, Sybil (1984) *Spinsters of this Parish. The Life and times of F. M. Major and Mary Sheepshanks*, Virago.

Peterson, M. Jeanne (1989) *Family Love and Work in the Lives of Victorian Gentlewomen*, Bloomington: Indiana University Press.

Peterson, William S. (1976) *Victorian Heretic. Mrs Humphry Ward's Robert Elsmere*, Leicester: Leicester University Press.

Poovey, Mary (1984) *The Proper Lady and the Woman Writer*, Chicago: Chicago University Press.

Poovey, Mary (1989) *Uneven Developments. The Ideological Work of Gender in Mid-Victorian England*, Virago, 1st edn 1988.

Power, Anne (1987) *Property Before People*, Allen & Unwin.

Prochaska, Frank (1980) *Women and Philanthropy in Nineteenth-Century England*, Oxford: Clarendon.

Prochaska, Frank (1988) *The Voluntary Impulse. Philanthropy in Modern Britain*, Faber & Faber.

Rendall, Jane (ed.) (1987) *Equal or Different? Women's Politics, 1800–1914*, Oxford: Blackwell.

Richter, Melvin (1964) *The Politics of Conscience: T. H. Green and his Age*, Weidenfeld & Nicolson.

Riley, Denise (1988) *Am I That Name?* Macmillan.

Roof, Madeleine (1962) *A Hundred Years of Family Welfare*, Michael Joseph.

Rose, Phyllis (1984) *Parallel Lives. Five Victorian Marriages*, New York: Knopf.

Russet, Cynthia Eagle (1989) *Sexual Science. The Victorian Construction of Womanhood*, Cambridge, Mass.: Harvard University Press.

Scott, Joan (1988) *Gender and the Politics of History*, New York: Columbia University Press.

Searle, G. R. (1971) *The Quest for National Efficiency*, Oxford: Blackwell.

Stedman-Jones, Gareth (1976) *Outcast London*, Harmondsworth: Penguin.

Steedman, Carolyn (1990) *Childhood, Culture and Class in Britain. Margaret McMillan, 1860–1931*, Virago.

Summers, Anne (1988) *Angels and Citizens. British Women as Military Nurses, 1854–1914*, Routledge & Kegan Paul.

Sutherland, John (1990) *Mrs Humphry Ward. Eminent Victorian, Pre-eminent Edwardian*, Oxford: Oxford University Press.

Tebbut, Melanie (1983) *Making Ends Meet. Pawnbroking and Working-Class Credit*, Leicester: Leicester University Press.

Thomson, T. (ed.) (1987) *Dear Girl. The Diaries and Letters of Two Working Women, 1897–1917*, The Women's Press.

Vicinus, Martha (1985) *Independent Women. Work and Community for Single Women, 1850–1920*, Virago.

Vincent, Andrew (ed.) (1986) *The Philosophy of T. H. Green*, Gower.

Vincent, Andrew and Plant, Raymond (1984) *Philosophy, Politics and Citizenship*, Oxford: Blackwell.

Vogeler, Martha S. (1984) *Frederic Harrison. The Vocations of a Positivist*, Oxford: Clarendon.

Waites, Bernard (1987) *A Class Society at War, Britain 1914–18*, Leamington Spa: Berg.

Walton, Ronald G. (1975) *Women in Social Work*, Routledge & Kegan Paul.

Wilmer, Clive (ed.) (1985) *John Ruskin: Unto This Last and Other Writings*, Harmondsworth: Penguin.

Articles published post-1960

Baker, Paula (1984) 'The Domestication of Politics: Women in American Political Society, 1780–1920', *American Historical Review* 89.

Bland, Lucy (1986) 'Marriage Laid Bare: Middle-Class Women and Marital Sex, 1880–1940', in J. Lewis (ed.) *Labour and Love: Women's Experience of Home and Family, 1850–1940*, Oxford: Blackwell.

Bland, Lucy (1987) 'The Married Woman, the "New Woman" and the Feminist: Sexual Politics of the 1890s', in J. Rendall (ed.) *Equal or Different? Women's Politics 1800–1914*, Oxford: Blackwell.

Cahill, M. and Jowitt, T. (1980) 'The New Philanthropy: The Emergence of the Bradford City Guild of Help', *Journal of Social Policy* 9 (July).

Clarke, P. F. (1974) 'The Progressive Movement in England', *Transactions of the Royal Historical Society* 24.

Cole, M. (1961) 'The Webbs and Social Theory', *British Journal of Sociology* 12 (June).

Collini, Stefan (1976) 'Hobhouse, Bosanquet and the State: Philosophical Idealism and Political Argument in England, 1880–1918', *Past and Present* 72.

Collini, Stefan (1980) 'Political Theory and the "Science of Society" in Victorian Britain', *Historical Journal* 23.

Collini, Stefan (1985) 'The Idea of "Character" in Victorian Political Thought', *Transactions of the Royal Historical Society* 35.

Conway, Jill (1973) 'Stereotypes of Femininity in a Theory of Sexual Evolution', in M. Vicinus (ed.) *Suffer and be Still*, Bloomington: Indiana University Press.

Davies, Celia (1988) 'The Health Visitor as Mother's Friend: A Woman's Place in Public Health, 1900–1914', *Social History of Medicine* 1.

Dyhouse, Carol (1976) 'Social Darwinistic Ideas and the Development of Women's Education in England, 1880–1920', *History of Education* 5 (Feb.).

Fido, Judith (1977) 'The Charity Organisation Society and Social Casework in London, 1869–1900', in A. P. Donajgrodski (ed.) *Social Control in Nineteenth-Century Britain*, Croom Helm.

Harris, José (1983) 'The Transition to High Politics in English Social Policy, 1880–1914', in M. Bentley and J. Stevenson, *High and Low Politics in Modern Britain*, Oxford: Clarendon.

Harris, José (1989) 'The Webbs, the COS and the Ratan Tata Foundation: Social Policy from the Perspective of 1912', in M. A. Bulmer, J. Lewis and D. Piachaud (eds) *The Goals of Social Policy*, Unwin Hyman.

Harrison, Brian (1966) 'Philanthropy and the Victorians', *Victorian Studies* 9.

Harrison, Brian (1976) 'Miss Butler's Oxford Survey', in A. H. Halsey (ed.) *Traditions of Social Policy. Essays in Honour of Violet Butler*, Oxford: Blackwell.

McKibbin, Ross (1978) 'Social Class and Social Observation in Edwardian England', *Transactions of the Royal Historical Society* 28.

Minor, Iris (1979) 'Working-Class Women and Matrimonial Law Reform, 1890–1914', in D. E. Martin and D. Rubinstein (eds) *Ideology and the Labour Movement*, Croom Helm.

Moore, M. J. (1977) 'Social Work and Social Welfare: The Organisation of Philanthropic Resources in Britain, 1900–1914', *Journal of British Studies* XVI.

Nicolson, P. (1987) 'A Moral View of Politics: T. H. Green and the British Idealists', *Political Studies* 35.

Offen, Karen (1988) 'Defining Feminism: A Comparative Historical Approach', *Signs* 14 (Autumn).

Pedersen, Susan (1989) 'The Failure of Feminism in the Making of the British Welfare State', *Radical History Review* 43 (Winter).

Rose, Michael (1981) 'The Crisis of Poor Relief in England, 1860–1890', in W. J. Mommsen (ed.) *The Emergence of the Welfare State in Britain and Germany*, Croom Helm.

Ross, Ellen (1982) ' "Fierce Questions and Taunts": Married Life in Working-Class London, 1870–1914', *Feminist Studies* 8.

Scott, Ann Firor (1984) 'On Seeing and Not Seeing: A Case of Historical Invisibility', *Journal of American History* 71.

Simey, T. (1961) 'The Contribution of Sidney and Beatrice Webb to Sociology', *British Journal of Sociology* 12 (June).

Stone, Donald (1972) 'Victorian Feminism in the Nineteenth-Century Novel', *Women's Studies* 1.

Summers, Anne (1979) 'A Home from Home: Women's Philanthropic Work in the Nineteenth Century', in S. Burman (ed.) *Fit Work for Women*, Croom Helm.

Thane, Pat (1984) 'The Working Class and State "Welfare" in Britain, 1880–1914', *Historical Journal* 27.

Thompson, Dorothy (1987) 'Women, Work and Politics in Nineteenth-Century England: The Problem of Authority', in Jane Rendall (ed.) *Equal or Different? Women's Politics, 1800–1914*, Oxford: Blackwell.

Vincent, A. W. (1984) 'The Poor Law Reports of 1909 and the Social Theory of the Charity Organisation Society', *Victorian Studies* 27.

Wohl, A. (1971) 'Octavia Hill and the Homes of the London Poor', *Journal of British Studies* 10.

Zimmeck, Meta (1984) 'Strategies and Stratagems for the Employment of Women in the Civil Service, 1919–1939', *Historical Journal* 27.

Zimmeck, Meta (1986) 'Jobs for the Girls: 'The Expansion of Clerical Work for Women, 1850–1914', in Angela V. John (ed.) *Unequal Opportunities. Women's Employment in England, 1800–1918*, Oxford: Blackwell.

Books published before 1960
(Entries for Mrs Humphry Ward's novels are to the edition used for textual references.)
Arnold, Matthew (1889) *Culture and Anarchy*, Smith Elder, 1st edn 1869.
Barnett, Henrietta (1881) *The Work of Lady Visitors*, Metropolitan Association for Befriending Young Servants.
Barnett, S. A. (1888) *Practicable Socialism*, Longman.
Bell, Lady Florence (1985) *At the Works. A Study of a Manufacturing Town*, Virago, 1st edn 1907.
Bibby, Miss, Colles, Miss, Petty, Miss and Sykes, Dr (circa 1910) *The Pudding Lady. A New Departure in Social Work*, Stead's Publishing House.
Booth, Charles (1892) *Life and Labour of the People in London*, Vols 1 and 3, Macmillan.
Bosanquet, Bernard (ed.) (1895) *Aspects of Social Reform*, Macmillan.
Bosanquet, Bernard (1899) *The Philosophical Theory of the State*, Macmillan.
Bosanquet, Charles (1874) *A Handy Book for Visitors of the Poor in London*, Longman.
Bosanquet, Helen (1896) *Rich and Poor*, Macmillan.
Bosanquet, Helen (1898) *The Administration of Charitable Relief*, National Union of Women Workers.
Bosanquet, Helen (1898) *The Standard of Life and Other Studies*, Macmillan.
Bosanquet, Helen (1900) *The Education of Women*, np.
Bosanquet, Helen (1903) *The Strength of the People. A Study in Social Economics*, Macmillan.
Bosanquet, Helen (1906) *The Family*, Macmillan.
Bosanquet, Helen (1907) *The Economics of Women's Work*, National Liberal Club.
Bosanquet, Helen (1909) *The Poor Law Report of 1909*, Macmillan.
Burdett Coutts, Baroness (1893) *Women's Mission to Women*, Sampson Low Marston & Co.
Charity Organisation Society (1893) *The Epileptic and Crippled Child and Adult*, Swann Sonnenschein.

Charity Organisation Society (1893) *The Feeble-Minded Child and Adult*, Swann Sonnenschein.

Chase, Ellen (1929) *Tenant Friends in Old Deptford*, Williams & Norgate.

Cole, M. (1949) *The Webbs and their Work*, Frederick Muller Ltd.

Courtney, W. L. (1904) *The Feminine Note in Fiction*, Chapman Hall.

Hill, Octavia (1875) *Homes of the London Poor*, Macmillan.

Hill, Octavia (1877) *Our Common Land*, Macmillan.

Hill, William Thompson (1956) *Octavia Hill: Pioneer of the National Trust and Housing Reformer*, Hutchins.

Hodson, A. L. (1909) *Letters from a Settlement*, Edward Arnold.

Houghton, Walter E. (1957) *The Victorian Frame of Mind, 1830–1870*, New Haven: Yale University Press.

Jameson, Anna (1859) *Sisters of Charity and the Communism of Labour*, Longman.

Knapp, J. M. (ed.) (1895) *The Universities and the Social Problem. An Account of University Settlements in East London*, Rivington, Percival & Co.

Loane, M. (1908) *From their Point of View*, Edward Arnold.

Loane, M. (1909) *An Englishman's Castle*, Edward Arnold.

Loane, M. (1910) *Neighbours and Friends*, Edward Arnold.

Loane, M. (1910) *The Queen's Poor*, Edward Arnold.

Loch, C. S. (1910) *Charity and Social Life*, Macmillan.

Macadam, Elizabeth (1925) *The Equipment of the Social Worker*, Allen & Unwin.

Macadam, Elizabeth (1934) *The New Philanthropy: A Study of the Relations between the Statutory and the Voluntary Social Services*, Allen & Unwin.

MacDonald, Ramsay (1912) *Margaret Ethel MacDonald*, Allen & Unwin.

Markham, Violet (1953) *Return Passage*, Oxford: Oxford University Press.

Markham, Violet (1956) *Friendship's Harvest*, Max Reinhardt.

Martin, Anna (1911) *Married Working Women*, National Union of Women's Suffrage Societies.

Maurice, C. Edmund (1913) *Life of Octavia Hill*, Macmillan.

Maurice, Emily (ed.) (1928) *Octavia Hill: Early Ideals*, Allen & Unwin.

Maurice, F. D. (1855) *Lectures to Ladies on Practical Subjects*, Macmillan.

Maurice, F. D. (1893) *Social Morality*, Macmillan.

Muirhead, J. H. (ed.) (1935) *Bernard Bosanquet and his Friends*, Allen & Unwin.

Nevinson, Wynne (1920) *Life's Fitful Fever*, A. & C. Black.

Potter, B. (1930) *The Cooperative Movement in Great Britain*, Allen & Unwin, 1st edn 1891.

Reason, W. (ed.) (1898) *University and Social Settlements*, Methuen.

Stronach, Alice (1901) *A Newnham Friendship*, Blackie & Son.

Trevelyan, Janet Penrose (1920) *Evening Play Centres for Children*, Methuen.

Trevelyan, Janet Penrose (1923) *The Life of Mrs Humphry Ward*, Constable.

Urwick, E. J. (1912) *A Philosophy of Social Progress*, Methuen.

Ward, Mrs Humphry (1891) *University Hall: Opening Address*, Smith Elder.

Ward, Mrs Humphry (1892) *New Forms of Christian Education*, Smith Elder.

Ward, Mrs Humphry (1892) *The Future of University Hall. An Address*, Smith Elder.

Ward, Mrs Humphry (1892) *The History of David Grieve*, Smith Elder.

Ward, Mrs Humphry (1894) *Marcella*, Thomas Nelson.

Ward, Mrs Humphry (1894) *Unitarians and the Future*, Philip Green.

Ward, Mrs Humphry (1896) *Sir George Tressady*, Smith Elder.

Ward, Mrs Humphry (1899) *Robert Elsmere*, George Newnes, 1st edn 1888.

Ward, Mrs Humphry (1900) *Eleanor*, Macmillan.

Ward, Mrs Humphry (1906) *Fenwick's Career*, Harper Bros.

Ward, Mrs Humphry (1907) *The Marriage of William Ashe*, Nelson, 1st edn 1905.

Ward, Mrs Humphry (1908) *The Testing of Diana Mallory*, Harper Bros.

Ward, Mrs Humphry (1909) *Daphne, or Marriage à la Mode*, Cassell.

Ward, Mrs Humphry (1911) *Lady Rose's Daughter*, Smith Elder, 1st edn 1903.

Ward, Mrs Humphry (1911) *The Case of Richard Meynell*, Smith Elder.

Ward, Mrs Humphry (1913) *The Coryston Family*, Smith Elder.

Ward, Mrs Humphry (1913) *The Mating of Lydia*, Garden City, New York: Doubleday Page & Co.

Ward, Mrs Humphry (1915) *Delia Blanchflower*, Ward Lock, 1st edn 1914.

Ward, Mrs Humphry (1915) *Eltham House*, Cassell.

Ward, Mrs Humphry (1916) *England's Effort. Six Letters to an American Friend*, Smith Elder.

Ward, Mrs Humphry (1916) *Lady Connie*, Smith Elder.

Ward, Mrs Humphry (1917) *Missing*, Collins.

Ward, Mrs Humphry (1918) *A Writer's Recollections*, Collins.
Ward, Mrs Humphry (1918) *The War and Elizabeth*, Collins.
Ward, Mrs Humphry (1919) *Cousin Philip*, Collins.
Ward, Mrs Humphry (1920) *Harvest*, Collins.
Ward, Mrs Humphry (1983) *Helbeck of Bannisdale*, Harmondsworth: Penguin, 1st edn 1898.
Webb, Beatrice (1896) *Women and the Factory Acts*, Fabian Tract No. 67.
Webb, Beatrice (ed.) (1901) *The Case for the Factory Acts*.
Webb, Beatrice (1975) *Our Partnership*, ed. B. Drake and M. I. Cole, Cambridge: Cambridge University Press, 1st edn 1948.
Webb, Beatrice (1979) *My Apprenticeship*, Cambridge: Cambridge University Press, 1st edn 1926.
Webb, Sidney and Webb, Beatrice (1897) *Industrial Democracy*, Longman.
Webb, Sidney and Webb, Beatrice (1975) *Methods of Social Study*, Cambridge: Cambridge University Press, 1st edn 1932.

Name index

Subject index